Epistles from Perpetua

Epistles from Perpetua

Praying Through a Pandemic

CATHERINE HALSALL

Foreword by Robin Hall, PhD

RESOURCE *Publications* · Eugene, Oregon

EPISTLES FROM PERPETUA
Praying Through a Pandemic

Copyright © 2025 Catherine Halsall. All rights reserved. Except for brief quotations in critical publications or reviews, no part of this book may be reproduced in any manner without prior written permission from the publisher. Write: Permissions, Wipf and Stock Publishers, 199 W. 8th Ave., Suite 3, Eugene, OR 97401.

Wipf & Stock
An Imprint of Wipf and Stock Publishers
199 W. 8th Ave., Suite 3
Eugene, OR 97401

www.wipfandstock.com

PAPERBACK ISBN: 979-8-3852-1082-4
HARDCOVER ISBN: 979-8-3852-1083-1
EBOOK ISBN: 979-8-3852-1084-8

Scripture quotations from New Revised Standard Version Bible copyright © 1989. National Council of Churches of Christ in the United States of America. Used by permission. All rights reserved worldwide.

Scripture quotations from The Holy Bible. New International Version copyright © 1973, 1978, 1984, 2011 by Biblica, Inc. Used by permission. All rights reserved worldwide.

Scripture quotations from the New English Bible copyright © 1970. The Delegates of the Oxford University Press and The Syndics of the Cambridge University Press. Used by permission. All rights reserved worldwide.

Scripture quotations from the Holy Bible. Authorised King James Version copyright © 1950, 1953. William Collins. Used by permission. All rights reserved worldwide.

Scripture quotations from The New Testament in Modern Speech by Richard Francis Weymouth. 3rd ed. London: James Clarke, 1914. Used by permission. All rights reserved worldwide.

Quotations from The Martyrdom of Saints Perpetua and Felicitas. Acts of the Christian Martyrs. Chapter 8. Translated and edited by Herbert Musurilla. Oxford University Press. Permission granted PLSclear Licence ID47890.

Lines from Hildegard of Bingen's Poem on the Holy Spirit, translated and paraphrased for modern English by Matt Thiele and used with his permission.

Dedicated to

Jennifer Ruth
A precious gift from God

Contents

Foreword | xi
Acknowledgments | xiii
List of Abbreviations | xv

Epistle 1 | 1
Epistle 2 | 4
Epistle 3 | 7
Epistle 4 | 10
Epistle 5 | 13
Epistle 6 | 16
Epistle 7 | 19
Epistle 8 | 22
Epistle 9 | 25
Epistle 10 | 28
Epistle 11 | 32
Epistle 12 | 35
Epistle 13 | 38
Epistle 14 | 41
Epistle 15 | 44
Epistle 16 | 47
Epistle 17 | 50
Epistle 18 | 53
Epistle 19 | 56
Epistle 20 | 59
Epistle 21 | 62
Epistle 22 | 65
Epistle 23 | 68
Epistle 24 | 71
Epistle 25 | 74

Epistle 26 | 77
Epistle 27 | 80
Epistle 28 | 83
Epistle 29 | 86
Epistle 30 | 89
Epistle 31 | 92
Epistle 32 | 95
Epistle 33 | 98
Epistle 34 | 101
Epistle 35 | 104
Epistle 36 | 109
Epistle 37 | 112
Epistle 38 | 115
Epistle 39 | 118
Epistle 40 | 121
Epistle 41 | 124
Epistle 42 | 127
Epistle 43 | 130
Epistle 44 | 133
Epistle 45 | 136
Epistle 46 | 139
Epistle 47 | 144
Epistle 48 | 147
Epistle 49 | 150
Epistle 50 | 153
Epistle 51 | 156
Epistle 52 | 159
Epistle 53 | 162
Epistle 54 | 165
Epistle 55 | 168
Epistle 56 | 171
Epistle 57 | 174
Epistle 58 | 177
Epistle 59 | 180
Epistle 60 | 183
Epistle 61 | 186
Epistle 62 | 189
Epistle 63 | 192
Epistle 64 | 195

Epistle 65	198
Epistle 66	201
Epistle 67	204
Epistle 68	207
Epistle 69	210
Epistle 70	213
Epistle 71	216
Epistle 72	219
Epistle 73	222
Epistle 74	225
Epistle 75	228
Epistle 76	231
Epistle 77	234
Epistle 78	237
Epistle 79	240
Epistle 80	243
Epistle 81	246
Epistle 82	249
Epistle 83	252
Epistle 84	255
Epistle 85	258
Epistle 86	263
Epistle 87	266
Epistle 88	269
Epistle 89	272
Epistle 90	275
Epistle 91	278
Epistle 92	281
Epistle 93	284
Epistle 94	288
Epistle 95	291
Epistle 96	294
Epistle 97	297
Epistle 98	300
Epistle 99	303
Epistle 100	306
Epistle 101	309
Epistle 102	312
Epistle 103	315

Epistle 104 | 317
Epistle 105 | 320
Epistle 106 | 323
Epistle 107 | 326
Epistle 108 | 329
Epistle 109 | 332
Epistle 110 | 335
Epistle 111 | 338
Epistle 112 | 341
Epistle 113 | 344
Epistle 114 | 347
Epistle 115 | 350
Epistle 116 | 353
Epistle 117 | 356
Epistle 118 | 359
Epistle 119 | 362
Epistle 120 | 365
Epistle 121 | 368
Epistle 122 | 371
Epistle 123 | 372
Epistle 124 | 375
Epistle 125 | 378
Epistle 126 | 381
Epistle 127 | 384
Epistle 128 | 387
Epistle 129 | 390
A Final Epistle from Perpetua | 393

Bibliography | 395

Foreword

Under the name of one of the earliest female martyrs known, and fashioned in the style of her diary penned in a Carthage prison in 203 AD, Catherine Halsall has created an extraordinarily insightful collection of tools for prayer. As did this young woman, Perpetua, with baby at breast, face the horrifying prospect of being thrown to the beasts for declaring, "I cannot be called anything other than what I am, a Christian," so the author foresaw the severe social and economic disruption, the physical and mental suffering, caused by the global pandemic of the coronavirus disease 2019 (COVID-19) and sought to nurture the heart relationship of today's believers with their heavenly Father.

In a series of 130 weekly epistles, the Bible is opened in tantalizing and rewarding ways to reveal the daily prayer lives of Old Testament heroes and New Testament evangelists. The prayer patterns of men and women of faith across the ages are described and puzzling questions confronted head-on: How can God listen to millions of prayers, all in the same instant? When our prayers don't formulate as we would like, what do we do? When the loneliness of circumstances overwhelm, how can we keep our hearts and souls alive? Perpetua's words of long ago, "I knew that I could speak with the Lord," is shown to resonate with Christians today.

Robin Hall, PhD

Acknowledgments

In the writing of this work I extend much gratitude to the following people:

All members of my family—my children, grandchildren, and my special niece—who over a period of some time were always there with support, encouragement, and practical help. Written anonymously, these epistles were sent by email to members of St. Swithun's Anglican Church, Pymble, each week. I express gratitude to the Reverend Doctor Roger Chilton, who thought this venture would be a worthwhile endeavor, and to The Right Reverend Donald Cameron, who unknowingly gave me ongoing encouragement. There were often a number of responses sent to the Office Staff and these heartened and motivated me to continue with this project for over one hundred weeks. I originally approached the writing with some trepidation but eventually was led to believe it was worthwhile to many. I am grateful for the contribution of Ann Powell for two of the Epistles and thank also Peter and Judy Taylor for the use of their material on methods of prayer. To those few who became aware of the authorship I am particularly indebted. Thank you to Robin Hall for the publishing support with her recommendation and foreword.

The inspiration for everything written here on prayer is the eternal Word of God our Father.

As with everything I have accomplished—in loving memory of Ian.

List of Abbreviations

Chr	Chronicles
Col	Colossians
Cor	Corinthians
Dan	Daniel
Deut	Deuteronomy
Eccl	Ecclesiastes
Eph	Ephesians
Esth	Esther
Exod	Exodus
Gal	Galatians
Gen	Genesis
Hab	Habakkuk
Heb	Hebrews
Hos	Hosea
Isa	Isaiah
Jas	James
Jer	Jeremiah
Josh	Joshua
Kgs	Kings
Lam	Lamentations
Matt	Matthew
Mic	Micah
Neh	Nehemiah
Num	Numbers
Pet	Peter
Phil	Philippians
Prov	Proverbs
Ps	Psalms
Rev	Revelation

Rom	Romans
Sam	Samuel
Sir	Sirach
Thess	Thessalonians
Tim	Timothy
Zech	Zechariah

Epistle 1

This little screed is going to come to you, by virtual means, each week. Now a screed can mean a number of things—an informal letter or other account; a wooden strip serving as a guide for making a true level surface; a fragment of cloth. In Scotland this fragment is to be torn, ripped apart, or shredded. In that country it can also be meant for a drinking bout! Hopefully you will welcome the screed as a loving regular epistle and a tool for leveling your heart and mind. Being virtual you cannot put it through the paper shredder and its purpose is not to send you on a drinking bout.

The subject we are going to embrace each week is *Prayer*. Many of you are able to become lost in prayer in a dedicated quiet place; others pray differently, for example, having conversations with God while driving or walking. Some may use the Psalms or a Prayer Book to guide them. Then again, there are always believers who find a prayer life difficult. For those that do, perhaps the following plan of action could help, and, in the process, draw you ever closer to your Savior. Even using this following strategy for quiet contemplation would enrich your life, particularly at this frightening time.

It is aimed to help and encourage you in your conversing with God. It involves a physical exercise, which may be hard at first but, as time and practice proceeds, it will become something to which you will look forward with great anticipation.

- Set a time, and day; each Wednesday, for example.
- Put a notice on your front door—"Please do not knock or ring the bell at this time," or something similar.
- If you are a business man or woman who is constantly engaged in Zoom meetings, inform your colleagues you are not available at this prescribed time. Your time with Perpetua is as regular as the

business meetings. Similarly, inform your family and friends that you cannot be in touch virtually at this prescribed time.

- Turn your phone and computer onto silent.
- Turn off the radio and the television.
- Close off any other noise in your home.
- Set a timer (perhaps on the oven)—starting with five to ten minutes.
- Choose the most comfortable chair you have.
- Read the words of the screed carefully.
- Spend the first five minutes thinking about the weekly screed.
- Engage your heart and your mind.
- Spend the second five minutes talking to God.

Richard L. Pratt Jr., an American theologian and author, wrote a book entitled, *Pray with Your Eyes Open*. He does not mean necessarily keeping our eyes open when we pray, but pray with the eyes of our hearts open. Benedict, an Italian Mystic who lived from 480–547, encouraged his followers to "Listen with the ear of the heart." Talking to God—praying—is about engaging fully our hearts.

Now, today's screed is going to be a little short because you need to digest all of the above—slowly and carefully.

When living in London for three months last year I found myself in a predominately Muslim area. Every time I went out the door I tried to smile and say hello to people (mainly women and children) I passed in the street. Women quickly bowed their heads or turned away. My hostess told me they were too frightened to be seen conversing with me. I also found it strange at night, when walking home, to see men sometimes sitting in cars generally engaged in cell phone conversations. Again, my hostess explained, that extended families living together in a small home, used this as an escape to gain some privacy or just some "alone" time. I found it all very sad. The families were very connected, the children were well dressed and well behaved, and, conversely, the men shop-keepers were friendly and happy for a chat. But, now, shopping in Sainsbury's with the current coronavirus situation has added drawbacks. Specifically, the ladies from Bangladesh are still shopping in groups surrounded by all their children. They don't observe social distancing, in fact, it is quite the opposite.

Why would they all be taking such risks? Women in these cultures are living in a country quite alien to their upbringing. Also, they grew up in a crowded country where human beings were unavoidably jostled in public places. Many of the emigrant women cannot speak English—sometimes they are unable to read and write in their own language, let alone in a language completely foreign to them. They may not have access to any understandable television or radio programs. They only know what their menfolk tell them. In our present situation isolation is difficult but some of us are able to tackle and enjoy tasks and pastimes we have neglected in our normal busy routine. Now with a virtual world, I have a relation who is having a beneficial time—away from work, in her lovely home, watching the sunset each evening and renewing and growing her relationships with family and friends virtually! She is missing a lot of her outside life but is filling her inside life with great substitutes.

Women who are isolated in their own culture, yet are still congregating with extended families in small spaces, and doing their shopping in their usual manner—ignorant of the dangers abounding—particularly need our prayers. Isolation in a new homeland, somewhat restricted by beliefs and customs that they nevertheless hold dear, will obviously be deeply impacted by a second isolation due to the pandemic. We have a hope they cannot envisage—when the world heals itself, we can return to a much fuller life. They cannot. Will you make these vulnerable people a vital part of your hearts and minds in your prayers at this regular "set-aside" time.

> Do not forget to remove your notice
> and turn on your phone and computer!

Epistle 2

This week's epistle comes with the hope that last week's communication found fertile ground—that you *prayed with your eyes open* and *listened with the ear of your heart!*

We know, through the present deluge of news reporting, that the coronavirus is the main priority of nations all over the world. There are many countries, however, which either are neglecting parts of the population in their regions or devoid of the facilities to cope. There are huge settlements of refugees in countries in the Middle East, Asia, and the continent of Europe. Families, generally of considerable size, exist in the most horrific conditions with poor shelter, few amenities, and little or no hope for the future. Take, for example, the Moria Camp on the Greek island of Lesbos. Here there is one water faucet for every 1,300 people and no soap available. Families of five or six sleep together in spaces no more than thirty square feet. The camp is surrounded by barbed wire in a compound originally designed for 3,000 people but now holds 20,000 men, women, and children. Four percent are children. They live in flimsy tents erected on wooden pallets because of the sub-zero temperatures and the accompanying mud and slush. There is no reliable electricity supply and few toilets.

The Boat Refugee Foundation runs the only medical clinic. This facility is available for acute care only and operates on restricted hours of 4–11 pm. because of lack of staffing. Presently there is an epidemic of meningococcal meningitis among the children. In addition to physical illnesses and injuries among adults, there is a great number of patients suffering from horrific episodes of post traumatic stress due to their life experiences. Thousands more people live outside the camp itself, in an area known as the "jungle," where there are generally no services of any type and where refugees are constantly subjected to vigilantes who want the camps closed.

How blessed we are in Australia with our present situation. There are many people in financial difficulties, who have lost their jobs, and have little or no money to keep paying rents and mortgage instalments. But the governments—both Federal and State—are certainly working constantly to keep our country safe; to ensure that our population is able to have access to essential needs; and doing all they can to extend some form of financial security to those who desperately need it. The most disadvantaged appear to be the very ones who are normally helped by various charity organizations. Now, because of imposed social distancing and other government restrictions, they are struggling to cope with a shortage of funds and the lack of volunteer helpers. People who live on the streets do not have a ready supply of soap, water, and disinfectants. They are always isolated because of their situation alone. We can give practical support with ongoing donations to the various charities, but we need to be keeping them in our prayers. We know that we share a God who listens and is able to perform wondrous works. How wonderful that we have such a glorious God whom we can always approach.

We can ask: The Light of the World to break forth into the darkness:

I am the light of the world. Whoever follows me will never walk in darkness but will have the light of life. John 8:12 (NRSV)

The Prince of Peace to bring an end to all wars:

. . . they shall beat their swords into plowshares, and their spears into pruning hooks; nation shall not lift up sword against nation, neither shall they learn war any more. Isa 2:4b (NRSV)

The Cornerstone of the Earth to establish us on a strong footing:

Come to him, a living stone, though rejected by mortals yet chosen and precious in God's sight, and like living stones, let yourself be built into a spiritual house, to be a holy priesthood . . . 1 Pet 2:4 (NRSV)

The Fortress amidst the world to enable us to fight the devil:

. . . those who are born of God do not sin, but the one who was born of God protects them, and the evil one does not touch them. 1 John 5:18 (NRSV)

The Master Potter to mold us into the image of Christ:

Yet, O LORD, you are the Father; we are the clay, and you are our potter; we are all the work of your hand. Isa 64:8 (NRSV)

The Fountain of Wisdom to guide the world to a safer place:

> *For the LORD gives wisdom; from his mouth come knowledge and understanding.* Prov 2:6 (NRSV)

The Compassionate Father to aid the needy and the distressed:

> *I love the LORD, because he has heard my voice and my supplications.* Ps 116:1 (NRSV)

The Bread of Life to fill our hungry souls:

> *I am the bread of life. Whoever comes to me will never be hungry, and whoever believes in me will never be thirsty.* John 6:35 (NRSV)

> *Those who love me, I will deliver*
> *I will protect those who know my name.*
> *When they call to me, I will answer them.* Ps 91:14–15a (NRSV)

Epistle 3

Today we will look at the importance of touch—of being able to touch those we love, to hold hands, to embrace, to hug, to kiss. In these present days we are forced to abandon these loving gestures. The item of affection that is often missed more than any other is that of holding hands. I can remember as a small child, then later as a middle-aged daughter, holding my mother's hand. I loved holding my grandfather's hand when we went for walks and examining the small cancer sores he had from gardening in Brisbane's constant sun. My husband and I always held hands when we went out; we even held hands sitting on the couch watching television or just talking. Starved of such affection for a long time, could this make us dry and withered inside? How long before we can throw caution to the wind and be wild with our greetings, especially with our grandchildren?

I was blessed that, when my husband died, I was with him—just the two of us at home—and my holding him when I saw him pass away from me to the "touch of God." When my son arrived, he went straight to the bedside and kissed his father—he needed that communion of touch with his dad. Many people do not have that blessing—loved ones die suddenly away from home, sometimes away traveling in another state or another country. Some carers, after spending day and night beside hospital beds, might go home for just one night's sleep and their loved one dies in that short time away. But they have been physically there in the last stages, if not the final hour.

Today, with the fear of the spread of the coronavirus, elderly and chronically ill patients have been completely isolated from their families. Aged facilities are in lockdown; hospitals are restricting visitors. The suffering of those in isolation must be heartbreaking, especially for those who rely on such visits for loving stimulation and even survival. My brother-in-law has had Alzheimer's for more than twelve years. He is obviously in the last stages although he is still able to eat well. When

I visit with his wife I feel that, although he doesn't know exactly who I am, he responds to my kiss or my grip of his hand. When he first was diagnosed, being a man who spent his life aiming to follow the example of Christ, he said he was determined not to become angry or bitter about his condition. Whenever we visited his home, he would greet us by saying, "I don't know who you are—but I know I love you and you love me!" When I sit talking to his wife, she holds his hand and if she takes it away for any reason, he grasps it to bring her back.

Alan's family have moved him to a dementia home where he can look out the window and see a familiar street and look over the road and see the church he attended for many years. They have set up a virtual link so he can see them on screen but he appears to be unresponsive to all these attempts to be with him. Only touch brings some kind of recognition. All the elderly in aged care facilities must be finding life so very difficult and bewildering. Those who are in places where the virus has struck must also be very frightened—not only of becoming ill but of undergoing it alone.

My sister-in-law has, over the past few years, gradually become very embittered about her husband's deteriorating condition. She looked after him at home until it became a physical impossibility and has been a faithful visitor since. But she does not cope with being surrounded by a whole group of dementia patients and seeing them, as well as her husband, getting gradually worse. Now she cannot visit at all, she has become very, very angry. And whom has she become angry with? In my last phone-call she distressingly ranted against God. Alan, the sufferer, still maintains a strong faith. He has always responded to the Mass when he was able to attend, before he moved into his present abode. He appears to be patiently at peace—enveloped by the love of God. How important is it that we must all keep our faith no matter how life throws what seems to be impossible trials and tribulations in our path.

It is amazing that the one factor in all this—the inability to touch—is causing so much distress. Can we not pray that we can all survive this physical loss while crawling through such a time of uncertainty. Loss is not just about death: There are many losses that cause sometimes as much grief as death itself. God made us for relationships—a relationship with him and relationships with other human beings.

Pray for strength for ourselves and for others in this time of aloneness.

Pray especially for those who are only finding anger and bitterness.

Pray for the bereaved who, having been with their loved one when dying, are forced to self-isolate for fourteen days without the comfort of family.

Epistle 4

Over fifty years ago, in the *Presbyterian Life* (later entitled *Australian Presbyterian Life*), there was a writer called Geneva Gown who, in each edition, answered questions from the various parishioners of Victoria. Some people challenged him on theological questions; others on procedural queries. Who was Geneva Gown? For years people in the many congregations tried to establish his identity but never succeeded. He certainly kept them guessing!

So, who is Perpetua? Perpetua was a young Christian in the African city of Carthage, and was nearing the end of the time of training that every new believer received. She was being instructed with several other new believers—Saturninus, Secundulus, Revocatus, and Felicitas. Perpetua was twenty-two, born to a wealthy family, and the mother of an infant son. Revocatus and Felicitas, who was pregnant, were both slaves. The Roman authorities of the province arrested them for refusing to worship the Empire's deities. They were kept captive to await trial but Perpetua was permitted to keep her baby. Saturus, another member of the group, had not been arrested but, in solidarity, he turned himself in. Perpetua kept a journal of her imprisonment.

> *While we were still under arrest my father out of love for me was trying to persuade me and shake my resolution. I said, "I cannot be called anything that what I am, a Christian." At this my father was so angered by the word Christian that he moved towards me as though he would pluck my eyes out. But he left it at that and departed, vanquished along with his diabolical arguments. For a few days afterwards I gave thanks to the Lord that I was separated from my father, and I was comforted by his absence. During those few days I was baptized, and I was inspired by the Spirit not to ask for any other favor after the water but simply the perseverance of the flesh. A few days later we were lodged in the prison; and I was*

> *terrified, as I had never before been in such a dark hole . . . I was tortured with worry for my baby there.*

Perpetua's brother, who was also a believer, visited and begged her to ask for a vision:

> *to discover whether you are to be condemned or free . . . Then I made my request and this was the vision I had. I saw a ladder of tremendous height made of bronze, reaching all the way to the heavens, but it was so narrow that only one person could climb up at a time . . . At the foot of the ladder lay a dragon of enormous size, and it would attack those who tried to climb up and try to terrify them from doing so. "He will not harm me," I said, "in the name of Christ Jesus." Slowly, as though he was afraid of me, the dragon stuck his head out from underneath the ladder. Then, using it as my first step, I trod on his head and went up. Then I saw an immense garden, and in it a gray-haired man sat in shepherd's garb; tall he was, and milking sheep. And standing around him were many thousands of people clad in white garments. He raised his head, looked at me, and said: "I am glad you have come, my child." He called me over to him and gave me, as it were, a mouthful of the milk he was drawing; and I took it in my cupped hands and consumed it. And all those who stood around said: "Amen!" At the sound of this word I came to, with the taste of something sweet still in my mouth. I at once told this to my brother, and we realized that we would have to suffer, and that from now on we would no longer have any hope in this world.*

When it came time for the trial, Perpetua was taken from the prison for questioning. Her father again arrived to plead with her to recant: "Give up your pride! You will destroy all of us! None of us will ever be able to speak freely again if anything happens to you." Cruelly he took her baby son with him when he left. He came a second time but to no avail. After a sentence of execution by the beasts in the arena, Perpetua "sent the deacon Pomponius straight away to my father to ask for the baby. But my father refused to give him over."

When the Day of their Victory dawned, they marched from the prison to the amphitheater ecstatically, as though they were going to heaven, trembling with joy rather than fear. The men were to be savaged by a wild boar, a leopard, and a bear. A mad heifer was prepared for the women. After surviving the attack by the heifer, Perpetua was eventually slain by a gladiator—she screamed as she was struck on the bone; then she took the terror-stricken hand of the young gladiator and guided the sword to her throat.

This, then, is Perpetua. Today there are still martyrs suffering for their belief in Christ as their only Savior. Pray for these servants of the Lord.

When you meditate on the life of Perpetua, note the words of reasoning of her father! Note also that her husband is strangely absent. When a husband and wife encountered trials and suffering the marriage should become stronger:

> *We are here to help each other*
> *walk the mile and bear the load.*
> *I will hold the Christ-light for you*
> *in the night-time of your fear.*[1]

Statistics show that, when a child has a terminal illness, the father often leaves. Read the detailed story of Perpetua in the *Acts of the Christian Martyrs*, edited by Herbert Musurilla. Or, on the internet, by searching: *The Martyrdom of Saints Perpetua and Felicitas*.

---

1. P. C. A., *Rejoice*, 310: 7–10

Epistle 5

How are you going with the reading and the thinking? Or the close reading and the meditating? The English language alters the thought process with the change of a word. Remember that! (The use of the word "doom" in Moffatt's Version of Romans 8:1 really brings home what condemnation is!)

We are going to look at close reading in today's epistle from Perpetua. This should be an incredible help in establishing the Bible as inerrant. Pamela Tamarkin Reis is an American Jewish woman and an independent student of the Hebrew scriptures. However, she is held in such respect that her articles have been published in leading scholarly journals such as *The Journal for the Study of the Old Testament and Vetus Testamentum*. In her book, *Reading the Lines: A Fresh Look at the Hebrew Bible*, she relates how she came to believe that the scriptures were a true record. When her father told her that there were no mistakes in the Torah, she said "I was not shy to sass and did not hesitate to rebut, 'Oh, there probably *are* mistakes.' 'No,' my father said patiently, 'If you think there's a mistake, it's because you're too dumb to figure it out.'"[1] This led her on a magnificent voyage of discovery because, when you believe that the Bible is inerrant, you have to spend time and scrutiny trying to work out the intricacies that arise.

Too many times in theological studies, lecturers, when coming upon controversial subjects that do not fit their personal agendas, blithely claim mistakes—if not the author's—the scribe's, the redactor's, the translator's. With textual criticism, source criticism, hermeneutics, etc. they think they can find what is correct and what is added or detracted. Ancient writers they find unsophisticated, uncultivated, and ignorant. Reis calls them "kill-joys" destroying the challenge and amusement of finding out what a passage means. We could also say that there is great doubt about

---

1. Reis, *Reading the Lines*, 4.

the so-called shortcomings of ancient writers. In addition, we must remember that the Hebrew language does not use elaboration—the Old Testament uses words sparingly and thus demands reader participation. The ancient writer, unlike the modern writer, does not set the tone of a scene with description or guide us with adjectives and adverbs, he recounts sparingly—and that is all. Therefore, the modern reader has to be more intuitive.

So, let us all be detectives! Reis uses the example of when Joseph was brought hastily out of a filthy Egyptian dungeon to meet with Pharaoh. Obviously, he would have bathed before going to the court but the scripture says that Joseph shaved and changed clothes. Would he shave without bathing? Bathing is assumed; but shaving and changing clothes are the only important actions that are mentioned. Why? (Genesis 41:14)

Going backward in time to Genesis 22:3–8 we read where Abraham and Isaac are going up a hill to make the sacrifice to God: "Abraham took the wood of the burnt offering and laid it on his son Isaac, and he himself carried the fire and the knife." Isaac says, "The fire and the wood are here, but where is the lamb for a burnt offering?" Abraham has three items; Isaac mentions two of them. Why doesn't he list the knife? Reis says "the reader is supposed to notice the missing third and to reflect on it. The pathos and terror of the scene becomes excruciating once the reader realizes that Isaac knows what is to befall him."[2] The following silence of Abraham and his son "is far more effective and chilling than any amount of piled-on adjectives describing Isaac's dread and Abraham's torment."[3]

Going back even further in Genesis 18:12 when the visitors tell Abraham and Sarah about the future birth of their child, Sarah laughed. We are often told of her action of disbelief, which does appear to be involuntary and quickly regretted. In the preceding chapter when God gave Abraham the same promise: "Abraham fell on his face and laughed, and said to himself, Can a child be born to a man who is a hundred years old?" Genesis 17:17 (NRSV) Compare the two.

Keep alert, we are now going forward, again to Joseph, but before he was taken to Egypt. His father sent him to Schechem to check on his brothers who were pasturing the sheep. When Joseph arrived, his brothers were nowhere to be seen. He met a man who told him that they had gone to Dothan. It is always assumed that this man was a messenger from

---

2. Reis, *Reading the Lines*, 10.
3. Reis, *Reading the Lines*, 10.

God—an angel. We know that angels carry divine tidings. Why would God send an angel to Joseph to merely give him street directions? It must mean that the city they went to—Dothan—has some significance. (Genesis 37:17)

Let's jump to the Book of Judges. One of my Sunday School children was fascinated by the death of Eglon. In a few words we have a picture that does not require the movie makers to demonstrate it to us. (Judges 3:17–22) Further on, is it right that the life and bravery of Deborah is allowed to be denigrated by modern interpreters because she is a woman? (Judges 4) Later still, does Jephthah make a foolish vow or is his daughter willful and spoiled? (Judges 11)

Happy meditating! It will be wonderful to develop the ability to understand God's word and enjoy its heights and depths; its twists and turns—then to pray responsively. When we get to know people well in the Bible, we begin to understand how they faced life's enormous challenges—solely with the strength of their faith in God. We can gain from their examples. We can pray for that strength for ourselves and pray for those we love as they too struggle in today's path of fear and uncertainty.

May we always be receptive. May we ever be perceptive.

Epistle 6

Isolation and anxiety are the experiences of today's world. Even when the situation begins to abate and there are opportunities for regaining closer contact with family and friends, there will be for many, more months of fear—people who have not been as blessed as we in Australia. The continent of Africa encompasses many countries that will be in dire distress and need. The most critical piece of lifesaving equipment of this present pandemic is in desperately short supply. As at the second week of April the World Health Organization reported that there are fewer than 2,000 ventilators across forty-one countries in Africa. Investigating journalists write that Somalia's health ministry still does not have a single one! The Central African Republic has three; South Sudan, four; Liberia, five; Nigeria, with a population two-thirds that of the United States, has fewer than one hundred.

As the average cost is $25,000 for one ventilator, hopefully there will be donations of these vital machines over the coming months. A Chinese billionaire has been known to have donated five hundred but these are to be dispersed throughout the entire continent. Additionally, there are not many doctors who have the expertise to use them and there are very few medical people who are able to intubate patients or supervise the whole process. At most treatment centers there are beds—but no oxygen, no ventilators, no protective equipment for staff. Some of these countries already have the poorest healthcare systems in the world and yet they have enormous populations. Then, of course, in rural areas of many of these places where rebels control the people, there are no facilities at all.

While we are all entering a somewhat exciting new world of Zoom technology, pause to think of African medical personnel sitting six feet apart in hospital conference rooms, following demonstrations of the correct use of ventilators on Zoom, by doctors from the more fortunate countries. Previously the demonstrator flew in with the technology to give a hands-on approach! We know that being physically together in Bible-study groups, home groups, church services, and meetings, is much more rewarding than meeting on Zoom—even if Zoom is an interesting challenge.

The other aspect of the coronavirus is the incorrect reporting of deaths. Some countries are only reporting deaths in hospitals; others report deaths in hospitals and nursing homes; few record virus deaths at home. Perhaps it makes the leaders of these countries look as if they are having a very successful result with the restrictions they imposed—the "we are doing better than you" philosophy! Looking at this scenario from a personal viewpoint seems to illustrate that some deaths are important and some are not. Let us suppress the deaths that fade away into obscurity is the practice. But each life is important to God; each death to life as we know it, is important to God; each resurrection life is important to God. God watches over each one of us:

> *The LORD looks down from heaven; he sees all humankind.*
> *From where he sits enthroned he watches all the inhabitants of the earth.* Ps 33:13–14 (NRSV)

When my mother was a child, there was a picture on her wall of Hagar, lost and bereft in the desert. Above her the whole sky was dominated by an enormous eye—the eye of God watching Hagar and her son Ishmael. This picture frightened my mother. To her it meant that God was taking note of her behavior and there was nowhere to go to escape his watchful eye. But as she grew in Christian knowledge, she realized it meant that, wherever she went, and whatever trouble she endured, God was there, ever watching over her with compassion. As Hagar discovered:

> *When the water in the skin was gone, she cast the child under one of the bushes. Then she went and sat down opposite him a good way off, about the distance of a bowshot; for she said, "Do not let me look on the death of the child." And as she sat opposite him, she lifted up her voice and wept. And God heard the voice of the boy, and the angel of God called to Hagar from heaven, and said to her, "What troubles you, Hagar? Do not be afraid; for God has heard the voice of the boy where he is. Come, lift up the boy and hold him fast with your hand, for I will make a great nation of him." Then God opened her eyes and she saw a well of water. She went, and filled the skin with water, and gave the boy a drink.* Gen 21:15–19 (NRSV)

Next, turn to Psalm 139—the psalm of a loving, all-knowing, and faithful God who knows each one of us intimately:

For it was you who formed my inward parts,
you knit me together in my mother's womb.
I praise you, for I am fearfully and wonderfully made.
Wonderful are your works; that I know very well.
My frame was not hidden from you, when I was made in secret,
intricately woven in the depths of the earth.
Your eyes beheld my unformed substance.
In your book were written
all the days that were formed for me,
when none of them as yet existed. Ps 139:13–18 (NRSV)

When we read this psalm in its entirety, we see that we can never escape God's compassionate care. This, for us, means eternal hope, grace, and security.

Make this psalm your prayer for today;
make it your meditation for all time.

Epistle 7

My Soul Finds Rest. This is the title of a book by Dietrich Bonhoeffer. It is a book of reflections on a number of the Psalms. Perpetua talked earlier about using the Psalms to guide and develop your prayer life. You may have encountered people who claim that using the Psalms is not realistic praying because you can become like a parrot—just learning by rote and praying the words without depth. Would they say the same if you quoted a poem you love, for example:

> *If I should die think only this of me;*
> *That there's some corner of a foreign field*
> *That is forever England.*[1]

or,

> *I wandered lonely as a cloud*
> *That floats on high o'er vales and hills . . .*[2]

or,

> *The Assyrian came down like a wolf on the fold*
> *And his cohorts were gleaming in purple and gold.*[3]

You just don't recite these lines verbatim without your heart wrenching for the lost generation of the First World War; or, seeing in your mind's eye coming over a hill and being confronted with a host of golden daffodils; or, picturing the mighty Assyrian army preparing to surge down on the Israelites with all its mighty noise and clamor, only to be slain by the angel of the LORD. (Byron does use poetic liberties but, nevertheless, symbolizes the fear of the besieged Jerusalem.) Sometimes

---

1. Brooke, *The Poetical Works*, 23.
2. Wordsworth, *The Works of William Wordsworth*, 186.
3. Byron, *Selections from Byron*, 103.

you only need one line to take you to another time when ill-thought-out orders brought chaos and death.

Into the valley of death rode the six hundred.[4]

In exactly the same way the Psalms read, recited, and meditated upon, bring us a glorious picture; a picture of a holy, righteous, and faithful God. We see all his patience and all his forgiveness. We worship him yet we also rage against him. We communicate with him on all levels and he is always there, always our strength and our refuge. The Israelites prayed these psalms for thousands of years, Jesus himself prayed the Psalms. How can these songs of worship be said without stirring our spirits, expressing our deepest needs, and glorifying our God. Many times, we are desolate and torn apart in life but the God of the Psalms will never let us go. Prayer, i.e., communication with God, can be hard. He is holy; we are sinful. The Psalms teach us to learn God's language, to take on a real earnestness in our walk with our Father. We must persist until the soul awakes, the soul gains strength, the soul finds rest. Augustine of Hippo said of God of the Psalms: "You stir man to take pleasure in praising you, because you have made us for yourself, and our heart is restless until it rests in you."[5]

With our eyes wide open and the ear of our hearts listening, we can see the glory and the depth of the words in the Psalms. Dietrich Bonhoeffer urges us to use the Psalms to come close to God. He says we should practice prayer with great earnestness. Every knee should bow and with a Psalm in your heart, "let the mind go free and the soul finds its way into the Father's house, returning home to find rest."[6] Bonhoeffer also wrote of the Psalms as "a strange journey of ups and downs, falling and rising, despair and exaltation."[7] Martin Luther "believed that you could hear the voice of Christ in every psalm—praying with us and for us."[8] The Psalms of love, of worship, of anguish, of yearning for forgiveness, give us the right words to speak to God and demonstrate to us how amazingly deep his love is for us.

Of all the words of scripture the Psalms seem to demand that we go to a place of quiet. We need to block out the world—its noise and its

---

4. Tennyson, *The Works of Alfred Tennyson*, 260.
5. Levering, *The Theology of Augustine*, 91.
6. Bonhoeffer, *My Soul Finds Rest*, 31.
7. Bonhoeffer, *My Soul Finds Rest*, 10.
8. Bonhoeffer, *My Soul Finds Rest*, 11.

demands. Our brains become overloaded; our bodies become fatigued; our souls become bereft. Bruce Demarest says: "Head-centered people *need* to quiet their minds to allow the heart to develop through the discipline of quiet."[9] When we are deeply quiet our spiritual self grows in anticipation and hope. The Psalms fill that anticipation and that hope. In the stillness God reveals himself.

> *Our soul waits for the LORD; he is our help and shield.*
> *Our heart is glad in him, because we trust in his holy name.*
> *Let your steadfast love, O LORD, be upon us, even as we hope in you.*
> Ps 33:20–22 (NRSV)

When we are afraid; when we fear what the morrow will bring, we can, like David when he was hiding from Absalom, say:

> *I lie down and sleep; I wake again, for the LORD sustains me.* Ps 3:5 (NRSV)

We can sleep peacefully because the LORD watches over us—he is always awake. And we know, when we ask for forgiveness, we will receive it through his Promised One, the Savior:

> *Have mercy on me, O God, according to your steadfast love;*
> *according to your abundant mercy blot out my transgressions.*
> *Wash me thoroughly from my iniquity, and cleanse me from my sin.*
> Ps 51:1–2 (NRSV)

We can walk in assurance. God says:

> *Those who love me, I will deliver;*
> *I will protect those who know my name.*
> *When they call to me, I will answer them;*
> *I will be with them in trouble, I will rescue them and honor them.*
> Ps 91:14–15 (NRSV)

---

9. Demarest, *Satisfy Your Soul*, 127.

Epistle 8

Here is an order sent to the French Marshal Grouchy from Marshal Soult, concerning Napoleon's requirements for him during the Battle of Waterloo:

> *The Emperor directs me to tell you that at this moment his Majesty is going to attack the English army, which has taken position at Waterloo . . . Thus his Majesty desires that you direct your movements on Wavre in order to draw near to us, place yourself in touch with our operations, and link up your communications with us, driving before you those portions of the Prussian army that have taken this direction and may have stopped at Wavre, where you should arrive as soon as possible. You will follow the enemy's column on your right, using some light troops to observe their movements and gather up their stragglers. Inform me immediately about your dispositions and your march, also about any news of the enemy, and do not neglect to link up your communications with us. The Emperor desires to have news from you very often.*[1]

The author of *Waterloo*, Bernard Cornwell, calls this order impenetrable nonsense. "Grouchy, instead of asking for elucidation, seized on the single command to direct his movements towards Wavre. What Napoleon seemed to have wanted was for Grouchy to position his army between Blücher [i.e., the Prussian army] and the field of Waterloo."[2]

In our epistles we have previously looked at the amplitude of the Old Testament and how the nature of the Hebrew language encourages us in a process of "close reading" of narratives to establish the complete scenario and to attain a clear meaning of different passages. In addition, we discovered we have the literature of the Psalms and the wisdom literature to begird us and guide us in our prayer life. We have also noted

---

1. Cornwell, *Waterloo*, 146.
2. Cornwell, *Waterloo*, 146.

that many modern theologians do not give enough credit to the ancient writers—people who were educated in grammar and rhetoric from an early age.

When we look at the New Testament, we see Jesus using an extraordinary pattern of language forms in his teaching, which needs our acknowledgment so that we can clearly understand his revelation. He uses *Overstatement, Hyperbole, Puns, Similes, Metaphors, Proverbs, Irony, Paradoxes, Parables, Riddles, Argument, Questioning, Poetry*. Although many of his listeners may not have immediately understood some of these lessons, they were not spoken without the expectation that disciples, priests, scribes, Sadducees, centurions, tax-gatherers, fishermen, and ordinary men and women would understand. Certainly today, they provide an extraordinary succession of fascinating writing whilst revealing to us the great news of true salvation.

The most important aspect of the gospels and the remainder of the New Testament is that it is so clear that there is no possibility of any misunderstanding—very different from some of the orders parlayed about on a battlefield: both dealing with life and death. Paul, in his letters, is also a master of language and its forms. Interestingly Marva Dawn, an American theologian, who specializes in writing on the splendor of worship, records her sermon on 1 Corinthians 12 (NRSV) where she points out that Paul is hilariously funny! Yes! Very funny! She cites 12–13:

> *For just as the body is one and has many members, and all the members of the body, though many, are one body, so it is with Christ. For in the one Spirit we were all baptized into one body— Jews or Greeks, slaves or free—and we were all made to drink of one Spirit.*

Then, she continues, Paul develops the other side of the illustration portrayed here: "The foot can't say, 'Oh dear, give me a hand here; I guess I don't fit in since I'm only a foot.'"[3] Marva, using Paul's words, continues: "If the whole body were an eye, where would the hearing be?" What a ludicrous picture! Can you envision this great big eyeball rolling down the street?"[4] Read all these verses and imagine what a wonderful cartoon could be created for children (and us)! It brings to memory the First World War Digger who was being escorted to the casualty tent because

---

3. Dawn, *A Royal Waste of Time*, 173.
4. Dawn, *A Royal Waste of Time*, 174.

he had lost his hand when hit by the remnants of a shell. In macabre humor he kept asking soldiers he passed—Give us a hand, mate!

What is this scripture about? It is working together as the church, uniting as one body. We must all work together, appreciating each other and supporting each other. We will suffer together; we will rejoice together. In these days when we cannot gather together as one body, we must use every facility and every opportunity to be together in spirit. Even though, during this time of a world pandemic, we cannot have real church services in our real church building, we cannot let the devil divide us and persecute us in our worry and loneliness. The message of the gospel is clear, the commandment of Jesus is clear: "Just as I have loved you, you also should love one another." John 13:34 (NRSV) Paul's theology is clear: "For I am not ashamed of the gospel, it is the power of God for salvation to everyone who has faith." Romans 1:16 (NRSV)

Let us pray for ourselves for godly wisdom, unity, fellowship and encouragement, love and discernment, knowledge of God's will, perseverance, faith that endures, fruits of the Spirit, the armor of God, and a responsive gratitude for saving grace. Let us pray for the world for belief in the Savior Jesus Christ, for a love of peace and unity, for bravery under persecution and tyranny, for courage in these present times, for care and love for one another.

Our hearts are never fully at rest until we rest in him. .

Epistle 9

Do you ever feel that God is far away; that you cannot reach him or feel his presence; that something blocks your prayers from reaching the heights? Might it be a barrier that we have created? For, in the Prophets we read:

> *Am I not a God nearby, says the LORD, and not a God far off? Who can hide in secret places so that I cannot see them? says the LORD. Do I not fill heaven and earth? says the LORD.* Jer 23:23–24. (NRSV)

In the Psalms David writes:

> *You search out my path and my lying down, and are acquainted with all my ways.* Ps 139:3 (NRSV)

> *Where can I go from your spirit? Or where can I flee from your presence? If I ascend to heaven, you are there. If I make my bed in Sheol, you are there.* Ps 139:7–8 (NRSV)

> *If I say, "Surely the darkness shall cover me, and the light around me become night," even the darkness is not dark to you; the night is as bright as the day, for darkness is as light to you.* Ps 139:11–12 (NRSV)

God is always there, within our reach, waiting for us to put our hand in his:

> *Draw near to God, and he will draw near to you.* Jas 4:8a (NRSV)

We must seek after God as we pray. Richard Pratt, in his work *Praying With Your Eyes Open*, says: "We must devote our hearts to communing with him in a vibrant and personal way."[1] Then we will come to the realization that "One of the greatest privileges believers have is the freedom to approach God in his heavenly dwelling place . . . when we

---

1. Pratt, *Pray With Your Eyes Open*, 57.

lift our hearts to heaven, we can discover an ever-increasing assurance that our prayers are reaching God and that He is giving us His personal attention."[2]

We can meditate on descriptions of heaven
Job 1:6–12   Isaiah 6:1–13   Daniel 7:9–11   Acts 7:55–56   Revelation 4:2–8a

The Orthodox Church believes that heaven and earth meet in the Church through the Divine Liturgy. The architecture and embellishments of the church complement the liturgy and are designed, not unlike the Old Testament temples, to proceed from the secular to the holy. The entry or the narthex is the transitional space for worshippers; the nave is the ark or the ship where prayers, hymns, and readings are enacted; and finally, the Sanctuary, divided from the nave by a wall or screen, is the domain of the priests and is called the holy of holies. When Russians came to Constantinople to investigate Christian churches, they returned to their homeland convinced that they must erect similar edifices because these represented heaven on earth.

Solomon built a house for God to live in on earth using exacting measurements and specific interiors to create an extension of heaven: "Yet the Most High does not dwell in houses made with human hands." Acts 7:48 (NRSV) Nevertheless, we can reflect on heaven from the biblical visions mentioned above and remember also the vision of Perpetua.

> *Bless the LORD, O my soul*
>   *O LORD my God, you are very great.*
> *You are clothed with honor and majesty,*
>   *wrapped in light as with a garment.*
> *You stretch out the heavens like a tent,*
>   *you set the beams of your chambers on the waters,*
>   *you make the clouds your chariot,*
>   *you ride on the wings of the wind,*
>   *you make the winds your messengers,*
>   *fire and flame your ministers. Ps 104:1–4 (NRSV)*

Exploring the heavenly home of God demonstrates the holiness of our God.

---

2. Pratt, *Pray With Your Eyes Open*, 58.

It also gives us a picture of our future home.

When we meditate on Isaiah's vision of heaven we see that Isaiah, overcome with the glory of God's holiness, says:

> "*Woe to me! I am lost, for I am a man of unclean lips, and I live among a people of unclean lips; yet my eyes have seen the King, the LORD of hosts!" Then one of the seraphs flew to me, holding a live coal that had been taken from the altar with a pair of tongs. The seraph touched my mouth with it and said: "Now that this has touched your lips, your guilt has departed and your sin is blotted out."* Isa 6:5–7 (NRSV)

With the coming of Jesus to earth from heaven, to die on the cross for us, our sins have been blotted out. Now, in John's first epistle, the apostle calls us "children of God." Scripture tells us that God is the perfect Father, the all-loving Father, the eternal Father. A perfect father does not cut himself off from his children. He loves them, he guides them, and he disciplines them: your rod and your staff—they comfort me.

In Harper Lee's *To Kill a Mockingbird*, the boy Jem is attacked and nearly murdered. His arm is broken. After the doctor left, his father Atticus "turned out the light and went into Jem's room. He would be there all night, and he would be there when Jem waked up in the morning."[3] Our Father God in Heaven is always with us; he is beside us in every agony of our lives.

God is enthroned in heaven yet he is—*omnipresent*. Through the gift of the Holy Spirit we can come to know him intimately. Let us open our hearts to the Spirit with our prayers for, as John Calvin states: "The testimony of the Spirit is more excellent than all reasons . . . the Word will not find acceptance in [human] hearts before it is sealed by the inward testimony of the Spirit."[4]

---

3. Lee, *To Kill a Mockingbird*, 309.
4. Piper, *God Is the Gospel*, 78.

Epistle 10

WITH THE CURRENT SITUATION, where many of us are still living in some type of isolation, some people have been indulging in the formerly neglected enjoyment of reading. Fiction is often a difficult genre—because of the vast amount available it becomes so difficult to make a choice. However, we can always resort to the classics. *Agnes Grey*, by Anne Brontë, which the critic George Moore called "the most perfect prose narrative in English literature,"[1] was originally censored because of the portrayal of how the aristocracy in England treated its governesses. *The Moonstone*, by Wilkie Collins, was considered the first modern English detective tale and established many of the ground rules of the modern detective novel. *The Riddle of the Sands*, by Erskine Childers, was the introduction to the reading public of the spy novel. This gripping work would also be enjoyed by erstwhile sailors. It was a forecast of the possibility of a war with Germany at the beginning of the twentieth century.

Following the publication of the *Riddle of the Sands* came another spy thriller, *The Thirty-Nine Steps*, by John Buchan. John Buchan was a son of the Free Kirk, a scholar, barrister, colonial administrator, journal editor, critic, publisher, war correspondent and advisor, member of Parliament, Lord High Commissioner of the Church of Scotland, and Governor-General of Canada. He wrote prolifically, with many of his novels based in countries where he lived and worked, e.g., *John McNab* (Scotland), *Prester John* (South Africa), and *Sick Heart River* (Canada). *The Thirty-Nine Steps* supposedly was given its name for the thirty-nine steps counted by his six-year-old daughter, from his holiday home to the sea. Thirty-nine is a suggestive religious number—The Thirty-Nine Articles of the Church of England, plus St. Paul submitted to thirty-nine lashes. (1 Corinthians 11:24.) The Old Testament law prescribed: "Forty

---

1. Brontë, *Agnes Grey*, cover.

lashes may be given but no more; if more lashes than these are given, your neighbor will be degraded in your sight." Deuteronomy 25:3–4 (NRSV) How prudent was the flogger—keep it to thirty-nine in case there was a miscount!

All of Buchan's books are exquisitely written, though dated. However, his descriptions are still relevant because they are so memorable. When writing of his sojourn in South Africa he penned these words:

> *I bathed in one of the Malmani pools—and icy cold it was—and then basked in the early sunshine while breakfast was cooking. The water made a pleasant music, and nearby was a covert of willows filled with singing birds. Then and there came on me the hour of revelation . . . Scents, sights and sounds blended into a harmony so perfect that it transcended human expression, even human thought. It was like a glimpse of the peace of eternity . . . The world was a place of inexhaustible beauty, but still more was the husk of something infinite, ineffable, and immortal, in very truth the garment of God.*[2]

All of the above books are engrossingly alive because each author used his or her own experiences when writing.

Sara Nelson, who wrote *So Many Books, So Little Time*, comments that books are personalities in their own right. Many people regard their books as their friends. This seems often to be the case for people living alone. Between the covers of each volume is someone alive and close by. Sara Nelson adds that when things are going well for her, she reads! When the opposite happens, she reads more! In her book she sets out to chronicle a year's worth of passionate reading of all types and genres, in amidst her normal frenetic life of husband, children, and work. It is a fascinating account—thoughtful, quirky, and funny. She illustrates how the first words of a book immediately grab our attention!

> "*The Miracle Life of Edgar Mint* by Brady Udall has a great one:
> If I could tell you only one thing about my life it would be this: when I was seven years old the mailman ran over my head."[3]

Sara Nelson goes on to illustrate how a reader can be immediately entranced by a first line:

---

2. Buchan, *Beyond the Thirty-Nine Steps*, 91.
3. Nelson, *So Many Books, So Little Time*, 208.

"Here are some that belong in my very own First Line Hall of Fame:

The first time I had sex with a man for money, it was September.
—Laura Kasischke, *Suspicious River.*

I have noticed when someone asks for you on the telephone and, finding you out, leaves a message begging you to call him up the moment you come in, as it's important, the matter is often more important to him than to you.
—W. Somerset Maugham, *Cakes and Ale.*

My name is Salmon, like the fish, first name Susie. I was fourteen when I was murdered.
—Alice Sebold, *The Lovely Bones.*

I am always drawn back to places where I have lived, the houses and their neighborhoods.
—Truman Capote, *Breakfast at Tiffany's.*

Many years later, as he faced the firing squad, Colonel Aureliano Buendia was to remember that distant afternoon when his father took him to discover ice.
—Gabriel Garcia Márquez, *One Hundred Years of Solitude.*"[4]

The most magnificent book ever written is enthralling because it was penned by witnesses to the times—people who experienced the happenings they related. Faithful servants wrote under the direction of God himself. There are so many great introductory lines to its different parts.

In the beginning when God created the heavens and the earth . . . Gen 1:1 (NRSV)

This happened in the days of Ahasuerus, the same Ahasuerus who ruled over one hundred twenty-seven provinces from India to Ethiopia. Esth 1:1 (NRSV)

In the beginning was the Word, and the Word was with God, and the Word was God. John 1:1 (NRSV)

There is therefore now no condemnation . . . Rom 8:1 (NRSV)

I wish you would bear with me in a little foolishness. Do bear with me! 2 Cor 11:1 (NRSV)

---

4. Nelson, *So Many Books, So Little Time*, 211–212.

Now faith is the assurance of things hoped for, the conviction of things not seen. Heb 11:1 (NRSV)

In a beautifully written book, we come to know the writer as well as the characters. We must read the Bible to achieve God consciousness, to develop biblical spirituality, but never to just gain head knowledge. Heart knowledge is what we need; what our souls crave for. To follow God's plan and see its culmination in the life, death, and resurrection of our Savior Jesus, cannot be compared with any earthly writing. Let us say like Paul, "I want to know Christ and the power of the resurrection." Philippians 3:10a (NRSV)

Keep this desire in your heart when you pray.

Epistle 11

I was deeply impressed with the simplicity and fervor of his prayer, and felt that he was speaking to a familiar friend in whom he had perfect confidence and from whom real blessing was confidently expected.[1]

This was written about Hudson Taylor when he spoke at a conference in Perth, Scotland, after he had been given the opportunity to talk about the work of spreading the gospel in inland China. Hudson Taylor, when answering a call from God to go to China, greatly upset the missionaries who were already in this huge country—living as Europeans and stationed in reasonably safe coastal towns and villages. Taylor saw the great need to go inland to the millions of unreached, dressed in Chinese clothes with shaven head and a long pigtail down his back. He was untrained as a Christian worker and, although originally with some financial backing, he very soon divorced himself from the group who had sent him and spent the rest of his life with no set income. All his financial aid came solely from prayer. On his sojourns back to Britain, when he spoke at various gatherings, he refused to have a collection at the end. He believed, and was proven right, that much more money would come in after people had gone home and thought deeply about the needs of the heathen Chinese. "Poor neglected China, scarcely any one cares about it. And that immense country, containing nearly a fourth of the human race, is left in ignorance and darkness."[2]

Although Hudson had a fine intellect, when he married Maria Dyer, the marriage enabled him to further his dreams. Maria had a more thorough education. She improved his cumbrous style, teaching him to write

1. Pollock, *Hudson Taylor and Maria*, 149.
2. Pollock, *Hudson Taylor and Maria*, 20.

good English and, helping him with his Greek and the local Chinese colloquial.

At one stage, overburdened with work, away from Maria, and in ill-health, Hudson Taylor experienced a paucity in his prayer life. He agonized, fasted, and read the Bible without effect. After a visit with a fellow missionary, John McCarthy, he received a letter from him. McCarthy wrote, "I seem to have sipped only of that which can fully satisfy." [He had found the answer to Hudson's crisis] "To let my loving Saviour work in me his will. Abiding, not striving or struggling."[3]

Hudson was overcome: ". . . and I looked to Jesus and saw (and when I saw, oh, how the joy overflowed) that he had said, 'I will never leave you' . . . Hudson grasped that he must not struggle to have strength or peace but rest in the strength and peace of Christ."[4]

Years later, advanced in years and visiting Europe, Hudson Taylor was spreading the message of the desperate needs of an unevangelized China when the Boxer Rebellion occurred in that land. It was an uprising against foreigners begun by peasants but supported by the government. Missionaries and their families, and Chinese converts, were massacred. Many of those from the China Inland Mission living as their founder—as Chinese with no set income—failed to escape. The following is an extract of a letter written to her family at home, by a Mrs Atwater, newly pregnant.

> *My Dear, Dear ones,*
>
> *I have tried to gather courage to write to you once more. How am I to write all the horrible details of these days? I would rather spare you. The dear ones at Shouyang, seven in all, including our lovely girls, were taken prisoners and brought to T'aiyuan in irons, and there by the Governor's orders beheaded, together with the T'aiyuan friends, thirty-three souls. The following day the Roman Catholic priests and nuns from T'aiyuan were also beheaded, ten souls yesterday. Three weeks after these had perished, our Mission at Taku was attacked, and our six friends there, and several brave Christians who stood by them, were beheaded. We are now waiting our call home. We have tried to get away to the hills but the plans did not work. Our things are being stolen right and left, for the people know that we are condemned. Why our lives have been spared we cannot tell. The Proclamation says that whoever*

---

3. Pollock, *Hudson Taylor and Maria*, 222.
4. Pollock, *Hudson Taylor and Maria*, 222.

kills us will be doing the Governor a great service. Our Magistrate has kept peace so far, but if these men come from Taku there is not much hope, and there seems none any way we turn. The foreign soldiers are in Pao-ting-fu and it is said that peace is made. This would save us in any civilized land, no matter what people may say. The Governor seems to be in haste to finish his bloody work, for which there is little doubt he was sent to Shansi.

Dear ones, I long for a sight of your dear faces, but I fear we shall not meet on earth. I have loved you all so much, and know you will not forget the one who lies in China. There never were sisters and brothers like mine. I am preparing for the end very quietly and calmly. The Lord is wonderfully near, and He will not fail me. I was very restless and excited while there seemed a chance of life, but God has taken away that feeling, and now I just pray for grace to meet the terrible end bravely. The pain will soon be over, and oh the sweetness of the welcome above!

My little baby will go with me. I think God will give it to me in Heaven, and my dear mother will be so glad to see us. I cannot imagine the Saviour's welcome. Oh, that will compensate for all these days of suspense. Dear ones, live near to God and cling less closely to earth. There is no other way by which we can receive that Peace from God which passeth understanding. I would like to send a special message to each of you, but it tries me too much. I must keep calm and still these hours. I do not regret coming to China, but I am sorry I have done so little. My married life, two precious years, has been so full of happiness. We will die together, my dear husband and I. I used to dread separation. If we escape now it will be a miracle. I send my love to you all, and the dear friends who remember me.

Your loving sister, Lizzie."[5]

Pray that we will be conscious always that the Holy Spirit is sent to abide in us. Pray that today's missionaries will live ever in the joy of an abiding Spirit.

---

5. Broomhall, *Martyred Missionaries of the China Inland Mission*, 127–28.

Epistle 12

One of the greatest early writers and thinkers of the Patristic Age was Augustine, bp. of Hippo. In his work, *Satisfy Your Soul*, Bruce Demarest outlines one of Augustine's themes for reflection: the believer's growth into spiritual maturity in Christ. Augustine's *Commentary on the Lord's Sermon on the Mount* weaves together two other sections of scripture with the Beatitudes.

Isaiah 11:2–3	*Seven graces of the Spirit*
Matthew 5:3–10	*Seven Beatitudes*
Matthew 6:9–13	*Seven petitions of the Lord's Prayer*

[The number seven is one of great significance in scripture. It symbolizes the unity of the four corners of the earth with the Trinity. It occurs more than 700 times throughout the Bible and fifty-four times in the Book of Revelation with its seven churches, seven angels, seven seals, seven trumpets, seven stars.]

Augustine believed that every step forward in the spiritual life is a divine enablement (the Spirit's graces); the power of the Spirit inscribes on the believing heart a new law (the Beatitudes); and, the new law, which is the Spirit-enabled life, expresses itself in a habit of prayer (the Lord's Prayer).

He uses these three passages of scripture to list the seven stages to maturity in Christ:

First step: your decision for Christ is the first stage. With this decision comes a holy awe of God. Augustine links Isaiah 11:2a, 3 (NRSV) "The spirit of the LORD shall rest on him . . . the spirit of knowledge and the fear of the LORD. His delight shall be in the fear of the LORD" with the beatitude, "Blessed are the poor in Spirit, for theirs is the kingdom of heaven." Matthew 5:3 (NRSV) The humble Christian prays, "Our father in heaven, hallowed be your name."

Second step: is "acquaintance with biblical teaching in a spirit of docility."[1] "The spirit of the LORD shall rest on him . . ." Isaiah 11:2a, (NRSV) godliness (but with awe of the LORD) is coupled with the beatitude "Blessed are the meek, for they shall inherit the earth." Matthew 5:5 (NRSV) The godly Christian in humility prays, "Your kingdom come."

Third step: Now the Christian "understands sin's damaging effects upon the soul and grieves his unholy condition,"[2] "the spirit of knowledge" Isaiah 11:2b (NRSV) with the beatitude "Blessed are those who mourn, for they shall be comforted." Matthew 5:4 (NRSV) "Knowing the gulf that exists between his own performance and God's perfections, the Christian prays from the heart,"[3] "Your will be done on earth as it is in heaven."

Fourth step: a step to maturity, which involves the hard work of combatting sin and pursuing righteousness. So, Augustine connects the Spirit's grace of fortitude and might from Isaiah 11:2b (NRSV) with the beatitude "Blessed are those who hunger and thirst for righteousness, for they shall be filled." Matthew 5:6 (NRSV) Those who truly hunger for inner virtue pray, "Give us this day our daily bread", "the spiritual resources needed to win the battle against sin and Satan."[4]

Fifth step: "the Spirit's enlightenment causes love to reign as the rule of one's life, thereby fulfilling the Great Commandment. Love purifies the heart so that it may see God."[5] The Christian is then greatly moved to perform acts of mercy: "the spirit of counsel" Isaiah 11:2 (NRSV) is joined with the beatitude "Blessed are the merciful, for they will be shown mercy" Matthew 5:7 (NRSV) and the prayer, "Forgive us our sins, as we forgive those who sin against us."

---

1. Demarest, *Satisfy Your Soul*, 265.
2. Demarest, *Satisfy Your Soul*, 265.
3. Demarest, *Satisfy Your Soul*, 265.
4. Demarest, *Satisfy Your Soul*, 266.
5. Demarest, *Satisfy Your Soul*, 266.

Sixth step: "Purity of life, born out of love, opens the Christian's eyes to see the face of God as in a mirror."[6] In Ephesians 1:17–18 (NRSV) Paul says, "I pray that the God of our Lord Jesus Christ, the Father of glory, may give you a spirit of wisdom and revelation as you come to know him, so that with the eyes of your heart enlightened, you may know what is the hope to which he has called you, what are the riches of his glorious inheritance amongst the saints." The heart beholds God! From the spirit of understanding in Isaiah 11:2 to the beatitude "Blessed are the pure in heart, for they will see God." Matthew 5:8 (NRSV) But sin blinds our sight of God's face, thus we pray "Lead us not into temptation."

Seventh step: the Christian attains the practical knowledge—the spirit of wisdom in Isaiah 11:2 Wisdom brings peace to the person growing in likeness to Christ. "Blessed are the peacemakers, for they shall be called sons of God." Matthew 5:9 (NRSV) But as Satan himself continually badgers us to fracture the peace of God Christians must pray, with great earnestness, "Deliver us from evil."

What can we learn from this promulgation? God's spirit comes to us all through the Old and the New Testament. We are called with a holy calling according to God's own purpose and grace—this grace was given to us in Christ Jesus before the ages began and the Christ who was revealed to us, taught us the way of truth and love. We respond to God's grace by communing with him in prayer.

> Augustine's seven stages to maturity in Christ weave seven graces, seven beatitudes, and seven petitions into a rich tapestry of prayer, holiness, love, empowerment, contemplation of God, and service in gratitude. Cling to the gift of prayer, keep your hearts open to God's Spirit, and follow this rich tapestry presented throughout God's word.

---

6. Demarest, *Satisfy Your Soul*, 266.

Epistle 13

The Assembly of Divines at Westminster, commonly known as the Westminster Assembly, was a council of English and Scottish theologians and members of the English Parliament, which was intended to bring the Church of England into greater conformity with the Church of Scotland. It was in session from 1643–1653 when England was experimenting with a Puritan Commonwealth. The works that came out of this Assembly included *The Westminster Confession of Faith*, *The Larger Catechism*, and *The Shorter Catechism with Scripture Proofs*. However, England's initial commitment to this congress and its works was eclipsed by its return to the traditional monarchy in 1660. Charles II, the "Merry Monarch," caused the theological mood of the 1640s to be supplanted by a more fashionable pose of pragmatic skepticism.

The results of the Assembly were nevertheless held in higher honor in Scotland. John Knox, when he had returned to Scotland from his long exile, had instigated the use of catechisms for children, setting aside the afternoon of each sabbath day for instruction. Thus Scotland, in the seventeenth century, was familiar with catechisms and embraced both the Confession and the Catechisms of the Assembly. Even today there are still older Presbyterian folk who can recite the Shorter Catechism, or, at least, remember their parents doing so. It is a series of questions with answers elaborated with scripture proofs.

Question 1 What is the chief end of man?
Answer Man's chief end is to glorify God, and to enjoy him for ever.

1 Corinthians 10:31 "So, whether you eat or drink, or whatever you do, do everything for the glory of God" (KJV)

Psalm 73:25–6 "Whom have I in heaven but you? And there is nothing on earth that I desire other than you. My flesh and my heart may fail, but God is the strength of my heart and my portion forever." (KJV)

Question 2 What rule hath God given to direct us how we may glorify and enjoy him?
Answer The word of God, which is contained in the Scriptures of the Old and New Testaments, is the only rule to direct us how we may glorify and enjoy him.

Ephesians 2:20 ". . . built upon the foundations of the apostles and prophets, with Christ Jesus himself as the cornerstone." (KJV)

2 Timothy 3:16 "All scripture is inspired by God and is useful for teaching, for reproof, for correction, and for training in righteousness." (KJV)

1 John 1:3–4 "we declare to you what we have seen and heard so that you also may have fellowship with us; and truly our fellowship is with the Father and with his Son Jesus Christ.
We are writing these things so that our joy may be complete." (KJV)

Question 98 What is prayer?
Answer Prayer is an offering up of our desires unto God for things agreeable to his will in the name of Christ with the confession of our sins and thankful acknowledgment of his mercies.

Psalm 62:8 "Trust in him at all times, O people; pour out your heart before him; God is a refuge for us." (KJV)

Romans 8:27 "And God, who searches the heart, knows what is the mind of the Spirit, because the Spirit intercedes for the saints according to the will of God." (KJV)

John 16:23b "Very truly, I tell you, if you ask anything of the Father in my name, he will give it to you." (KJV)

Daniel 9:4 "I prayed to the LORD my God and made my confession." (KJV)

Philippians 4:6 "Do not worry about anything, but in everything in prayer and supplication with thanksgiving let your requests be made known to God." (KJV)

Question 99 What rule hath God given for our direction in prayer?
Answer The whole word of God is of use to direct us in prayer but the special rule of direction is that form of prayer that Christ taught his disciples, commonly called *The Lord's Prayer.*

1 John 5:14 "And this is the boldness we have in him, that if we ask anything according to his will, he hears us." (KJV)

Matthew 6:9–13 "Pray then this way: Our Father in heaven, hallowed be your name.
Your kingdom come. Your will be done, on earth as it is in heaven.
Give us this day our daily bread.
And forgive us our debts, as we also have forgiven our debtors.
And do not bring us to the time of trial, but rescue us from the evil one." (KJV)

Question 107 What does the conclusion of the Lord's Prayer teach us?
Answer The conclusion of the Lord's Prayer (which is, "For thine is the kingdom, and the power, and the glory, for ever, Amen") teacheth us, to take our encouragement in prayer from God only, and in our prayers to praise him, ascribing kingdom, power and glory to him. And in testimony of our desire, and assurance to be heard, we say, Amen.

Daniel 9:18b–19 "We do not present our supplication before you on the ground of our righteousness, but on the ground of your great mercies. O Lord, hear; O Lord, forgive; O Lord, listen and act and do not delay! For your own sake, O God." (KJV)

I Chronicles 29:11–13 "Yours, O Lord, are the greatness, the power, the glory, the victory, and the majesty; for all that is in the heavens and on earth is yours, yours is the kingdom O Lord, and you are exalted as head above all. Riches and honour come from you, and you rule over all. In your hand are power and might; and it is in your hand to make great and to give strength to all. And now, our God, we give thanks to you and praise your glorious name." (KJV)

Epistle 14

In recent years there has been a deal of interest in trivia, so much so, that there are regularly groups that play a game of trivia in competition. The cell phone is very handy when you know you can secretly ring your mother to get some answers about the Academy Awards in the 1940s and 1950s. There are also a lot of people who have brains full of what other people think are useless facts, but which often make interesting listening. Here are a few examples...

1. Contrary to numerous film portrayals, Elizabeth I and Mary, Queen of Scots, never met in person.
2. Australian Prime Minister Robert Menzies refused a knighthood in 1954.
3. The first Hanoverian King of Great Britain, George I, was actually fifty-eighth in line for the throne—but the first Protestant!
4. There were more women and children who died of brutality or starvation in British concentration camps during the Boer War, than soldiers who died in the actual conflict.
5. In 1962, a computer programmer at NASA omitted a hyphen from Mariner 1's flight program and, as a consequence, the space probe headed off course and had to be destroyed at a cost of more than 7,000,000 dollars.
6. Again, to do with space exploration—there was only eight seconds of fuel left when the lunar module landed on the moon in 1969.

Can you think of anything in the Bible that is worthless trivia? One book that many people might put in this category is the Book of Leviticus. When men in a Japanese POW camp asked the chaplain if they could use the fine India paper of the Bible to roll their ersatz tobacco, he, knowing how desperate they were for any kind of relief from their bleak existence, said yes—but begin with the Book of Leviticus! Nevertheless, even considering that Jesus came so that we would not need to abide by all the interminable laws listed in Leviticus, he himself said, "Do not think that I have come to abolish the law or the prophets; I have come not to abolish but to fulfill." Matthew 5:17 (NRSV) All the books of the Bible fit together to tell the grand narrative of God's story. But, "it does not purport to be just one more story of humankind's search for God. No, this is God's story, the account of his search for us, a story essentially told in four chapters: Creation, Fall, Redemption, Consummation. In this story, God is the divine protagonist, Satan the antagonist, God's people the agonists (although too often also the antagonists), with redemption and reconciliation as the plot resolution."[1]

Leviticus talks of holiness: "For I am the LORD your God; sanctify yourselves therefore, and be holy, for I am holy." Leviticus 11:44a (NRSV) The first section deals with ritual purity—laws for the priest; the second section with moral holiness—love to others. The last section contains covenant curses and blessings, which brings a formal conclusion to the covenant structure that began in Exodus. Leviticus, as with all books of the Bible, can only be fully understood in the light of what goes before it and what follows it!

This book of Holiness sends the same message we encounter throughout both the Old and New Testaments. When we accept Christ as our Savior, we need to continually put aside our sin and, with the help of the Holy Spirit, strive to live a life of holiness . . .

> *Who shall ascend the hill of the LORD? And who shall stand in*
> *his holy place? Those who have clean hands and pure hearts . . .*
> Ps 24:3–5 (NRSV)

Irrespective of our skills, or lack of skills in prayer, we must strive to continue in prayer. With reading God's Word and praying we will develop a passion for a holy life, a life lived in response to the sacrifice of Jesus. The scriptures provide the key for living this life of holiness.

> *I appeal to you therefore, brothers and sisters, by the mercies of*
> *God, to present your bodies as a living sacrifice, holy and accept-*
> *able to God, which is your spiritual worship. Do not be conformed*
> *to this world, but be transformed by the renewing of your minds,*

---

1. Fee and Stuart, *How to Read the Bible Book by Book*, 14.

so that you may discern what is the will of God—what is good and acceptable and perfect. Rom 12:1–2 (NRSV)

Blessed be the God and Father of our Lord Jesus Christ, who has blessed us in Christ with every spiritual blessing in the heavenly places just as he chose us in Christ before the foundation of the world to be holy and blameless before him in love. Eph 1:3–4 (NRSV)

Always remember: "For the eyes of the Lord are on the righteous, and his ears are open to their prayer." 1 Pet 3:12 (NRSV)

We can always find, in God's Word advice relevant to our life in modern times. In the Book of Leviticus where we looked at Chapter 11, v 44a, it appears as if v 44b is very relevant to our present frightening times. Trivia is true, and generally just a disclosure of strange facts or events that don't seem relevant enough to remember. But trivia can send the brain on an interesting journey, often pushing you to find out more! We can come across trivial facts in the Bible—or what seem to be trivial facts—but these facts are a guide to realizing that brief accounts bring a much more involved story than that presented in the text. We talked about that previously when we looked at the practice of "close reading" in the Hebrew of the Old Testament.

Epistle 15

Have you ever worried that God hears all your prayers when there must be millions of prayers raised to him every night and day? This is the great wonder of God. We cannot judge him by human standards—in fact, we cannot possibly fathom the being of God at all. God's attributes are essential and inherent dimensions of his very nature. Further, his attributes are inseparable from his very essence. God is spirit; not composed of matter and does not possess a physical nature. He is alive and personal, capable of feeling and choosing. He is infinite—unlimited and unlimitable in terms of space, time, knowledge, and power. He is unchanging; he is constant; he is faithful. God is holy; just and true; full of mercy and grace. Most of all he is sovereign. Then of course you hear people quoting the "o" words in relation to his character:

Omnipotence—all powerful

Omnipresence—present everywhere

Omniscience—all knowing.

This is the great wonder that such a God loves each one of us and knows well each one of us, "O LORD, you have searched me and known me . . ." The wondrous words of Psalm 139:9 ensure that we are loved and known "If I take the wings of the morning and settle at the farthest limits of the sea, even there your hand shall lead me." (NRSV) Our name is inscribed on the palms of his hands. His law is written on our hearts. What a wondrous God he is!

In Psalm 147:4–5 (NRSV) we read:

> *He determines the number of the stars;*
> *he gives to all of them their names.*
> *Great is our LORD, and abundant in power;*
> *his understanding is beyond measure.*

There are various estimates of the number of stars in our universe; we do not always see the possibilities in the city sky. Forty sextillion is one estimate; another is 1 billion million; or 1 quadrillion. Yet he names each one of them! In Matthew 10:29–31 (NRSV) we read, "Are not two sparrows sold for a penny? Yet not one of them will fall to the ground apart from your Father. And even the hairs of your head are counted. So do not be afraid, you are of more value than many sparrows." Do you ever think on this when you see a bird fall to the ground or discover one splattered on the road?

Not only does God know us but, because of the suffering and sacrifice of his son Jesus, we can now come to him with our sins blotted out. "This was in accordance with the eternal purpose he has carried out in Christ Jesus our Lord, in whom we have access to God in boldness and confidence through faith in him." Ephesians 3:11–12 (NRSV) We are now adopted as God's sons and daughters:

> *But when the fullness of time had come, God sent his Son, born of a woman, born under the law, in order to redeem those who were under the law, so that we might receive adoption as children. And because you are children, God has sent the Spirit of his Son into our hearts, crying, "Abba! Father!" So you are no longer a slave but a child, and if a child then also an heir, through God.* Gal 4:4–7 (NRSV)

Our wondrous God knows us, loves us, and he will take us by the hand and lead us out of the land of sin and slavery. We are his children and his heirs.

> *Blessed be the God and Father of our Lord Jesus Christ! By his great mercy he has given us a new birth into a living hope through the resurrection of Jesus Christ from the dead, and into an inheritance that is imperishable, undefiled, and unfading, kept in heaven for you, who are being protected by the power of God through faith for a salvation ready to be revealed in the last time. In this you rejoice, even if now for a little while you have had to suffer various trials, so that the genuineness of your faith—being more precious than gold that, though perishable, is tested by fire—may be found to result in praise and glory and honor when Christ is revealed. Although you have not seen him, you love him; and even though you do not see him now, you believe in him and rejoice with an indescribable and glorious joy, for you are receiving the outcome of your faith, the salvation of your souls.* 1 Pet 1:3–9 (NRSV)

Confidently we know that we now have access to God. We can reach out to our heavenly Father and pour out all our petitions in prayer to him. He is faithful, he is listening, he will comfort and strengthen us—no matter when, no matter where, no matter what is involved, we shall be heard.

> *Let us approach with a true heart in full assurance of faith, with our hearts sprinkled clean from an evil conscience and our bodies washed with pure water.* Heb 10:22 (NRSV)

If you are further troubled, go into a secret place, and read through Psalm 139.

Epistle 16

Do you believe that Julius Caesar existed? Or Marco Polo? Or Archimedes? Homer, Herodotus, Thucydides, Boadicea, Cleopatra, Metternich, Galileo, Machiavelli? Why do you believe all these people existed?

. . . because there is recorded proof—written by eye-witnesses who lived in the times or by later people who had talked to such witnesses.

We can even read that Thucydides criticized Herodotus for handling the truth loosely! Herodotus is often referred to as the "Father of History" because he was considered to be very systematic in his historical investigations. Thucydides, a historian from the same period (latter part of the fifth century BC), was also an army general who set strict standards of impartiality, evidence gathering, and analysis of cause and effect. Thus, when he felt Herodotus had given exaggerated accounts of battle numbers, etc. he called him to task. Herodotus did admit that one couldn't always believe the stories he related. Thus, we not only have evidence of the existence of both these men (before Christ walked the earth) but we can find dialogue between them. If this is believed, because of witnesses of the times, why do so many people challenge the existence of Jesus and the story of his life on earth?

We don't have to rely exclusively on the gospels and the writings of Paul and the other apostles. There are non-Christian writers of the times, for example, who testify to Jesus. Cornelius Tacticus, born in AD 56, was a Roman historian and politician who was openly hostile to Christianity. He was an admirable historian using official records and talking to many people about actual events. He gives a very honest account of Nero and his overly cruel persecutions of the Christians; actions that aroused pity among the witnesses. The writings of Tacticus also include an accurate date of the death of Christ. His friend, Pliny the Younger, was a lawyer and magistrate of ancient Rome. He wrote an enormous number of missives that remain a unique testimony to everyday life in the first century AD. The two most important of these describe the eruption of Mount Vesuvius and the request to the Emperor for instructions regarding official policy concerning Christians. Of interest in all these documents is the fact that the followers of Christ were originally called Christians by the pagans.

The first-century Jewish historian, Flavius Josephus, contains in his *Antiquities of the Jews*, two references to Jesus of Nazareth and one to John the Baptist. In Book 18, he states that Jesus was the Messiah and a wise teacher who was crucified by Pilate. However, most scholars feel that this passage is not authentic considering the insertion of the word Messiah. Yet the second reference where Josephus refers to James, the brother of Jesus called the Christ, is considered authentic. In the case of the reference to John the Baptist and the account of his arrest and death, there are differences, but this points to a definite possibility of it being genuine, because any Christian redactions would have striven to make the account align with the view in the Gospels.

Then, of course, we have the writings of the witnesses to Christ in the New Testament. When the letters of Paul were available to the people and then the later Gospels, there would have been alive actual witnesses to Christ and others who had known such witnesses. Would not these people have risen up in agitation if these writings had been false—just as Thucydides had criticized Herodotus for false reporting?

Peter Williams, in his book *Can We Trust the Gospels?*, makes the salient point that four Gospels, containing such an abundance of material about one person in ancient times, was a rarity. The Gospels do not conflict but supplement and complement each other, sometimes recording similar events; sometimes looking at a different aspect of the same event. In relating the nativity story in the Gospels, for example, Luke relates the happenings from Mary's aspect whereas Matthew uses Joseph as his source. All were written close to the time of the events recorded. All have a familiarity with the circumstances and the places their authors wrote about. More than that, there is an intimate knowledge of Jesus himself. Even though the disciples didn't always understand the extent of Jesus' mission, they followed him faithfully. Their writings confirm their Jewishness but often reveal the nuances of their backgrounds—a doctor, a fisherman, a tax-collector.

Not only did the gospel writers come from a background of oral tradition but scribes of the New Testament times were mainly Christian—in fact the Christian scribes can be recognized as also saving the literature of the pagans, as they were expert and conscientious copyists in anything they undertook. In addition, their honesty determined that the four Gospels were produced with all the individual styles and subtle differences that make them so unique. We have today many manuscripts—in fact over 1,000 Greek manuscripts of the Gospels, which have been discovered and identified. They are from the second century, the third century, and the fourth century. Hence the gap between the earliest available manuscripts and the writing of the Gospels themselves has narrowed massively.

In his last chapter Williams asks the question: "Who would make all this up?"[1] We can believe that Jesus walked the earth and went to the cross to die for us. Paul writes: be "in Christ" "So if anyone is in Christ, there is a new creation: everything old has passed away, see, everything has become new!" 2 Corinthians 5:17 (NRSV)

> Most of all, because the death of Christ has torn down the temple curtain, we can enter the Holy of Holies and commune with our God in prayer.

---

1. Williams, *Can We Trust the Gospels?* 129.

Epistle 17

In Epistle 15 we discussed how God is a great and wondrous God yet he is our personal Father. He knows us, he loves us, he guides us, he comforts us. Through his son, Jesus Christ, we can approach him with confidence and joy. But how do we discover what God's will is for each of us in this earthly life?

We must read our Bible—the Word of God—and we must read it regularly and systematically. We achieve little if we just randomly choose a particular verse or if we impose our own ideas on the text. Nor will our personal experiences be the avenue to guide us to find answers. Only study, careful meditation, and prayer will enlighten our minds. We need to rejoice, give thanks, and seek after God. Our characters will develop, we will be changed, and we will draw closer to God. "Rejoice always, pray without ceasing, give thanks in all circumstances for this is the will of God in Christ Jesus for you." 1 Thessalonians 5:16–18 (NRSV) Plus, we have something that the Old Testament saints lacked—we have the Holy Spirit in its fullest measure: "Do not quench the Spirit. Do not despise the words of the prophets but test everything; hold fast to what is good; abstain from every form or evil." Thessalonians 5:19–22 (NRSV)

We cannot discern the mind of God but, through the Bible and the Holy Spirit, we can develop a heart like his—a heart of virtue and of love. And remember, no matter how many Christian books might capture our interest, the Bible is the only book with God's direct message to us.

> *The unfolding of your words give light; it imparts understanding to the simple* Ps 119:130 (NRSV)

We must pray to God asking him to give us spiritual understanding as we read. Pray that God's Spirit would enlighten our hearts and minds so that we can be guided to do his will in our daily lives. Pray always before reading!

Bruce K. Waltke, Professor Emeritus at Regent College, Vancouver, writes:

> I used to read the Bible for its academic merit, and I will confess I got little spiritual benefit from it. God didn't speak to me; it didn't change my heart. Then I read about a scholar who found his Bible study dry until he asked God for enlightenment. He began praying, "Lord, speak to me through Your Word." He did not simply want to read the stories; he wanted to know God's heart. At first he noticed very little difference in his reading. But soon, within three weeks of praying that prayer as he read, his heart began to burn within him. God began revealing to him how His Word should change his life. He developed a love for His teaching. God heard his prayer and began to speak to him through His Word. When I worked on translating the book of Proverbs for the NIV, I spend 60 hours a week on that text. But after 10 weeks of work, I was farther away from God than when I began because I forgot to pray that scholar's prayer . . . Prayer can never be separated from reading God's Word.[1]

Though Christian books will never replace God's Book there are many that can help us to in our search of the scriptures. These usually take the form of a guide to work through the Bible itself detailing the background of each book of the Bible and telling something about the various biblical characters. There are also a number of Study Bibles that include helpful notes to explain difficult sections as we read through the text.

God has a plan for all of us. We may not discern it and, because it is beyond our control, we often lose patience and go our own way. But God is at work in all the circumstances of our life—whether great or small. He is faithful even though we are not. We must endeavor to learn all we can about him from his Word with prayer and, in doing so, discover his will for us.

> *O the depth of the riches and wisdom and knowledge of God! How unsearchable are his judgments and how inscrutable his ways!*
>
> *"For who has known the mind of the Lord?*
> *Or who has been his counselor?*
> *Or who has given a gift to him,*
> *to receive a gift in return?"*

---

1. Waltke, *Finding the Will of God*, 74–75.

For from him and through him and to him are all things. To him be the glory forever. Amen.

I appeal to you therefore, brothers and sisters, by the mercies of God, to present your bodies as a living sacrifice, holy and acceptable to God, which is your spiritual worship. Do not be conformed to this world, but be transformed by the renewing of your minds, so that you may discern what is the will of God—what is good and acceptable and perfect. Rom 11:33–12:2 (NRSV)

Epistle 18

The apostle Paul wrote:

> *For this reason I bow my knees before the Father, from whom every family in heaven and on earth takes its name. I pray that, according to the riches of his glory, he may grant that you may be strengthened in your inner being with power through his Spirit, and that Christ may dwell in your hearts through faith, as you are being rooted and grounded in love. I pray that you may have the power to comprehend, with all the saints, what is the breadth and length and height and depth, and to know the love of Christ that surpasses knowledge, so that you may be filled with all the fullness of God.* Eph 3:14–19 (NRSV)

The deep love relationship with Jesus Christ involves every aspect of the believer's being and it must be kindled with prayer—the prayer that comes from a heart that is open to the Holy Spirit.

All of Paul's letters encourage Christians to commune with God through prayer—for guidance and comfort but most of all—to enable men and women to come close to God and experience his peace. Often it is beneficial to us to look at different translations of Bible passages to bring to our attention to different aspects and emphases that can sometimes appear to be hidden! Gary Newton presents an analytical outline of Philippians 4:4–9 (from NRSV).

    4 *Rejoice* in the Lord always.
    I will say it again: *Rejoice!*
    5 Let your graciousness be known to everyone.
        The Lord is near.
    6 Don't worry about anything.
        but in everything,
            through prayer and petition
                with thanksgiving,

> let your requests be made known to God.
>> 7 *And* the peace of God,
>>> which surpasses every thought,
>> will guard your hearts
>>> and your minds in Christ Jesus.
>> 8 Finally, brothers and sisters,
>>> whatever is true,
>>> whatever is honorable,
>>> whatever is just,
>>> whatever is pure,
>>> whatever is lovely,
>>> whatever is commendable—
>>> if there is any moral excellence and
>>> if there is any praise—
>
> dwell on these things,
>
> 9 Do what you have learned and
>> received and
>> heard and
>> seen in me.
>>> And *the God of peace* will be with you."[1]

- No matter what emotions we may be experiencing, we should seek joy in our relationship with Jesus Christ *(v.4)*

- The fact that the Lord is always by our side helps us be more relaxed in the midst of difficulty *(v.5)*

- The best antidote for worry is prayer *(v.6)*

- In order to experience God's presence and peace, we must bring our emotions, thoughts, and behavior under his Lordship *(vv.4–9)*

- Even in the midst of horrible circumstances, we can pray with thanksgiving because God is close to us and in control *(vv.4–7)*

- Although we may not always understand how and when God answers prayer, we should pray about everything that concerns us *(vv.6–7)*

- When we rejoice in the Lord and talk to him about all our needs, his peace guards our hearts and minds *(vv.4–7)*

- When we discipline our minds according to God's Word, and obey God consistently, the God of peace promises to be with us *(vv.8–9)*

---

1. Newton, *Heart-Deep Teaching*, 64.

- Our thoughts influence our actions for either good or evil *(vv.8–9)*
- Experiencing God's presence and his peace involves more than just our emotions *(vv.4–9)*
- The peace of God seems to be intimately connected to the indwelling of the Holy Spirit in our very being *(vv.7–9)*
- While the peace of God may be beyond our human understanding, the path to experiencing it is simple *(vv.4–7)*[2]

We must open our hearts to the Holy Spirit when we pray these words from Philippians, and the Spirit will search, cleanse, and mold us, and bring peace to our hearts, our minds, and our souls.

---

2. Newton, *Heart-Deep Teaching*, 73.

Epistle 19

Have you ever watched an eagle fly overhead—perhaps not in the coastal areas of Australia but certainly on film or television? Strangely, eagles do not move their wings like other birds. They sit on the high crags of cliffs and wait until they sense the wind currents then they launch out and *soar*. Hitting turbulence on a flight at 30,000 feet can cause quite a bumpy ride but eagles soaring high in the sky seek this turbulence for a free, energy-saving lift. This technique is called thermal soaring. They can find hot rising pockets of air and use the currents to stay aloft—flying higher and longer than other birds. There are many fluctuations in the speed of air and, eagles in particular, are able to navigate within this environment.

Eagles are majestic, powerful, monogamous, and faithful parents to their eaglets. "Saul and Jonathan, beloved and lovely! In life and death they were not divided; they were swifter than eagles, they were stronger than lions." 2 Samuel 1:23 (NRSV) Eagles are also patient—waiting for the right time and suitable wind to hunt for prey; generally from hundreds of feet in the air. Strangely they have both monocular and binocular vision meaning they can use their eyes independently of each other. With swift attack they grab their prey in their talons and soar to their eyrie. God instructed Moses to say to the Israelites: "You have seen what I did to the Egyptians, and how I bore you on eagles' wings and brought you to myself." Exodus 19:4 (NRSV) And, then in the wilderness, God did not desert the Israelites. In the song of Moses, we read: "the LORD's own portion was his people, Jacob his allotted share. He sustained him in a desert land, in a howling wilderness waste; he shielded him, cared for him, and guarded him as the apple of his eye. As an eagle stirs up his nest and hovers over his young." Deuteronomy 32:9–11a (NRSV)

In the Old Testament, God also uses the allegory of the eagle to warn his disobedient people of the consequences of their wickedness: "The LORD will bring a nation from far away, from the end of the earth, to swoop down on you like an eagle, a nation whose language you do not understand, a grim-faced nation showing no respect to the old or favor to the young. It shall consume the fruit of your livestock and the fruit of your ground until you are destroyed, leaving you neither grain, wine, and oil, nor the increase of your cattle and the issue of your flock, until it has made you perish." Deuteronomy 28:49–51 (NRSV)

But the LORD is a God of mercy and forgiveness. The most wonderful illustration of all the attributes of the eagle is found in Psalm 91. Although the eagle is not mentioned in name, we see the similarity in an assurance of God's protection just as the eagle protects its young fledglings as they learn to leave the nest.

> *You who live in the shelter of the Most High; who abide in the shadow of the Almighty, will say to the LORD, "My refuge and my fortress; my God in whom I trust." For he will deliver you from the snare of the fowler and from the deadly pestilence; he will cover you with his pinions, and under his wings you will find refuge; his faithfulness is a shield and a buckler. You will not fear the terror of the night, or the arrow that flies by day, or the pestilence that stalks in darkness, or the destruction that wastes at noonday.* Ps 91:1–6 (NRSV)

We will not fear the loneliness of the day or night; we will not fear the onset of the pandemic. God is with us and wraps his wings around us. Sometimes fear kills more than the plague itself!

> *Those who love me, I will deliver; I will protect those who know my name. When they call to me, I will deliver them; I will be with them in trouble, I will rescue them and honor them. With long life I will satisfy them, and show them my salvation.* Ps 91:14–16 (NRSV)

We sometimes need repeated practice to leave the eyrie. But, eventually, we can catch the current of wind and soar. We can catch the breath of the Holy Spirit and soar to realms unknown. We read and study the Word with our eyes but we must grasp the Holy Spirit who dwells there, with the eyes of faith—our monocular and binocular vision. We must listen for the rush of the violent wind as it fills the place where we are; we must look for the divided tongues, as of fire, resting on the heads of the apostles. We must listen for the Spirit to give us the ability to feel and know him. We can proclaim: *Come, breathe on me, Holy Spirit. I will rise up on eagles' wings and soar!*

Remember above, the words of Psalm 91:15 (NRSV), "When they call to me, I will answer them." We must pray; we must call to him; we must wait for the Spirit.

Have you not known? Have you not heard?
The LORD is the everlasting God,
the Creator of the ends of the earth.
He does not faint or grow weary; his understanding is
unsearchable.
He gives power to the faint,
and strengthens the powerless.
Even youths will faint and be weary,
and the young will fall exhausted;
but those who wait for the LORD shall
renew their strength,
they shall mount up with wings like eagles,
they shall run and not be weary,
they shall walk and not faint. Isa 40:28–31 (NRSV)

Epistle 20

Then, what I had waited for, pounced upon me. The stars went out, and I fell. Like something come alive, the rope lashed violently against my face and I fell silently, endlessly into nothingness, as if dreaming of falling. I fell fast, faster than thought, and my stomach protested at the swooping speed of it. I swept down, and from far above I saw myself falling and felt nothing. No thoughts, and all fears gone away. So this is it!

A whoomphing impact on my back broke the dream, and the snow engulfed me. I felt cold wetness on my cheeks. I wasn't stopping, and for an instant blinding moment I was frightened. Now, the crevasse! Ahhh . . . NO!!

The acceleration took me again, mercifully fast, too fast for the scream which died above me . . .[1]

Joe Simpson had just summitted the South Ridge of Cerro Yantauri in the Peruvian Andes with his climbing companion Simon Yates. Coming down he experienced a fall and broke his right leg badly. The two were now descending with Simon lowering Joe down with ropes from a belay seat. In the midst of a storm and battling exhaustion Joe gathered speed on a slope and went over the edge. Hanging freely, he realized at once Simon would not be able to pull him up. After over an hour of battling to hold onto the rope Simon knew he could no longer hold on. To save himself he cut the rope.

This is a story of survival entitled *Touching the Void*. After surviving the fall and with a useless leg, Joe faced the near impossibility of climbing 130 feet up a slope at a difficult angle. After hours of determination, setbacks, and perseverance, he rolled out of the yawning top. This was just the beginning—he still had six miles to crawl or hop to the base camp. He

1. Simpson, *Touching the Void*, 108.

was entirely alone in the silence of the mountain. Through his jumbled mind he heard a voice. "The *voice* was clean and sharp and commanding. [The book then traces his horrific journey to safety following the voice.] . . . The *voice* told me exactly how to go about it . . . The *voice* would interrupt any reverie."[2] . . . "The *voice,* and the watch, urged me into motion whenever the heat from the glacier halted me in a drowsy exhausted daze . . . the *voice* told me to reach that point in half an hour . . . the *voice* would tell me I was late, and I would wake with a start and crawl again."[3] ". . . the *voice* said, Go on, keep going, faster . . . I tried to ignore the *voice* but couldn't—don't sleep, not here, find a snow hole."[4] "Get moving now, move! . . . Look how far you've gone. Just do it, don't think about it."[5]

The most incredible part of this tale of survival is the *"voice!"* Since Joe Simpson's book was published in 1988, he has still continued to embrace his love of mountaineering but his income is from writing and speaking tours. In any of the interviews broadcast no-one seems to ask about this voice. The persistent question is how he felt about the fact that Simon cut the rope.

He writes that, when facing what seemed impossible, his mind was a mess of negative thoughts but the voice took over as if it was alien from his own brain. Could it have just been Joe's inner positive self? Mountaineers need to be strong in mind as well as body, self-sufficient, relying entirely on their own strength and ability. Or was it more than that? We are all so conditioned by today's world when men and women are driven high achievers and believe everything they attain is achieved by self. Thus, being enamored with the created rather than the Creator, men and women are like Pharaoh—with hardened hearts and wayward souls.

In 1 Kings 19:11–12 Elijah was instructed to "'Go out and stand on the mountain before the LORD, for the LORD is about to pass by. Now there was a great wind, so strong that it was splitting mountains and breaking rocks in pieces before the LORD, but the LORD was not in the wind; and after the wind an earthquake, but he LORD was not in the earthquake; and after the earthquake a fire, but the LORD was not in the fire; and after the fire a sound of sheer silence." (NRSV) Elijah's encounter with God was at one of his lowest points in his life. He had fled from Jezebel into the wilderness. "I have been very zealous for the LORD,

---

2. Simpson, *Touching the Void*, 141.
3. Simpson, *Touching the Void*, 144–45.
4. Simpson, *Touching the Void*, 160.
5. Simpson, *Touching the Void*, 163.

the God of hosts; for the Israelites have forsaken your covenant, thrown down your altars, and killed your prophets with the sword. I alone am left and they are seeking my life, to take it away." Kings 19:10 (NRSV) In our times of great fear or sorrow do we want to flee? Are the noises of the world so strong that we do not stop to listen to the *sound of silence—God himself*?

God does speak to us in our hearts and minds. We can speak to him in a quiet place and stay still for our souls to be refreshed. God often speaks to us when we least expect it. In his book *The Problem of Pain*, C. S. Lewis writes, "God whispers to us in our pleasures, speaks in our conscience, but shouts in our pains: it is his megaphone to rouse a deaf world."[6]

> *O let me hear you speaking*
> *in accents clear and still,*
> *above the storms of passion,*
> *the murmurs of self-will.*
> *O speak to re-assure me,*
> *to hasten or control,*
> *and speak to make me listen,*
> *O Guardian of my soul.*[7]

---

6. Lewis, *The Problem of Pain*, 3.
7. Bode, "O Jesus I have Promised," v3.

Epistle 21

Christopher De Vinck is a teacher, poet, and writer who, in 1985, wrote an article about his disabled brother for the *Reader's Digest*. This article was later reprinted in the *Wall Street Journal*, *Catholic Digest*, the *Chicago Sun*, the *New York Post*, *Read Magazine*, *New Covenant*, *Catholic New York*, and *Campus Life*. It was read by many ordinary people but also by leaders in the Church, and the United States President, affecting all of them profoundly.

The following is a precis of the article:

> *I grew up in a house where my brother was on his back in his bed for thirty-two years, in the same corner of his room, under the same window, beside the same yellow walls. He was blind, mute. His legs were twisted. He didn't have the strength to lift his head or the intelligence to learn anything. Oliver was born with severe brain damage which left him and his body in a permanent state of helplessness . . . My family and I fed Oliver. We changed his diapers, bathed him, tickled his chest to make him laugh. We pulled the shade down on the window over his head in the morning to keep the sun from burning his tender skin. We listened to him laugh as we watched television downstairs. We listened to him rock his arms up and down to make the bed squeak . . . Oliver's case was hopeless.*
>
> > *Well, I guess you could call him a vegetable.*
> > *I called him Oliver, my brother.*
> > *You would have loved him.*
>
> *Oliver grew to the size of a ten-year-old. He had a big chest, a large head. His hands and feet were those of a five-year-old, small and soft. We'd wrap a box of baby cereal for him at Christmas and place it under the tree. We'd pat his head with a damp cloth in the middle of a heat wave. His baptismal certificate hung on the wall above his head. A bishop came to the house and confirmed him.*

> We were fortunate that Oliver's case was so severe. The best we could do for him was feed him three times a day, bathe him, and keep him warm. He never knew what his condition was. We were blessed with his presence, a true presence of peace . . . We lived with him moment by moment.
>
> Feeding him was like feeding an eight-month-old child. His head was always propped up to a slight incline on pillows. A teaspoon of food was brought to his lips. He would feel the spoon, open his mouth, close his mouth, and swallow. I still today, can hear the sound of the spoon ticking and tapping against his red bowl in the silence of his room . . . once my mother said to me, "When you go to heaven, Oliver will run to you, embrace you, and the first thing he will say is 'Thank you.'" . . . When Oliver died, my mother held him in her arms, and said "Goodbye, my angel."[1]

De Vinck believes that Oliver created a certain power around him and his family, which changed all their lives. He cannot explain Oliver's influence except to say that the powerless in our world do hold great power. The weak do confound the mighty. "But God chose what is foolish in the world to shame the wise; God chose what is weak in the world to shame the strong." 1 Corinthians 1:27 (NRSV) Oliver's family once took him to a Healing Service at their church. De Vinck knew his whole being was aching to ask for healing for his brother, but he felt a prayer rise from his heart asking only that Oliver would always remain as he was—pure in heart. A child with no apparent usefulness of meaning was a holy innocent, a child of light. How many priests or ministers today would refuse to confirm Oliver because he could not mentally respond to his vows?

From Oliver we can learn to pray and minister to those who suffer and grieve. We can learn compassion; we can pray with compassion. The ways of our Father are hidden to us but we can somehow understand that a child who lives in apparent emptiness can see God and know his peace. At the other end of our life span we can also believe that Christians who suffer from dementia can still know the love and comfort of their Savior. God knows their hearts. We think because the mind is gone, all that is precious is gone. Our memory is a mental activity—it depicts our mindset and constructs our identity. Being the essence of the individual, it is consumed with self and, we wrongly think, essential for existence. God's memory is different. God never forgets; he is faithful; his memory is entirely governed by fidelity. It is God's remembering that confers on us

---

1. De Vinck, *The Power of the Powerless*, 9, 11–14.

our identity. We are never lost to God. We may forget, whether by disease or by will, but God never forgets. Then again, in the face of the naïve assumptions of modernity with its limited version of personhood, many patients with dementia have an extraordinary ability to recall hidden narrative from their lives, plus ever-loving partners experience constant evidence of loving recognition. Dementia cannot rob the heart!

We need constant prayer for the families of the so-called powerless. Pray with compassion for people who are prevented from being with those who are so precious to them at these fearful times. Pray that they will always know that "the steadfast love of the LORD is from everlasting to everlasting on those who fear him." Psalm 103:17 (NRSV)

Jesus said: "I am the good shepherd. I know my own and my own know me, just as the Father knows me and I know the Father." John 10:14–15 (NRSV)

Epistle 22

How often do we hear people using quotations to illustrate their standpoint? Unfortunately, not only do many quotations fail to stand up to scrutiny, but they are often misquotations! "God helps those who help themselves" is a perfect example of such a misquotation plus it is an incorrect theology. It appears in a tale by Aesop, the writer of fables in ancient times. A waggoner was once driving a heavy load along a muddy road. He came to a section where the wheels sank halfway in the mire. The more the horses pulled the deeper sank the wheels. The waggoner threw down his whip, knelt down, and prayed to Hercules the Strong saying "Help me in my hour of distress!" Hercules appeared to him and said "Tut, now don't sprawl there. Get up and put your shoulder to the wheel: *'The gods help those who help themselves.'*" The Bible teaches the exact opposite because our God makes special provision to help the helpless—he acts first.

Another, "No rest for the wicked," is often used for people staying up late at night overwhelmed with a copious amount of work. This is a misquote from Isaiah 48:22 (NRSV), "'There is no peace,' says the LORD, 'for the wicked.'" This is not "tongue in cheek" about gaining some sleep but, an injunction from the prophet that we must reject our sinful ways to find a wonderful peace and solace in the LORD. "Blood is thicker than water" is often thought to be a biblical quotation, but it is an eighteenth-century English proverb. It refers to the precedence of everyday familial relationships, whereas blood in the Bible refers to sacrifice and the theology of the covenant.

Prayer is often misinterpreted. This important part of the life of a Christian is often looked at from a worldly perspective—an extra just to be used on occasions of need! Perhaps it is unnecessary? Someone will often say: Does God not know, even without being reminded, both in what respect we are troubled and what is best for us, so that it may seem in a sense superfluous that he should be stirred up by our prayers—as if he were drowsily blinking or even sleeping until he is aroused by our voice? And, if he is all-wise, doesn't he already know what is best for us? And, if he is all-good, won't he do it whether we pray or not? C. S. Lewis considers the actions we take on our own initiative with our work, for example. "The kind of causality we exercise by work is, so to speak, divinely guaranteed, and therefore ruthless. By it we are free to do ourselves as much harm as we please. But the kind which we exercise by prayer is not like that; God has left himself a discretionary power. Had he not done so, prayer would be an activity too dangerous for man and we should have the horrible state of things envisaged by Juvenal: 'Enormous prayers which Heaven in anger grants.' (*Satires*, Book IV, Satire x, line 111)."[1]

Our God instructs us to call upon his name. Through the sacrifice of his son Jesus on the cross, we have been absolved from our sin and have become adopted sons and daughters who can now confidently cry, "Abba! Father!" By communing with him we can experience all the treasures and promises he ordains for us. Calvin gives succinct reasons for prayer.

> *First, so that our hearts may be fired with a zealous and burning desire ever to seek, love and serve him while we become accustomed in every need to flee to him as to a sacred anchor. Secondly, that there may enter our hearts no desire and no wish at all of which we should be ashamed to make him a witness, while we learn to set all our wishes before his eyes, and even to pour out our whole hearts. Thirdly, that we be prepared to receive his benefits with true gratitude of heart and thanksgiving, benefits that our prayer reminds us come from his hand. Fourthly, moreover, that having obtained what we are seeking, and being convinced he has answered our prayers, we should be led to meditate upon his kindness more ardently. And fifthly, that at the same time we embrace with greater delight those things which we acknowledge to have been obtained by prayer. Finally, that use and experience may, according to the measure of our feebleness, confirm his providence.*[2]

Even pagans acknowledge the necessity and power of prayer. Three days before the brutal execution of the Tsar of Russia and his family in July 1918, the Commandant at Ipatiev House allowed Father Ivan Storozhev to conduct an Orthodox Service for the Imperial Family. The traditional prayer for the dead: "With the saints give rest, O Christ, to

---

1. Lewis, *How to Pray*, 21–22.
2. Calvin, *Prayer*, 8.

the soul of your servant where there is neither pain, nor sorrow, nor suffering but life everlasting" was sung—upon which the Romanovs had all silently fallen to their knees. Storozhev had sensed, in that moment, the great spiritual comfort it had given them. After the Service, he went to the commandant's office to change his vestments. Yakov Yurovsky, the man who planned and led the eventual killings, remarked, "Well, they've said their prayers and unburdened themselves."[3] When the priest replied he believed that faith was always fortified by prayer, Yurovsky said, "I have never discounted the power of religion and say that to you in all honesty."[4] Perhaps this hardened Bolshevik and Jewish apostate was recalling long-forgotten moments of family prayer around the Friday night table and the profound significance to his own Jewish race of the mourners' *Kaddish*—the prayers for the dead. The prayers of our childhood cannot be erased.

---

3. Rappaport, *Ekaterinburg*, 162.
4. Rappaport, *Ekaterinburg*, 162–63.

Epistle 23

In the first chapter of the Gospel of Mark we read where Jesus began his ministry in Capernaum, firstly healing a man with an unclean spirit, "And the unclean spirit, convulsing him and crying with a loud voice, came out of him." v.26 (NRSV) Jesus then healed Peter's mother-in-law and later in the day many who were sick or possessed by demons came to him. "And he cured many who were sick with various diseases and cast out many demons; and he would not permit the demons to speak, because they knew him." v.34 (NRSV) These healings were not quiet affairs—the demons convulsing and crying out as they were defeated!

In Acts 3, after the Day of Pentecost when the Holy Spirit came in tongues of fire and rested on the heads of the apostles, Peter and John came to the temple and found a crippled beggar at the Beautiful Gate. Instead of giving him alms, Peter healed him of his infliction with the power of the Spirit. Again, we see a reaction of noise and clamor! "And he took him by the right hand and raised him up; and immediately his feet and ankles were made strong. Jumping up, he stood and began to walk, and he entered the temple with them, walking and leaping and praising God." v.7–8 (NRSV) Recently this healing was presented in our Daily Devotions accompanied by that wonderful Sunday School song: . . . *walking and leaping and praising God . . .*

In *Going Solo*, a biographical memoir by Roald Dahl, he tells how, when he was sitting on the verandah of the home of the British District Officer at Tabora in Tanganyika, his servant boy, Mdisho, came running from the back of the house yelling:

> "Come quick bwana! Come quick! Come quick! A huge lion is eating the wife of the cook! . . . the cook is chasing the lion and trying to save his wife!"[1] Round the back of the house four or five houseboys were leaping about and shrieking, "Simba! Simba! Simba!"

1. Dahl, *Going Solo*, 35.

> The massive, sandy-coloured lion was not more than eighty or ninety yards off and trotting away from the house. He had a fine bushy collar of fur around his neck, and in his jaws he was holding the wife of the cook. The lion had the woman by the waist so that her head and arms hung down on one side and her legs on the other . . . the lion, so startlingly close, was loping away from us in the calmest possible manner with a slow, long-striding, springy lope, and behind the lion, no more than the length of a tennis court behind, ran the cook . . . running most bravely and waving his arms like a whirlwind leaping, clapping his hands, screaming, shouting, shouting, shouting, "Simba! Simba! Simba! Simba! Let go of my wife! Let go of my wife!"[2]

The District Officer now had his rifle and was imploring the cook to get out of his way so he could shoot the simba!

> But the cook ignored him and kept on running, and the lion ignored everybody, not altering his pace at all but continuing to lope along with slow springy strides and with the head held high and carrying the woman proudly in his jaws, rather like a dog who is trotting off with a good bone.[3]

Both the cook and the District Officer were catching up. About fifty yards behind the gun was raised and a shot was deliberately aimed in front of the lion. As the spurt of dust arose,

> the lion stopped dead and turned his head, still holding the woman in his jaws. He saw his pursuers, he had heard the rifle shot . . . he dropped the cook's wife on to the ground and broke for cover. [Dahl said] I have never seen anything accelerate so fast from a standing start. With great leaping bounding strides he was in among the jungle trees on the hillock before Robert Sandford could ram another cartridge onto his gun.[4]
>
> All were certain that those terrible jaws would have ripped the woman's waist and stomach almost in two. She lay on the ground and said, "That old lion he couldn't scare me. I just lay there in his mouth pretending I was dead and he didn't even bite through my clothes." She stood and smoothed her dress which was drenched with the lion's saliva and she and her husband embraced and did a

---

2. Dahl, *Going Solo*, 36.
3. Dahl, *Going Solo*, 36.
4. Dahl, *Going Solo*, 37.

> *little dance of joy in the twilight . . . The cook ran into the kitchen, clapping his hands and leaping for joy.*[5]

Christians are somewhat reserved in showing their joy—especially the older generation. Yet when we experience the Holy Spirit in our lives we can often feel a great leap of faith and assurance in our hearts. The closer we come to our Father the stronger the response of our soul.

> *Clap your hands all you peoples; shout to the God with loud songs of joy. For the LORD, the Most High, is awesome. A great King over all the earth.* Ps 47:1–2 (NRSV)

But Jesus did not confine his ministry to what he did in public. The next morning, after the healings, he rose "while it was still very dark and went to a deserted place, and there he prayed." Mark 1:35 (NRSV) The Greek text says that he "prayed continually." He began his day with his Father, knowing that only then could he be led and empowered fully for all the day would bring. For Jesus, spirituality was about more than what we do in public. In fact, what we do in private prepares us for what we do in public. We need to start each day with prayer.

---

5. Dahl, *Going Solo*, 38.

Epistle 24

We sometimes are shallow in our relationship with God—we want his blessings and his power to solve our problems, but we do not seek after a "soul intimacy" with our Father. We can deepen our relationship with prayer and our guide to prayer is always found in God's Word, the Bible. We have seen how wonderful the Psalms are to help us come closer to God. There are many other prayers in the Old Testament—prayers of Moses, David, Jeremiah, Daniel, etc. Jesus teaches us exactly how to pray in the Gospels, and Paul, in his epistles, gives us a theology of prayer.

Prayer, as we know, is talking with God, but it must not be idle chatter or casual conversation. God is Holy. When we pray to him it should be planned, disciplined, and prioritized. Setting aside times and places for prayer has been outlined before and it is the ultimate for our approach. Jesus went away to lonely places to pray to the Father. Yet, we know that this is not always an easy task. There may be the constant demands of children, young and old; debilitating or chronic illness; the care of the elderly; or, jobs or businesses with no set structures or time frames. Acknowledging our problems of commitment to earthly ties can be the first step to planning to pray even if it is only initially for short periods of time amidst the intermittent chaos of life.

> *We need to develop a 'habit' for praying.*
> *We need to reach a point when we cannot live without prayer. We need to cry with Jacob: "I will not let you go, unless you bless me."*
> *Genesis 32:26 (NRSV)*

Reading through prayers in the Bible, meditating on them, and finding meaning for them in our lives, is a grand beginning. By taking the examples of praying people in both the Old Testament and the New Testament we can see how those that prayed nurtured their relationship with God. This can be our guide to engaging in "God talk!" Read, for example,

David's prayer for safety from Absalom in Psalm 3; Daniel's prayer for the people in Daniel 9:1–19; The prayer of Moses in Exodus 32:11–14 when he pleads with God for forgiveness for the Israelites. These prayers all display a real intimacy with God. [*The Prayer of Azariah and the Song of the Three Jews* in the Apocrypha is quite wonderful, expressing a confident and steadfast faith: "Then the three with one voice praised and glorified and blessed God in the furnace." v.28]

Jesus talks continually to his Father. He teaches his followers how to pray in Matthew 6:9–14 in the words of what the Church calls *The Lord's Prayer*. He taught his followers how to pray, where to pray, and what to say! Thus, Jesus gives us the foundation for our intimate conversations with God. Even if these are the only words we use each day we are at the beginning of life's great adventure. Paul, in his epistles, guides us in prayer. He encourages us to believe and persevere in prayer. Even when we do not know what to pray for and how to express our prayers, Paul writes: "Likewise the Spirit helps us in our weakness, for we do not know how to pray as we ought, but that very Spirit intercedes with sighs too deep for words. And God, who searches the heart, knows what is the mind of the Spirit, because the Spirit intercedes for the saints according to the will of God." Romans 8:26–27 (NRSV) Clumsy and ineffectual we may feel, but the Holy Spirit abides in us as an advocate and a counselor. Thus, we must learn to completely rely on his power.

In the Old Testament we read:

> *Then the King said to me, "What do you request?" So I prayed to the God of Heaven.* Neh 2:4 (NRSV)

Only the Spirit of his God could truly guide him.

In the New Testament we read:

> *God is spirit, and those who worship him must worship in spirit and truth.* John 4:24 (NRSV)

> *Pray in the Spirit at all times in every prayer and supplication. To that end keep alert and always persevere in supplication for all the saints.* Eph 6:18 (NRSV)

> *But you, beloved, build yourselves up on your most holy faith; pray in the Holy Spirit.* Jude 20 (NRSV)

James Packer says, ". . . praying is the active exercise of a personal relationship; a kind of friendship with the living God and his son Jesus Christ, and the way it goes is more under divine control than under ours."[1] The control of the Spirit!

John Chapman says, "pray as you can and don't try to pray as you can't."[2] Do not let us make it harder than it is—relinquish it to the Spirit!

Martyn Lloyd-Jones says, "We must come face to face with our tendency to try to pray on our own."[3] We need the Holy Spirit.

The Puritans exhorted one another to "pray until you pray."

---

1. Hanes, *In My Path of Prayer*, 57.
2. Hanes, *In My Path of Prayer*, 58.
3. Lloyd-Jones, *Living Water*, 86.

Epistle 25

In the last epistle we finished with the Puritan exhortation: "pray until you pray!" What does this mean and how is it helpful?

The Puritans were a group of English Protestants in the late sixteenth-century and seventeenth-century church who regarded the reformation of the Elizabethan Church as incomplete and sought to simplify and regulate forms of worship. Elizabeth I was in many ways the ultimate tyrant but, in regard to religious matters, she was unfathomably tolerant. "There is only one Christ, Jesus, one faith," she once proclaimed, "All else is a dispute over trifles."[1] And there were disputes! The Puritans wanted a church that was no longer based on episcopal principles but one which was governed by a powerful group of ordained and elected elders or presbyters—some of these to supervise; some to discipline; some to preach; some to teach. There was to be an educated and informed laity whilst the clergy themselves were to be closely regimented by their colleagues. Worship would be approached in a learned manner.

The Puritan expression "pray until you pray," meant that the people in the pews should pray long enough and honestly enough to achieve two objectives—to get past the formalism of set prayers and to overcome the unreality that is experienced in short, infrequent praying. Although prayer must come from the heart rather than the printed word, it should not be rushed, crammed into minutes between the innumerable tasks of each day. American Research Professor, Donald Carson, says: "If we pray until we pray, eventually we come to delight in God's presence, to rest in his love, to cherish his will. Even in dark or agonized praying, we somehow know we are doing business with God."[2] "For it is God who is at work in you, enabling you both to will and to work for his good pleasure." Philippians 2:13 (NRSV)

1. Ronald, *Heretic Queen*, Front Book Jacket.
2. Carson, *Praying with Paul*, 18.

Nevertheless, we should not put aside the prayers we find in the Psalms or the Book of Common Prayer, or even good Christian hymns, for example, as these can be the first stepping stones to our prayerful walk with the Father. They lead us to an understanding of the majesty and holiness of our God and keep us aware of our failings and our need for his forgiveness, and for his empowering and enduring strength. The more frequently we pray; the more time we take to pray; the more we humble ourselves in prayer—the more we will become aware of the Spirit lifting our prayers to the LORD of all. Each of us is so different with different lives and different gifts and abilities. We must all find our own way on our prayer journey. We can use the examples of men and women in the Bible and even the examples of Christians we know today.

How hard it is to have a regular, disciplined prayer life. There are so many excuses in today's world. But these must be overcome. Even when we set aside time specifically for prayer, we may still find we feel too discouraged, too stressed, or too empty to pray. Then we justify putting off prayer until a better time. Prayer is not reliant on whether we feel we are dressed in body and soul in the right manner before we pray. Surely when we are discouraged, stressed, or empty, that is when we must pray. "Is not the basis of any Christian's approach to the heavenly Father the sufficiency of Christ's mediating work on our behalf? Is not this a part of what we mean when we pray 'in Jesus' name.'"[3] The second unacceptable presupposition behind this attitude is that any obligation to pray is somehow diminished when we do not feel like praying! ". . . this is unbearably self-centered. It means, that I, and I alone, determine what is my duty, my obligation. In short, it means that I am my own god."[4] "Rejoice in hope, be patient in suffering, persevere in prayer." Romans 12:12 (NRSV)

Sometimes we feel there is no need to pray. Our life might be going so well that we can put off our conversations with God. We enjoy our independence and revel in our achievements. How many examples do we find in the Old Testaments of the Israelites, time and time again, going their own way and ending up in a disastrous situation—in famine, in defeat, in exile. Do we not think that sometimes our very self-confidence might have led us along the wrong path to confusion and despair? Then we become too bitter to pray! Sometimes we bring ourselves to our own bitterness. But often it is illness, or grief, or any amount of earthly losses.

3. Carson, *Praying with Paul*, 94.
4. Carson, *Praying with Paul*, 95.

We live in anger, raging at the unjust world and the enemies that assail us. When we read the Psalms, we see the anger of God's people in many of them. Taking our anger and losses to our heavenly Father will provide a refuge and an anchor for our souls.

> *Put away from you all bitterness and wrath and anger and wrangling and slander, together with all malice, and be kind to one another, tenderhearted, forgiving one another, as God in Christ has forgiven you.* Eph 4:31–32 (NRSV)

Nor should we be too ashamed to pray—nothing is hidden from God.

> *Then I acknowledged my sin to you, and I did not hide my iniquity;*
> *I said, " will confess my transgressions to the LORD,"*
> *and you forgave the guilt of my sin.* Ps 32:5 (NRSV)

Epistle 26

In past epistles we have talked about the discipline of prayer and having times specifically set aside for prayer. This means we know and love the Lord and constantly build our relationship with him. However, it does not mean we cannot communicate with God at different moments during the day. When we have an intimacy with God we can call on him anytime and anywhere. Charles Haddon Spurgeon, the preaching sensation of London Metropolitan Tabernacle in the late nineteenth century, had a personal prayer life that was remarkable. Peter Morden, in his illustrated biography of Spurgeon, writes:

> *His basic pattern was to pray morning and evening, as the title of his famous book of daily readings suggests. Sometimes he would pray with his family; sometimes he would be alone. But his prayer life certainly did not stop there; Spurgeon wanted to maintain continued communion with God throughout the day. One of the ways he sought to do this was by praying short, one-sentence prayers as he went about his daily work. Friends spoke of seeing him pray as he wrote a letter, as he was reading a book, or whilst he was out walking. Speaking of his own experiences, he said, "Some of us could honestly say that we are seldom a quarter of an hour without speaking to God." These short pithy prayers are what have sometimes been called "arrow prayers," prayers addressed to God in the midst of a day full of all sorts of different tasks. They were a vital part of Spurgeon's devotional life.*[1]

Spurgeon also believed in setting aside longer periods for prayer and reflection, seeking to spend quality time with God. This statement sounds a bit like the modern adage of spending "quality time with the children" quoted by the working parents. Unfortunately, the time parents set aside for quality time isn't always the time when the children are

---

1. Morden, *C. H. Spurgeon*, 85–86.

responsive. "Arrow" moments of real intimacy are often snatched in the car or watching television or at sports grounds! We know that we need to set aside time for regular prayer but grabbing the special small moments are important too! Unlike humans God is always available.

Often our prayers don't instantly formulate as we would like. Spurgeon once said, "I like sometimes in prayer, when I do not feel I can say anything, just to sit still, and look up."[2] When he did this, in "solemn silence," Spurgeon experienced fellowship with Jesus of a closer form than words could possibly express. There are often many times when we want to pray and think our hearts are empty and find our voices silent. Quiet contemplation can heal and comfort. For our hearts are not empty. God abides at the very depth and center of our soul; he lies within our very selves. In Romans 8, Paul regularly links the work of the Spirit with the atoning work of Christ. The Christian has died and risen with Christ and now this same Christ lives in the believer by his Spirit. Michael Raiter writes of the conversion of Muslim girl, Bilquis Sheikh, when she encountered the Spirit of God:

> "Oh Father, my Father . . . Father God." Hesitantly, I spoke his name aloud. I tried different ways of speaking to Him. And then, as if something broke through for me I found myself trusting that He was indeed hearing me, just as my earthly father had always done. "Father, oh my Father God" I cried, with growing confidence. My voice seemed unusually loud in the large bedroom as I knelt on the rug beside my bed. But suddenly that room wasn't empty any more. He was there![3]

We must not become legalistic in our approach to prayer and parrot-like in our actual words. We must seek to find the expression of our love for the Father. We must look to the Spirit who is there within us—guiding us, upholding us, strengthening us. From a Spirit-filled heart will flow our words to the Father.

The Psalmist cries:

> As a deer longs for flowing streams, so my soul longs for you, O God. My soul thirsts for God, for the living God. Ps 42:1–2a (NRSV)

Jesus says to the Samaritan woman at the well:

---

2. Morden, *C. H. Spurgeon*, 86.
3. Raiter, *Stirrings of the Soul*, 206–207.

Everyone who drinks of this water will be thirsty again, but those who drink of the water that I will give them will never be thirsty. The water I will give them will become in them a spring of water gushing up to eternal life. John 4:13–14 (NRSV)

These words of Jesus reveal to us the quenching of our spiritual thirst; the Holy Spirit draws us back to these words again and again, so that we may know our Savior and deepen our fellowship with the Father through a continuing affinity. Personalities differ. We are naturally individuals—yet all precious in the sight of the Creator. We will develop our own prayer-life. Nevertheless, when we pray, we must all look to the first and great commandment—to love the Lord our God with all our hearts, minds, souls, and strength. The Spirit shall always be our constant guide and counselor.

Epistle 27

In Mark 12:30 Jesus said that the first commandment was "you shall love the Lord your God with all your heart, and with all your soul, and with all your mind, and with all your strength." (NRSV)

Heart, soul, mind, strength.
Let us look at . . . mind and soul; heart and strength!
The soul suffers intellectually if we fail to use our minds

> *Buy truth, and do not sell it; buy wisdom, instruction, and understanding.* Prov 23:23 (NRSV)

> *You were taught to put away your former way of life, your old self, corrupt and deluded by its lusts, and to be renewed in the spirit of your minds, and to clothe yourselves with the new self, created according to the likeness of God in true righteousness and holiness.* Eph 4:22–24 (NRSV)

> *For this reason, since the day we heard it, we have not ceased praying for you and asking that you may be filled with the knowledge of God's will in all spiritual wisdom and understanding.* Col 1:9 (NRSV)

> *Therefore prepare your minds for action; discipline yourselves; set all your hope on the grace that Jesus Christ will bring you when he is revealed.* 1 Pet 1:13 (NRSV)

The soul suffers morally when we fail to keep God's wise commandments:

> *How can young people keep their way pure? By guarding it according to your word. With my whole heart I seek you; do not let me stray from your commandments.* Ps 119:9–10 (NRSV)

> *But be doers of the word, and not merely hearers who deceive themselves. For if any are hearers of the word and not doers, they are like those who look at themselves in a mirror, for they look at themselves and, on going away, immediately forget what they were like. But those who look into the perfect law, the law of liberty, and persevere, being not hearers who forget but doers who act—they will be blessed in their doing.* Jas 1:22–25 (NRSV)

> *An important quality of the spiritual person is that he is growing in obedience to God's commands because he loves God so deeply he does not want to cause any break—through guilt or through shame—between himself and the love he experiences in closeness with God. Keeping the commands is not a burden then, it is freedom from heaviness and the sense of spiritual separation.*[1]

The soul suffers deeply when emotions are dead or out of control:

> *"Come," my heart says, "seek his face!" Your face, LORD, do I seek.* Ps 27:8 (NRSV)

> *No one has ever seen God; if we love one another, God lives in us, and his love is perfected in us.* 1 John 4:12 (NRSV)

> *Be imitators of God, as beloved children, and live in love, as Christ loved us and gave himself up for us, a fragrant offering and sacrifice to God.* Eph 5:1–2 (NRSV)

We need to love God deeply. In the Augustinian Stations of the Cross are these words: "O Lord my God, you alone do I love; you alone do I follow; you alone do I seek; you alone am I prepared to serve." Soliloquies 1,1. As our hearts are filled with his Spirit, so our hearts will be moved to love one another.

The soul suffers helplessly if we fail to build our courage and strength:

> *When they brought the kings out to Joshua, Joshua summoned all the Israelites, and said to the chiefs of the warriors who had gone with him, "Come near, put your feet on the necks of these kings." Then they came near and put their feet on their necks. And Joshua said to them, "Do not be afraid or dismayed; be strong and courageous; for thus the LORD will do to all the enemies against whom you fight."* Josh 10:24–25 (NRSV)

> *The LORD is my strength and my might, and he has become my salvation; this is my God, and I will praise him, my father's God,*

---

1. Demarest, *Satisfy Your Soul*, 54.

> *and I will exalt him. The LORD is a warrior; the LORD is his name.* Exod 15:2–3 (NRSV)
>
> *For who is God except the LORD? And who is a rock besides our God?—the God who girded me with strength, and made my way safe. He made my feet like the feet of a deer, and set me secure on the heights.* Ps 18:31–33 (NRSV)
>
> *My flesh and my heart may fail, but God is the strength of my heart and my portion forever.* Ps 73:26 (NRSV)
>
> *May you be made strong with all the strength that comes from his glorious power, and may you be prepared to endure everything with patience, while joyfully giving thanks to the Father, who has enabled you to share in the inheritance of the saints in the light.* Col 1:11–12 (NRSV)

In the Hebrew *Ethics of the Fathers*, we read: "Be as strong as a leopard, as light as an eagle, run like the deer and be as mighty as the lion to do the bidding of your Father in Heaven." Mishnah 23 Ch. 5

> Loving God with all our hearts, and with all our souls, and with all our minds, and with all our strength, will enable us to know him fully. To know God is to worship him in his holiness and in our humility. With complete trust we can go to our God with prayers and petitions and wait upon him.

Epistle 28

Sometimes we look at prayer as our seeking after God. But in Genesis 3 it is the LORD God who is the One who comes seeking, taking a walk in the cool breezes of the evening. God has been pursuing us ever since—especially in the person of Jesus the Christ becoming incarnate to search for the lost—and of the Holy Spirit with his gentle brooding over us as early as Genesis 1:2 (NRSV), "the earth was a formless void and darkness covered the face of the deep, while a wind from God swept over the face of the waters." From the creation onwards God has been extraordinarily patient with humankind; always faithful and always sure—no matter how the created world and its peoples become endlessly abusive and corrupted. The biggest barrier is when the created beings want to be gods themselves. Then there is an inadequate comprehension of God.

A modern theologian commented that people today are being taught to read the Bible with a "hermeneutics of suspicion." Basically, the method of interpretation with which they read is infused with great doubt concerning the reliability of the Bible. Eugene Peterson expresses it this way: "But as we narrow our eyes in suspicion, the world is correspondingly narrowed down. And when we take these reading habits to our reading of Holy Scripture, we end up with a small sawdust heap of facts."[1] How often do we doubt many parts of scripture, picking and choosing which facts we want to accept and which we readily question? Do we also challenge the many attributes of the LORD God himself?

We are surrounded day and night by lies and omens; by people never accepting responsibility for their actions; by evil spirits in the guise of a true religion. We need to work hard to distinguish truth, trust, and honor from the secular way of the hedonistic culture that encompasses us. Paul Ricoeur encourages us to:

---

1. Peterson, *Eat This Book*, 68–69

> *. . . look at the world with childlike wonder, ready to be startled into surprised delight by the profuse abundance of truth and beauty and goodness that is spilling out of the skies at every moment. Cultivate a hermeneutics of adoration—see how large, how splendid, how magnificent life is. And then practice this hermeneutic of adoration in the reading of Holy Scripture. Plan on spending the rest of your lives exploring and enjoying the world both vast and intricate that is revealed by this text.*[2]

Sometimes, when a text is read aloud, instead of following it in your Bible, close your eyes and put all your mind and energy into imagining the picture portrayed. Listening to Isaiah this way would bring to the heart and soul a wonderful experience of the majesty and glory of God.

> *In the year that King Uzziah died, I saw the Lord sitting on a throne, high and lofty, and the hem of his robe filled the temple. Seraphs were in attendance above him; each had six wings: with two they covered their faces, and with two they covered their feet, and with two they flew. And one called to another and said: "Holy, holy, holy is the LORD of hosts; the whole earth is full of his glory." The pivots on the thresholds shook at the voice of those that called, and the house filled with smoke.* Isa 6:1–4 (NRSV)

We need also to approach God with *fascination*. When God revealed himself to Moses in the burning bush—burning but not consumed—Moses was fascinated to investigate what was happening. It was only when God saw that he had caught the attention of Moses, that he warned him to come no closer. Moses had been receptive to the glorious presence of Yahweh, "I must turn aside and look at this great sight, and see why the bush is not burned up." Exodus 3:3 (NRSV) We must find that fascination: "O taste and see that the LORD is good; happy are those who take refuge in him." Psalm 34:8 (NRSV)

How long is it since you have felt a profound sense of *astonishment and wonder* before God? At the transfiguration, Peter, James, and John were astonished at the revelation of Christ's glory: "he was transfigured before them, and his face shone like the sun, and his clothes became dazzling white." Matthew 17:2 (NRSV) Then the great wonder when Moses and Elijah appeared with him. "Lord it is good for us to be here." 4b (NRSV) This is another great reading to capture in our imagination with eyes closed and our body stilled with expectation.

---

2. Ricoeur, *The Symbolism of Evil*, 351.

Do we experience *awe* in the presence of God? In response to Israel's miraculous escape from Egypt, Moses sang a song of deliverance: "Who is like you, O LORD, among the gods? Who is like you, majestic in holiness, awesome in splendor, doing wonders?" Exodus 15:11 (NRSV) At the Day of Pentecost after the coming of the Holy Spirit upon those who were gathered together in the one place. "Awe came upon everyone, because many wonders and signs were being done by the apostles." Acts 2:43 (NRSV) . . . A third reading for the imagination!

And in our dedicated reading we can experience *ecstasy!* Paul tells of his visions and revelations in 2 Corinthians 12:1–7. This is a rare gift that God may grant us but we can experience a glimpse of this spiritual exaltation when we become lost in the wonderful love and grace of our Father. Our souls will be fortified and strengthened for our worldly pilgrimage. Sometimes when singing a beautiful hymn by Charles or John Wesley, for example, we can be transported to a higher realm for a precious short time.

"Pray, and praise Thee, without ceasing. Glory in Thy perfect love."[3]

Let us approach our God with confidence. He is our God and we are his people.

---

3. Church of Scotland, *The Church Hymnary*. Rev. ed. Hymn 479.

Epistle 29

In this Epistle we are looking to God's Word to encourage us in our prayer life. Reading the scriptures slowly and deeply brings us a vision of a holy and righteous God. Yet this is a God we can know personally. Christians of the past have found the Bible their mainstay in their earthly pilgrimage.

In 1549, in correspondence to his ward Mistress Penelope Pye, daughter of Sir William Pye, John Cheke, tutor to Edward VI, wrote these words:

> *In prayer, either public or private, you are to remember that you speak to God. In conversation, either open or secret, in close place or in hidden thought, you are not to forget that you walk in the eye and sight of God. When you speak to God, know that you speak to him who understands the bottom of your heart.*[1]

> *On the day I called, you answered me,*
> *You increased my strength of soul. Ps 138:3 (NRSV)*

Dietrich Bonhoeffer talks about our eyes: "It is our daily prayer each morning when our eyes open and the night is past that God should enlighten the eyes of our heart."[2] ". . . so that, with the eyes of your heart enlightened, you may know what is the hope to which he has called you." Ephesians 1:18a (NRSV)

In his Rule, St. Benedict talks about our ears: "Listen carefully . . . and incline the ear of the heart."[3]

> *The eyes of the LORD are on the righteous,*
> *and his ears are open to their cry. Ps 34:15 (NRSV)*

---

1. Religious Tract Society, *Writings of Edward the Sixth*, 23–24.
2. Bonhoeffer, *My Soul Finds Rest*, 87–88.
3. Neal, *worldonfire.org*, July 11, 2017.

When we are fearful, we can turn to our faithful God. John G. Paton, the Scottish missionary to the New Hebrides in the middle of the nineteenth century, suffered extreme hardship and danger living amongst naked and painted cannibals who had no concept of right and wrong. Early in his mission a friendly native warned him to hide in a large chestnut tree. Paton recounted in his autobiography:

> *The hours I spent there live all before me as if it were but of yesterday. I heard the frequent discharging of muskets, and the yells of the savages. Yet I sat there among the branches, as safe as in the arms of Jesus. Never, in all my sorrows, did my Lord draw nearer to me, and speak more soothingly in my soul, than when the moonlight flickered among those chestnut leaves, and the night air played on my throbbing brow, as I told all my heart to Jesus. Alone, yet not alone! If it be to glorify my God, I will not grudge to spend many nights alone in such a tree, to feel again my Saviour's spiritual presence, to enjoy his consoling fellowship. If thus thrown back upon your own soul, alone, all alone, in the midnight in the bush, in the very embrace of death itself have you a Friend, that will not fail you then?*[4]

> *I've found a Friend; O such a Friend! He loved me ere I knew him;*
> *He drew me with the cords of love, and thus He bound me to Him,*
> *And round my heart still closely twine those ties which nought can sever,*
> *For I am His, and He is mine, forever and forever.*[5]

> *O taste and see that the LORD is good;*
> *happy are those who take refuge in him. Ps 34:8 (NRSV)*

On a later occasion, when Paton's home was beset by hostile tribesmen, he and his wife prayed throughout the night for safety and deliverance. In the morning the natives were gone—they had fled because men, dressed in garments of dazzling white, had surrounded the house until day broke.

> *The angel of the LORD encamps around those who fear him;*
> *and delivers them. Ps 34:7 (NRSV)*

Do we neglect our prayer life, especially when life is going well? Do we rely on ourselves to provide wisdom for each day? Do we try to build up our own courage and strength to tackle the trials and tribulation; the

---

4. Paton, *John G. Paton*, 200.
5. P. C. A., *Rejoice*, 416.

sorrows and griefs of life? Our insight is poor—it lacks understanding; it lacks knowledge! Only a dependence on a loving faithful Father will keep us safe and secure.

> *Trust in the LORD with all your heart,*
> *and do not rely on your own insight. Prov 3:5 (NRSV)*

> *I want their hearts to be encouraged and united in love, so that they may have all the riches of assured understanding and have the knowledge of God's mystery, that is, Christ himself, in whom are hidden all the treasures of wisdom and knowledge. Col 2:2–3 (NRSV)*

By reading the Word and meditating on it daily we can come to know our loving Father and rejoice in the sacrifice that his beloved Son made for us. Through prayer we can find a firm rock for our feet; a safe refuge for our lives; a mighty anchor for our souls. We can face each day with clear minds knowing the purpose that God has in store for us. In confidence we can pray the words of Catherine Parr, as found in her *Prayers or Meditations* of 1545:

> *Send forth the hot flow of thy love to burn and consume the cloudy fantasies of my mind.*[6]

In whom shall we put our trust?

> *Some take pride in chariots, and some in horses,*
> *but our pride is in the name of the LORD our God.*
> *They will collapse and fall, but we shall rise and stand upright.*
> *Ps 20:7–8 (NRSV)*

---

6. Religious Tract Society, *Writings of Queen Catherine Parr*, 55.

Epistle 30

How important do you have to be to have a conversation with God? In the Old Testament we read of conversations that the leaders of God's chosen people Israel had with YHWH, the LORD and Creator. Abraham and Moses, for example, were given instructions by God. Sometimes God received complete obedience and sometimes he encountered numerous excuses! The Judges and the Prophets all conversed with God. However, it is empowering for us to know that this intimacy of relationship was not confined to the VIPs of the Bible. Ordinary men and women could know God also and so can we!

Take for instance the story of Abraham's servant in Genesis 24. He is instructed by Abraham to journey to Abraham's homeland to find a bride for his son Isaac, from amongst Abraham's own relatives. The servant has momentous doubts that his mission will succeed. When he came to the well where he was destined to watch the women come in the evening to fetch water, he says "O LORD, God of my master Abraham, please grant me success today and show steadfast love to my master Abraham." 24:12 (NRSV)

Theologian John Goldingay says:

> . . . this might suggest that the head of the family fulfills a quasi-priestly function for the rest of the family, and that an ordinary person like the servant does not think of God as "his." But he may simply speak this way because of the nature of the task he is undertaking . . . in due course the servant asks God to make it come about that the girl he asks for a drink of water, who not only gives him a drink but offers to water his camels, is the one for Isaac. He is extraordinarily specific and confident in his expectation regarding what YHWH is to do. It is as if he imagines himself to be dealing with a different kind of being than the august and imperious one we have seen in action with Abraham, the one who deals in vast territories and aeons of time and who, when offended, sends

> *down fire and brimstone from the sky. In the First Testament, the one God has to have both the characteristics of the awesome creator and those of the personal god who looks after an individual. And God does as the servant specifies. YHWH's being the God of the clan chief does not mean this ordinary person cannot relate to God. While the servant here does so in connection with his commission from Abraham, there is sufficient ease in his relating to God to imply that this was no new experience. He would talk to God the same way about a wife for his own son, or about his own wife's difficulty in conceiving. This underlines the likelihood that the story of a family head such as Abraham points to dynamics of ordinary people's relationship with God.*[1]

There are so many unnamed people in the Bible. Yet many of these people play important roles in their stories. Does that mean that they are unimportant? Definitely not! Each person, named or unnamed, is known by our God and loved by our God. In the first letter he wrote to the Corinthians, Paul encourages his co-workers, even though they are treated as unknown in the world, that they (and thus, we ourselves) are known to God. In the war cemeteries of Europe, Asia, and the Middle East, are the earthly resting places of millions of soldiers, thousands of whom could not be identified—in fact, many whose bodies could not be located or whose bodies were pulverized into the earth. On the tombstones of the unidentified are engraved: *Known to God.* Unrecoverable bodies have memorial markers with the same: *Known to God.*

Moses said to the Israelites: "the LORD your God has chosen you out of all the peoples on earth to be his people, his treasured possession. It was not because you were more numerous than any other people that the LORD set his heart on you and chose you—for you were the fewest of all peoples." Deuteronomy 7:6–7 (NRSV)

Other nations were far greater in number with greater lands and standing armies. So too, in the New Testament, we witness a new people of God growing from a small number of apostles. At the Day of Pentecost "those who welcomed Peter's message were baptized, and that day about three thousand persons were added" Acts 2:41 (NRSV); each individual believer treasured and known by God. God speaks to us! God calls to us! "And when you turn to the right or when you turn to the left, your ears shall hear a word behind you, saying, 'This is the way; walk in it.'" Isaiah 30:21 (NRSV)

---

1. Goldingay, *Old Testament Theology. Volume 1*, 286.

When we respond and open our hearts to God, we are likely to experience a strong sense of God's undeserved love for us and feel welcomed as his children. We will perceive that we are accepted in spite of our painful imperfections. We will find love, joy, peace, and gratitude. Our spiritual hunger will be satisfied and our strength renewed. Even our emptiness and loneliness will be vanquished. God hears all who seek him.

> *Christians must not stop at the word God speaks, but press on until we encounter the God who speaks the Word.*[2]

> God wills that we should push into his presence and live our whole life there. This is to be known to us in conscious experience. It is more than a doctrine to be held; it is a life to be enjoyed every moment of every day.[3]

---

2. Demarest, *Satisfy Your Soul*, 98.
3. Tozer, *The Pursuit of God*, 36.

Epistle 31

In Isaiah 57 we read these words:

> *Peace, peace, to the far and the near, says the LORD;*
> *and I will heal them.*
> *But the wicked are like the tossing sea that cannot keep still;*
> *its waters toss up mire and mud.*
> *There is no peace, says my God, for the wicked.* 19–21 (NRSV)

The wicked are not only the evil-doers—they are also those who turn away from God—those who turn to the gods of hedonism and materialism. Lasting peace and enduring healing can only be found in God. If there is somebody or something in this world that we love more than God we will never find true satisfaction and comfort. We will coast along but, as Augustine of Hippo and many modern theologians say, we will be constantly restless—like a tossing sea—always anxious; never wholly at peace. We must know God and know him intimately. But how can we know our God intimately? When Thomas said: "How can we know the way?" Jesus said to him, "I am the way, and the truth, and the life. No one comes to the Father except through me. If you know me, you will know my Father also. From now on you do know him and have seen him." John 14:5b–7 (NRSV) Through Jesus and, what he has done for us on the cross, we can know our God intimately and have deep restfulness.

Horatio Spafford was born in New York in 1828, but it was in Chicago that he became well known for his clear Christian testimony. He and his wife, Anna, were active in their Presbyterian parish and had met and grown a friendship with the famous evangelist Dwight Moody. Horatio was a successful lawyer who had amassed a great deal of property in his home city. He and Anna were to experience much tragedy in their lives. Their son Horatio Jr. died of scarlet fever at the age of four. A year later, in 1871, the Great Fire of Chicago devastated many of Horatio's properties. Two years on, the family decided to travel to Europe to attend some of Moody's gatherings. However, Horatio was delayed by business demands—zoning issues arising from the Fire—and Anna and the four girls went on ahead, sailing on the *Ville de Havre*. On November 22, 1873, while crossing the Atlantic, the ship was struck by an iron sailing vessel. The family was thrown into the tempestuous ocean as their ship sank within twelve minutes. Anna, 11, Margaret Lee, 9, Elizabeth, 5, and Tanetta aged 2 were all drowned. Their mother was found floating on a plank of wood in an unconscious state. On arrival in Cardiff she telegraphed her husband with the words, "Saved Alone—what shall I do?"

Horatio embarked immediately to reach her. As his ship was passing over the very place that the *Ville de Havre* had sunk, the captain summoned Horatio to the bridge to show him his charts. Horatio Stafford returned to his cabin and wrote the words of the following hymn:

> When peace, like a river,
> Flows all through my life,
> when sorrows like sea billows roll;
> whatever my lot,
> You have taught me to say:
>
> *It is well, it is well*
> *with my soul, with my soul,*
> *it is well, it is well with my soul*
>
> Though Satan should buffet,
> though trials should come,
> let this blest assurance control:
> that Christ has regarded
> my helpless estate
> and has shed His own blood for my soul.
>
> *It is well, it is well . . .*
>
> My sin, O the bliss
> of this glorious thought,
> my sin, not in part, but the whole,
> is nailed to the cross,
> and I bear it no more:
> praise the Lord, praise the Lord, O my soul.
>
> *It is well, it is well . . .*

And, Lord, haste the day
when my faith shall be sight,
the clouds be rolled back as a scroll;
the trumpet shall sound
and the Lord shall descend,
"Even so"—it is well with my soul.

It is well, it is well . . . [1]

Following these tragedies, Anna gave birth to three more children: Horatio named for his brother, Bertha, and Grace. In 1880, this second precious son died. After a decade of financial loss and personal grief, and with a sad lack of support from their church, Horatio made the decision to take his family from the land where material success was so important—on a spiritual pilgrimage—to Jerusalem in the Holy Land. A party of thirteen adults and three children set up an American Colony there in 1881. Joined later by Swedish Christians, the group engaged in philanthropic work embracing all religious communities. Their desire was always to show those living around them the love of Jesus. Amidst the billowing waves God brought healing and peace. He will bring healing and peace to us, whatever our trials and griefs.

---

1. P.C.A., *Rejoice*, 586.

Epistle 32

In the previous epistle we were presented with the words of a hymn written by Horatio Spafford in the late nineteenth century. We read that peace is like a river and that sorrows roll with the billows of the sea. Satan will buffet our lives but sin has been nailed to the cross therefore we can praise the LORD because it is well with our soul. The old hymns can be a wondrous source of comfort and delight often giving us a dazzling picture of the Father, the Son, and the Spirit, verse by verse. The music of course is so vital, carrying the words with our voices to praise and glorify our God. But many of the modern songs of praise are equally inspiring. One of these illustrates the same belief in trusting in Jesus our Savior to overcome devasting losses, as does Spafford's great hymn: *I Will Trust You in the Darkness*, written by Rob Smith. Often these modern songs of praise invite us to not only sing, but to clap and move with the music. This is not a new mode of worship by any means! We read in the Book of Samuel, when the ark of God was carried in glory to Jerusalem . . .

"David and all the house of Israel were dancing before the LORD with all their might, with songs and lyres and harps and tambourines and castanets and cymbals." 2 Samuel 6:5 (NRSV) How many of us remember in past years watching the local band of the Salvation Army marching to their Gospel Hall each Sunday evening the brass instrument, the drums, and the tambourines flashing in the early evening light—all bands-people smartly attired in their uniforms; the young lasses adorned with rib-boned bonnets. How stirring was that sight of Christian witness—young and old "gospeling" to young and old!

We all can, especially children, participate in modern music joyfully like David.

Hymns and songs can inspire our prayer life. After all they are words of praise and prayer raised to the Father in the name of his son Jesus. Poetry also can mold our thinking and conversation with the Lord

God. Emily Dickinson, the reclusive American poet of the nineteenth century, suffered from agoraphobia and possibly also anorexia. She refused to go to church and never received visitors. But through her family and a wide network of correspondents she still knew and experienced the world around her. All her life she struggled with belief and wrestled with God. Nevertheless, she would never let go of him. In one of her succinct poems, she compared the call of prayer to a bird stamping its foot and crying: "Give me." She battled against an age when unbelief was taking hold of prominent thinkers and philosophers. Some found that her poems appeared to be simple but they are truly profound:

> *I never saw a moor;*
> *I never saw the sea;*
> *Yet know I how the heather looks,*
> *And what a billow be.*
>> *I never spoke with God,*
>> *Nor visited in heaven;*
>> *Yet certain am I of the spot*
>> *As if the checks were given.*[1]

She has never seen these things—from the natural world to metaphysics—she is yet certain of them. Earthly thought cannot breach heaven but she believes her thoughts can. If she can believe in nature's reality by thinking it, she can believe the divine also. She maps out heaven by sheer force of imagination!

In these days of the pandemic where people are isolated for months at a time, we are blessed to be able to go to our God in prayer. We are alone, but never alone. Our prayers are not like the angry bird stamping its foot; our prayers are the spoken and sung words of a people to their Creator springing from the deep feelings of the heart. Calvin says that the tongue was peculiarly created to tell and proclaim the praise of God . . . so we must, with gratitude in our hearts, sing psalms, hymns, and spiritual songs to God. One of Martin Luther's great gifts to the Church was the instigation of congregational singing and his masterpiece here was the hymn *A Mighty Fortress is our God*!

> And though this world, with devils filled,
> should threaten to undo us,
> we will not fear, for God has willed
> His truth to triumph through us.

---

1. Dickinson, *Poems*, 156.

The prince of darkness grim,
we tremble not for him;
his rage we can endure,
we know his doom is sure,
the Word of God shall fell him.[2]

In Colossians 3:16 (NRSV) we read: "Let the word of Christ dwell in you richly; teach and admonish one another in all wisdom; and with gratitude in your hearts sing psalms, hymns and spiritual songs to God." And in 1 Corinthians 14:15 (NRSV) "What should I do then? I will pray with the spirit, but I will pray with the mind also; I will sing praise with the spirit, but I will sing praise with the mind also."

---

2. P.C.A., *Rejoice*, 316.

Epistle 33

Sadly, many people today think that if they live good lives as good people, bad things should not happen to them. But the real picture, unfortunately, can be far different. The world is broken by sin, and bad things happen to people regardless of how well they live! God has allowed us to "run the world" but he is constantly there, with comfort and strength for us. He is a refuge from our tribulations and an anchor for our souls. Often, we need him but other times we feel quite self-sufficient, living comfortable lives with many benefits—or perhaps we should say, with many blessings. When bad things happen, we are often at a loss to understand why!

Timothy Keller says:

> *We should love God for himself alone, not for the benefits he brings. How do you develop a love like that? Let's say you initially fall in love with a person, and, if you are honest, it was partly because of some of the person's "assets"—his or her looks or connections, for instance. But as the relationship progresses, you begin to love the person for himself alone, and then when some of the assets go away, you don't mind. We call that growth in love and character. Now, what if you grew in your love for God like that? What if you could grow in your love for him so that he became increasingly satisfying in himself to you? That would mean that circumstances wouldn't rattle you as much, since you had God and his love enriching and nourishing you regardless of the circumstances of life.*[1]

Unfortunately, this may often only be achieved by experiencing hardships and perhaps heartbreak. It may be a loss of income, ill-health, death of a loved one, a horrific accident, or just merely the onset of old age with all its frailties. But, no matter what adversity we encounter:

> *The LORD is near to the broken hearted,*
>   *and saves the crushed in spirit.* Ps 34:18 (NRSV)

1. Keller, *Walking with God through Pain and Suffering*, 273–74.

and,

> The LORD upholds those who are falling,
> and raises up all who are bowed down. Ps 145:14 (NRSV)

In the Book of Job, we see a conflict between good and evil and, more importantly, a confrontation between God and Satan, with God allowing Satan to torment Job to test his faith. We find a righteous man who loves and worships God yet he loses everything he possesses. Job was one of the richest men in the East. Furthermore, God allows Satan to afflict Job with painful diseases. But, incredibly, as Job's suffering increases, he moves deeper and closer to God.

> For I know that my Redeemer lives, and that at the last he will stand upon the earth and after my skin has been thus destroyed, then in my flesh I shall see God, whom I shall see on my side, and my eyes shall behold, and not another. My heart faints within me! Job 19:25–28 (NRSV)

Timothy Keller comments on Job and his suffering in this way,

> The crucial thing to notice is this: Through it all, Job never stopped praying. Yes, he complained, but he complained to *God*. He doubted, but he doubted to *God*. He screamed and yelled, but he did it in God's presence. No matter how much in agony he was, he continued to address God. He kept seeking him. And, in the end, God and Job triumphed. How wonderful that our God sees the grief and anger and questioning, and is still willing to say "you triumphed"—not because it was all fine, not because Job's heart and motives were always right, but because Job's doggedness in seeking the face and presence of God meant that *the suffering did not drive him away from God but toward him*. And that made all the difference.[2]

In times of trouble and loss we must be like Job. We must seek God; we must go to him. We can be honest, we can argue and plead, we can open our hearts and souls to him. But always we must pray continuously putting our hope only in him. God says to believers in Christ, "I will never leave you or forsake you." Hebrews 13:5b (NRSV) Jesus says we are his sheep and "no one will snatch them out of my hand." John 10:28b (NRSV)

---

2. Keller, *Walking with God through Pain and Suffering*, 287–88.

Our love for God must be greater than our love for anything else. It doesn't mean that we must not love our family and all the blessings we are given, but that we need to reorder our loves. By loving God supremely, we will capture the calm, the tranquility, the peace of God. We will find the strength for life on earth with all its temptations and evils if we make Christ the cornerstone of our being. We will cope with the suffering that comes with our earthly existence. We will bear loneliness knowing that God is always there.

And, the only way we can grow that love to maturity is through prayer. The more we pray the closer we will come to the Father. We will find one in whom we can put all our trust. We can trust his wisdom; we can trust his love.

> *Come to me, all you that are weary and are carrying heavy burdens, and I will give you rest. Take my yoke upon you, and learn from me; for I am gentle and humble in heart, and you will find rest for your souls. For my yoke is easy and my burden is light.*
> Matt 11:28–30 (NRSV)

Epistle 34

During the first two centuries of Christianity there was strong opposition to recognizing birthdays of martyrs and, for that matter, the birthday of Jesus. Many of the Church Fathers reasoned that it was far more appropriate that saints and martyrs should be honored on the day of their martyrdom—these were their true birthdays from the Church's perspective—the day they celebrated their journey into Paradise. Although it cannot be established that December 25 was the day Jesus was born, some early reasoning calculated the date of his conception! It was identified that the spring equinox was the date of the creation of the world; the fourth day being when light was created. Therefore, March 25 became the date that Jesus was conceived and, nine months later, December 25 became the date of his birth.

Sadly, none of the contemporary customs of Christmas has their origin in theological or liturgical affirmations. Many have grown out of quite mundane happenings, for example, it is thought that the Advent Calendar, loved by children, was created in the nineteenth century by a Munich housewife who tired of having to answer endlessly when Christmas would come. In the world of today, Christmas, like Easter, is simply a time for holidays from the normal humdrum of life. It has become secularized and commercialized. This seems incredible considering that the virgin conception and the virgin birth is the most astonishing miracle of human history. It is the birth of a baby who is fully human and fully divine. How can so many people today ignore the great wonder and majesty of this act of God? How can people make the whole season commonplace; a flashy production devoid of real meaning? Ask anyone today what Christmas is about and most will answer it is for the children!

No, it is for all of humankind, no matter what age – for "the people who walked in darkness have seen a great light; those who lived in a land of deep darkness—on them light has shined." Isaiah 9:2 (NRSV)

Remember in the first epistle how Perpetua encouraged you to set a time aside each week to spend a quiet period communing with God—no door bells, no television or radio, no phones, no availability to the world at all. When you are settled you could read the following from Luke 2:22–38

> *When the time came for their purification according to the law of Moses, they brought him up to Jerusalem to present him to the Lord (as it is written in the law of the Lord, "Every firstborn male shall be designated as holy to the Lord"), and they offered a sacrifice according to what is stated in the law of the Lord, "a pair of turtledoves or two young pigeons." Now there was a man in Jerusalem whose name was Simeon, this man was righteous and devout, looking forward to the consolation of Israel, and the Holy Spirit rested on him. It had been revealed to him by the Holy Spirit that he would not see death before he had seen the Lord's Messiah. Guided by the Spirit, Simeon came into the temple; and when the parents brought in the child Jesus, to do for him what was customary under the law, Simeon took him in his arms and praised God, saying,*
>
> > *"Master, now you are dismissing your servant in peace,*
> > > *according to your word;*
> > *for my eyes have seen your salvation,*
> > > *which you have prepared in the*
> > > > *presence of all peoples,*
> > *a light for revelation to the Gentiles*
> > > *and for glory to your people Israel."*
>
> *And the child's father and mother were amazed at what was being said about him. Then Simeon blessed them and said to his mother Mary, "This child is destined for the falling and the rising of many in Israel, and to be a sign that will be opposed so that the inner thoughts of many will be revealed—and a sword will pierce your own soul too."*
>
> *There was also a prophet, Anna the daughter of Phanuel, of the tribe of Asher. She was of a great age, having lived with her husband seven years after her marriage, then as a widow to the age of eighty-four. She never left the temple but worshiped there with fasting and prayer, night and day. At that moment she came, and began to praise God and to speak about the child to all who were looking for the redemption of Jerusalem.* (NRSV)

Meditate on this scripture. Pray that you understand every aspect of it.

- The keeping of the Law by the parents of Jesus
- The extraordinary patient faith of both Simeon and Anna
- The guidance of the Holy Spirit in both their vigils
- The intense gratitude of Simeon and his prophetic words to the parents
- The joyful praise of Anna after so many long years
- The amazement of Mary and Joseph at the words of Simeon
- The witness of Anna to all who would listen

Mary had trusted in all the miraculous events that happened to her—the conception and the birth of her child; the worship of the shepherds and the Wise Men; the flight to Egypt. She had been an obedient servant of her God even though she did not fully understand all it entailed. "But Mary treasured all these words and pondered them in her heart." Luke 2:19 (NRSV)

Pray that we can believe and accept what we may not understand through the Holy Spirit. Pray that we can be faithful and righteous like Mary and Joseph.

Epistle 35

With this Epistle we are looking at the beginning of a new year—a year that may bring the promise of relief from the traumatic events of the past year. Certainly, through all these long months, we have been able to feel the constant presence of our God—nurturing, comforting, and strengthening us. During these coming three weeks Perpetua will be unable to send out a regular weekly epistle. Thus, this message today is in three parts with a meditation for each week—the last Wednesday of the old year and the first two Wednesdays of the new year.

The Bible illustrates how prayer moves from the level of a type of magic to the pinnacle of a spiritual communion and identification with God. It helps us to develop a creation of personal contact to affect the nature and develop the course of our relationship with the Father. From our somewhat prosaic efforts we too can commune with God just as the people of the Old Testament and those of the new covenant in the New Testament did. Our prayer life can reach great heights of wisdom and comfort—day by day, week by week.

Week 1: Let us meditate on prayer in the Old Testament

> *Now Moses used to take the tent and pitch it outside the camp, far off from the camp; he called it the tent of meeting. And everyone who sought the LORD would go out to the tent of meeting, which was outside the camp. Whenever Moses went out to the tent, all the people would rise and stand, each of them, at the entrance of their tents and watch Moses until he had gone into the tent. When Moses entered the tent, the pillar of cloud would descend and stand at the entrance to the tent, and the LORD would speak with Moses. When all the people saw the pillar of cloud standing at the entrance to the tent, all the people would rise and bow down, all of them, at the entrance of their tent. Thus the LORD used to speak*

to Moses face to face, as one speaks to a friend. Then he would return to the camp; but his young assistant, Joshua son of Nun, would not leave the tent. Exod 33:7–11 (NRSV)

And Hezekiah prayed before the LORD, and said: "O LORD, the God of Israel, who are enthroned above the cherubim, you are God, you alone, of all the kingdoms of the earth; you have made heaven and earth. Incline your ear, O LORD, and hear; open your eyes, O LORD, and see; hear the words of Sennacherib, which he has sent to mock the living God. Truly, O LORD, the kings of Assyria have laid waste the nations and their lands, and have hurled their gods into the fire, though they were no gods but the work of human hands—wood and stone—and so they were destroyed. So now, O LORD our God, save us, I pray you, from his hand, so that all the kingdoms of the earth may know that you, O LORD, are God alone." 2 Kgs 19:15–19 (NRSV)

Therefore thus says the LORD concerning the king of Assyria: He shall not come into this city, shoot an arrow there, come before it with a shield, or cast up a siege ramp against it. By the way that he came, by the same he shall return; he shall not come into this city, says the LORD. For I will defend this city to save it for my own sake and for the sake of my servant David. 2 Kgs 19:32–34 (NRSV)

I, Daniel, alone saw the vision; the people who were with me did not see the vision, though a great trembling fell upon them, and they fled and hid themselves. So I was left alone to see this great vision. My strength left me, and my complexion grew deathly pale, and I retained no strength. Then I heard the sound of his words; and when I heard the sound of his words, I fell into a trance, face to the ground. But then a hand touched me and roused me to my hands and knees. He said to me, "Daniel greatly beloved, pay attention to the words that I am going to speak to you. Stand on your feet, for I have now been sent to you." So while he was speaking this word to me, I stood up trembling. He said to me, "Do not fear, Daniel, for from the first day that you set your mind to gain understanding and to humble yourself before your God, your words have been heard, and I have come because of your words." Dan 10:8–12 (NRSV)

Week 2: Let us meditate on prayer in the Gospels

> *So I say to you, Ask, and it will be given you; search, and you will find; knock, and the door will be opened for you. For everyone who asks receives, and everyone who searches finds, and for everyone who knocks, the door will be opened. Is there anyone among you, who, if your child asks for a fish, will give a snake instead of a fish? Or if the child asks for an egg, will give a scorpion? If you then, who are evil, know how to give good gifts to your children, how much more will the heavenly Father give the Holy Spirit to those who ask him!* Luke 11:9–13 (NRSV)

Jesus prays for his disciples . . .

> *I have made your name known to those whom you gave me from the world. They were yours, and you gave them to me, and they have kept your word. Now they know that everything you have given me is from you; for the words that you gave to me I have given to them, and they have received them and know in truth that I came from you; and they have believed that you sent me. I am asking on their behalf; I am not asking on behalf of the world, but on behalf of those whom you gave me, because they are yours. All mine are yours, and yours are mine; and I have been glorified in them. And now I am no longer in the world, but they are in the world, and I am coming to you. Holy Father, protect them in your name that you have given me, so that they may be one, as we are one. While I was with them, I protected them in your name that you have given me. I guarded them, and not one of them was lost except the one destined to be lost, so that the scripture might be fulfilled. But now I am coming to you, and I speak these things in the world so that they may have my joy made complete in themselves. I have given them your word, and the world has hated them because they do not belong to the world, just as I do not belong to the world. I am not asking you to take them out of the world, but I ask you to protect them from the evil one. They do not belong to the world, just as I do not belong to the world. Sanctify them in truth; your word is truth. As you have sent me into the world, so I have sent them into the world.* John 17:6–18 (NRSV)

Jesus prays for us . . .

I ask not only on behalf of these, but also on behalf of those who will believe in me through their word, that they may all be one. As you, Father are in me and I am in you, may they also be in us, so that the world may believe that you have sent me. The glory that you have given me I have given them, so that they may be one, as we are one, I in them and you in me, that they may become completely one, so that the world may know that you have sent me and have loved them even as you have loved me. Father, I desire that those also, whom you have given me, may be with me where I am, to see my glory, which you have given me because you loved me before the foundation of the world. John 17:20-24 (NRSV)

Week 3: Let us meditate on prayer in the early Church

For this reason, since the day we heard it, we have not ceased praying for you and asking that you be filled with the knowledge of God's will in all spiritual wisdom and understanding, so that you may lead lives worthy of the Lord, fully pleasing to him, as you bear fruit in every good work and as you grow in the knowledge of God. May you be made strong with all the strength that comes from his glorious power, and may you be prepared to endure everything with patience, while joyfully giving thanks to the Father who has enabled you to share in the inheritance of the saints in the light. Col 1:9-12 (NRSV)

Since, then, we have a great high priest who has passed through the heavens, Jesus, the Son of God, let us hold fast to our confession. For we do not have a high priest who is unable to sympathize with our weaknesses, but we have one who in every respect has been tested as we are, yet without sin. Let us therefore approach the throne of grace with boldness, so that we may receive mercy and find grace to help in time of need. Heb 4:14-16 (NRSV)

Therefore, my friends, since we have confidence to enter the sanctuary by the blood of Jesus, by the new and living way that he opened for us through the curtain (that is, through his flesh), and since we have a great high priest over the house of God, let us approach with a true heart in full assurance of faith, with our hearts sprinkled clean from an evil conscience and our bodies washed with pure water. Heb 10: 19-22 (NRSV)

But ask in faith, never doubting, for the one who doubts is like a wave of the sea, driven and tossed by the wind; for the doubter, being double-minded and unstable in every way, must not expect to receive anything from the Lord. Jas 1:6–8 (NRSV)

Epistle 36

C. S. Lewis, the well-known Christian apologist of the twentieth century, studied Christianity for many years before he came to a complete inner faith. Debates and arguments with fellow scholars at Oxford and Cambridge played a role, but this was largely a preparatory one. "He became a Christian not through accepting a particular set of arguments but through learning to read a story the right way. And maybe others could move closer to Christian belief by the same path."[1]

Objections to Christianity are phrased in words that miss the heart of Christianity; words in defense of Christianity are often ineffective as they miss the depth and the commitment. Alan Jacobs, the author of *The Narnian: The Life and Imagination of C.S. Lewis*, recounts that the worldly success of the writings of Lewis was pushing him to a feeling of unwanted pride.

> *I am going to be (if I live long enough) one of those men who was a famous writer in his forties and dies unknown—like Christian [in The Pilgrim's Progress] going down into the green valley of humiliation. Which is the most beautiful thing in Bunyan and can be the most beautiful thing in life if a man takes it quite rightly—a matter I think and pray about a great deal. One thing is certain: much better to begin (at least) learning humility on this side of the grave than to have it all as fresh problems on the other.*[2]

Did he feel his written words were too learned; too dispassionate; not reaching the heart so essential for real Christianity?

> Perhaps that is why Saint Francis, so the story goes, instructed his followers to "preach the Gospel always, using words if necessary." It is not simply and straight forwardly *wrong* to make arguments in defense of the Christian faith, but it is a relatively

---

1. Jacobs, *The Narnian*, 238.
2. Jacobs, *The Narnian*, 237.

> superficial activity; it fails to address the core issues . . . After all, an apologist for Christianity, to some degree at least, commits himself or herself to answering questions that Jesus himself consistently refused to answer.[3]

Peter turned and saw the disciple whom Jesus loved following them; he was the one who had reclined next to Jesus at the supper and had said, "Lord, who is it that is going to betray you?" When Peter saw him, he said to Jesus, "Lord, what about him?" Jesus said to him, "If it is my will that he remain until I come, what is that to you? Follow me!" John 21:20–22 (NRSV)

This epistle is not intended to condemn the practice of apologetics—it is, in its way, a necessary boon in the world of today. But we should always acknowledge that our reading of the Word should be penetrating our hearts as well as our minds. For our personal growth we should be talking to God as well as talking about God. We should be praying and— through our prayer life— witnessing! Each narrative in the Bible is vitally important.

Over the years, biblical scholarship has given us a preponderance of commentators who seem to go to extremes with suggestions of multiple authors and redactors; and intricate studies of style, source, and text; so that the narrative has been bogged down in questions and criticism. But there is always a story there—a story that enlightens us and shows us a purpose and a meaning. Perhaps that is what Lewis meant when he said we can become a Christian "through learning to read a story the right way."

Take, for example, the story of Judah and Tamar in Genesis 38. [Perhaps read Genesis 37:12–39:12 first?] This narrative leaves the story of Joseph and launches into a somewhat unrelated episode in the life of Judah. Some commentators often see this as a "completely independent unit," which does not have any connection with the "drama of Joseph." However, Robert Alter points out that there are continual intimate significances through motif and theme with the main story. Some of these are—Judah "goes down from his brothers" cf. Joseph is "brought down to Egypt"; Jacob's desperate mourning for his lost son cf. with Judah's almost indifference to the loss of his first two sons; by suggesting the brothers sell Joseph to the Egyptians, Judah is the deceiver of his father when he

---

3. Jacobs, *The Narnian*, 242.

brings to him the cherished tunic of Joseph's dipped in goat's blood cf. when Judah himself is deceived by Tamar who received his seal and his cord as a pledge for the gift of a goat from his flock and then brings it to him. Later we see a righteous Joseph fleeing Potiphar's wife forced to leave his garment in her hand cf. the unrighteous Judah willingly giving his revered seal and cord to Tamar.

Actually, "the entire book of Genesis is about the reversal of the iron law of primogeniture, about the election through some devious twist of destiny of a younger son to carry on the line."[4] It is ironic that Joseph, the second youngest, ruled over his brothers, and Judah, the fourth born was the progenitor of the Kings of Israel. But, in reading the story we see God's great plan fulfilled right up until the genealogical table in Matthew that culminates in the birth of Jesus.

We can read the "story." We can pray to God with thanksgiving:

> Yes God, we are beginning to understand the faithfulness and perseverance you have shown to your people by reading the narratives in your Word. Help us to understand your purposes for us today so that we can come ever closer to you.

---

4. Alter, *The Art of Biblical Narrative*, 6.

Epistle 37

In these epistles we are often acknowledging that delving into God's Word is not only going to increase our knowledge of our Heavenly Father, but is going to teach us how to converse with him; how to pray to him. Reading the Bible demands our participation. In this Epistle we are going to be specifically considering the Old Testament. When you read a story, a parable, a record of a historical event, the text rarely tells us what the narrator is thinking or feeling. Nor is there always a lot of description with excessive word content. Sometimes words seem to be deliberately left out! With modern writing and, with the advent of movies and television, we have become lazy. We expect everything to be explained to us. Even when we are left baffled at the end of a movie, we often rewind the disc to try and find out what we imagine we missed—just a few words that would explain the mystery confounding us. (Of course, when you are old it is because you had an unscheduled mid-movie nap!) The "technological" reader of today needs to be spoon-fed; the brain has become apathetic!

The reader needs to participate in God's Word; needs to look for what is missing; and then, decide why these things are missing. Nevertheless, we must be intuitive and must not read into the book what we *guess* might be there. Complicated it may seem, but we must *discover* what should be there. That way when we read out of the book, we fill the gaps and discover the full story in all its importance. We need to set some kind of criteria—what we discover must fit in; it must be logical; it must be supported by the rest of the story. How much more vital is something we detect ourselves than something we are taught in a lecture for example?

This does not mean though that modernity has stifled all our thinking but just that, in surface reading the Bible, we fail to find the message for our modern age in its pages. One of the helpful steps in Bible publication today is the Bible that has what is termed "Cultural Studies Background" notes in addition to the actual text. This enables the reader to gain a better understanding as to what the author and/or the original audience of each book was experiencing in the life and culture of the time. Thus, it helps the modern reader to apply the message of the scripture to his or her life today more accurately. The chronicle of Lot and his daughters and the story of Tamar and Judah are both examples that can be interpreted in the mind of today. These have always been used to demonstrate and emphasize the fall to sin of some of the men of the Old Testament. With cultural notations we can begin to understand the huge responsibility to Israel of the Old Testament Patriarchs. And with the experience of today's culture, we can also see the desperation and despair of the women who were pledged to these men. Not only can we see it, we can also feel it. We can dwell on Zipporah and begin to understand her suffering and her anger. We can see the deep hurt of women in the practice of polygamy; a hurt of which men were completely blind.

The Book of Psalms, in contrast to most of the Old Testament, does not push us to delve into the texts to grow the whole story in our minds. In contrast to the rest of the Testament, this is one of the rare places when we now hear what the narrator is feeling. Individual Psalms are not relating historical events—but they are related to historical events. The background to each can be found in other parts of the Old Testament. Psalm 3 for example, contains the words of King David, calling to his Father in his desperate hour of need. 2 Samuel 15–18 relates how David came to this point. He is hiding in a cave in flight from his son Absalom who is endeavoring to slay him and take the throne.

> *O LORD, how many are my foes!*
>   *Many are rising against me; many are saying to me,*
> *"There is no help for you in God."*
>   *But you, O LORD, are a shield around me,*
> *my glory, and the one who lifts up my head,*
>   *I cry aloud to the LORD, and he answers me from his holy hill.*
> *I lie down to sleep;*
>   *I wake again, for the LORD sustains me.*
> *I am not afraid . . .* Ps 3:1–6a (NRSV)

How much more deeply do these words resonate in our souls when we take time to look at the background, And, yet, we can use these words of comfort in a modern-day situation. When fearful of an approaching operation we can say with David: "I lie down to sleep; I wake again, for the LORD sustains me."

Many people become bored with prayer, perhaps due to a somewhat exciting frenetic lifestyle. But this is largely because our perception of God is too narrow. We must deepen our knowledge and awareness of God. We can do this by studying the text of his Word to find the complete story and by treasuring the heartfelt words of his people Israel in the Psalms. The more we study; the more we remember in our hearts and our minds.

> Aristotle once said that "memory is the scribe of the soul." Let us fill our memory with food for the soul.

Epistle 38

Let us reflect on your Christian life and experiences. At what time in your life did you delight in spiritual heights; and, at what time in your life did you suffer spiritual depths. Perhaps you have not had these spiritual extremes but, nevertheless, there were probably periods when you felt especially close to God and other periods when you felt abandoned.

The Psalmist says with joy:

> *The LORD is my strength and my shield; in him my heart trusts;*
> *so I am helped, and my heart exults,*
> *and with my song I give thanks to him.* Ps 28:7 (NRSV)

... and in despair:

> *Wait for the LORD; be strong, and let your heart take courage;*
> *wait for the LORD.* Ps 27:14 (NRSV)

In the depths of our souls God has planted a desire for him; an insatiable hunger. We can have a hunger in our physical bodies, which has to be continually satisfied, but we also have a hunger in our souls, which can only be sated by spiritual food. The difference is emphasized throughout God's Word:

> *You shall eat, but not be satisfied, and there shall be a gnawing hunger within you.* Mic 6:14 (NRSV)

> *All human toil is for the mouth, yet the appetite is not satisfied.* Eccl 6:7 (NRSV)

To be whole we must respond; by responding he feeds our hunger and completely satisfies our need ...

> *My soul is satisfied with a rich feast, and my mouth praises you with joyful lips.* Ps 63:5 (NRSV)

> *For he satisfies the thirsty, and the hungry he fills with good things.*
> Ps 107:9 (NRSV)

No greater clarity can be found than in the words of Jesus in John's Gospel when he addressed those in the synagogue at Capernaum:

> *Do not work for the food that perishes, but for the food that endures for eternal life, which the Son of Man will give you. For it is on him that God the Father has set his seal . . . I am the bread of life. Whoever comes to me will never be hungry and whoever believes in me will never be thirsty.* John 6:27, 35 (NRSV)

And again, when he was talking to the woman of Samaria at the well:

> *Everyone who drinks of this water will be thirsty again, but those who drink of the water that I will give them will never be thirsty. The water that I will give will become in them a spring of water gushing up to eternal life.* John 4:13–14 (NRSV)

The Gospel of John presents a much larger measure of theological interpretation than Matthew, Mark, and Luke. There is a fascinating emphasis on dualism throughout. The earlier gospels talk about the two ages—the present age and the Age to Come. John seems to go a step further to contrast the two worlds—the world of evil ruled by the devil and the world above ruled by God. John talks about Darkness and Light—Jesus himself is the Light, come from above; and about Flesh and Spirit—flesh synonymous with humankind, the Spirit synonymous with God. Flesh cannot reach up into the world above; it must be born of the Spirit. The Light shines in the darkness; the Bread of Life feeds the soul and the Water of Life quenches the thirst. The gift of the Spirit enables us to worship in a new way. The Temple is no longer; the road to the Father is through the teaching of Jesus. Jesus is now our High Priest and through him we can directly converse in prayer with God. We receive the Kingdom of God as a preliminary blessing here on earth: "John proclaims a present salvation in the person and mission of Jesus that will have an eschatological consummation."[1]

We will always have, on earth, times of spiritual assuredness and times of spiritual desperation. Is this not a type of dualism—a suggestion of a battle for our souls between God and the devil? The Bible provides great contrast to the folly of doubt and disbelief and to the emptiness of suffering and grief. Reading, meditating, and writing biblical words

---

1. Ladd, *A Theology of the New Testament*, 236.

on our hearts carves a path to prayer. Even when our own words fail to materialize we can pray a repetitive line of scripture to bring us closer to the Father.

> *O give thanks to the LORD, for he is good,*
>   *for his steadfast love endures forever.*
> *Who by understanding made the heavens,*
>   *for his steadfast love endures forever;*
> *who spread out the earth on the waters,*
>   *for his steadfast love endures forever;*
> *who made the great lights,*
>   *for his steadfast love endures forever;*
> *the sun to rule over the day,*
>   *for his steadfast love endures forever;*
> *the moon and stars to rule over the night,*
>   *for his steadfast love endures forever.*
> *It is he who remembered us in our low estate,*
>   *for his steadfast love endures forever;*
> *and rescues us from our foes,*
>   *for his steadfast love endures forever;*
> *who gives food to all flesh,*
>   *for his steadfast love endures forever.*
> *O give thanks to the God of heaven,*
>   *for his steadfast love endures forever.*
> Ps 136:1, 5–9, 23–26 (NRSV)

Epistle 39

In the last Epistle we talked about using God's Word as inspiration for prayer—just repeating a biblical verse or a line of scripture can help us to begin a conversation with our Father. With these words concentrate on completely relaxing in silence—waiting on the LORD. In Psalm 1 we read:

> *Happy are those who do not follow the advice of the wicked, or take the path that sinners tread, or sit in the seat of scoffers; but their delight is in the law of the LORD, and on his law they meditate day and night.* 1–2 (NRSV)

Richard of St. Victor, a medieval Scottish philosopher (b. 1173), goes one step further when he states that "meditation investigates but contemplation wonders." Meditation reveals the message of the passage and then contemplation brings understanding and, with it, calm, depth, and strength. When we are conscious only of our inner self we can reach out in prayer. The first step could be to talk to God about what we have derived from his words or, if that is not the case, asking him to help us understand.

Thomas à Kempis says "All sacred scriptures should be read in the spirit in which they were written. In them, therefore, we should seek food for our souls . . . let the love of pure truth draw you to read."[1] We can use the scripture to help us form the words of prayer. We don't have to give voice to what people might think is a "good" prayer. Rather we should concentrate on it being a "real" prayer. Such a prayer, a prayer from the heart, can be brief and sometimes simple, but it will be a prayer that exclusively centers on God. Just be with God. If words do not form, rest with unspoken prayer, in the encompassing beauty of silence. "O Jesus, Brightness of eternal glory and comfort of the pilgrim soul, hear my cry,

---

1. Thomas à Kempis, *The Imitation of Christ*, 33.

and regard my utter desolation. Words fail me in your presence; let my silence speak for me."[2]

Praying to Jesus—always in gratitude for his sacrifice—helps us to understand what it is to really love Jesus. We must love him above all else because his love for us is faithful and enduring. We end all our prayers in the name of Jesus but do we really fathom the depth of those words? Jesus bore rejection and humiliation for us; he suffered on the cross for us; he was forsaken by the Father for us. All he asks is our love for him. But that love must be great; never must we forget what he has done for us.

> *Jesus has many who love His Kingdom in Heaven, but few who bear His Cross. He has many who desire comfort, but few who desire suffering. He finds many to share His feast, but few His fasting. All desire to rejoice with Him, but few are willing to suffer for His sake. Many follow Jesus to the Breaking of the Bread, but few to the drinking of the Cup of His Passion. Many admire His miracles but few follow Him in the humiliation of His Cross ... how powerful is the pure love of Jesus, free from all self-interest and self-love!*[3]

You must never hold back in the depth and intensity of your love for God and his beloved son, Jesus. Reading many of the Church Fathers and the medieval mystics we discover how personal their adoration and worship was—that is how ours should be. All the words of scripture are for each one of us—not just for the Church Leaders and the erudite theologians of past and present. The relationship with God that Jesus re-established was for each one of us.

> *You stand assembled today, all of you, before the LORD your God—the leaders of your tribes, your elders, and your officials, all the men of Israel, your children, your women, and the aliens who are in your camp, both those who cut your wood and those who draw your water—to enter into the covenant of the LORD your God, sworn by oath, which the LORD your God is making with you today; in order that he may establish you today as his people, and that he may be your God, as he promised you and he swore to your ancestors, to Abraham, to Isaac, and to Jacob. I am making this covenant, sworn by an oath, not only with you who stand here with us today before the LORD our God, but also with those who are not here with us today.* Deut 29:10–15 (NRSV)

---

2. Thomas à Kempis, *The Imitation of Christ*, 121.
3. Thomas à Kempis, *The Imitation of Christ*, 83.

Pamela Tamarkin Reis, wrote of listening to this part of scripture in the Synagogue. After the service she asked the rabbi who were those who were not there. "He said, 'You,' 'Do you mean,' I said, 'that according to the Bible, I received the Torah on the same day as everybody else?'" [When he confirmed this] "I felt a heady rush of entitlement."[4] We are the people of God in the new covenant. When the Bible was published in recent years with vocabulary for both men and women, many women experienced a similar rush of entitlement in their hearts!

> If Martha came into your room right now and said: "The Teacher is here and is calling for you" do not hesitate—go in haste to meet your beloved friend! If you seek Jesus in prayer in all things, you will surely find him.

---

4. Reis, *Reading the Lines*, 12.

Epistle 40

A valuable aid to our prayer life is an openness to God's magnificence. Our senses need to be receptive. One writer has termed it a willingness to be enchanted! We must engage our senses not just our minds when delving into God's Word. That way every part of our body is awakened to the holy worship of the Creator. Often, in the midst of the modern world, we find this difficult, especially when our prayers are snatched in the tiny seconds of available time! Nevertheless, our souls need to be immersed in His glory.

One of the great advantages in our path to true reflection is the liturgy of the Church Service, but sadly, during the COVID period, this is not always available to us. Liturgy can become absorbed in our minds, our spirits, even our physical bodies. It awakens a personal experience and our very senses become enriched. We are not here considering the worship of idols or icons nor any representation by man of God and his precious son Jesus. Clearly, we know that is forbidden from the Ten Commandments and the Israelites were constantly reminded of this:

> *The idols of the nations are silver and gold, the work of human hands.*
> *They have mouths, but they do not speak; they have eyes but do not see;*
> *they have ears, but they do not hear; and there is no breath in their mouths.*
> *Those who make them and all who trust them shall become like them.*
> Ps 135:15–18 (NRSV)

Surprisingly, even with the discarding of the Temple practices of the Old Testament, we can find a liturgical framework in the New Testament. The word "liturgy" has its roots in the Greek, bringing together service, ministry, people and work. "Liturgy, therefore, is the labor of the laity or the soul-work of the people. It is the spiritual work that Christians perform in their seasons of public worship."[1] Liturgy just means reading the Bible, congregation responses either by spoken word or in song, reciting creeds, praying together, celebrating the Lord's Supper, even the lighting of candles in remembrance. It doesn't involve the elaborate practices that worry the Reforming Churches! "Calvin believed that liturgy limits levity and giddiness in worship."[2] A modern theologian believes that "faithful liturgy is a tool the Spirit uses to move Christians deeper into the Christian reality. When internalized by faith, biblical and creedal responses in the liturgy restore and reshape the Christian's soul."[3] Christians, therefore, should never be non-participants in the liturgy of the Service; it is integral!

We can embrace the following readings even though we are presently unable to gather together in great numbers. At home, following a Service online, we can still sing and even in a much-reduced congregation we can sing in our hearts.

> *. . . be filled with the Spirit, as you sing psalms and hymns and spiritual songs among yourselves, singing and making melody to the Lord in your hearts, giving thanks to God the Father at all times and for everything in the name of our Lord Jesus Christ.* Eph 5:18b–20 (NRSV)

> *What should be done then, my friends? When you come together, each one has a hymn, a lesson, a revelation, a tongue, or an interpretation. Let all things be done for building up.* 1 Cor 14:26 (NRSV)

Even communion can be celebrated in our home if we are isolated:

> *For I received from the Lord what I also handed onto you, that the Lord Jesus on the night he was betrayed took a loaf of bread, and when he had given thanks, he broke it and said, "This is my body that is for you. Do this in remembrance of me." In the same way he took the cup also, after supper, saying, "This is the cup of the new covenant in my blood. Do this, as often as you drink it, in remembrance of me." For as often as you eat this bread and drink the cup, you proclaim the Lord's death until he comes.* 1 Cor 11:23–26 (NRSV)

1. Demarest, *Satisfy Your Soul*, 173.
2. Demarest, *Satisfy Your Soul*, 174.
3. Demarest, *Satisfy Your Soul*, 174.

Not only our senses, but our bodies can be involved in the liturgy. We can re-enact the washing of the feet, the blessing of hands, the anointing with oil. In the Baptism Service when the water is sprinkled or the body immersed, the congregation participates by reciting or singing the Aaronic Blessing. All liturgy awakens in us a personal experience and enables us to become enriched. Somebody once wrote that liturgy was a hook on which to hang our contemplation; another profound thought is that it is a sign to begin on a path to enrichment.

With a real consciousness of liturgy our senses can drown in the splendor of God. We can hear the Word of God being applied to us personally. We can pray together to build up our confidence and our strength. We can partake in all that is offered to us and increase our knowledge of God in all his holiness and mercy. As we gradually come closer to God, we will find it a natural act to talk with him, and to pray constantly. The more we come to know people, the more we share our lives through talking on an intimate basis. How much more wonderful will conversations with God become if we become truly intimate with him. Conversations all possible because of a loving Savior.

Jesus, Shepherd of your sheep, you have given us a place for prayer,
Give us, we beseech you, a heart to ever pray.

Epistle 41

When we study the Word of God in the Old Testament, we find that the prominent figures, both men and women, are faithful prayers. They talk with God constantly in praise and gratitude and in distress and failure. We have looked before in our Epistles, at the words of Psalm 3 when David, hiding in a cave from his son Absalom, was calling on God in fear:

> *O LORD, how many are my foes! Many are rising up against me.*
> Ps 3:1 (NRSV)

He is comforted—he feels that God has wrapped him in a protective shield; the LORD God has heard his cry and answered him from on high. Thus, David is then able to say:

> *I lie down and sleep; I wake again, for the LORD sustains me.* Ps 3:5 (NRSV)

In Psalm 4 David seems to have gained courage from the response of God to his initial trauma:

> *Answer me when I call to you, O God of my right.*
> *You gave me room when I was in distress.*
> *Be gracious to me and hear my prayer.*
> *How long, you people, shall my honor suffer shame?*
> *How long will you love vain words and seek after lies?*
> *But know that the LORD has set apart the faithful for himself;*
> *the LORD hears when I call to him.*
> *When you are disturbed do not sin;*
> *ponder it on your beds, and be silent,*
> *Offer right sacrifices and put your trust in the LORD.*
> *There are many who say, "O that we might see some good!"*
> *Let the light of your face shine upon us, O LORD.*
> *You have put gladness in my heart*
> *more than when their grain and wine abound.*
> *I will both lie down and sleep in peace;*

For you alone, O LORD, make me lie down in safety.
Ps 4:1–8 (NRSV)

Notice how once again David is voicing his plea for help but nevertheless, he now appears most confident that God will answer—if he approaches in humility his God will be righteous; he will hear him; he will be merciful.

The *Psalms of David* are deeply personal.

In fact, all the Psalms illustrate a great interaction between God and his people. Some Psalms, like Psalm 4, portray a real conversation:

David talking to God, pleading for an answer!
God lamenting—how long will his people behave this way?

The people of Israel were being led astray worshipping gods of other nations; with the well-to-do putting their trust in earthly possessions and seeking the praise of the world in the process. They were in rebellion to David, God's special king. The words that David writes in v.2 are as if God himself speaks them. But there is a confident plea for deliverance. David knows that the LORD God has always set aside the righteous for himself; he will always hear them. The people will come to him, they will be overwhelmed by their sinfulness. Even though they have turned away, God is in control and will hear them. David knows this—he calls on the people to stifle their anger at the end of the day. They must be self-controlled: "Do not let the sun go down on your anger and do not make room for the devil." Ephesians 4:26a–27 (NRSV) They need to search their hearts and be silent—to reflect on their wayward path and seek forgiveness.

Then, in the last section: "Let the light of your face shine on us, O Lord!, You have filled my heart with greater joy . . . Psalm 4:7" (NRSV) than all the things the world could possibly offer.

The "light of your face" can be a metaphor for the sun. The sun brings us light; it brings us warmth and comfort. In Psalm 80: *A Prayer for Israel's Restoration*, we read in v.3 "Restore us, O God. Let your face shine, that we may be saved." in v.7 "Restore us, O God of hosts. Let your face shine that we may be saved." And, in v.19 "Restore us, O LORD God of hosts. Let your face shine, that we may be saved . . ." (NRSV)

This is our God; the God of all people who is LORD, worthy of praise and adoration. In Psalm 84: *The Joy of Worship in the Temple* we read in v.11 "For the LORD God is a sun and a shield, he bestows favor and honor. No good thing does the LORD withhold from those who walk uprightly." (NRSV)

> God is faithful; God hears; God shields us from harm,
> He honors we who walk in his paths, He gives us joy and peace.

When we repent and throw away our anger and our fear we will lie down and sleep in peace, for you alone, O LORD, make me dwell in safety.

The West Highland Way in Scotland is divided into stages. The last stage takes an average walker some eight hours to complete. Approximately midway among the hills, devoid of trees, there is an incredible silence—no sound of bird or beast! Looking up to the light of the midday sun—to the heights—there appears to be a real presence. The famous Scottish poet, Robbie Burns, once wrote:

> *My heart's in the Highlands, my heart is not here,*
> *My heart's in the Highlands, a-chasing the deer . . .*
> *My heart's in the Highlands, wherever I go.*

Let us pray, today and always, that our hearts are not riveted on worldly desires but our hearts are in the heights—not a-chasing deer—but seeking the face of God that shines on us always, wherever we go!

Epistle 42

In this epistle we are going to discover what some of our Christian forebears said about prayer! Lancelot Andrewes, an English bishop and theologian who lived from 1555–1626 wrote: "There is never a time we do not stand in need of God's particular assistance; nor a place in which we cannot pray." For Andrewes prayer should be ceaseless; it was like the burning of incense ever rising to the court of heaven. "Let our prayer go up to him that his grace may come down to us," so to lighten us in our way and works that we may in the end come to dwell in him, in the light where there is no even-tide. "Prayer giveth up; pity cometh down."[1]

John Calvin, Genevan Reformer, 1509–1564, said we "lay open before him our infirmities which we would be ashamed to confess before men."[2] He believed that we cannot pray without the Holy Spirit anticipating the great need to commune with God. The Spirit directs our words and in so doing prays with us.

> *Calvin taught that prayer was the chief exercise of the faith and that faith opened up the way to prayer. By approaching God faith goes before to illumine the way, giving us the full impression that he is our Father, then the gate is opened and we may converse freely with him and he with us . . . And yet our prayers are acceptable to God only in so far as Christ sprinkles and sanctifies them with the perfume of his own sacrifice.*[3]

Dietrich Bonhoeffer, founder of the Confessing Church in Germany, executed on Hitler's orders in April 1945—a mere two weeks before liberation—believed that, in prayer, we confuse man and God. The heart of man cannot pray by itself. Prayer does not mean we simply pour out one's heart. It means rather to find the way to God and to speak with him,

---

1. Dorman, "Lancelot Andrewes and Prayer," 1.
2. Wallace, *Calvin, Geneva and the Reformation*, 212,
3. Wallace, *Calvin, Geneva and the Reformation*, 213.

whether the heart is full or empty. We cannot do this by ourselves. We need to do that through Jesus Christ. Only by understanding fully the sacrifice Jesus made and accepting that he died for our sins, so that the wrath of God would be borne by him, can we come to an intimate relationship with the Father. As Calvin said—our prayers must be sprinkled with the perfume of Christ's sacrifice!

Bonhoeffer's faith was sure. When a pastor in London, he once preached "Death is mild; death is sweet and gentle; it beckons to us with heavenly power, if only we realize that it is the gateway to our homeland, the tabernacle of joy, the everlasting kingdom of peace."[4] It is the culmination of our prayer life when we come before the throne of grace to worship the God with whom we have communed in our earthly life through prayer.

We come to God in prayer through the loving sacrifice of Jesus but we are still faltering in our weakness. In Paul's Letter to the Romans, we learn how the Holy Spirit intercedes for us when we find it hard to express the depth of our desires. We can even sit silently with God. John Stott in his commentary on Romans 5–8 entitled *Men Made New* writes:

> *We should not be ashamed of such wordless prayers. God the Father understands prayers which are sighed rather than said, because he searches our hearts, and can read our thoughts. He knows too what is the mind of the Spirit, because the Holy Spirit always prays according to the will of God. And so the Father in heaven answers the prayers which are prompted by the Spirit in our hearts.*[5]

Today, some Christians are rediscovering an ancient prayer practice. A prayer labyrinth is a geometrically designed walking path that leads into and out of a central point. It is not a maze as it has a distinctive route. This practice is readily condemned by some claiming it to be a pagan rite. It was used by pagans in the past but, like a book, a painting, a score of music, it is the content and the purpose that denotes its character. There are many ways you can pray through a labyrinth, for example, during the walk inwards you can vocalize a prayer of confession with reflection at the center and renewal and commitment on the outward journey. Or, on the inward path you could ask questions or plead for help with enduring problems, reflect at the center and praise God with gratitude on

---

4. Metaxas, *Bonhoeffer*, 531.
5. Stott, *Men Made New*, 98–99.

the outward path. What is vital that we keep in our minds all that our theologians of today's epistle have taught us.

Praying to God the Father in the heights; sprinkling our prayers with the sacrifice of Jesus the Son on this earth; looking to the purity of the Holy Spirit to guide us in our weakness.

The greatest contribution to our communion with God is the perseverance of our prayer life. Not only do we have the words of the Church Fathers and theologians of all ages to aid us and meditate upon, there are the innumerable examples of men and women in the Bible itself who never ceased praying.

Let us commit ourselves to be like them.

Epistle 43

I am sure many of us have children, siblings, relatives, or close friends who, in their youth, were brought up in the family of Christ, but after living in the secular world of today, have strayed from the narrow way. We can constantly pray for our loved ones—and we do—but sometimes we become dispirited when we don't reap anything from our frequent prayers. We must remember that our prayers are never in vain. We may not see results now; we might never see results in our lifetime, but God is in control and will guide his chosen ones forever. Remember the words of *The Parable of the Lost Sheep* . . .

> *Take care that you do not despise one of these little ones; for, I tell you, in heaven their angels continually see the face of my Father in heaven. What do you think? If a shepherd has a hundred sheep, and one of them has gone astray, does he not leave the ninety-nine on the mountains and go in search of the one that went astray? And if he finds it, truly I tell you, he rejoices over it more than over the ninety-nine that never went astray. So it is not the will of your Father in heaven that one of these little ones should be lost.* Matt 18:10–14 (NRSV)

We have shown the way of life to those who now appear lost. We have to be strong enough to always believe that God has them in his care. By living our lives in the faith and being always there for encouragement—sometimes silent; sometimes spoken—we can rest in the knowledge that a far greater being than us is compassionate to all those who have fallen away.

How precious is every lamb to God the Father: "He will feed his flock like a shepherd; he will gather the lambs in his arms, and carry them in his bosom, and gently lead the mother sheep." Isaiah 40:11 (NRSV) . . . Our lambs in his arms . . .

> *Then I myself will gather the remnant of my flock out of all the lands where I have driven them and I will bring them back into the fold . . . I will raise up shepherds over them who will shepherd them, and they shall not fear any longer, or be dismayed, nor shall any be missing, says the LORD.* Jer 23:3–4 (NRSV)

> *But David said to Saul, "Your servant used to keep sheep for his father; and whenever a lion or a bear came, and took a lamb from the flock, I went after it and struck it down, rescuing the lamb from its mouth, and if it turned against me, I would catch it by the jaw, strike it down, and kill it."* 1 Sam 17:34–35 (NRSV)

Our Shepherd has struck down Satan, and in the last days he will destroy him.

Elizabeth Cecilia Clephane, the daughter of the Sheriff of Fife in Scotland, was born in 1830. She was the author of many hymns popularized in the times by Ira Sankey. When she wrote her hymn, *The Lost Sheep*, in 1868, she was facing imminent death. It was published in *The Children's Hour* (1868) and later in *The Family Treasury* (1872). When Ira Sankey read the text, a tune was composed and the whole included in his *Gospel Hymns and Sacred Songs*, which was published in 1875. The lines expressed the experiences, the hopes, and the longings of a young Christian facing release from illness. Written on the very edge of this life, with the better land fully in view through faith, they seem to be footsteps printed on the sands of time, where these sands touch the ocean of eternity.

> *There were ninety and nine that safely lay*
> *In the shelter of the fold;*
> *But one was out on the hills away,*
> *Far off from the gates of gold.*
> *Away on the mountains wild and bare;*
> *Away from the tender Shepherd's care.*
>
> *Lord Thou hast here Thy ninety and nine;*
> *Are they not enough for Thee?*
> *But the Shepherd made answer: This of Mine*
> *Has wandered away from Me.*
> *And although the road be rough and steep,*
> *I go to the desert to find My sheep.*
>
> *But none of the ransomed ever knew*
> *How deep were the waters crossed;*

Nor how dark was the night that the Lord passed through
Ere he found His sheep that was lost.
Far out in the desert He heard its cry;
Twas sick and helpless and ready to die.

Lord, whence are those blood-drops all the way,
That mark out the mountain's track?
They were shed for one who had gone astray
Ere the Shepherd could bring him back.
Lord, whence are They hands so rent and torn?
They're pierced tonight by many a thorn.

And all through the mountains, thunder-riv'n,
And up from the rocky steep,
There arose a glad cry to the gate of heav'n,
Rejoice! I have found My sheep!
And the angels echoed around the throne,
Rejoice, for the Lord brings back His own![1]

---

1. Sankey. *Gospel Hymns and Sacred Songs*, no. 9.

Epistle 44

Anselm of Canterbury (1033-1109) was an outstanding philosopher and theologian of the eleventh century. In his famous work *The Proslogion*, he set out to illustrate the relationship between faith and understanding. What do you think comes first? Do we have to understand the Bible to come to a belief in God; or, do we find faith first and then try to understand what we are to believe? *Anselm believed that you do not understand so that you believe but that you believe so that you might understand. Furthermore, he reasoned that, unless you first believe, you shall not understand.* He felt very strongly that once we came to believe; once we came to faith in Christ; it was essential that we proceed to study the Word and so come to a deep well of understanding. When we believe, when we find faith, we leap over the deep chasm between the intellect and the heart. With an enlightened heart our whole being is altered and our outlook and concerns are transformed.

This can be somewhat confusing. Some people study the Bible and yet are not moved to believe; others, like the actor David Suchet, may read *The Letter to the Romans* from a Bible left by the Gideons in a hotel room—and believe! Other people have a momentous event in their lives that impacts so much that they find faith and then they go to the Bible. Many can pinpoint the exact day and time they became a convert, whereas for some they cannot remember a time when they did not believe in God. Whatever your situation your faith must be nurtured and strengthened, and this happens principally in two ways—studying the Word and growing an ardent prayer life. This way we satisfy our souls.

Take comfort in the fact we do not have to be theologians or any other type of academic to understand God's Word. The Bible is written for all peoples. Jesus spoke to both the learned and the illiterate and his message was understood by those who listened with the ear of their hearts. In fact, amazingly, it was the learned of the day—the Pharisees, the scribes, the priests, and the rabbis who failed to understand. Right through the ages other scholars have added more meaning to the words of the Bible than is necessary. Of course, we need to study the words, to meditate on the meaning of the message, but never to put our own presumptive thoughts into the narrative.

We know that a prime method Jesus used was to teach in parables—simple stories that evolved into a teaching about God or about the Kingdom. All these parables reveal a wonderful clarification, for example, in the Prodigal Son, when the son realized how far he had fallen by sinning against his father and heaven, he resolved to return home in repentance and prepared to take the lowest place in his father's house. Then comes the vital part of the parable—not the sins of the younger son or the jealousy of the older son—but the reaction of the father: "But while he was still far off, his father saw him and was filled with compassion; he ran and put his arms around him and kissed him." Luke 15:20 (NRSV) We have a story of ourselves, turning to our own way trying to grasp the treasures of the world. When we fall and acknowledge our need to return to our Father God, he will welcome us and put his arms around us.

> *I will render thank offerings to you. For you have delivered my soul from death, and my feet from falling, so that I may walk before God in the light of life.* Ps 56:12b–13 (NRSV)

Many of the Church Fathers, instead of looking at the parables to find a simple straightforward message, found in them lessons that they were never designed to teach. Augustine, bp. of Hippo, identified the Innkeeper in the Good Samaritan with the apostle Paul; Tertullian equated the fatted calf in the Prodigal Son as slain for the feast with the Savior himself. We must not see things that are not there! We just need quick insight and good sense. Sometimes the details do not need any special interpretation and if we try to find something that is not there, we lose the impact of the message. When Paul wrote to the Colossians he said:

> *For I want you to know how much I am struggling for you, and for those in Laodicea, and for all who have not seen me face to face. I want their hearts to be encouraged and united in love, so that they may have all the riches of assured understanding and have the knowledge of God's mystery, that is, Christ himself, in whom are hidden all the treasures of wisdom and knowledge.* Col 2:1–3 (NRSV)

Wisdom is skill, experience, expertise; understanding is discernment and perception. The Holy Spirit opens God's insights and discernment to us so that we can overcome the problems and challenges we face day by day. Through Christ our Savior we can come to belief; the Holy Spirit is our ultimate aid in coming to an understanding. The Spirit aids us in our prayer life guiding us always to the Father. When we have a new acquaintance, we engage in conversation with them to find out who they really are. The more we converse the closer we become. So it is with prayer—the more we talk to God, the more we learn of the depth of his love and compassion and know how special we are to him.

> *You turn things upside down! Shall the potter be regarded as the clay?*
> *Shall the thing made say of its maker, "He did not make me";*
> *or the thing formed say of the one who formed it,*
> *He has no understanding?* Isa 29:16 (NRSV)

God understands us—even with our human limitations we can come to a deep understanding of him through prayer.

Epistle 45

Don't you feel sorry for all those people who have discarded the faithful book for the Kindle. I have just purchased a book on the natural history of the Bible and am smelling the pages and running my fingers over the exquisite sketches, paintings, and photographs of animals, birds, and plants! The book jacket is just like a protective cloak around a precious art form. Each page is beautifully arranged with Bible readings and little commentaries. What magic! Spinning slowly through the pages with my thumb brings a myriad of color.

Much older books have an unchallenged beauty in content, presentation, and history. Illuminated manuscripts illicit gasps of wonder and delight. Despite the dour predictions of modern youth, libraries of books will continue to exist.

What about our Bibles? Every time there is a new translation, we must have it! Different translations bring so many different aspects and provide even more food for thought. My mother loved her Weymouth translation of the New Testament; I love the Phillips version of 1 Corinthians 13. But, no matter how much clearer modern translations are, I still need the Authorized King James Version, as I cherish the wording, which is often more direct, more powerful, more beautiful. Of course, a Kindle is handy; it never wears out; its pages are never torn! Bibles invariably become battered, the pages creased, and the corners curled! They become repositories for Bible Study notes, for programs from Services, for favorite bookmarks, for special photographs, for notes from Sunday School children, for important mementos. Sometimes they fall open at the parts we love—no doubt due to our constant reference.

Our faith with God needs to be like both of these vehicles of reading. Pristine, clearly set out, easy to consult and carry, free from wear and tear, like a Kindle—but also worn from constant use, loved for its memories, precious for its intimacy, like an old Bible. Our prayer life should also be like both—clear and fresh but precious and intimate—but also righteous.

> *The sacrifice of the wicked is an abomination to the LORD, but the prayer of the upright is his delight.* Prov 15:8 (NRSV)

Our prayer life should also be ongoing—day by day.

> *Rejoice in hope, be patient in suffering, persevere in prayer.* Rom 12:12 (NRSV)

We must pray for fellow believers, just as Paul prayed for the early converts.

> *I thank God every time I remember you, constantly praying with joy in every one of my prayers for all of you, because of your sharing in the gospel from the first day until now.* Phil 1:3–5 (NRSV)

We can pray in complete confidence; without disquiet.

> *Do not worry about anything, but in everything by prayer and supplication with thanksgiving let your requests be known to God.* Phil 4:6 (NRSV)

And, remember always, that even when we fall from the narrow way,

> *The LORD has heard my supplication; the LORD accepts my prayer.* Ps 6:9 (NRSV)

When we go into our Kindles or open our Bibles, we are on the way to developing a heart for God.

> *If you will spend time with him in his Word and if you will talk with him in prayer each day, you will soon develop what Paul calls "the mind of Christ." As you come to love him, he will conform the desires of your heart to match his desires. Then there will no longer be a question of seeking his will so much as a desire to please him.*[1]

> *My child, if you accept my words*
> *and treasure up my commandments within you,*
> *making your ear attentive to wisdom*
> *and inclining your heart to understanding;*
> *if you indeed cry out for insight,*
> *and raise your voice for understanding,*
> *if you seek it like silver,*
> *and search for it as for hidden treasures—*

---

1. Waltke, *Finding the Will of God*, 89–90.

> *then you will understand the fear of the LORD*
> *and find the knowledge of God.*
> Prov 2:1–5 (NRSV)

With such words in our hearts and minds we need to mature in our knowledge of God. By spending more time with him in prayer we will become closer to him and so love him more deeply. Ultimately his desires for us will become our desires. But you must never cease talking with him. "When you stop talking, you stop understanding what God wants."[2]

If you have ever had sons who attended an all-boys school with a Christian foundation, you will know that the most deliberately battered Bible brings the greatest respect amongst peers. This, unfortunately, is not because it is the most well-read Bible, but probably so that you would not be regarded as a genuine "Bible-Basher" (an oxymoron!) in this wild and attractive world of secularism. At the other end of the spectrum, older people are finding a large-print Bible a very attractive option for reading but not for carrying! The Kindle could in both cases prove to be a far more useful tool to enable us to know the heart of God!

---

2. Waltke, *Finding the Will of God*, 101.

Epistle 46

This week we are meditating on the journey of Jesus to the cross on Calvary. We are going to have a much longer epistle and it comes from the pen of Ann Powell. Perpetua feels very blessed that Ann has allowed us to use her words to enable us to experience and understand the miracle at Bethany.

> It would be great to study the N.T. reading first!
> *Lazarus*   John 11: 1–45 (NIV)

Well, it was a long reading, wasn't it? There are ways of shortening it but how can you take out a single word? It is so complete that in a sense there is nothing more to say. But this is John's Gospel and there are always layers of meaning to peel away.

The setting of this story is a family.

I'm an only child! I expect there are other singletons out there today. I longed for a sibling but it was not to be. But there were bonuses; there were, and still are, people who are as dear to me as a blood relative. My husband Oliver's family say to me, "You aren't our sister-in-law. You are our sister." My address file has many names labelled, "Ann's almost sister or brother." There's a glue that holds adoptive relationships together with as much strength as filial love.

That is the feeling I get about Jesus' relationship with Lazarus, Martha, and Mary. The humanity of their relationship creates a wonderful backdrop to the divinity of Jesus in their midst. We have met Martha and Mary before in Luke 10. Traditionally Mary is the spiritual sister, longing to learn from Jesus, to sit at his feet like the disciples. Impetuous, she will pour expensive perfume over Jesus' feet in a later story. Martha has a different temperament. She has the responsibility of being the head of the household, the hostess with the guests to care and cater for and decisions to make.

In this story we meet their brother Lazarus for the first time and clearly there is a great bond between Jesus and the whole family . . .

It's not hard to imagine the situation when Lazarus is taken ill. As the sisters watch over him and see his condition deteriorating, there evolves a discussion which may be familiar. "Should we let Jesus know? Is Lazarus really that sick?" And finally, they take the decision to send the message.

> *Lord, the one you love is sick.* John 11:3b

Did they not realize the gravity of the illness or did their brother take a sudden turn for the worst? On a human level these are obvious questions, but the words of Jesus give us the first inkling that this is no ordinary story.

> *This sickness will not end in death. No, it is for God's glory so that God's Son may be glorified through it.* 4

And he waits for two days before saying: "Let us go back to Judea." 7 The disciples react strongly: "A short while ago the Jews tried to stone you, and yet you are going back there?" 8

Then Jesus talks enigmatically about walking in the light of day. The rocks one might stumble over in the dark are also those people who are looking to trip Jesus up metaphorically.

> *Our friend Lazarus has fallen asleep, but I am going there to wake him up.* 11b

How would you react to that news? With relief? As the disciples did? Oh, that's okay then. He'll get better.

Patiently Jesus explains that actually Lazarus is dead—that what he is talking about is the sleep of death. It's a euphemism that is often used. And that what is about to happen will be to their benefit so that they might believe!

A key theme in John's Gospel—Thomas, always practical and down to earth, says well we might as well go and die with him. They have no idea what's going to happen. And the scene is set.

In our western culture it is hard for us to understand the great demonstration of grief that was taking place—the wailing and the moaning, the heart-wrenching cries, and the shaking bodies. We are told that Bethany was less than two miles away from Jerusalem and many Jews had come to the house to extend comfort. So, gathered there at Martha's house were not just family and friends, but professional mourners with their noisy instruments. The first four days were of intense mourning, the next three a little less, then continued support for the bereaved. Lazarus must have died just after the messenger had been sent with the news of his sickness, and Jesus must have known supernaturally that this had happened. Yet he waited two days. Why?

When somebody we love is seriously ill our instinct is to go to them; to spend precious time with them; maybe even to say goodbye.

Bishop Tom Wright believes that those two days were a time of deep prayer, of wrestling with God in a similar way to the struggle in the Garden of Gethsemane on the night before Jesus died—that this time was a preparation for the miracle, the sixth miraculous sign in John's Gospel.

At Cana, Jesus had turned water into wine. Later, also at Cana, he had healed an official's son from a distance. At Bethesda, Jesus had given mobility to a man who had been waiting for healing for thirty-eight years. Then there was the miraculous feeding of 5,000 men, not to mention women and children. The healing of the man blind from birth had raised many issues with the Pharisees. But all of these will be crowned by the miraculous sign of the raising of Lazarus from the dead.

So, it was four days since Lazarus had died and they had laid him in the tomb, sealing it with a large stone. The noisy mourning was still continuing when Martha went out to meet Jesus. How easy it is to identify with her cry, "Lord, if you had been here, my brother would not have died." 21 How often do we say "If only I had or hadn't done that, this would not have happened." The common belief was that the soul hovered around the body for three days. After that, decomposition set in and there was no more chance of resuscitation. And it was now the fourth day! But even so, Martha then makes an extraordinary statement: "But I know that even now God will give you whatever you ask." 21b After four days!! Jesus said to her: "Your brother will rise again." "I know he will rise again in the resurrection at the last day" 11:23–24, says Martha, faithful to the belief of the Pharisees.

> But now allow yourself to feel the full weight of the words of Jesus.

> > I am [the name of God Almighty] *the resurrection and the life. He who believes in me will live even though he dies, and whoever lives and believes in me will never die. Do you believe this?* 25

Martha's affirmation is magnificent. In the midst of her grief, maybe even because of her grief, she makes this great declaration of faith because she has been privileged to hear the words of the great I AM.

> Yes Lord, I believe that you are the Christ, the Son of God, who has come into the world. 27

But we have only heard part of the story . . .

Martha hurries back and whispers to Mary that Jesus has arrived and is asking for her and Mary tries to slip away quietly, but she is noticed and followed because the Jews think she is going to weep at the tomb. Meeting Jesus, she throws herself weeping at his feet and repeats her sister's words: "Lord, if you had been here, my brother would not have died." 32b And, in the shortest verse in the Bible, we are told that "Jesus wept." 35 Now, this is not the Greek word used for official mourning of the crowds but a word describing deep emotion, floods of tears. Jesus wept for the grief of his much-loved friends. Perhaps he wept in compassion for the pain that they were suffering, but, in a sense, these are the tears with which he identifies with the weeping world. If only things could be different!

"Jesus, once more deeply moved, came to the tomb . . . 'take away the stone,' he said." 38–39 Martha, in spite of her earlier affirmation, is still perhaps believing in the resurrection on the last day. It is four days since Lazarus died. Surely decomposition must have begun. How can she bear the sight of her beloved brother? How can they bear the stench?

> But Lord . . . by this time there is a bad odour, for he has been there four days. Then Jesus said, "Did I not tell you that if you believed, you would see the glory of God?" 39b–40

So, they took away the stone.

Jesus looked up to heaven in the attitude of prayer and said: "Father I thank you that you have heard me." 41a Thank you that you have heard my prayer during those two days of waiting and the time of journeying. Thank you that you have heard the prayer of my weeping! Thank you that you always hear me and thank you that all these people now know that this is so and believe.

What a wonderful example of how to pray!

Then Jesus shouts with the voice of authority: "Lazarus! Come out!" 43b What did the people expect? Were they watching in apprehension, fear, disbelief? And Lazarus comes out wrapped in the linen cloths of burial.

"Jesus said to them, 'Take off the grave cloths and let him go.'" 44b Take off those things that bind him and stop him from living a full life. Take off the petty restrictions and the rituals.

Take off those things that hinder his relationship with God.

And I wonder what are those things that bind us, making us spiritually dead? Preventing us from living a life of fulfillment, preventing us, like Martha, from fully believing?

> This great final miraculous sign, this raising of Lazarus from the dead, points us to Jesus' death. He too was laid in a tomb, wrapped in grave cloths. But, on Easter day, he burst forth from the grave leaving behind all the restrictions and promising resurrection to all who believe. As we walk the way of the cross towards Good Friday, we know that it is not the end, for Jesus is the resurrection and the life—whoever believes in him will never die.

Epistle 47

In the last epistle we were following Jesus on his way to Jerusalem. We read of the miraculous healing of a dead man, the loved friend of Jesus. We saw Lazarus coming out of the tomb bound in the grave cloths and Jesus telling the people to take off these cloths so he was no longer restricted. This narrative equates with Jesus coming out of the tomb on Easter Sunday leaving the grave cloths behind.

All through the gospels we take the journey with Jesus on his way to Jerusalem and ultimately to his death on the cross—the sacrifice for our sins so that we can approach a righteous God. And all through the gospels Jesus talked to the people in parables and taught the disciples the deep meaning of these parables, so that they could understand what was going to happen. The parable of the noble vineyard owner and his son in Luke 20:9–18 is a startling example of what the Jews will do to their Savior. A rich man planted a large vineyard and then went away to another country. He rented out his vineyard to greedy, unscrupulous men. When he sent his servant to the vineyard to collect the rent; the tenants beat him and he returned emptyhanded. He sent another servant; he was also treated badly and returned emptyhanded! A third one was cast out. Then the owner of the vineyard decided to send his beloved son—surely, they would respect him. The tenants killed him. Not only that, but "they drag the son outside the vineyard because if they KILL him within the vineyard, their grapes will become defiled and thereby worthless."[1] Amazingly they observe an added minor law concerning financial gain and yet ignore one of the Ten Commandments concerning love for a fellow Israelite!

The noble man took the vineyard off the tenants and gave it to others.

1. Bailey, *Jesus Through Middle Eastern Eyes*, 420.

The vineyard owner was entitled, by Jewish law, to contact the authorities to send armed men into the vineyard to deal with the usurpers. He chooses not to take this action. "The owner experiences anger, frustration, pain, anguish, rejection, desire for retributive justice and finally a costly peace out of which he chooses to act—*I will send my beloved son.*"[2] Remember in the Old Testament, when David was standing over the sleeping body of King Saul, against the advice of his companion, he stays his hand and spares the life of Saul who is plotting to kill him. Saul was anointed as King by God.

> The beloved son of the owner is sent into the vineyard alone and unarmed; the appearance of the Son will shame them . . . How is the phrase "my beloved son" to be understood? In Psalm 2:7 the Lord tell the new enthroned king of Israel, "You are my son, today I have begotten you." (NRSV) See the startling parallel with God, sending his anointed son, not fully armed on a white charger, but on a donkey with a blanket for a saddle and no escort, into Jerusalem, to die on the cross.
>
> The vineyard owner sent his anointed son—not at the head of company of armed men, but as another servant coming to collect the rent. Incredibly, in this parable, as in most of the parables of Jesus, God offers grace and judgment. He did not kill the tenants; he took the vineyard from them and gave it to others.
>
> All through these times the Jewish Leaders were battling to keep their authority. "Israel's high priestly establishment controlled an institution with a set of buildings. They also spoke for the heritage of Israel. In the first century the house of Annas, with his five sons (each of whom became high priests) and Caiaphas (his son-in-law), controlled the high priestly establishment for decades. They were no doubt confident that their administration would continue indefinitely."[3]

But could the people go straight to the LORD in prayer—no; only through the high priest in the holy of holies. This is the great difference. Their authority was with buildings and endless ritual.

Jesus is *our* High Priest—he died for us, he rose again to conquer death for ever. *How great is Easter Sunday! He is risen!* The temple curtain

---

2. Bailey, *Jesus Through Middle Eastern Eyes*, 417.
3. Bailey, *Jesus Through Middle Eastern Eyes*, 421.

is torn away so that, through Jesus, we can approach our God and pray to him personally and intimately.

> *And every priest stands day after day at his service, offering again and again the same sacrifices that can never take away sins. But when Christ had offered for all times a single sacrifice for sins, "he sat down at the right hand of God," and since than has been waiting "until his enemies would be made a footstool for his feet." For by a single offering he has perfected for all times those who are sanctified. And the Holy Spirit also testifies to us, for after saying, "This is the covenant that I will make with them,*
> > *after these days said the Lord:*
> > *I will put my laws in their hearts,*
> > *and will write them on their minds,"*
> *He also adds, "I will remember their sins and lawless deeds no more." Where there is forgiveness of these, there is no longer any offering for sin.* Heb 10:11–18 (NRSV)

Jesus, our Great High Priest, has made the sacrifice for us.

Epistle 48

Many of us remember the great film, *Chariots of Fire*—a film that won four Oscars in 1982, including Best Picture. It is the story of Eric Liddell, a twenty-two-year-old Edinburgh student and already one of the fastest sprinters in the world, who sacrificed his chance to win the 100-meter race at the Paris Olympics of 1924 because the heats were to be run on a Sunday. Eric believed in the sanctity of the Lord's Day. Of course, as is the case of many movies, facts were somewhat distorted to maintain the drama of events, for example, in the case of the handling of his initial stance and in the resultant entry in the 400 meters. Nevertheless, his character stood true; his faith was resolute, and this came through in the movie. Certainly, his success in the 400 meters was portrayed with true drama. When asked about the secret of his 400 meters success, the reply was: "I run the first 200 metres as hard as I can. Then, for the second 200 meters, with God's help, I run harder."[1]

Eric's father, James Liddell, was originally a Scottish draper and, following a call to the ministry and ordination, was sent to China under the umbrella of the London Missionary Society. After a six-year engagement his fiancée, Mary, arrived, and they were married in Shanghai in 1899. Eric, their second son, was born in 1902 in a compound in Siaochang on the Great Plain where peasant farmers continually toiled amongst drought, flooding, locust plagues, and bandits. Of course, it was the time of the Boxer Rebellion! In this far-flung part of the great expanse of China, Eric always saw himself as Chinese—he dressed as a Chinese and learned their language. This was his life until the family returned to Scotland on furlough in 1907. He was told he was going home but home to him was always China!

---

1. Hamilton, *For the Glory*, 121.

So began a life of education, university, and sport. Sport became a solace with the separation from his parents who had returned to their missionary work. He shone at rugby and all classes of athletics. All through these years of study and sport, Eric knew in his heart that he too would eventually return to the country he loved with a plan to follow in his father's footsteps. For this reason, whilst still winning races after the Games and certainly capable of winning again in 1928, he refused to commit himself to another Olympics. Instead, he preached far and wide at a variety of gatherings. They came to hear this wondrous sportsman. "He talked about faith, prayer and the spirit of competitiveness and fairness on the field."[2] He remembered his Olympic success as a glorious week but added, "I am needed in China. And I am going to run a different race there."[3]

Eric returned to a China that was continually changing. The year 1921 saw the newly formed Communist Party of China. Fighting eventuated between Communists and the ancient remnants of war lords. China became ungovernable and, in the civil war that evolved, hate crimes against foreigners again took hold. "Missionaries were wedged between rival armies and rival warlords and also the bedraggled but belligerent assortment of bandits who took advantage of the anarchy."[4] Eric was engaged in teaching at the Anglo-Chinese College and, after his marriage in 1934 to Florence MacKenzie, the daughter of Canadian missionaries, he served in the mission at Sioachang, his birthplace. By the time two daughters were born, Eric was regularly journeying there from Teintsin, which proved safer for his little family.

In 1937 the Japanese began their steady advance from Manchuria originally infiltrating through goods, currency, and schools. By 1941 Eric came to the conclusion that his family should leave China for the safety of Canada. Florence, pregnant with their third daughter, left with the two girls, with Eric planning to follow. But the Japanese did not honor an agreement to allow the missionaries to leave. In early 1943 they were incarcerated with other civilians in a camp called Weihsien. Here Eric, admired for his "unruffled spirit" and "serene temper," was considered a modest man who took part in every duty of the camp. Inmates marveled at his unflagging energy and constant encouragement. His advice was always: "First of all, have a prayer hour. Secondly, keep it." He was rigid

2. Hamilton, *For the Glory*, 123.
3. Hamilton, *For the Glory*, 124.
4. Hamilton, *For the Glory*, 174.

on that point because he believed that "Anyone who, neglecting that fixed hour of prayer, [will] say he can pray at all times [and] will probably end in praying at no time."[5] Amongst other tasks, he had been organizing sport for the young people but locked the sports gear in a cupboard on Sundays. One Sunday youths broke in, took the equipment, and played a game, which resulted in a violent brawl. The next Sunday Eric decided that, in order to have fair and enjoyable sport, he would observe a continental sabbath, and opened the cupboard after midday and umpired the resultant game.

By 1945 Eric was suffering from extreme depression and lethargy. He desperately missed his precious family and began to blame his condition on a lack of faith. He pushed himself to preach and still joined in camp duties. Everybody considered he was suffering from over-work but a stroke signified the presence of a brain tumor. He died early in the year after a second stroke. He prayed faithfully to the end, praying for all—even the Japanese guards.

> Eric Liddell is mostly remembered for his outstanding performance at the Paris Olympics but his most vital life was in China serving his beloved Savior.

---

5. Hamilton, *For the Glory*, 242.

Epistle 49

Over these last months we have often looked at the lives of Christian missionaries and preachers and been inspired by the fact that all were men of prayer. John Calvin, the great Reformist, commented that we can confess to our Father in prayer the sins we would not acknowledge before men and women. Hudson Taylor impressed people deeply with his fervor for prayer. Yet, at one stage, Hudson felt his prayer life was failing. By letting his Savior work in him he was mightily revived with a renewed joy of communing. When John Paton was hiding in a large tree from marauding cannibals of the New Hebrides, he enjoyed the consoling fellowship of his Savior. Charles Spurgeon set aside long periods for prayer but, in the daily round of activities he talked to God incessantly, sending him short "arrow" prayers. Dietrich Bonhoeffer believed that to really reach God in prayer we need to go through Jesus, our Savior. Last week we read of Eric Liddell, faithful in prayer—in days of glory and nights of tribulation—when blessed with a loving family and when bereft with loved ones far away.

Inspired by these people and turning to a biography of David Livingstone it was distressing to discover that he did not seem to be a man of constant prayer. He conducted family prayers each morning after marriage and did much soul-searching over the following years but this appeared to be directed to the supposedly rightful fulfillment of his ambitions. Visiting Westminster Abbey and reading the memorial to this giant of a man it would have been more accurate to have written at the end, [erstwhile] missionary rather than at the beginning. He was a contradictory hero who resolutely explored the continent of Africa and stubbornly made claims that were at variance with others. When he first went to Africa, he understood the native people far more than other missionaries. He argued incessantly with them regarding their methods. Livingstone fought for the abolition of slavery with success but ultimately his life was spent obsessively in exploration, sometimes with family, sometimes with like-minded companions, often impatiently on his own. On marriage he declared: "I have never found two agreeing unless one were a cypher."[1] When he first decided to begin exploring the surrounding regions, he took his wife and children with him. At one stage they had to go without water for five days. "Livingstone, with his unique gift of being humorous after the event, put it, 'the less there was of water, the more thirsty the little rogues became.'"[2] Eventually he sent his family back to Scotland whilst he traveled alone. There his wife Mary, with little support from the Missionary Society and no other income, went from place to place in extreme poverty for four years. Livingstone, for all his great achievements, seems to have a paucity of prayer.

In the Old Testament, through all his fearful inflictions, Job continually prayed. Many times, in these Epistles, we have read the prayers of David in the Psalms. Here we see an intimate relationship of an earthly king with his heavenly king. In the New Testament when Peter attempted to walk on water and fear overcame him, he uttered a panic prayer to Jesus. Nicky Gumbel, in his commentary on this incident in the Gospel of Matthew, endorsed the fact that, like Peter, our panic prayers are always answered—and answered immediately. We can see how vitally important prayer is.

In the Book of Hebrews, as in other books of the New Testament, there is a keen depiction *of* the compassion of Christ. But also here, there is a wonderful compassion *for* Christ—let us feel how incredibly great was his sacrifice!

> *In the days of his flesh, Jesus offered up prayers and supplications, with loud cries and tears, to the one who was able to save him from death, and he was heard because of his reverent submission. Although he was a Son, he learned obedience through what he suffered, and having been made perfect, he became the source of eternal salvation for all who obey him having been designated by God a high priest according to the order of Melchizedek.* Heb 5:7–10 (NRSV)
>
> *Therefore, since we are surrounded by so great a cloud of witnesses, let us also lay aside every weight and the sin that clings so closely, and let us run with perseverance the race that is set before us, looking to Jesus the pioneer and perfecter of our faith, who*

---

1. Deal, *Livingstone*, 61.
2. Deal, *Livingstone*, 99.

> *for the sake of the joy that was set before him endured the cross, disregarding its shame, and has taken his seat at the right hand of the throne of God. Consider him who endured such hostility against himself from sinners so that you may not grow weary or lose heart. In your struggle against sin you have not yet resisted to the point of shedding your blood.* Heb 12:1–4 (NRSV)

Jesus endured physical and psychological suffering for us!

Throughout Hebrews we are encouraged by the heroes and heroines of faith—the examples of Abel, Enoch, and Noah, of Abraham and Moses, Rahab protecting the spies, the Judges, David and Samuel, the Prophets, the unnamed who suffered torture, mocking, flogging, imprisonment, stoning, and more. We are still surrounded by heroes of the faith—men and women of prayer—who put their complete trust in Jesus by heeding his call, following his path, and bearing all in his name. What bliss that through Jesus we can nightly commune with God, our Father, to find comfort, solace, and strength with the promise of joy for each new day.

> *Weeping may linger for the night, but joy comes with the morning.*
> Ps 30:5 (NRSV)

Epistle 50

We have come to a fiftieth epistle over a period of almost twelve months. These days there are probably few people who have written so many letters in such a period. In past times the postman would deliver twice a day during the week and also on Saturday mornings. In this technological age the postman is only calling every second week day! Of course, people receive and send countless emails daily. These could take any form as there are no strict guidelines for address and form. Nor are they called letters, epistles, or missives! They don't need stamps to ensure official delivery nor do they warrant human messengers or professional couriers.

There have been epistles since ancient times. In the Old Testament they took an abbreviated form, being mainly terse messages from one king to another—perhaps requesting a favor of some kind—or orders from a king to his various subordinates. In the New Testament we encounter epistles galore! Paul's letters to his fledging congregations and to his faithful followers comprise his theology of the cross and his instructions on a right relationship to the risen Christ. Sometimes, as in the Letters to the Corinthians, Paul presents a frank discussion on the scandalous conditions in certain local congregations. Then follows the *Letter to the Hebrews*, a literary and theological masterpiece, and the *Letters of Peter, John, James,* and *Jude*. Peter speaks much of suffering; some of the others are presented as types of homilies. Just as with our letters today, all have a specific audience in mind. Our erstwhile letters began with Dear cousin, Dear friend, etc. Greek letters of Apocryphal and New Testament times began with "Greetings" or "Rejoice." Paul's letters open with the terms "Grace" and "Peace" to the recipients.

Unlike our letters in which we identify ourselves at the very end, Paul identifies the sender at the very beginning: "Paul, a servant of Jesus Christ, called to be an apostle, set apart for the gospel of God . . ." Romans 1:1 (NRSV) and then sends his greeting to the recipient: "To all God's beloved in Rome, who are called to be saints: Grace to you and peace from God our Father and the Lord Jesus Christ." Romans 1:7 (NRSV) What a wonderful beginning—"Love and peace to you from . . . praying that this letter finds you well and my message comforts you?" Would not receiving such an introduction impel you to begin to read the rest with a glow of anticipation? Paul follows with thanksgiving to God, for example, in 1 Corinthians 1:4–8 (NRSV)

> *I give thanks to my God always for you because of the grace of God that has been given to you in Christ Jesus, for in every way you have been enriched in him, in speech and knowledge of every kind— just as the testimony of Christ has been strengthened among you—so that you are not lacking in any spiritual gift as you wait for the revealing of our Lord Jesus Christ. He will also strengthen you to the end, so that you may be blameless on the day of our Lord Jesus Christ. God is faithful; by him you are called into the fellowship of his Son, Jesus Christ our Lord.*

How beautifully Paul pens such an amazing personal greeting encompassing a complete theology in a few potent words. A prayer of thanksgiving for the grace of God. "The Corinthians had received a great deal of grace. Their responses to that grace were deeply flawed."[1] We too, like the Corinthians, have received a great deal of grace. How has our response been to the grace of God? But: "Regardless of all the ethical and theological failings that Paul found in the Church in Corinth, he was confident that the Corinthians would stand 'guiltless in the day of our Lord Jesus Christ.' O that the antagonists in church fights in every age might maintain this amazing confidence."[2] God is faithful even if we are not.

> This densely packed introduction and thanksgiving is like a diamond that sheds light in many directions.[3]

"[Paul] was a narrative theologian, writing letters to churches to help them see more clearly how God had written them into the cosmic story of salvation."[4]

The way these Pauline letters were written spurs us to pattern our Christian lives on his example. When we communicate with God our Father—when we pray—we need to begin with thanksgiving for God's

1. Bailey, *Paul Through Mediterranean Eyes*, 61.
2. Bailey, *Paul Through Mediterranean Eyes*, 62.
3. Bailey, *Paul Through Mediterranean Eyes*, 63.
4. Kirk, *Jesus Have I Loved, but Paul?* 27.

grace; we need to remember that we are God's new creation through the sacrifice of his beloved son; we need to bring our needs to him with trust in his faithfulness; we need to come always in the depth of humility; we need to accept his righteousness in all we seek. *We must first seek God before we seek his blessings.* We must plan our prayers not just drift into prayer without any real purpose.

In the *Letter to the Ephesians*, Paul prays for all his readers of yesterday and today:

> *. . . I bow my knees before the Father, from whom every family in heaven and on earth takes its name. I pray that, according to the riches of his glory, he may grant that you may be strengthened in your inner being with power through his Spirit, and that Christ may dwell in your hearts through faith, as you are being rooted and grounded in love. I pray that you may have the power to comprehend, with all the saints, what is the breadth and length and height and depth, and to know the love of Christ that surpasses knowledge, so that you may be filled with all the fullness of God.*
> Eph 3:14–19 (NRSV)

Epistle 51

> *How long, O LORD!*
> *Will you forget me forever?*
> *How long will you hide your face from me?*
> Ps 13:1 (NRSV)

A distressed cry to our LORD God but he appears to have turned away! A feeling of divine abandonment!

Have you read and followed the story of Joseph and his brothers in the Old Testament? Joseph, the much-loved son of Jacob, was a tittle-tattler and bragged about the dreams he had; dreams that depicted his brothers bowing down before him. His brothers, having him out in distant fields, see the opportunity to be rid of him—firstly contemplating killing him, but then selling him to a passing caravan of Ishmaelite traders. Joseph, languishing in fear at the bottom of a deep pit of darkness—a cold and dank abyss—must have felt far from the protection of his God.

He was taken down to Egypt.

But: "The LORD was with Joseph" Genesis 39:2 (NRSV) He had not abandoned him. Joseph was purchased by Potiphar, an officer of Pharaoh, and he fared well serving in his household, until his master's wife accused him of molesting her and he was thrown into prison.

> *But the LORD was with Joseph and showed him steadfast love; he gave him favor in the sight of the chief jailer.* Gen 39:21 (NRSV)

Under God's love and protection Joseph, in following years, was released from jail when he successfully interpreted Pharaoh's dreams—or should we say his nightmares. Then Joseph was appointed, by Pharaoh, as his authority over the land of Egypt. When famine was experienced throughout all the lands, Jacob sent his sons to Egypt to buy grain. But

Benjamin, his youngest, he kept with him. When they came before him Joseph recognized his brothers and dealt harshly with them. They did not know him—he turned aside and wept. He took Simeon, bound him and incarcerated him. He then sent his other brothers back to Jacob telling them he would release Simeon if they returned with Benjamin. Now Jacob is distressed and desolate. He has lost the first son of his beloved Rachel; now he might lose the second son. Nevertheless, he says:

> *If it must be so, then do this: take some of the choice fruits of the land in your bags, and carry down as a present to the man . . . Take your brother also, and be on your way again to the man; may God Almighty grant you mercy before the man, so that he may send back your other brother and Benjamin. As for me, if I am bereaved of my children, I am bereaved.* Gen 43: 11a, 13–14 (NRSV)

Is the LORD God hiding his face from him?

The word "face" is often used in the Bible—"the face of the deep" and "the face of the waters." Genesis 1:2 (NRSV); "the face of the ground" Genesis 2:6 (NRSV); "the face of the sky" Matthew 16:3b (KJV) With the present-day emphasis on "body language" we can agree that the face is the part of the body through which a person's attitudes are best expressed. Often, we have to be careful to keep a "poker" face, which in itself expresses certain feelings! To avert or hide the face indicates displeasure or disappointment: "So I hid my face from them and gave them into the hands of my adversaries." Ezekiel 39:23 (NRSV) To set the face against one is to express hostility: "For I have set my face against this city for evil and not for good, says the LORD, it shall be given into the hands of the king of Babylon and he shall burn it with fire." Jeremiah 21:10 (NRSV) Yet, an illustration of determination: "When the days drew near for him to be taken up, [Jesus] set his face to go to Jerusalem." Luke 9:51 (NRSV)

Then, elsewhere, we find a wonderful indication of loving acceptance:

> *The LORD bless you and keep you;*
> *the LORD make his face to shine upon you, and be gracious to you;*
> *the LORD lift up his countenance upon you, and give you peace.*
> Num 6:24–26 (NRSV)

Most importantly, since a person's face reflects personality and character, face can be indicative of presence. Read "presence" for "face":

> *Hear O LORD, when I cry aloud, be gracious to me and answer me! "Come," my heart says, "seek his face!" Your face, LORD, do I seek. Do not hide your face from me.* Ps 27:7–9 (NRSV)

In Old Testament times to see the King's face was an expression denoting access to the King—now an entry into the palace of the King of Glory but only an entry through the sacrifice of his beloved son, Jesus.

> *And even if our gospel is veiled, it is veiled to those who are perishing. In their case the god of this world has blinded the minds of the unbelievers, to keep them from seeing the light of the gospel of the glory of Christ, who is the image of God. For we do not proclaim ourselves, we proclaim Jesus Christ as Lord and ourselves as slaves for Jesus' sake. For it is the God who said, "Let light shine out of darkness" who has shone in our hearts to give the light of the knowledge of the glory of God in the face of Jesus Christ.* 2 Cor 4:3–6 (NRSV)

Eventually Joseph revealed to his brothers who he was. They returned to their father Jacob and told him: "Joseph is still alive! He is even ruler over the land of Egypt. He was stunned; he could not believe them." Genesis 45:26 (NRSV) When Jacob was reunited with Joseph he said "I can die now, having seen for myself that you are still alive." Genesis 46:30 (NRSV)

Could not Jacob, no longer bereft, now turn to the end of Psalm 13:

> *I will sing to the LORD,*
> *because he has dealt bountifully with me.* Ps 13:6 (NRSV)

We also can sing to the Lord God in abundant gratitude.
At the end of our pilgrimage, we shall see God's face in the heavenly city—he does not abandon his faithful servants.

Epistle 52

One of the activities that many may have missed during COVID restrictions is dining on beautiful food at a fine restaurant. It often seems to be like a scrumptious banquet in comparison with some of the day-to-day cooking at our homes. Banquets are a feature in biblical times in both the Testaments. In Amos 6:4–5 the guests "lie in on beds inlaid with ivory, and lounge on their couches, and dine on choice lambs and fattened calves . . . drink wine by the bowlful and use the finest lotions." (NIV) Banquets were held on various occasions—the arrival of a stranger, for example. When the three men appeared before Abraham:

> *Abraham hurried into the tent to Sarah. "Quick," he said, "get three seahs of the finest flour and knead it and bake some bread." Then he ran to the herd and selected a choice, tender calf and gave it to the servant, who hurried to prepare it. He then brought some curds and milk and the calf that had been prepared, and set these before them.* Gen 18:6–8 (NIV)

At other times banquets were customary—when a child was weaned; after the sheep-shearing; at the grape harvest; after the completion of a public building; when a treaty was ratified; at a wedding. Jesus himself was feasting at the wedding in Cana when the wine ran out and, at the bidding of his mother Mary, he turned water into wine. John 2:1–11

It would not be a complete surprise to learn that King Henry VIII was a great instigator of gargantuan banquets. "Between five hundred and a thousand people ate from King Henry's bounty every day; on special occasions the number could rise to fifteen hundred."[1] Henry's much extended family, his favorites, Court officials, visiting nobles and their retinues, household servants, outdoor staff, even vagabonds found their way to the feast. "Grooms armed with whips and bells patrolled the dining

---

1. Erickson, *Great Harry*, 97.

hall in an effort 'to fear them away withal' but there were too many."[2] "In one day of feasting his courtiers consumed eleven entire carcasses of beef, six sheep, seventeen hogs and pigs, forty-five dozen chickens, fifteen swans, six cranes, thirty-two dozen pigeons and fifty-four dozen larks, nearly six dozen geese and four peacocks. Three thousand pears and thirteen hundred apples went to flavor the meat and fowl, while the bakers provided three thousand loaves of bread and the buttery nearly four hundred dishes of butter."[3] This, of course, was all supplemented in the cooking with garlic, ginger, salt, cinnamon, many exotic sauces, and much offal. There were often minnows, porpoises, and dolphins. These banquets had no other purpose than to indulge in greed and gluttony.

The greatest of all banquets is the Messianic Banquet!

> *On this mountain the LORD Almighty will prepare a feast of rich food for all peoples, a banquet of aged wine—the best of meats and the finest of wines. On this mountain he will destroy the shroud that enfolds all peoples, the shroud that covers all nations; he will swallow up death forever. The sovereign LORD will wipe away the tears from all faces; he will remove his people's disgrace from all the earth. The LORD has spoken. In that day they will say, "Surely this is our God; we trusted in him, and he saved us. This is the LORD, we trusted in him; let us rejoice and be glad in his salvation."* Isa 25:6–9 (NIV)

This banquet has desideratum.

Jesus has much to say on this banquet. In a parable in Luke 14:16–24 he emphasizes who will be the guests at this great feast—it will be those whose wait has been rewarded and they are glad and rejoicing in his salvation:

> *A certain man was preparing a great banquet and invited many guests. At the time of the banquet he sent his servant to tell those who had been invited, 'Come, for everything is now ready.' The slave was bombarded with excuses: 'I have just bought a field, and I must go and see it . . . I have just bought five yoke of oxen, and I'm on my way to try them out . . . I just got married so I cannot come.'* (NIV)

Even the wording of their excuses is offensive and unacceptable—perhaps padding it out and including an apology might be slightly more

---

2. Erickson, *Great Harry*, 97.
3. Erickson, *Great Harry*, 106.

acceptable. What does the man do? He instructs his servant to go out further afield and gather all the "outcasts of Israel"—not once but also a second time!

The people who do come are not the pious leaders of the Jews but, as Isaiah predicted, the people of other nations—the Gentiles—as well as the believing Jews. The invitation is limitless. "Those who hear the good news must accept and the enter the banquet hall or reject and stand aloof."[4]

This banquet is an inauguration:

> The Eucharist can be understood as a foreshadowing of the great banquet. At communion, believers are invited, in the present, to participate in the messianic banquet of the end time. We remember the past, celebrate in the present and look forward to the marriage supper of the Lamb. The parable assures the faithful that they already have a place at that banquet.[5]

---

4. Bailey, *Jesus Through Middle Eastern Eyes*, 220.
5. Bailey, *Jesus Through Middle Eastern Eyes*, 219.

Epistle 53

The readers of today are often engrossed in the latest mystery stories! In the past children were introduced to this genre quite early in some of the books of Enid Blyton—*The Mystery of the Burnt Cottage, The Mystery of the Secret Room, The Mystery of the Disappearing Cat.* Then, moving into the young adult years, the books of Agatha Christie—*The Mystery of the Blue Train, The Mysterious Affair at Styles, The Seven Dials Mystery.* Additionally, *The Great Mystery Collection* can be purchased: this contains the macabre writings of Edgar Allan Poe, and the Sherlock Holmes detective stories of Arthur Conan Doyle, plus the mystery of *Crime and Punishment* by Fyodor Dostoevsky, amongst others.

The word "mystery" seems to have had its earliest known appearance as a Greek religious term meaning "to close the eyes." It did not always have a religious connotation in the Old Testament although the Wisdom Literature used it in connection with the sin of divulging secrets. In pagan society it came to be understood as a secret of any type. However, in the New Testament, "mystery" did come to be used exclusively as a religious term. It often referred to as a divine plan that was to be revealed to a select few and perhaps only at some future time. The parables, for example, were spoken to the crowds of people following Jesus, and then afterwards, explained in more detail to the disciples. Often the word "mystery" is equated with the word "gospel"—a divine secret that would become an open secret through Christ.

> *When he was alone, the Twelve and the others around him asked him about parables. He told them, "The secret of the kingdom of God has been given to you. But to those on the outside everything is said in parables so that, they may be ever seeing but never perceiving, and ever hearing but never understanding; otherwise they might turn and be forgiven!"* Mark 4:10–12 (NIV)

Importantly, Jesus, in v 13–20, relates the Parable of the Sower, which clarifies his reasoning.

Jesus the Christ, in his ministry and teaching, reveals the Kingdom of God.

Paul, in his letters, recognizes that there is a divine missionary plan that is slowly being revealed to us. Read his doxology in Romans:

> *Now to him who is able to establish you in accordance with my gospel, the message I proclaim about Jesus Christ, in keeping with the revelation of the mystery hidden for long ages past, but now revealed and made known through the prophetic writings by the command of the eternal God, so that all the Gentiles might come to the obedience that comes from faith—to the only wise God be glory forever through Jesus Christ! Amen.* Rom 16:25–27 (NIV)

Also:

> *We do, however, speak a message of wisdom among the mature, but not the wisdom of this age or of the rulers of this age, who are coming to nothing. No, we declare God's wisdom, a mystery that has been hidden and that God destined for our glory before time began. None of the rulers of this age understood it, for if they had, they would not have crucified the Lord of glory. However, as it is written: "What no eye has seen, what no ear has heard, and what no human mind has conceived—the things God has prepared for those who love him—these are the things God has revealed to us by his Spirit."* 1 Cor 2:6–10 (NIV)

We are like the seed thrown on the good soil in Mark 4:20 "Others, like seed sown on good soil, hear the word, accept it, and produce a crop . . ." (NIV) Nevertheless, we will not understand these mysteries unless we have love, and search for understanding through the Spirit.

There are specific mysteries when we see that, we the Gentiles, are included in God's eternal promises and when, in Ephesians, we read of God's great plan to unite the universe—all things in him in Heaven and on earth. Then, when we exegete passages in the New Testament we can uncover its hidden meaning; we can reveal to our hearts its hidden mystery. Of course, we have in the Bible one book full of mystery! These mysteries stretch our minds to visualize an incredible heavenly aura of words and pictures. The Revelation to John reveals the end times—the heavenly worship, the scroll and the Lamb, the seven seals, the seven trumpets, the two witnesses, the woman and the dragon, Michael and his angels fighting the dragon, the bowls of God's wrath, the great whore, the fall of Babylon, the rider on the white horse, the beast and his armies defeated, and, the final defeat of Satan when he is cast into the lake of fire and sulfur. But there is final rejoicing—a New Heaven and a New Earth. Then one of the seven angels:

> *carried me away in the Spirit to a mountain great and high, and showed me the Holy City, Jerusalem, coming down out of heaven from God. It shone with the glory of God, and its brilliance was like that of a very precious jewel, like a jasper, clear as crystal.* Rev 21:10–11 (NIV)

A book of great mysteries but mysteries revealed and explained. Yet we must be vigilant yet.

> *Do not seal up the words of prophecy of this scroll, because the time is near. Let the one who does wrong continue to do wrong; let the vile person continue to be vile; let the one who does right continue to do right; and let the holy person continue to be holy.* Rev 22:10–11 (NIV)

There are mysteries still—the doctrine of the Trinity; the incredibility of the incarnation; the startling biblical promises; the wonder of the sacraments; the enigma of some of the liturgy; the puzzlement of some of the words we try to honor. "That is why a man leaves his father and his mother and is united to his wife, and they become one flesh." Genesis 2:24 (NIV) How strange and mystical this is in reality. But it occurs in a truly faithful marriage with years of growing love and commitment. Do not dismiss mystery for it is wondrous. All the teaching we receive can never take away its value. Only the Spirit can help us accept what we cannot understand. Cromwell once said: "Presbyterians who, with their rigid practices and methods 'laboured to hedge in the wind and bind up the sweet influence of the Spirit.'"[1]

---

1. Fraser, *Cromwell*, xxix.

Epistle 54

The world in which we live is daily dominated by political correctness. When this movement first began it was, in some ways, quite sensible because it made us think of ways we may have been offending people by thoughtless words and expressions. However, like any attempt to change society, political correctness has grown to an absurd degree. With the parallel growth of secularism and materialism, Christianity has become the victim. We must not insult people who hold any other religious beliefs yet we must not object when bookshops and stationery shops stock Christmas cards that make mocking jokes about Jesus! Every opportunity to tone down any pride in our faith is taken. A very recent example was taken at the funeral of Prince Philip, Duke of Edinburgh.

The Funeral Service was planned by Philip himself. The two readings were from Ecclesiasticus and the Gospel of John. Ecclesiasticus is one of the books of the Apocrypha, the intertestamental books between the Old and the New Testament. Although these books are not included in the canon, they are worthy of consultation, especially if only to follow the history of the Jewish people in those years of waiting for the promised Messiah, for example, 1 and 2 Maccabees. Ecclesiasticus is often entitled Book of Sirach, probably to eliminate confusion with the Ecclesiastes of the Old Testament. It is ascribed to Jesus (Hebrew Joshua; Aramaic Jeshua) the son of Sirach, who appears to have taught in Jerusalem during the first quarter of the second century BC. It is a most comprehensive work of Jewish Wisdom Literature, the objective of which can be compared to Proverbs of the Old Testament. The work has always been highly regarded in both Jewish and Christian circles.

> *Look at the rainbow, and praise him who made it;*
> > *it is exceedingly beautiful in its brightness.*
> *It encircles the sky with it glorious arc; the hands of the Most High have stretched it out.*
> *By his command he sends the driving snow and spreads the lightnings of his judgement.*
> *Therefore the storehouses are opened, and the clouds fly out like birds.*
> *In his majesty he gives the clouds their strength, and the hailstones are broken in pieces.*
> *The voice of his thunder rebukes the earth; when he appears, the mountains shake.*
> *At his will the south wind blows; so do the storm from the north and the whirlwind.*
> *He scatters the snow like birds flying down, and its descent is like locusts alighting.*
> *The eye is dazzled by the beauty of its whiteness, and the mind is amazed as it falls.*
> *He pours the frost over the earth like salt, and icicles form like pointed thorns.*
> *The cold north wind blows, and ice freezes on the water,*
> *it settles on every pool of water, and the water puts it on like a breastplate.*
> *He consumes the mountains and burns up the wilderness,*
> > *and withers the tender grass like fire,*
> *A mist quickly heals all things; the falling dew gives refreshment from the heat.*
> *By his plan he stilled the deep and planted islands in it.*
> *Those who sail the sea tell of its dangers, and we marvel at what we hear.*
> *In it are strange and marvelous creatures, all kind of living things, and huge sea monsters.*
> *Because of him each of his messengers succeeds,*
> > *and by his word all things hold together.* Sir 43:11–26 (NRSV)

We can easily see that this is not canonical but there are many parallels we can recognize from the Old Testament. In its way, this reading echoes the visions we see in Genesis and the creation story; and, in Psalms 29, 65, and 104. Psalm 104 was also included in the Funeral Service. The music of this Psalm had been composed and the words adapted in honor of Prince Philip, on the occasion of his seventy-fifth birthday, in recognition of his service at sea. He wished it to be sung again at his Funeral. It is

EPISTLE 54

a much deeper and more comprehensive praise of God the Creator than our reading from Ecclesiasticus yet similar in content.

> *How many are your works, LORD!*
> *In wisdom you made them all; the earth is full of your creatures.*
> *There is the sea, vast and spacious,*
> *teeming with creatures beyond number—living things both large and small.*
> *There the ships go to and fro,*
> *and Leviathan, which you formed to frolic there.* Ps 104:24-26 (NIV)

The gospel reading at the Service was as follows:

> *"Lord," Martha said to Jesus, "if you had been here, my brother would not have died. And even now I know that whatever you ask from God, God will give you[.]" Jesus said to her, "Your brother will rise again." Martha said to him, "I know that he will rise again in the resurrection at the last day." Jesus said to her, "I am the resurrection and the life; he who believes in me, though he die, yet shall he live, and whoever lives and believes in me shall never die. Do you believe this?" She said to him, "Yes Lord; I believe you are the Christ, the Son of God, he who is coming into the world."* John 11:21-27 (NIV)

Thus, we see the belief of Prince Philip—firstly that God is the great Creator and that he rules over all: "each of his messengers succeeds and by his Word all things hold together" and—secondly, that Jesus was the resurrection and the life. By believing in him he will never die. This was Philip's theology—a Creator and all-powerful God who sent his Son to die in his place and thus give him everlasting life.

> But according to the political correctness of the British commentator it was Nature, not God, who was the creator and the readings therefore reflected Philip's interest in the environment and his overall philosophy!

Epistle 55

Autumn is a wonderful season—we have sometimes grown weary with heavy and humid days when suddenly the cooling breeze of autumn is felt and the trees blaze with beautiful russet browns, golden hues, and crimson intensity. How beautiful are trees! Even the trees that autumn does not touch all come in a vast display of differing greens. Trees produce fruit; they give shade; they provide shelter. Trees are mentioned in the Bible more than any living thing other than God and people, and are used in a great variety of symbolic meaning—fertile trees, trees that prosper, trees that die, trees that are forbidden, and, mighty trees that the LORD God destroys as in Ezekiel 31.

We read about the Garden of Eden: "The LORD God made all kinds of trees grow out of the ground—trees that were pleasing to the eye and good for food. In the middle of the garden were the tree of life and the tree of the knowledge of good and evil." He said to Adam and Eve: "You are free to eat from any tree in the garden; but you must not eat from the tree of the knowledge of good and evil, for when you eat from it you will certainly die." Genesis 2: 9,16b–17 (NIV) But did the first man and woman take heed of God's warning? Nevertheless, trees continued to be included in the model of the new garden; the promised garden. Ezekiel was brought to the entrance of the temple; ". . . and I saw water coming out from under the threshold of the temple," it flowed as a river towards the sea: "Fruit trees of all kinds will grow on both banks of the river. Their leaves will not wither, nor will their fruit fail. Every month they will bear fruit, because the water from the sanctuary flows to them. Their fruit will serve for food and their leaves for healing." Ezekiel 47:1,12 (NIV)

Lastly, we will see the Tree of Life in Paradise:

> *Then the angel showed me the river of the water of life, as clear as crystal, flowing from the throne of God and of the Lamb down the middle of the great street of the city. On each side of the river stood*

> *the tree of life bearing twelve crops of fruit, yielding its fruit each month; and the leaves of the tree are for the healing of the nations.*
> Rev 22:1–2 (NIV)

How often do we read or sing of the nations, beating their swords into plowshares; and their spears into pruning hooks, "Nation will not take up sword against nation, nor will they train for war anymore." Isaiah 2:4b (NIV) But, what do the warriors do then? "Everyone will sit under their own vine and under their own fig tree, and no one will make them afraid, for the LORD Almighty has spoken. All the nations may walk in the name of their gods, but we will walk in the name of the LORD our God for ever and ever." Micah 4:4–5 (NIV) . . . a tree of peace and rest. When Elijah was fleeing in fear from Jezebel, he ran for his life, leaving his servant behind.

> *He, himself went a day's journey into the wilderness. He came to a broom bush, sat down under it and prayed that he might die. "I have had enough, LORD," he said. "Take my life; I am no better than my ancestors." Then he lay down under the bush and fell asleep. All at once an angel touched him and said, "Get up and eat." He looked around, and there by his head was some bread baked over hot coals, and a jar of water. He ate and drank and then lay down again. The angel of the LORD came back a second time and touched him and said, "Get up and eat, for the journey is too much for you." So he got up and ate and drank. Strengthened by that food, he traveled forty days and forty nights until he reached Horeb, the mountain of God. There he went into a cave and spent the night.* 1 Kgs 19:4–9a (NIV)

A single spindly broom tree provided respite at his lowest point!

Palm trees are prevalent in bible lands. "Now, Deborah, a prophet, the wife of Lappidoth, was leading Israel at that time. She held court under the Palm of Deborah between Ramah and Bethel, in the hill country of Ephraim, and the Israelites came up to her to have their disputes decided." Judges 4:4–5 (NIV)

How significant that Our Righteous Judge was welcomed into Jerusalem with the branches of palm trees held by a crowd singing loud Hosannas! Following this triumph, he was betrayed and crucified on a tree, the depth of degradation:

> *If someone guilty of a capital offense is put to death and their body is exposed on a pole, you must not leave the body hanging on the*

> *pole overnight. Be sure to bury it the same day, because anyone who is hung on a pole is under God's curse.* Deut 21:22–23 (NIV)

Truly Jesus was under a curse—the curse of our sins. Have you noticed that we are often likened to trees: One who delights in the law of the LORD and meditates on it day and night:

> *. . . is like a tree planted by streams of water, which yields its fruit in season, and whose leaf does not wither—whatever they do prospers.* Ps 1:3 (NIV)

and,

> *Blessed is the one who trusts in the LORD, whose confidence is in him. They will be like a tree planted by water, that sends out its roots by the stream. It does not fear when heat comes; its leaves are always green. It has no worries in a year of drought and never fails to bear fruit.* Jer 17:7–8 (NIV)

Tongues receive a mention!

> *The soothing tongue is a tree of life.* Prov 15:4 (NIV)

Remember—in today's world—these words of Jesus:

> *Watch out for false prophets. They come to you in sheep's clothing, but inwardly they are ferocious wolves. By their fruit you will recognize them. Do people pick grapes from thornbushes, or figs from thistles? Like-wise every good tree bears good fruit, but a bad tree bears bad fruit. A good tree cannot bear bad fruit, and a bad tree cannot bear food fruit. Every tree that does not bear good fruit is cut down and thrown into the fire. Thus, by their fruit you will recognize them.* Matt 7:15–20 (NIV)

Epistle 56

In Psalm 97 we read these opening verses:

> *The LORD reigns, let the earth be glad;*
> *Let the distant shores rejoice!*
> *Clouds and thick darkness surround him;*
> *righteousness and justice are the foundation of his throne.* 1–2
> (NIV)

Maybe we cannot see him clearly because clouds and thick darkness are all around him? There is an old hymn which begins:

> Thou hidden Love of God, whose height,
> Whose depth unfathomed, no man knows. . .[1]

We cannot see through the clouds and thick darkness; we cannot climb the great heights; we cannot swim to the deepest depths to find him. But we have God's Word, which we can read and meditate upon. Surely we can find our God. But so many people look at the teachings of Jesus, for example, and find them ethical, admirable, and comforting but do they experience the deep meaning of what Jesus is saying? Knowing and understanding the message is only the beginning. Do we deeply comprehend in our hearts and souls all that is being presented to us? Do we really feel that we have an intimate relationship with Jesus rather than just a companionship of a casual and useful friend? What about the miracles—are they are a step too far for us to take on board? Even Jews and Islam acknowledge that Jesus existed on earth—a good man—perhaps the last of the great prophets!

The affirmations of Oswald Chambers, a great biblical preacher and writer who died in 1917, still have significance for Christians today:

---

1. Church of Scotland. *Church Hymnary*, 459.

> If we have never had the experience of taking our commonplace religious shoes off our commonplace religious feet, and getting rid of all the undue familiarity with which we approach God, it is questionable whether we have ever stood in his presence. The people who are flippant and familiar are those who have never yet been introduced to Jesus Christ. After the amazing delight and liberty of realising what Jesus Christ does, comes the impenetrable darkness of realizing Who He is.[2]

Yes, the words of Jesus are on the pages we read but do we "plumb the depths" of them?

> *For the word of God is alive and active. Sharper than any double-edged sword, it penetrates even to dividing soul and spirit, joints and marrow; it judges the thoughts and attitudes of the heart. Nothing in all creation is hidden from God's sight. Everything is uncovered and laid bare before the eyes of him to whom we must give account.* Heb 4:12–13 (NIV)

Do we know ourselves? Sometimes we come to realize that we do not know ourselves very deeply. The disciple Peter thought he knew himself. He declared that he would lay his life down for his Lord yet he denied him three times when he was tested. Nonetheless, later, Peter did find the courage to follow Jesus with constant strength and unfailing commitment. How and when did this momentous change come about? When Jesus ascended to heaven, he did not leave Peter and his disciples bereft—he sent his Holy Spirit to them.

> *When the day of Pentecost came, they were all together in one place. Suddenly a sound like the blowing of a violent wind came from heaven and filled the whole house where they were sitting. They saw what seemed to be tongues of fire that separated and came to rest on each of them. All of them were filled with the Holy Spirit and began to speak in other tongues as the Spirit enabled them.* Acts 2:1–4 (NIV)

This is the answer for us! We must open ourselves to the Holy Spirit. We must wait on our God in prayer saying: "Come, Holy Spirit, Come!" The words spoken to us by Jesus must come alive in the Spirit so that we *can* plumb the depths and be filled with passion and understanding. We find in the Bible, especially in the Old Testament, so many words of "clouds and darkness"—Jesus respeaks these words in the New Testament

---

2. Chambers, *My Utmost for His Highest*, 3.

and they become spirit and life; clarity and joy. Our friendship with Jesus is not a casual one; it needs to be the most intimate relationship we can ever have.

> *You study the Scriptures diligently because you think that in them you have eternal life. These are the very Scriptures that testify about me, yet you refuse to come to me to have life.* John 5:39–40 (NIV)

and,

> *From this time many of his disciples turned back and no longer followed him. "You do not want to leave too, do you?" Jesus asked the Twelve. Simon Peter answered him, "Lord, to whom shall we go? You have the words of eternal life. We have come to believe and to know that you are the Holy One of God."* John 6:66–68 (NIV)

Resolutely, Paul prays for us:

> *I pray that out of his glorious riches he may strengthen you with power through his Spirit in your inner being, so that Christ may dwell in your hearts through faith. And I pray that you, being rooted and established in love, may have power, together with all the Lord's holy people, to grasp how wide and long and high and deep is the love of Christ and to know this love that surpasses knowledge— that you may be filled to the measure of all the fullness of God.* Eph 3:16–19 (NIV)

Epistle 57

A common misconception today is that the God of the Old Testament is a God of anger and the God of the New Testament is a God of love; the Old Testament identifies with war while the New Testament identifies with pacificism. An in-depth study and deep reflection on God's Word beginning with *Genesis* and ending with *The Revelation to John*, reveals the complete saga of God and Man. The New Testament could not exist in any sort of intelligent form without the Old Testament as its foundation. It is the same God throughout and he is unchangeable. In fact, a study of the Old Testament divulges a God who loves his people so much that he never deserts them. No matter that his chosen people turn away from him on many occasions; refuse to keep his commandments; build idols to other gods; intermarry with people from alien races; plead for an earthly king like other nations; commit sexual immorality; erect towers in an attempt to outshine him—God was always there chastising them, yes, but also loving and guiding them. He raised up leaders and prophets who battled to keep the people in God's holy ways. Yes, God's wrath is often obvious in the Old Testament but "Yahweh's wrath is only the expression of a deep and holy love which ardently seeks to correct, discipline, and ultimately make possible a new relationship."[1] Psalm 23 cautions that the rod of discipline and the staff of comfort are always there together, leading God's people through the valley of darkness and protecting them from evil. This then is the message of the God of the Old Testament—the LORD who was always there for an errant people, the God of a covenant of faithfulness.

The love of God manifests itself most strongly in Israel's history.

In the Old Testament the chosen people of Israel constantly prayed to Yahweh.

---

1. Buttrick. *The Interpreter's Dictionary of the Bible. Volume 2, D–J*, 426.

The Psalms, for example, are full of praise for the LORD as well as cries for help from the LORD. It is in the Psalms that prayer reaches the utmost heights. There is great joy in many of them and yet distress and anguish in others. Through them we can detect a developing personal relationship with the LORD God. Yet when we move into the Book of Job, we find this man of prayer is pleading for an intermediary. In the New Testament the new people of God, the followers of the Son of God, now have a mediator. No longer does sin prevent them, or us, from approaching the throne of God the Father—the God of love yet still the God who judges. Jesus, the mediator, prays constantly to his Father and teaches his disciples, and us, how to pray with the Lord's Prayer as our guide.

When we turn to the *Letters of Paul*, we see the Christian prayer in all its fullness. Almost every letter begins and ends with grace: "To the church of the Thessalonians in God the Father and the Lord Jesus Christ: Grace and peace to you." 1:1 (NIV) and "The grace of our Lord Jesus Christ be with you." 5:28 (NIV) He includes assurances of constant prayer on behalf of his readers! It is evident that Paul is convinced of the faithfulness of God and of Christ. "May the God who gives endurance and encouragement give you the same attitude of mind toward each other that Jesus Christ had, so that with one mind and one voice you may glorify the God and Father of our Lord Jesus Christ." Romans 15:5–6 (NIV) Endlessly Paul prays for the early Christians and these prayers apply directly to us today.

> *And this is my prayer, that your love may abound more and more in knowledge and depth of insight, so that you may be able to discern what is best and may be pure and blameless for the day of Christ, filled with the fruit of righteousness that comes through Jesus Christ—to the glory and praise of God.* Phil 1:9–11 (NIV)

To the God of all comfort, we pray:

> *Praise be to the God and Father of our Lord Jesus Christ, the Father of compassion and the God of all comfort, who comforts us in all our troubles so that we can comfort those in any trouble with the comfort we ourselves receive from God.* 2 Cor 1:3–4 (NIV)

To the God of hope, we pray for joy and peace:

> *May the God of hope fill you with all joy and peace as you trust in him, so that you may overflow with hope by the power of the Holy Spirit.* Rom 15:13 (NIV)

Notice that in each of these prayers of Paul he prays for a specific need for us which, when it comes, produces results in us—our desire to praise and glorify our God; a harvest of righteousness; the ability to bring consolation to others; and, an overflow of the power of the Holy Spirit.

The writer of the *Letter to the Hebrews* emphasizes that faith is essential. To draw near to God, we must believe: "And without faith it is impossible to please God, because anyone who comes to him must believe that he exists, and that he rewards those who earnestly seek him." Heb 11:6 (NIV) This appears to be a fact that we take for granted but perhaps it is something we really need to address. How strong is our faith; how grounded is our belief?

> *Everyone who believes that Jesus is the Christ is born of God, and everyone who loves the father loves his child as well. This is how we know that we love the children of God: by loving God and carrying out his commands. In fact, this is love for God: to keep his commands. And his commands are not burdensome, for everyone born of God overcomes the world. This is the victory that has overcome the world, even our faith. Who is it that overcomes the world? Only the one who believes that Jesus is the Son of God.* 1 John 5:1–5 (NIV)

We can conquer the world!

Epistle 58

How would you describe the Bible? Wikipedia describes the Bible as a collection of religious texts, writings, or scriptures sacred to Jews, Samaritans, Christians, Muslims, and others. We could state it is the story of God's special people—the Israelites descended from Adam and Eve recorded in the Old Testament; and, the birth of Christianity with the establishment of God's new Elect in the New Testament. Then, we could say that it is the story of God's creation of the world; or, the story of God's creation of humankind. But the Bible is more than a collection of writings or a historical story from the Middle East. It is the narrative of the Creator God and his created beings. It tells us the great love God has for his people even when, time and time again, they turn away from his law and his authority. Through the Bible God speaks to the people—and the people speak to God. They commune with prayer.

Still, there are many people today who see the Bible more as a historical saga involving people of thousands of years ago. They would be quick to deny that it has any great relevance to the men and women of the twenty-first century. In fact, the interest in history has been devalued in recent years, specifically in the education system. Stephen Hawking, our famous atheist of recent times, commented that we spend a great deal of time studying history, which he thinks is mostly the history of stupidity. He leaves God out of the equation. The historical saga of the Bible is the history of God and his people—God's everlasting love and his saving grace. It is not just a story for the people who lived in those times but for all people who live in God's world today.

It is written for us.

When God made his covenant with Noah, promising never again to send a flood to destroy the earth, he said: "This is the sign of the covenant that I am making between me and you and every living creature with you, a covenant for all generations to come." Genesis 9:12 (NIV) That sign was the bow he placed in the clouds above; it is the rainbow that we of the future generations can see as a reminder of his promise. In the Book of Deuteronomy, Moses says: "Know therefore that the LORD your God is God; he is the faithful God, keeping his covenant of love to a thousand generations of those who love him and keep his commandments." 7:9 (NIV) and, later, when Moses addressed all Israel in the wilderness, he said:

> *All of you are standing today in the presence of the LORD your God—your leaders and chief men, your elders and officials, and all the other men of Israel, together with your children and your wives, and the foreigners living in your camps who chop your wood and carry your water. You are standing here in order to enter into a covenant with the LORD your God, a covenant the LORD is making with you this day and sealing with an oath, to confirm you this day as his people, that he may be your God as he promised you and as he swore to your fathers, Abraham, Isaac and Jacob. I am making this covenant, with its oath, not only with you who are standing here with us today in the presence of the LORD our God but also with those who are not here today.* Deut 29:10–15 (NIV)

(Remember we have stirred our hearts with this statement in a previous epistle.)

In the famous Davidic Psalm containing a plea for deliverance from suffering and hostility we recognize the opening words as those that Jesus spoke as he was abandoned on the cross: "My God, my God, why have you forsaken me?" Psalm 22:1 (NIV) The closing lines of the Psalm speak about us: "Posterity will serve him; future generations will be told about the Lord. They will proclaim his righteousness, declaring to a people yet unborn: he has done it!" Psalm 22:30 (NIV)

Chapter 17 of the Gospel of John is often referred to as the "High Priestly Prayer of Jesus." In it he prays that all believers may be perfected so as to see Jesus—that is, all believers—believers in the New Testament times and believers today! After praying for his disciples, Jesus continues by praying for all believers:

> *My prayer is not for them alone. I pray also for those who will believe in me through their message, that all of them may be one, Father, just as you are in me and I am in you. May they also be in us so that the world may believe that you have sent me. I have given them the glory that you gave me, that they may be as one*

as we are one—I in them and you in me—so that they may be brought to complete unity. Then the world will know that you sent me and have loved them even as you have loved me. Father, I want those you have given me to be with me where I am, and to see my glory, the glory you have given me because you loved me before the creation of the world. John 17:20–24 (NIV)

And through the words of the disciples, we today become believers: "See what great love the Father has lavished on us, that we should be called children of God! And that is what we are!" 1 John 3:1a (NIV)

By reading the Word and praying, we will come to the Father and the Son through the Spirit: "Jesus replied, 'Anyone who loves me will obey my teaching. My Father will love them, and we will come to them and make our home with them.'" John 14:23 (NIV)

Epistle 59

Have you ever heard of the Fun Theory? This is an initiative based on the idea that something as simple as fun is the easiest way to change people's behavior for the future. In Sweden there were some subway stairs located next to the escalators but these stairs were rarely used. People would daily crowd onto the escalators instead. The stairs were cleverly transformed into a working piano. They were so popular that similar "piano stairs" were constructed in Stockholm, Melbourne, Auckland, Milan, Istanbul, and Colombia.

Now, no doubt, this venture would provide a temporary lift for the day—perhaps constant use would revitalize your life-style—but a more permanent change could be achieved with the use of poetic words to supplement the music!

Our worship today is greatly enhanced by the wonderful psalms, hymns, and other spiritual songs that form part of our Services. There is one denomination that operates on the regulative principle. Here we observe that God commands the churches to conduct public services of worship using only certain distinct elements affirmatively found in scripture by command or example. Conversely God prohibits any and all other practices in public worship. This of course means that only Psalms are to be sung and only with the aid of a tuning fork. We have the beautiful words of the Psalms but, without accompanying music, they could seem to lack a certain amount of joy. We know that the Psalms, which are a litany of triumph, grief, anger, exaltation and adoration, sadness and weeping, were sung in Old Testament times as well in the days of Jesus. The Psalter of the Second Temple came about in the time of the restoration of the temple worship by Ezra and Nehemiah. Also, in the Old Testament we find the instruments of music. King David, when bringing the Ark of the Covenant to Jerusalem, leads the house of Israel in dancing before the LORD with songs, and lyres, and harps, and tambourines, castanets, and cymbals. There was a pause in the procession when God struck Uzziah dead but this was because he put out his hand out to hold the Ark and not to do with the use of instruments.

Jesus often quoted the Psalms. The Psalm sung by Jesus and the disciples at the conclusion of the Last Supper was probably the Hallel or Psalm 113–118, particularly associated with the celebration of Jewish festivals. When Paul and Silas were imprisoned: "About midnight Paul and Silas were praying and singing hymns to God, and the other prisoners were listening to them." Acts 16:25 (NIV) Here we see the use of hymns as a form of prayerful devotion. Paul encouraged the new Christians at Colossae, "Let the message of Christ dwell among you richly as you teach and admonish one another with all wisdom through psalms, hymns, and songs from the Spirit, singing to God with gratitude in your hearts." Colossians 3:16 (NIV) Of course, we don't know if music was included on all these occasions or with any of the other examples we find in the New Testament where the basis of a hymn can be distinguished.

Christian hymnody blossomed in the worship of the fourth century and most was metrical in form. With the Reformation there was a surge in hymn singing with the German chorale. As mentioned in a former epistle, Martin Luther's hymn, *A Mighty Fortress is our God,* was a wonderful example of a stirring joy in God's mighty strength and power. Then we have the great development of religious music in the late Baroque period—Bach's *St. Matthew's Passion* and Handel's *Messiah*. Continuing with hymns we are blessed with many from John and Charles Wesley during the Methodist Revival. There was a plethora of hymn writers in England at this time—Isaac Watts, John Newton, Augustus Toplady. Later people, like Vaughan Williams for example, incorporated the music of folk songs in hymns—singing and making melody to the Lord!

How can you not sing with gratitude in our hearts. Hymns are a great strength and encouragement; a depth of feeling for the soul; poetry filled with biblical wisdom and transformed by glorious music. Nor are hymns tied to specific denominations—rather they are for every tradition binding all together.

Many of the older hymns are still sung regularly in churches today but there are many modern hymns that are also notable and soul stirring. Unfortunately, the updating of the words of the older hymns, which was carried out in the 1980s, often somewhat destroys the beauty of the poetic flow.

Like Paul and Silas, we use our hymns as a devotion. Hymns are prayers. When we are bereft of our own words the singing of a hymn can bring comfort to us and others. When people are reaching the end of life on earth, hymns are often the last remnant of memory. Witnessing family members singing hymns to hospital patients is experiencing a beautiful holy prayer to above. Many people can remember explicitly the words of a hymn because of the music whereas it may be a struggle to remember the exact wording of a long piece of scripture. We keep many of our favorite hymns in our hearts . . .

The following is a listing of the first lines of a number of much loved hymns:

>Be still my soul, the Lord is on your side
>Guide me, O my great Jehovah
>Love divine, all loves excelling
>O the deep, deep love of Jesus
>And can it be that I should gain
>I heard the voice of Jesus say
>To God be the glory
>In Christ alone my hope is found
>When peace like a river attendeth my way
>When I survey the wondrous cross
>Be thou my vision, O Lord of my heart

Epistle 60

We know that God created many animals—both wild and domesticated. "And God said, 'Let the land produce living creatures according to their kinds: the livestock, the creatures that move along the ground, and the wild animals, each according to its kind.' And it was so." Genesis 1:24 (NIV)

Probably the most majestic of the wild animals was the lion. In Bible times they were widespread across North Africa and the Middle East—the Romans kept lions in menageries and in New Testament times used them to tear apart and eat the Christians as entertainment for the Roman Emperor and his audiences. They are mentioned in both testaments:

> *The lions roar for their prey.* Ps 104:21a (NIV)
>
> *A king's wrath strikes terror like the roar of a lion.* Prov 20:2a (NIV)
>
> *Be alert and of sober mind. Your enemy the devil prowls around like a roaring lion looking for someone to devour.* 1 Pet 5:8 (NIV)
>
> *[A mighty angel] was holding a little scroll, which lay open in his hand. He planted his right foot on the sea and his left foot on the land, and he gave a loud shout, like the roar of a lion.* Rev 10:2–3 (NIV)

Obviously, travel in Palestine in ancient times was precarious with the presence of many wild beasts. In the Book of Isaiah, we read numerous times of the danger of being attacked by lions, in particular. But Isaiah does state that God will bring his faithful people to a place of safety when they return to Zion.

> *And a highway will be there; it will be called the Way of Holiness;*
> *it will be for those who walk on that Way.*

> *The unclean will not journey on it; wicked fools will not go about on it.*
> *No lion will be there, nor any ravenous beast; they will not be found there.*
> *But only the redeemed will walk there,*
> *and those the LORD has rescued will return.*
> *They will enter Zion with singing; everlasting joy will crown their heads.*
> *Gladness and joy will overtake them, and sorrow and sighing will flee away.* Isa 35:8–10 (NIV)

We know, in Isaiah, there are deep references to the coming of the Messiah; a message that heralds that momentous happening when God's sovereign reign will be established among the new elect. "How beautiful on the mountains are the feet of those who bring good news, who proclaim peace, who announce salvation, who say to Zion, 'Your God reigns!'" Isaiah 52:7 (NIV)

Having faith in the LORD God means the Israelites can travel on the Holy Way; they will not go astray; they will be safe from marauding animals; they shall be the redeemed people. And how will the Israelites have enough faith to blindly follow—because of the knowledge of a great and wondrous God. And how will they gain this knowledge—by obedience in prayer. How can we today travel on the Way of Holiness? Our enemy the devil is constantly there courting and tempting us! We must "Fear the LORD, you his holy people, for those who fear him lack nothing. The lions may grow weak and hungry, but those who seek the LORD lack no good thing" Psalm 34:9–10 (NIV) The *Letter of James* says: "Submit yourselves, then, to God. Resist the devil, and he will flee from you. Come near to God and he will come near to you." James 4:7–8a (NIV) We can only come near to God by on-going prayer:

> *We think rightly or wrongly about prayer according to the conception we have in our minds of prayer. If we think of prayer as the breath in our lungs and the blood from our hearts, we think rightly. The blood flows ceaselessly, and breathing continues ceaselessly; we are not conscious of it, but it is always going on. We are not always conscious of Jesus keeping us in perfect joint with God, but if we are obeying him, He always is. Prayer is not an exercise, it is the life.*[1]

---

1. Chambers, *My Utmost for His Highest*, 26/5.

Our prayer needs to be constant; our prayers are always answered—perhaps not the way we expect or want, but they are heeded and answered. If we pray unceasingly, we will come closer to God. And the way is through Jesus. As foretold by Isaiah, we shall travel on the Holy Way, safe from all evil. We will be the redeemed people because of the ransom paid by Jesus our Savior.

> *Therefore Jesus said again, "Very truly, I tell you, I am the gate for the sheep. All who have come before me are thieves and robbers; but the sheep have not listened to them. I am the gate; whoever enters through me will be saved. They will come in and go out, and find pasture. The thief comes only to steal and kill and destroy; I have come that they may have life, and have it to the full . . . I am the good shepherd; I know my sheep and my sheep know me—just as the Father knows me and I know the Father—and I lay down my life for the sheep.* John 10: 7–10; 14–15 (NIV)

We, who know our Savior, will travel on the Holy Way and come to Zion with singing; everlasting joy will be upon our heads; we will obtain joy and gladness; and—sorrow and sighing will flee away.

Epistle 61

I can listen no longer in silence. I must speak to you by such means as are within my reach. You pierce my soul. I am half-agony, half-hope. Tell me not that I am too late, that such precious feelings are gone forever. I offer myself to you again with a heart even more your own than when you almost broke it, eight years and a half ago.[1]

This is Naval Captain Frederick Wentworth writing to Ann Elliot in Jane Austen's novel *Persuasion*. For those who have not enjoyed reading this classic, eight and a half years previously to this missive being penned, Ann had been persuaded to break off her commitment to Frederick by Lady Russell, a friend of the Elliot family, who saw herself as a surrogate mother to Ann and her sisters. Now Frederick, in being the hearer of a conversation between Ann and his close friend, has felt encouraged to renew his declaration of love. His heart, almost broken all those years before, has obviously leapt with joy, his soul has been pierced by the words he has overheard.

We read often, in novels, of people experiencing "broken hearts." Physically this does not seem possible but many can affirm that they have had such an experience. The pain caused by deep grief or intense suffering is so great and persistent that nothing seems to alleviate it. It can almost feel that the heart is shattered! How can it be brought whole again?

Only the LORD God can heal and restore us: "The righteous cry out and the LORD hears them; and delivers them from all their troubles. The LORD is close to the brokenhearted, and saves those who are crushed in spirit." Psalm 34:17–18 (NIV) "He heals the brokenhearted and binds up their wounds." Psalm 147:3 (NIV)

---

1. Austen, *Persuasion*, 496.

Any other solution we try is futile—it can only be temporary, at best. Even in the midst of turmoil we can find the peace of God. It might be a sad peace but nevertheless it is the peace of acceptance for our souls. "The eternal God is your refuge, and underneath are the everlasting arms. He will drive out your enemies before you saying, 'Destroy them!'" Deuteronomy 33:27 (NIV)

God will drive out the devil who constantly tempts us into the world of sin and sorrow. He will destroy him and support and uphold us. This verse in the Book of Deuteronomy is rendered in similar vein in many of the present-day translations of the Bible. However, in the New Revised Version we read: "He subdues the ancient gods, shatters the forces of old; he drove out the enemy before you, and said, 'Destroy!'" The slightly different wording expands the picture. At this time Israel had been in the Wilderness for forty years; they have been constantly surrounded by pagan nations who worshipped ancient gods. But the LORD guided and protected them; he drove away their enemies; he destroyed them and the powerless gods they worshipped. Are we not living in God's domain as the Elect, surrounded by an alien world full of persecuting enemies who worship ancient and modern gods—futile gods who cannot bring any comfort, strength, refuge, joy, or peace? The preceding verse of Deuteronomy reads: "There is no one like the God of Jeshurun, who rides across the heavens to help you and on the clouds in his majesty." 33:26 (NIV)

He comes—watch him riding towards you!

He destroys the pagan enemies! Faithfully he will always be our defense; lovingly he will always be our refuge—the everlasting arms of support!

Jesus said: "Come to me, all you that are weary and burdened, and I will give you rest. Take my yoke upon you, and learn from me, for I am gentle and humble in heart, and you will find rest for your souls. For my yoke is easy, and my burden is light." Matthew 11: 28–30 (NIV) How often do we savor these verses; we must keep them constantly in our modern minds. If your hearts are fragile through what the world has wrought, make sure that you are securely yoked to the Savior and he will lead you through the Valley of Despair.

We began by Frederick Wentworth writing that his soul was pierced. Thomas Watson, a famous Puritan, used this exquisitely powerful word when he said: "That prayer is most likely to pierce heaven which first pierces one's own heart."[2] So, piercing our hearts and souls may be deeply sorrowful, but it can also mean it invigorates our heart and vitalizes our senses. We must pray that God will mend our broken hearts; strengthen our weakened hearts; and, create in us—new hearts.

> *Create in me a pure heart, O God, and renew a steadfast spirit within me. Do not cast me from your presence, or take your Holy Spirit from me. Restore to me the joy of your salvation, and grant me a willing spirit to sustain me.* Ps 51:10–12 (NIV)

Recognize however, Watson was no doubt stating that the most effective prayer comes from a repentant heart. Hearts are pierced with the recognition of our sin, and though this too leads to shattered souls, it stirs in us the whole panorama of the wages of sin. When we realize this our poignant prayers will be truly heaven bound. We will pray for a right relationship through our redemption and then we will be yoked to Christ and will receive joy, comfort, and peace—a peace that surpasses all understanding.

> Remember, there are always many around us who are brokenhearted with life. Pray for them also that they may find the peace and strength they need.

---

2. Elmer, *Piercing Heaven*, i.

Epistle 62

> *My footsteps were the first to press the firm, unbroken sands—nothing before had trampled them since last night's flowing tide had obliterated the deepest marks of yesterday, and left it fair and even, except where the subsiding water had left behind it the traces of dimpled pools, and little running streams.*[1]

Is this not like a new day when we can put the failings and the griefs of the former day behind us and start afresh? All the problems and worries are trickling away in little running streams!

How then should we approach each new day?

Robert Hawker, an Anglican preacher with Puritan leanings wrote this prayer:

> Come, Lord, I pray that your sweet influences would fill my mouth with your words, and that you would warm my heart with your love. Bring me to your mercy seat today, this morning, as you loose my tongue and enlarge my heart with your grace.[2]

Sometimes the days and nights are so horrific that is hard to have hope in a new day, but in times like these, our emotions are often razor-sharp and subsequently receptive to every glimmer of hope. Walter Schmidt, a German student, fighting in the First World War, penned this letter:

> *I received your letter of July 1st the day before yesterday. It flowed over me like a golden stream of beauty and the joy of youth, and innumerable vivid memories, which the rigour of war had swamped, sprang up again impetuously to the surface of my mind.*[3]

1. Brontë, *Agnes Grey*, 241.
2. Elmer, *Piercing Heaven*, 261.
3. Witkop, *German Students' War Letters*, 306.

A new day is welcomed often in the Old Testament—perhaps the greatest of all is found in the Psalm 118:24 (NIV): "This is the day that the LORD has made; let us rejoice and be glad in it." For the new day which follows a night of turmoil and guilt we read: "For his anger lasts only a moment; but his favor lasts a lifetime; weeping may stay for the night, but rejoicing comes in the morning." Psalm 30:5 (NIV) When fear and weaknesses assail us: "God is in the midst of the city, she will not fall; God will help her at break of day." Psalm 46:5 (NIV) '

Our God is a great and wondrous God:

> *I remember my affliction and my wandering, the bitterness and the gall. I well remember them, and my soul is downcast within me. Yet this I call to mind and therefore I have hope: Because of the LORD's great love we are not consumed, for his compassions never fail. They are new every morning; great is your faithfulness. I say to myself, "The LORD is my portion; therefore I will wait for him." Lam 3:19–24 (NIV)*

Truly our hope is in him: "But for you who revere my name the sun of righteousness will rise with healing in its rays. And you will go out and frolic like well-fed calves." Malachi 4:2 (NIV)

Why should we maintain this hope? Because God has great plans for us:

> *"For I know the plans I have for you," declares the LORD, "plans to prosper you and not to harm you, plans to give you hope and a future. Then you will call on me and come and pray to me, and I will listen to you. You will seek me and find me when you seek me with all your heart. I will be found by you," declares the LORD, "and will bring you back from captivity." Jer 29:11–14a (NIV)*

This is a message to the Israelites in exile—but also a message to us today as we live in a world that can never give us any real hope.

In these uncertain days of the worldwide pandemic of COVID-19 we seem to be continually thrust from a false sense of security when we are able to live a semblance of a normal life—to a life of solitude in another lockdown!

Dietrich Bonhoeffer, the great German theologian, was pivotal in the establishment of the Confessing Church as a stalwart against Hitler in the Second World War. The Roman Catholic Church in Germany had agreed to be compliant with all of the Führer's demands even to the point of expelling Jewish Christians from its fellowship and turning a blind eye to the transportation of Jewish families to concentration camps. Bonhoeffer continued to train new pastors for the Confessing Church and help Jewish families escape to Switzerland. Eventually he was arrested as part of the plot to exterminate Hitler. He was imprisoned for the last two years of his life in Berlin's Tegel prison and then finally at Flossenbürg Concentration Camp, where he was executed days before liberation. He wrote many letters to friends and family whilst imprisoned. The most poignant are those he penned to his fiancée, Maria von Wedemeyer. In his Christmas letter of 1944, he wrote:

> *I have often found that the quieter my surroundings, the more vividly I sense my connection with you all. It's as if, in solitude, the soul develops organs of which we're hardly aware in everyday life. So I haven't for an instant felt lonely and forlorn . . . I live in a great unseen realm of whose real existence I'm in no doubt. The old children's song about the angels says "two to cover me, two to wake me," and today we grown-ups are no less in need than children of preservation, night and morning, by kindly, unseen powers.*
>
> > *By kindly powers so wondrously protected*
> > *we wait with confidence, befall what may.*
> > *We are with God at night and in the morning,*
> > *and, just as certainly, on each new day.*[4]

---

4. Bonhoeffer and von Wedemeyer, *Love Letters from Cell 92*, 227, 229.

Epistle 63

We well remember the outcry when the first of the Harry Potter books hit the bookshops. Many people thought they were an assault on Christianity—even works of the devil! (Yes, there are spirits/ghosts there, but not the devil.) In 2001, the Alamogordo Christ Community Church in New Mexico burned hundreds of copies of the Harry Potter books. In Lewiston, Maine, a minister was denied a city permit to do the same so he cut up books with scissors—annually—obviously his fingers could not cope with a "one-off"!

It is interesting that it is often the case that such people have never read the Harry Potter books. Similarly, people who decry the truth of the Bible have often not read God's Word!

There are, however, quite a number of theologians who support, or at least, do not condemn these books. There are themes of love triumphing over adversity and characters choosing what is right when the choices are complex. A Youth Leader in the Anglican Church in the United Kingdom, found a perfect grounding for worthwhile Christian discussion with his group. He highlighted the various situations in which Harry and his friends find themselves as being similar to the various quandaries that young people face today. A Sydney Youth Minister agrees. She does not believe that Rowling's books show magic as a solution: but rather that magic brings problems. The fantasy is entertaining and engaging and can also reveal hidden Christian messages. Voldemort's killing curse rebounded on him and finally ended his life once and for all. When Harry goes to *King's Cross Station*, he sees the broken and mangled soul of Voldemort in stunted form. Harry, a flawed hero, sacrifices himself for his friends; we have an unflawed Savior who sacrifices himself for his friends on *The King's Cross*. Unusually, an unforeseen advantage occurs in many families when both parents and children devour the books—opening a perfect forum for worthwhile discussion.

There is a great similarity with traditional fairy tales and literary classics such as Homer's Odyssey and the Iliad. More modern writers such as George MacDonald, J. R. R. Tolkien and C. S. Lewis use fantasy to thrill their readers—all these men were strong Christians and there is always good Christian teaching. Tolkien was a devout Roman Catholic from boyhood and his work is fundamentally Catholic and religious. It embodies many of the elements of Beowulf, the Old English epic poem about pagans, which nonetheless contains biblical tales from Genesis, Exodus, and Daniel. In the work of C. S. Lewis, *The Chronicles of Narnia*, Christianity shines through—the great lion Aslan is Jesus Christ—as is the lamb with the sweet milky voice. When the children come across the lamb cooking fish over an open fire, it symbolizes Jesus, cooking fish and breaking bread for his disciples over a charcoal fire on the shores of the Sea of Tiberias. John 21. The fish was the most wonderful food the children had ever tasted.

Is not the food from Jesus the best food we can ever taste?

The first mentioned author here, George MacDonald, a Scottish preacher, was forced to leave his congregation because he did not conform to one of the essential precepts of Calvinism. He settled in London where he earned his living by writing fantasy books for children. Victorian society had become very priggish and conservative. With the Industrial Revolution people had flocked to the cities to find work in the factories and the folk stories and songs of the rural villages and hamlets had been lost. MacDonald's writings came just at the right time. Much of what he wrote concerned the wonder and beauty of death. *The Golden Key* highlighted twilight—the time when day meets night—a kind of magical hinterland where time and eternity meet. In *The Fantastic Imagination* he tells you that wherever your imagination leads you will be rewarded. "You have tasted of death now," said the Old Man, "it is good!" "It is good," said Mossy "It is better than life." "No," said the Old Man "It is only more than life."[1]

Mossy is one of MacDonald's child characters and it is through him and other children that MacDonald depicts death with their eyes. Though it sounds depressing it is applicable to the times, when many children never lived to adulthood and parents existed in ongoing sorrow. Modern readers, unlike Tolkien and Lewis, find this treatment of death

---

1. Sadler, "Defining Death as 'More Life,'" 4.

difficult. But here is a message for Christians today—to understand death as being "dressed up into a fuller awareness of immortality."[2] Mossy and Tangle "climbed out of the earth; and, still climbing, rose above it. They were in the rainbow."[3] Beautiful beings climbed into the rainbow, far above the ocean and the land—up to the country where the shadows fall. We can interpret "more than life" as dying-into-life.

No doubt, in today's world, we would perhaps not recommend the works of MacDonald to our children. But are we wrong? Perhaps they are really fantasy books for adults? When we approach the Bible, we have more variety of literature than can ever be envisioned anywhere. But none of it is fantasy. It is real; it is true; it is eternal. Through a book we learn much about the author. Through the Bible we learn much about God. The more we read; the more our soul becomes involved. And the more we pray to the author, the more we are enlightened, rewarded, strengthened, and assuaged.

---

2. Sadler, "Defining Death as 'More Life,'" 18.
3. Sadler, "Defining Death as 'More Life,'" 18.

Epistle 64

In the Old Testament we read: "A thousand years in your sight are like a day that has just gone by, or like a watch in the night." Psalm 90:4 (NIV)

In the New Testament we read: "But do not forget this one thing, dear friends, that with the Lord a day is like a thousand years, and a thousand years are like a day." 2 Peter 3:8 (NIV)

What do these readings mean? More importantly, what do they mean for us?

It is relevant to try and understand these when someone asks us, "How does God hear all our prayers at the same time?" Not only does he hear all our prayers but, "Before a word is on my tongue you, LORD, know it completely." Psalm 139:4 (NIV)

In the Old Testament God reveals himself as the Lord over all—he is the one who created time! The Creation story in Genesis is the beginning of our history—our past, our present, and our future. But God was there before creation: "Now the earth was formless and empty, darkness was over the surface of the deep, and the Spirit of God was hovering over the waters. And God said, 'Let there be light'; and there was light." Genesis 1:2–3 (NIV)

In creation, God made the world as we know it today. He separated the light from the darkness and in so doing, he separated the time of day from the time of night!

We understand creation not by today's reasoning, but, by faith. In the New Testament we read: "By faith we understand that the universe was formed at God's command, so that what is seen was not made out of what is visible." Hebrews 11:3 (NIV)

After the wonder of creation God revealed himself now and then *in* time as the sole Lord; and thereby also as Lord *over* time! "Temporality, the breaking up of time into past, present, and future, distinguishes the creature from the Creator, who is not bound by the limits of time, who gives time and takes it again."[1]

He was before time began! "Before the mountains were born or you brought forth the whole world, from everlasting to everlasting you are God." Psalm 90:2 (NIV) Our Creator God—who made the world and all that is in it in divisions of his time—is Lord over the ends of the earth. He is the eternal God, unchangeable in his being. All his attributes—his promises, his covenants, his righteousness, his merciful goodness, salvation, and redemption—are in the transient creation as eternal values for the new creation. "The fact that God is not bound by time does not mean that he is not conscious of the succession of points of time. He is aware that events occur in a particular order. Yet he is equally aware of all points of that order simultaneously."[2] Millard Erickson likens it to someone on top of a tall building watching a parade—he sees all parts of the parade not just the people actually at the foot of the building. C. S. Lewis likens it to an author who writes part of a sentence, goes for a walk, and, completes the sentence on his return—the sentence is written over time but covering the same moment in time.

When we consider our prayers, "If a million people are praying to Him at ten-thirty tonight, He need not listen to them all in that one snippet which we call ten-thirty. Ten-thirty—and every other moment from the beginning of the world—is always the Present for Him."[3] Yet we can know that he hears all of us individually because he speaks back to us! "Because he loves me," says the LORD, "I will rescue him; I will protect him, for he acknowledges my name. He will call on me, and I will answer him; I will be with him in trouble, I will deliver him and honor him." Psalm 91:14–15 (NIV) God gives infinite attention to each one of us. We are as much alone with him as if we were the only person he created. And, when his Son, Jesus Christ, died for us he died for each one of us individually.

Remember that Paul tells us:

> In the same way, the Spirit helps us in our weakness. We do not know what we ought to pray for, but the Spirit himself intercedes for us through wordless groans. And he who searches our hearts knows the mind of the Spirit, because the Spirit intercedes for God's people in accordance with the will of God. Rom 8:26–27 (NIV)

1. Buttrick, *The Interpreter's Dictionary of the Bible. v.4. R–Z*, 647.
2. Erickson, *Introducing Christian Doctrine*, 95.
3. Lewis, *Mere Christianity*, 168.

God, in his deep compassion, knows our human weaknesses—we do not always know how to pray and what to pray for. The Spirit always intercedes, helping us with our burden of frailty. In our need he walks beside us; he watches over us every minute of the day. And we can know that he listens in our time and his time—so great is his dominion.

> We must accept what we do not fully understand.
> God is the God of glory and strength; of majesty and power;
> of mercy and compassion.
> We must open our hearts and say, "But I trust in you, LORD; I say, 'You are my God.' My times are in your hands; deliver me from the hands of my enemies, from those who pursue me."
> Psalm 31:14–15 (NIV)

Epistle 65

> *On the last and greatest day of the festival, Jesus stood and said in loud voice, "Let anyone who is thirsty come to me and drink. Whoever believes in me, as Scripture has said, rivers of living water will flow from within them."* John 7:37–38 (NIV)

Remember in John 4:13–14 (NIV) Jesus said to the Samaritan woman at the well: "Everyone who drinks of this water will be thirsty again, but whoever drinks the water that I give them will never thirst. Indeed, the water I give will become in them a spring of water welling up to eternal life." This has been predicted three times in the Book of Isaiah: "With joy you will draw water from the wells of salvation." 12:3 (NIV) "The LORD will guide you always; he will satisfy your needs in a sun–scorched land, and strengthen your frame. You will be like a well-watered garden, like a spring whose waters never fail." 58:11 (NIV) The third reading is more in line with our reading from the

Gospel of John: "For I will pour water on the thirsty land, and streams on the dry ground; I will pour out my Spirit on your offspring, and my blessing on your descendants." 44:3 (NIV) because in John 7:39 our gospel reading continues: "By this [Jesus] meant the Spirit, whom those who believed in him were later to receive. Up to that time the Spirit had not been given, since Jesus had not yet been glorified." (NIV) Nevertheless, both readings from John involve the Spirit. The living water from Jesus involves not a thirst for natural water, "but for God, for eternal life in the presence of God; and the thirst is met not by removing this aching desire but by pouring out the Spirit."[1] "The spirit gives life; the flesh counts for nothing." John 6:63a (NIV)

A river is narrow and generally fast at its source but gets steadily wider and slower at the mouth. A river is powerful enough to erode the

---

1. Carson, *The Gospel According to John*, 220.

land on its banks and create deep valleys and steep gorges. When a river encounters an obstacle, it may momentarily stop but will eventually make a pathway around the obstacle or develop a build-up to tumble over the obstacle. The source is sometimes difficult to establish, for example, the source of the Nile River, which is fed by two large lakes and two mighty rivers—the White Nile and the Blue Nile. The White Nile refers to all the stretches of rivers draining from Lake Victoria until its merge with the Blue Nile. The Kagera River, which flows into Lake Victoria, is the longest feeder river for this lake, hence the most distant source of the main river itself.

We, as Christians, can be like a river. Our source is the Spirit given to us from Christ. We can be excited and swift when we first encounter the grace and joy of God and then, as we flow, we encounter obstacles. "Be strong and courageous. Do not be afraid; do not be discouraged, for the LORD your God will be with you wherever you go." Joshua 1:8b–9 (NIV) and, also: "Do not be afraid or terrified because of them, for the LORD your God will never leave you nor forsake you." Deuteronomy 31:6b (NIV) Your river might become landlocked like a dam on a huge property; or, taking instead of giving like the Dead Sea; it might fall from sight and appear miles later broader and stronger than ever. "See to it that no one takes you captive through hollow and deceptive philosophy, which depends on human tradition, and the elemental spiritual forces of this world rather than on Christ." Colossians 2:8 (NIV) Your river should flow wide and be ever strong in the Spirit. "But let justice roll on like a river, righteousness like a never-failing stream." Amos 5:24 (NIV)

We must always cling to the source; never let anything or anyone separate us from the Spirit. God will never desert us; he will bring us from the source of our journey into the depth of his great love. There is only one way that we can make the flow of the river a journey of ultimate joy. We have to build a relationship with the Triune God through the setbacks, the obstacles, the loneliness, the fear, the suffering, and the sometime the deadness of life itself. And like growing any relationship we have to commune with God; we need to pray and ask for God's blessings, which the Psalmist likens to: "a river whose streams make glad the city of God, the holy place where the Most High dwells. God is within her, she will not fall." Psalm 46:4–5a (NIV)

Listening to the run of a river or the tumble of a waterfall brightens our world. Watching the white-capped waves crash in the surf is breathtaking in its beauty. The enormity of the sea itself is wondrous to behold.

But, in Psalm 42:7–8 we read of the terror of the deep: "Deep calls to deep in the roar of your waterfalls; all your waves and your breakers have swept over me. By day the LORD directs his love, at night his song is with me—a prayer to the God of my life." (NIV) Deep trials have overcome the writer; waves are sweeping over him and he is sinking to the deepest depths. Like an experienced surfer—take a huge breath of the love of God and sink to the depths—swim up to the world above when the terrifying billows have passed. The treasures of God are always there: "neither height nor depth, nor anything else in all creation, will be able to separate us from the love of God that is in Christ Jesus our Lord." Romans 8:39 (NIV)

At night his song is with us; a prayer to the God of our lives.

Epistle 66

> *The virgin will conceive, and will give birth to a son, and they will call him Immanuel—which means "God with us."* Matt 1:23 (NIV)

This was the promise from Isaiah that God would send a Savior to his people Israel to deliver them—not from their mortal enemies but from their spiritual enemy; not from the nations surrounding them in Canaan, nor the Romans whose enormous empire was yet to come—but from their sins!

God would be with them; he would gather them to him and make them a new people under his grace. Thus, Jesus was born in Bethlehem in Judea.

Many nations have used this expression "God with us," to justify their mighty actions, specifically in wars. During the First World War, known as the *War to End All Wars*, British and their Allied soldiers went to battle believing they were engaged in a Holy War. Many of the officer class, although on the whole keeping their religion private, saw themselves as leading men in God's work on earth—giving them courage in this almost spiritual journey. Even the soldiers from the lower ranks were sometimes the receiver of a spiritual experience. John Glubb wrote:

> *Suddenly I felt my whole self over-whelmed by waves of deep and intense joy, which is impossible to describe. Never before had I experienced such a feeling of deep interior joy, so that I could hardly contain myself. I sat for what must have been several minutes, filled with the passionate joy of heaven itself—then the feeling slowly faded away.*[1]

This was written in the bitter winter of 1917 at a time when many men had fallen away from the belief that God was with them. Of course, the

---

1. Lewis-Stempel, *Six Weeks*, 175.

chaplains were the ones who tried to hold on to this, convinced that it was in God's purpose. Chaplain James Green wrote:

> We are where God has placed us and, being in the line of His Providence and doing His will, can claim what He promised to Joshua—His presence and his blessing... My question is "Are we wholehearted in our consecration to God and His Work?"[2]

Green was a slightly pompous man who didn't always get on with fellow chaplains. Nevertheless, he held on to this dictum all through the war years and so did many others.

Conversely, the enemy, the Germans, also believed that God was with them! In August 1915, Eduard Bruhn wrote to his parents:

> I am lying on the battlefield badly wounded. Whether I recover is in God's hands. If I die, do not weep. I am going blissfully home. May God soon send you peace and grant me a blessed home-coming. Jesus is with me, so it is easy to die.[3]

In March 1916, in his letter to his mother, Hans Haas included these words: "God knows whether He intends me to be united with Konrad in a French grave, or whether He is preserving me for some other purpose. For God is the God of History, and in a small way we are all his co-workers in the History of the World."[4] Later that year in June, he wrote: "Dear Parents, I am lying on the battlefield wounded in the body. I think I am dying. I am glad to have time to prepare for the heavenly home-coming. Thank you, dear Parents. God be with you."[5]

By the Second World War, Christianity was on the wane in Europe. Many had lost their faith during the ensuing years. The German leaders were embracing a Nordic mythology when they did think about religion. Yet amazingly, the ordinary soldiers all wore a replica of the previous war—a buckle engraved with the words Gott mit uns (God with us). It was a phrase commonly used in heraldry in Prussia from 1701 so it was continued in all wars by the rank and file. During the First World War, British soldiers, often, disparagingly, called out across the trenches in winter, "We've got mittens too!" The high-ranking Nazis of the Second World War, because of their rejection of God, abandoned it for the

---

2. McKernan, *Padre*, 45
3. Witkop, *German Students' War Letters*, 155.
4. Witkop, *German Students' War Letters*, 206.
5. Witkop, *German Students' War Letters*, 207.

embellishment of the words: Meine Ehre heißt Treue. (My honor is called loyalty.) But loyalty to whom?

In the Old Testament God created man and woman in his image. It does not mean that we are a mirror image of God in the flesh. We are given authority, responsibility, and dignity to fit us for the task of governing his creation. In the New Testament we are given the true image of God—Jesus is God—on earth, "God with us!" Jesus said "If you really know me, you will know my Father as well. From now on, you do know him and have seen him." John 14:7 (NIV) Paul calls Jesus the image of the invisible God. It is God's plan for men and women that they be conformed as the image of his Son. Can we come before a holy God as such? We must strive for the spiritual whilst on this earth.

> *The first man was of the dust of the earth; the second man is of heaven. As was the earthly man, so are those who are of the earth; and as is the heavenly man, so also are those who are of heaven. And just as we have borne the image of the earthly man, so shall we bear the image of the heavenly man. 1 Cor 15:47–49 (NIV)*

Epistle 67

Question 98 in *The Shorter Catechism* agreed upon by the Assembly of Divines at Westminster is as follows: What is prayer?

Answer: Prayer is an offering up of our desires unto God for things agreeable to his will in the name of Christ, with confession of our sins, and thankful acknowledgment of his mercies.

We pray for the things that are troubling us, for the problems we want solved, for the sorrows we want assuaged—we pray in the name of Jesus—we know our God will hear and answer. We confess where we have gone wrong asking for forgiveness, and we give thanks for all God's mercies.

The Heidelberg Catechism says:
The essence of faith is being thankful to God.

But sometimes prayer can be a dilemma! Does God really hear us? Can we hear God speak to us? Do we say, "Speak to us Lord," and yet do not stop to listen? Yet, when we look back on life, do we not suddenly discover where God has answered time and time again. It is sad that we often seem to need hindsight to see clearly. When you approach God in anxiety say: "Speak, Lord" and then wait in contemplative silence. Open your soul slowly to the gift of the Spirit.

Remember in the Old Testament when the boy Samuel woke in the night and heard his name called. He ran to the old priest Eli and said: "Here I am, you called me." But Eli replied "I didn't call you—go back and lie down." Twice more this occurred. "Then Eli realized that the LORD was calling the boy. So Eli told Samuel, "Go and lie down; and if he calls you, say, 'Speak, LORD, for your servant is listening.'" 1 Samuel 3:8b–10 (NIV) When Samuel did as Eli instructed, God spoke and told the boy that, because of Eli's wicked sons, the House of Eli could never be atoned! In the morning Samuel was afraid to relate his vision to Eli, but the priest said he must not hide it from him or God would deal with him severely. So, Samuel told him. Like Samuel, we must obey and treasure the words that God speaks to us. "The LORD was with Samuel as he grew up, and he let none of Samuel's words fall to the ground." 1 Samuel 3:19 (NIV)

God speaks to us in many different ways. We know well the story of Elijah! The prophet Elijah was standing on the mountain waiting for God to speak—he had been told that the LORD was about to pass by!

> *Then a great and powerful wind tore the mountains apart and shattered the rocks before the LORD, but the LORD was not in the wind. After the wind there was an earthquake, but the LORD was not in the earthquake. After the earthquake came a fire, but the LORD was not in the fire. And after the fire came a gentle whisper. When Elijah heard it, he pulled his cloak over his face and went out and stood at the mouth of the cave.* 1 Kgs 19:11b–13a (NIV)

In *The Psalms*, King David talks about the voice of God:

> *The voice of the LORD is over the waters, the God of glory thunders,*
> *The LORD thunders over the mighty waters.*
> *The voice of the LORD is powerful; the voice of the LORD is majestic.*
> *The voice of the LORD breaks into pieces the cedars of Lebanon.*
> *The voice of the LORD strikes with flashes of lightning*
> *The voice of the LORD shakes the desert;*
> *The LORD shakes the wilderness of Kadesh.*
> *The voice of the LORD twists the oaks and strips the forests bare.*
> Ps 29:3–4, 5b, 7–9a (NIV)

This is the same God who whispered to Elijah!

This second reading appears at first to be less than comforting. But David is praising God's glory, his majesty, his might, and his power. The LORD God is in control of all his creative elements, for example, he is faithful to his covenant with Noah—never again will he cover the earth with water: his voice is more powerful than all the waters in the sea and the sky. David introduces this Psalm with these words:

> *Ascribe to the LORD, you heavenly beings,*
> *ascribe to the LORD glory and strength.*
> *Ascribe to the LORD the glory due his name;*
> *worship the LORD in the splendor of his holiness.* 1–2 (NIV)

The lightning clears our vision; the thunder energizes our hearing. In fact, Horace, the Roman poet, admitted that he was torn from atheism by the terror of lighting and thunder. The timbre of God's voice illustrates his omnipotence—his limits are higher and deeper and wider than anything a human could possibly imagine. The Psalm ends with a contrast to the noise and clamor:

> *The LORD sits enthroned over the flood;*
> *the LORD is enthroned as King forever.*
> *The LORD give strength to his people;*
> *the LORD blesses his people with peace.* 10–11 (NIV)

In John 14:27 (NIV) Jesus gives us a powerful declaration of this peace: "Peace I leave with you; my peace I give you. I do not give to you as the world gives. Do not let your hearts be troubled and do not be afraid." We listen to the voice of Jesus; in confidence we follow wherever he leads—he leads us beside quiet waters. As we tread on the paths of righteousness in our earthly life, we will be safe and secure, fearing no evil, and with goodness overflowing.

Thus, say in confidence:
Speak, LORD, for your servant is listening.

Epistle 68

In these days of continual lockdown to combat the spread of the pandemic we are faced with the problem of loneliness—particularly those of us who live alone. Henri Nouwen, the Dutch Roman Catholic priest who wrote prolifically, called loneliness "one of the most universal sources of human suffering."[1] Loneliness is the painful awareness that we lack close and meaningful contact with other people and, for us, this has been dramatically entailed with the restrictions imposed on us by government. This loneliness can develop into self-defeating attitudes, to a lack of control, helplessness, anxiety, depression, and even hostility. We might see some of these feelings within ourselves—depression often develops when we encounter situations over which we have no control and, certainly we see hostility in the recent protest marches.

God does not want us to be alone. At the time of creation, the LORD God declared: "It is not good for man to be alone. I will make a helper suitable for him." Genesis 2:18 (NIV) Woman became a suitable helper for him—"equal and adequate."[2] Nor would Adam and Eve be alone or lonely and but would be in fellowship with the Creator God. However, their disobeying of God led to sin entering the world and with it—selfishness, tension, and loneliness. This loneliness is consequently experienced by many in the Old Testament—Moses, Job, Nehemiah, Elijah, and Jeremiah. We read many times in the Psalms of the times when David felt afflicted with loneliness and despair. We cannot possibly contemplate how lonely our Savior Jesus was in the Garden of Gethsemane. The apostle John spent his last years, probably in loneliness, on the island of Patmos and, in Paul's last days in prison, he wrote to Timothy: "Do your best to come to me quickly." 2 Timothy 4:9 (NIV) Demas had deserted him for worldly pursuits; Titus had gone to Galatia; Alexander had done him

1. Nouwen, *Reaching Out*, 15
2. Waltke, *Genesis*, 88.

much harm, "At my first defense, no one came to my support, but everyone deserted me." 2 Timothy 4:16 (NIV)

But Paul rejoiced that the Lord had stood at his side and given him strength!

Many of us, during lockdowns, have taken the opportunity to tackle jobs that have been long neglected—tasks that have often annoyed us. It may involve having a huge clean-out of unwanted possessions; painting a bedroom that is in need of a new look; individually cleaning the hundreds of books on the bookshelves; unpacking moving boxes that have been around for months; reorganizing kitchen cupboards; clearing an overgrown garden; a giant cleaning program in the home. But how many of these chores do we really need to tackle? Perhaps some of us are not young enough, or fit enough, to undertake very much. Plus, have they solved the problem of loneliness and frustration? Or, have we run out of such challenges but now live in a pristine environment? We can pat ourselves on the back for our great efforts but we need normality—even if it is a new type of normality!

When Elijah lay down in depression, the angel tapped him on the shoulder and told him to "rise and eat." When Jesus found the disciples sleeping for the third time when he came from praying in the Garden, he said to them to "arise, let us go" because the hour of betrayal was approaching. When he had explained to the disciples the promise of the Holy Spirit he then said "Come now, let us leave." Oswald Chambers uses these episodes as examples of not engaging in huge mind-numbing projects to get us through—although on completion we do experience a great feeling of pleasure—but in involving ourselves in the process of getting on with the task that is always there. Sometimes this task is mundane but it is reassuring. Chatting to a loved relative, whom you cannot meet up with because she lives thousands of miles over the seas, can lift your day. It might be only about what cookies she should purchase at the grocery store for morning tea but it is a moment of normality with the promise that your loneliness will not last forever.

We can use today's technology to Zoom meetings with others for Bible Study and fellowship; watch Church Services which are regularly streamlined; phone and message loved ones; walk with another in the beauty of God's created world; organize the boxes of photographs in the various cupboards; file the untidy piles of paperwork; we can expand the scope of our reading. But we are still faced with some days of total isolation. Arise and do something normal! Looking for ways to cure depression often sends us deeper when we decide it hasn't worked! So, arise from your couch and do something normal!

The love of family and friends can still be expressed during the moments of the long days. But the love of God is always there—waiting for us to turn to him and voice our needs. Praise him for his faithfulness; thank him for our continued safety; laud him for his power over all that is happening. Pray continuously in faith and humility because the hope we have through the sacrifice of our great High Priest Jesus is the anchor for our souls. It is firm and secure. And, through Christ, we have a sure and certain hope for all time.

Epistle 69

The baobab tree is an icon of the continent of Africa. The baobab is a prehistoric species thought to have a life span of some 5,000 years. Strangely, it is native to the African savannah where the climate is extremely dry and arid. There is little else able to survive in such areas and with its odd appearance it has become a distinctive feature of the landscape. During the rainy season the baobab absorbs and stores water in a gargantuan trunk and, as a result, it has the ability to grow to approximately 100 feet and also to produce a nutrient fruit. With its protective shelter from the elements and, it being a source of food and water for both people and animals, many communities make their homes near baobab trees. These communities regard it as "The Tree of Life."

> *He who dwells in the shelter of the Most High will rest in the shadow of the Almighty.* Ps 91:1 (NIV)

> *You have been a refuge for the poor, a refuge for the needy in their distress, a shelter from the storm and a shade from the heat.* Isa 25:4 (NIV)

We need to establish an absolute trust in our Almighty God. Come to him in praise and humility to talk to him—to pray—bringing all our requests with the acknowledgment of our constant failings. As we come closer to the Father enveloped in his forgiveness and love, we will achieve an intimate friendship with him. And this relationship needs to be faithful on our part. If we choose to abide under God's shadow, we need to *stay* and dwell with him. We will echo the words of Psalm 36:7 (ESV) He will be our Tree of Life!

> *How priceless is your unfailing love, O God!*
> *People take refuge in the shadow of your wings.*

When we make our home in him, we will find the courage to endure hardship and troubles for he will be in the midst, compassionately strengthening us.

Jim Elliot, Nate Saint, Ed McCully, Peter Fleming, and Roger Youderian were five American missionaries who, with their families, went to Ecuador to evangelize the Huaorani people. The Huaorani were generally known then as the Acua, which roughly means "savages." They were a particularly violent tribe who settled all disputes among themselves (and with other tribes) by killing with spears and machetes. As a result, their tribe was gradually diminishing. All of the people had parents and other relatives who had been slaughtered over the years. Originally the missionaries flew over the area dropping small gifts and supplies to advertise the fact they were wanting to be friends. Eventually, on January 5, 1956, they landed their plane on a riverside beach and set up camp. Over the next few days, two of the Acua, a man and a woman, periodically visited them and one even consented to go on a short flight. This was an amazing achievement as it was customary to kill any intruder who entered the Acua domain. Then after a lie was perpetrated by one of the natives, many men came to the beach and speared each of the missionaries. The five men were armed with guns but had resolved to use them only for frightening the natives if attacked. They would not shoot at the Acua. Their reasoning?

> *The natives are not ready for heaven. We are!*

Jim's wife, Elisabeth, later lived with the Acua for two years and was able to witness to them. Her book about the death of the five loved husbands and fathers was wonderfully entitled *Shadow of the Almighty*. God's promise!

> *For in the day of trouble he will keep me safe in his dwelling; he will hide me in the shadow of his sacred tent and set me high upon a rock.* Ps 27:5 (NIV)

In the Book of Exodus, God instructed Moses to make a tabernacle for him. This would be a sanctuary for his people Israel; a holy place where the LORD their God would dwell amidst them. Moses pitched a tent where God would stretch out his protective shade for every-one who camped in his presence. A cloud covered the Tent of Meeting; the glory of the LORD filled the Tabernacle.

In many ways the whole of the Old Testament is the shadow of things to come. The shadow of God shields us in the Old Testament. In the New Testament the shadow is no longer a reflection of something without physical substance—it becomes real in the person of Christ. Jesus,

> *The Word became flesh and made his dwelling place among us.*
> *We have seen his glory, the glory of the one and only Son who*
> *came from the Father, full of grace and truth.* John 1:14 (NIV)

Jesus pitched his tent amongst us and his sacrifice for us on the cross rips the tent apart: "The curtain of the temple was torn in two from top to bottom. And when the centurion, who stood there in front of Jesus, saw how he died, he said, 'Surely this man was the Son of God!'" Mark 15:38–39 (NIV)

There is now no barrier → our Shelter now is the Cross.
Under the shadow of God → under the blood of the Messiah!
Through the Son we can pray directly to the Father.
Let us pray then with praise and thanksgiving!

Epistle 70

When the Germans invaded the Netherlands during the Second World War, the Dutch Royal Family left their beloved homeland. Queen Wilhelmina went to London from whence she governed her country. The Crown Princess, Juliana, went to Canada with her young family. The Canadians sheltered the Royal family for three long years, during which time Juliana gave birth to a third daughter, Margriet. Interestingly the maternity ward at the Ottawa Civic Hospital was temporarily declared to be extraterritorial by the Canadian Government, thereby allowing Princess Margriet's citizenship to be solely influenced by her mother's Dutch citizenship.

As the Germans were driven back to their home turf, the Canadians played an integral part in the liberation of the Netherlands. After these years residing in Canada, the Dutch Royal Family returned home. Juliana sent 100,000 tulip bulbs to Ottawa in gratitude for the part played by these Canadian soldiers and for the sheltering of herself and her family in Canada, Later, in 1946, Juliana sent another 20,500 bulbs requesting that a display be created for the hospital. In following years tulip bulbs were sent annually to Canada and a Tulip Festival evolved. Queen Juliana returned to Ottawa to celebrate this in 1967, and Princess Margriet later traveled there for the fiftieth anniversary. The tulip has become a symbol of international friendship—all from an expression of overwhelming gratitude. How momentous is this ongoing thanksgiving.

In 1 Samuel 2:1–10 we read a wonderful prayer from Hannah. Elkanah was a Hebrew man with two wives—Peninnah had children but Hannah had none—she had only the heartbreak of an empty womb. Remember that, often in the Old Testament, barrenness was sometimes a sign of God's displeasure. When Elkanah and his family went to the Temple to offer sacrifices, Hannah was so overwhelmed with grief that she wept profusely. Eli, the priest, thought she had indulged in too much wine, but she regaled him with her sorrow. Eli told her to trust in the LORD, so she left with the belief that God would grant her wish. Hannah vowed that her promised child would be given to the service of the LORD God in gratitude for his great blessing. Hannah's prayer is a beautiful utterance. In 1 Samuel 2:1–2 she begins with these words: "My heart rejoices in the LORD; in the LORD my horn is lifted high. My mouth boasts over my enemies, for I delight in your deliverance. There is no one holy like the LORD; there is no one besides you; there is no Rock like our God." (NIV) After Hannah's child Samuel was born, she took him to Eli to serve in the Temple. Each year, at the time of the sacrifices, she lovingly made her son a little robe and took it to the Temple. "And the LORD was gracious to Hannah, she conceived and gave birth to three sons and two daughters." 1 Samuel 2:21 (NIV)

In Luke 1:46–55 we have the beautiful song of Mary. Mary goes to visit her cousin Elizabeth who, after many years of almost hopeless barrenness, was now carrying a child—John the Baptist. When Mary arrived the baby in Elizabeth's womb leapt in her womb and she was filled with the Holy Spirit. She exclaimed to Mary: "Blessed are you among women, and blessed is the child you will bear!" Luke 1:42b (NIV) Then follows Mary's glorious song of praise:

> *My soul glorifies the Lord and my spirit rejoices in God my Savior. For he has been mindful of the humble state of his servant. From now on all generations will call me blessed, for the Mighty One has done great things for me— holy is his name.* Luke 1:46–49 (NIV)

These examples are all expressions of gratitude for God's blessings with specific events. We too praise God for the blessings we receive and for particular answers to prayers. But, do we have ongoing gratitude to God? Do we only express our thankfulness when we are rejoicing with obvious results or—do we live with thankfulness filling every moment of the day? How often does God unexpectedly bless us with something and we don't pause to appreciate it? Are a lot of our blessings gifts that we take for granted because they may appear mundane at first glance? Can we surrender our hearts and souls entirely to a gracious God who blesses us continually?

When Eric Liddell was imprisoned by the Japanese in China, thousands of miles away from his beloved wife and his precious daughters, he was a "Christ light" for all the internees. He took on every task and activity he could—even when his health began to fail. Thinking it was due to a loss of faith, he prayed earnestly for strength to continue and struggled on. It was only when he was completely bedridden that it was realized he was seriously ill. His last words to a faithful friend were: "It's complete surrender."[1] Eric Liddell gave his whole life to God—whether using his tremendous gift of speed at the Olympics in Paris or serving on the mission field in far-flung China. In death he went with supreme confidence, and with gratitude for all that the Father had given him.

Surrendering to God is showing complete faith in him and believing in his promises. We can become as children and walk in the confidence with the Father, knowing that he is the ultimate source of our happiness and well-being. Through our salvation by the sacrifice of the Son, we can trust him for our secure hope—hope for each day and hope for every tomorrow.

Pray continually with thankfulness—surrender all to him.

---

1. Hamilton, *For the Glory*, 295.

Epistle 71

In the United Kingdom there exists a society called:
Friends of Friendless Churches.

The Friends of Friendless Churches believe historic places of worship are a great architectural legacy to the nation. This might be so, but they are also a great historical legacy of a faithful worshipping people of the nation! Fortunately, the blurb of the Society continues by saying:

> A beautiful church, whether standing alone in the countryside or surrounded by wharves and warehouses, offices and houses, is a perpetual reminder of spiritual values . . . such churches are "sermons in stone" and their message is delivered—not for half an hour on Sundays but every hour of every day of every year and not merely to those who enter, but to all who pass by.[1]

(This reminds us of the book of history of St Swithun's Church, Pymble, entitled *Living Stones*!)

The charity, formed in 1957, seeks to raise funds to save disused but beautiful old places of worship from demolition, decay, and unsympathetic conversion. How often do we see shows on television with people converting old churches to family homes. This may save them from destruction but to what extent is the spiritual home desecrated?

In Australia with the decline of a Christian worshipping population, we notice many churches are closed and empty. Some have been converted for commercial purposes—a Dance School, an Antique Center, a Community Refuge, an Antiquarian Book Shop, a local Meeting Place, and so on. Their appearance is often smartened but they are still, in many ways, friendless. They have lost their initial purpose and it almost feels like an abuse to those pioneers who labored so doggedly to raise

---

1. Friends of Friendless Churches Blurb, 2.

the funds so they could have a place of worship for their families. It has become a difficult problem!

The once mighty Church that is famous for its history of changeable functions is Hagia Sophia. Turkish; Auasofya, Koine Greek; Ἁγία Σοφία, romanized; Hagia Sophia; Latin; Sancta Sophia, (literally, "Holy Wisdom"); officially the Holy Hagia Sophia Grand Mosque (Turkish: Ayasofya-i Kebir Cami-i Şerifi); and, formerly the Church of Hagia Sophia. This is a Late Antique place of worship designed by the Greek geometers Isidore of Miletus and Anthemius of Tralles. It was originally built in 537 as the patriarchal cathedral of the imperial capital of Constantinople and was the largest Christian Church of the Byzantine Empire and the Eastern Orthodox Church. For a short period, 1204–1261 it became the city's Latin Catholic Cathedral. In 1453, after the Fall of Constantinople to the Ottoman Empire, it was converted into a mosque. In 1935, the secular Turkish Republic established it as a museum. However, in July 2020, a decree by the Turkish President, reclassified this building again as a Mosque![2] What a turbulent life and a sad ending to a wonderful monument that was originally dedicated to the Holy Wisdom, the Logos, the second person of the Trinity: "In whom are hidden all the treasures of wisdom and knowledge." Colossians 2:3 (NIV) A huge sanctuary for Christians has become so friendless.

Recently a video was viewed showing two sisters seated in a car, one behind the other. The twelve-year-old was pretending to be a musical instrument—very successfully it might be added. The three-year-old was singing to the improvisation, her words were: "We sing a rainbow, we sing a rainbow!" When the music stopped, the face of the three-year-old was a sight to behold. Her little song had abruptly finished because there was no more music. Suddenly she looked very friendless! How appropriate that her song was about a rainbow. After God had delivered Noah, his family, and all the paired animals from the Great Flood, he declared:

> *Never again will I curse the ground because of humans, even though every inclination of the human heart is evil from childhood. And never again will I destroy all living creatures, as I have done. As long as the earth endures, seedtime and harvest, cold and heat, summer and winter, day and night, will never cease . . . This is the sign of the covenant I am making between me and you and every living creature with you, a covenant for all generations to come. I have set my rainbow in the clouds, and it will be the sign*

2. Wikipedia, 2021.

of the covenant between me and the earth. Gen 8:21–22; 9:12–13 (NIV)

All those churches that are no longer churches according to notice boards or some residential address, are not friendless. Faithful Christians once worshipped there and that can never be forgotten or diminished. The Mosque in Istanbul is still where Wisdom was once worshipped and that cannot be erased. God made a covenant with Noah, that no matter how people turned away from him, he would still be their friend. Whenever we see a rainbow—our hearts can be refreshed. And what a friend we have in the Son, the Logos, the Source of All Wisdom. Jesus took the punishment the people of the Old Testament, and we today, deserved. What a wonderful loving friend!

We may feel deserted and alone in these strange days of lockdown but we are not deserted and alone. We are not friendless. God is still there. We may think that the music has stopped. It is still there. Listen quietly and pray.

Epistle 72

In the city of Hanoi there is a byway called "Train Street!" A section of the local railroad enters a 765-yard long alley lined with small houses and shops. The alley is so narrow that people vanish through their doorways when the train passes along the track at 4 pm and 7 pm each day. Some residents religiously blow whistles to warn of the train's approach. Tourists abound—immediately settling into coffee shops to experience a rush of danger from the passing train.

The Corinth Canal connects the Gulf of Corinth in the Ionian Sea with the Saronic Gulf in the Aegean Sea. It is four miles long and only sixty-nine feet wide at its base. There were several efforts in ancient times to construct this canal—first in the seventh century BC and by three Roman emperors in the years before and after the coming of Christ. Nero personally struck a pickax into the soil in 67 AD. Six thousand Jewish prisoners dug about 765 yards before the project was abandoned. The Canal was eventually built between 1890 and 1893. Its high limestone walls proved unstable and landslides often occurred. The wake from passing ships caused further landslides. Today it is mainly only a tourist attraction. In 2019 the MS *Braemar* became the widest and longest ship to cruise through, with the space between the ship and the sides of the canal seemingly merely the length of an arm of a passenger. These man-made passages are narrow ways with narrow gateways both far different from the narrow way and narrow gate we find in the gospels of Matthew and Luke!

> *Enter through the narrow gate. For wide is the gate and broad is the road which leads to destruction, and many enter through it. But small is the gate and narrow the road that leads to life, and only a few find it.* Matt 7:13–14 (WNT)

Similarly:

> Then Jesus went through the towns and villages, teaching as he made his way to Jerusalem. Someone asked him, "Lord, are only a few people going to be saved?" He said to them, "Make every effort to enter through the narrow door, because many, I tell you, will try to enter and not be able to. Once the owner of the house gets up and closes the door, you will stand outside knocking and pleading, 'Sir, open the door for us.'" Luke 13:22–24 (WNT)

We are freed from the turmoil of sin by the sacrifice of Jesus—but we must value our freedom and live that freedom in gratitude. Jesus is telling us that we must "strain every nerve" to enter the narrow gate. It is an agonizing, intense struggle with great purpose. It can be likened to the athlete striving to win a victory in 1 Corinthians 9:25; or to Epaphras laboring fervently, wrestling in prayer for the new Christians in Colossians 4:12; or, like the Christian who fights the good fight of faith in 1 Timothy 6:12. It involves an extreme effort! Plus, few are able to find it—this implies that unless a person is looking diligently for the narrow gate and earnestly seeking to enter through it, he or she is not likely to succeed! Nor, when the gate is found, is a claim of status or achievement in the world a guarantee of admittance! We come with nothing, as Augustus Toplady wrote in his stirring hymn, *Rock of Ages*:

> Nothing in my hand I bring, simply to Your cross I cling;
> naked, come to You for dress, helpless, look to you for grace;
> stained by sin, to You I cry: "Wash me, Saviour, or I die!"[1]

In *The Pilgrim's Progress*, that wonderful Puritan book written by John Bunyan when he was imprisoned for outlawed preaching, we find the hero, Christian, in great distress. He was overwhelmed by the consciousness that he was a sinful man and that the scriptures laid great emphasis on the seriousness of sin. He is directed to steps that lead to a little wicket-gate but, because of worry, shame, and fear, he could not clearly see the steps. Thus, he is diverted from his path by Mr Worldly Wise (an alien), Mr Legality (a cheat), and his son Civility (a hypocrite). With God's grace, Evangelist encourages him to believe that the man at the gate will receive him.

---

1. P.C.A., *Rejoice*, 409.

So, in the process of time, Christian got up to the gate. Now, over the gate there was written, "Knock, and it shall be opened unto you."

> *He that will enter in must first without*
> *Stand knocking at the Gate, nor need he doubt*
> *That is A KNOCKER but to enter in;*
> *For God can love him, and forgive his sin.*

He knocked, therefore, more than once or twice, saying—

> *May I now enter here? Will he within*
> *Open to sorry me, though I have been*
> *An undeserving rebel? Then shall I*
> *Not fail to sing his lasting praise on high.*

At last there came a grave person to the gate, named Good-will, who asked who was there? and whence he came? and what he would have?

CHR. Here is a poor burdened sinner. I come from the City of Destruction, but am going to Mount Zion, that I may be delivered from the wrath to come. I would therefore, Sir, since I am informed that by this gate is the way thither, know if you are willing to let me in?

GOOD-WILL. I am willing with all my heart, said he; and with that he opened the gate.[2]

Pray that we will find that narrow way; that we will strive with all our strength and perseverance toward that wicket-gate; so that we may come to knock on the Entry to Life. How glorious will the answer be when we ask if he is willing to let us in—
and—the gate is opened wide.

---

2. Bunyan, *The Pilgrim's Progress*, 41, 43.

Epistle 73

In Egypt the Pharaohs of Egypt were greatly revered to the extent that they were seen as the intermediaries between the people and their gods. They were therefore the leaders in religion as well as civic affairs. Holding all power in earthly life, they were preserved in death for the journey to the afterlife. Probably the most famous of these kings was Tutankhamun, not because he reigned for a long time—as he was only a nineteen-year-old cripple when he died—but because of the extent of the wondrous collection of treasures and artifacts found in his tomb after most of the tombs of other Pharaohs in the Valley of the Kings had been plundered. The throne of Tutankhamun, some 3,300 years old, is a glory of gold and other precious metals but, ironically, considering the efforts made for his afterlife, it now remains empty!

The Emperors of Japan were revered as gods! Shōwa, known in English as Hirohito, was the 124th Emperor from 1929–1989. However, also being regarded as a god, very few people had ever been in his presence so, when he broadcast live at the cessation of hostilities in 1945, the populace was amazed at his squeaky high voice, and distraught at his message of surrender. People struggled with the concept that he was a not a great god. His family and his Privy Council urged him to abdicate without success—but he was forced to explicitly reject the claim that he was an arahitogami, that is, an incarnate divinity. To placate the general population, to gain vital information about war criminals, and to establish continuity and stability, the Allies did not prosecute him but allowed him to remain as Emperor.

On May 20, 1910, at the funeral of King Edward VII, there was a "Parade of Kings." There were ten European kings, two heirs to European thrones, plus princes, consorts, grand dukes, and archdukes. In the carriages there rode seven queens, and numerous princesses and duchesses. With the exception of some Eastern princes, most of these royal personages were related to each other plus all were widely regarded as divinely appointed and guided. The cavalcade appeared to represent the high point of a glorious reign by almighty kings. However, by the end of the First World War, very few of these remained on their thrones. Most were now powerless and impotent and those that had endured no longer epitomized the wonder of kingly rule.

In the Old Testament we read of the Kings of Israel and Judah. The first King of Israel failed his God. "After removing Saul, [God] made David their king. He testified concerning him: 'I have found David son of Jesse a man after my own heart; he will do everything I want him to do.'" Acts 13:22 (NIV) After David came many kings—some were good kings; most were not. Solomon was a wise king originally; Hezekiah became a righteous king.

In Daniel 2 we read of the great King of Babylon, Nebuchadnezzar. The LORD God had delivered Jehoiakim, King of Judah, into his hands and the Israelites were now under the captivity of the Babylonians. Some of the Israelites from the royal family and the nobility were assigned to the king's palace and trained for three years to enter the service of Nebuchadnezzar. Among these men was Daniel. When the King was suffering from troubling dreams which none of his astrologers could interpret, Daniel was eventually brought before him to reveal to him their meaning. Daniel said to the King

> *No wise man, enchanter, magician or diviner can explain to the king the mystery he has asked about, but there is a God in heaven who reveals mysteries. He has shown King Nebuchadnezzar what will happen in the days to come.* Dan 2:27–28 (NIV)

Then follows an interpretation that challenges the king to honor Daniel's God. Though God has granted Nebuchadnezzar dominion, power, might, and glory, the following kings and their kingdoms will be inferior and will be destroyed. After this:

> *In the time of those kings, the God of heaven will set up a kingdom that will never be destroyed, nor will it be left to another people. It will crush all those kingdoms and bring them to an end, but it will itself endure forever.* Dan 2:44 (NIV)

> *I met a Traveller from an antique land,*
> *Who said: "Two vast and trunkless legs of stone*
> *Stand in the desert. Near them, on the sand,*
> *Half sunk, a shattered visage lies, whose frown,*

> And wrinkled lip, and sneer of cold command,
> Tell that its sculptor well those passions read
> Which yet survive, stamped on these lifeless things,
> The hand that mocked them, and the heart that fed;
> And on the pedestal these words appear:
> 'My name is OZYMANDIAS, King of Kings;
> Look on my words, ye Mighty, and despair!'
> No thing beside remains. Round the decay
> Of that colossal wreck, boundless and bare
> The lone and level sands stretch far away.[1]

There is a King of Kings! Isaiah predicts the greatest King of all: "He brings princes to naught and reduces the rulers of this world to nothing." Isaiah 40:23 (NIV)

In the New Testament we read that:

> in these last days [God] has spoken to us by his son, whom he appointed heir of all things, and through him whom also he made the universe. The Son is the radiance of God's glory and the exact representation of his being, sustaining all things by his powerful word. After he had provided purification for sins, he sat down at the right hand of the Majesty in heaven. So he became as much superior to the angels as the name he has inherited is superior to theirs. Heb 1:2–4 (NIV)

In Revelation 19:13,16:

> He is dressed in a robe dipped in blood, and his name is the Word of God . . . On his robe and on his thigh he has this name written KING OF KINGS AND LORD OF LORDS. (NIV)

---

1. Shelley, *Selected Poems*, 358.

Epistle 74

How many letters do we regularly write today? If we do need to put pen to paper, we no doubt have great trouble finding a respectable writing pad (plus a matching envelope) to carry out the task. In an age of emails, Facebook, mobile calls, and messaging, we seldom write letters. Nor are these letters delivered in the same time that we can send a communication by some electronic means. Remember the superior pads that had a sheet of lines underneath the paper to guide our writing? We also endeavored to do our best script, especially with the obligatory thank you letters. Now, with lack of practice our writing is abysmal. The only saving grace of this technological age is that the chemist does not have to labor to understand the doctor's prescriptions!

Throughout history, letters have been written and faithfully delivered. In ancient times the Near East relied on a system of roads that had been built during the Israelite monarchy. During the intertestamental times when firstly the Greek, and then the Roman Empires, caused the Jewish kings to become mere titular heads owing allegiance to the greater power, the roads were greatly improved and expanded. Merchants not only carrying goods, but spreading news and even cultural practices and religious beliefs, now traveled in carts pulled by horses or even oxen, on properly built Roman highways. The Romans even laid flat stones in the river beds to smooth the way for wagon wheels. They also set up a system of mile markers—were they not a great way to amuse the children on long drives on the highway! There were still robbers throughout the lands—and pirates on the high seas—but as more communities were established there was safety in private homes for travelers. Merchant caravans on land, and trading vessels on sea, carried letters to the far corners of the Empire. The apostle Paul, often incarcerated in prison, sent letters far and wide, carried by faithful supporters.

The Letter to the Romans is distinctive in a number of ways. Unlike others it was written to a city that Paul had never visited and to a church he had not founded. Yet Chapter 16 illustrates that he knew of five house churches already established in Rome: verses 5, 10, 11, 14, 15. In the opening verses of the chapter Paul goes to some lengths to state his authority as an apostle and to attempt to build a relationship with the Christians there. The closing chapter varies in style from the closing greetings generally sent—it reads more like a transcript of recommendations. It certainly contains a long list and it may be questioned how Paul knew so many people in this unknown location. But we know that early Christians traveled much—especially those who had been exiled from a specific city. The people listed either had worked with Paul in spreading the gospel; were his relatives or relatives of his co-workers; or, had been in prison with him. There is even one who was the city's director of public works! It is thought that, of the twenty-six people mentioned, fourteen of these were not born in Rome. The chapter could also be deemed an introduction for Phoebe to those in Rome—both Jewish and Gentile Christians. It is a difficult situation for her as the Christians in Rome were somewhat divided. Paul knows that the Jews and the Gentiles must come together in the fellowship of the Spirit despite their preconceived ideas and practices. Phoebe is not just a carrier of mail—she is a co-worker with Paul charged with bringing spiritual maturity to the church of Rome. She leaves from Corinth's port of Cenchreae, from where she is a guardian of a Christian congregation, to sail to Rome.

> I commend to you our sister Phoebe, a deacon of the church in Cenchreae. I ask you to receive her in the Lord in a way worthy of his people and to give her any help she may need from you, for she has been the benefactor of many people, including me. Rom 16:1–2 (NIV)

Paul records his indebtedness to Phoebe!

It is not altogether strange that a woman was chosen to take this epistle to Rome. In these times women in Rome held a wide range of roles both in the home, and in business and commercial ventures.

> It is therefore not a surprise at all to find women like the eight that Paul mentions in Romans 16 playing a variety of roles in the Roman church, and indeed probably a wider variety than they could have played in the synagogue. This is probably one reason

women were attracted to the Christian movement as it spread west across the empire.[1]

And this is why many women today feel so spiritually stirred when they read the new Bible versions—the Word is really for them!

All the letters of Paul promote a dedication to prayer. Prayers of thanksgiving for the saving grace of God through Christ; prayers for spread of the gospel and prayers for those who face danger and tribulation in this work; prayers that the readers may grow in knowledge and love; prayers that all will be one in Christ.

> *The Lord is near. Do not be anxious about anything, but in every situation, by prayer and petition, with thanksgiving, present your requests to God. And the peace of God, which transcends all understanding, will guard your hearts and your minds in Christ Jesus.* Phil 4:5b–7 (NIV)

---

1. Witherington, *Paul's Letter to the Romans*, 392.

Epistle 75

Do you find it disappointing, when reading, that there is a repetition of the same words over and over again? The richness of the English language seems to becoming lost in mediocracy! Standard commonplace words are the order of the day in a fast-moving world where fewer and fewer people are taking the time to explore the joy of reading. Modern translations of old works have lost the fascination of language and the reader can often be misled as to the meaning of a passage because of benign wording. If you read older non-fiction works you may be more likely to challenge your thinking. The lazy reader will just gloss over a new word hoping to find some sort of meaning from the context of the sentence. However, keeping a journal of words you haven't before encountered, leads to the adventure of using them—sometimes to the consternation of your listeners. Using a thesaurus when writing makes it possible with one word to express a deeper, wider, or more relevant meaning! Following are different words which you might like to embrace:

Apolaustic	devoted to enjoyment; a buffoon who loves food
Blate	bashful, shy
Contumacious	willfully and obstinately disobedient
Discombobulate	to confuse or disconnect; upset; frustrate
Encomium	a formal expression of high praise
Munificence	unusual generosity
Pelagic	relating to open seas or oceans
Peroration	a long speech of lofty and pompous language
Rictus	the gaping or opening of the mouth
Snafu	a badly confused or ridiculously muddled situation

| Saudade | a deeply emotional state of melancholic longing for person or thing that is absent; a yearning |
| Tincture | a trace, a smack, or smattering, a tinge |

Perhaps none of the above would fit into normal conversation but they roll off the tongue beautifully and promote imagination. Perhaps also many of these are already familiar to you? The British Library has some suggestions:

Overmorrow	the day after tomorrow
Wamble	the rumbling of the stomach
Dysania	the condition of finding it difficult to get out of bed

Probably the most exciting are the distinctly Dickensian words! In his prolific writing Charles Dickens searched constantly to find the right word to put into the mouths of his characters to the extent that his biographical hero, David Copperfield once said "I wallow in words!" When Dickens failed to find a word to satisfy, he invented new words and phrases. A recently published book entitled *What the Dickens?!* has more than 200 examples of Dickensian words!

"Bonneting	knocking a man's hat off; pulling it over his eyes
Gormed	stupefied, confounded, staring blankly
Marplot	a meddlesome though well-meaning person
Spanker	something very fine
Comfoozled	exhausted, overcome
Connubialities	polite euphemism for marital arguments
Growlery	a place of refuge where one goes to vent frustrations
Rantipole	an ill-behaved and reckless person
Fanteeg	a state of anxiety or worry
Scrowdging	crushing, squeezing, crowding
Coriolanian	snobby
Mumchance	silent"[1]

---

1. Kozlowski, *What the Dickens?!* various pp.

When we look through the thesaurus the word "prayer" has numerous synonyms – some relevant; some only vaguely useful; some even incorrect: *appeal, invocation, plea, communion, entreaty, litany, orison, petition, call, supplication, adoration, imploration, request, paternoster, rogation.*

> Even an imprecation will be heard by God who can enable us to cope with the rage and the bitterness.
> Our Father can help us persevere with a person who is discombobulated by building up a response of patience and love.
> God can intervene when children are contumacious or partners become involved in connubialities.
> We may even find laughter when we experience bonneting.
> The behemoth of envy and pride can be overcome with prayer.
> Come to the Lord when you are weighed down with saudade.
> We should always pray with praise, confession, and thanksgiving, especially when we would prefer to go to the growlery!
> We would surely feel blessing if we wallow in the beauty of God's holiness.
> Our faith must not remain inchoate or suffer from insouciance.
> Open our hearts to the Spirit when we feel unable to pray—the Spirit helps us in our weakness; the Spirit intercedes for us even when we have no words.

Remember "Before a word is on my tongue you know it completely." Psalm 139:4 (NIV) We need to be ever conscious of this and pause before we speak!

> Each morning may we come anew into your glorious presence with new songs of thanksgiving in our mouths and "May the God of peace, who through the blood of the eternal covenant brought back from the dead our Lord Jesus, that great Shepherd of the sheep, equip you with everything good for doing his will, and may he work in us what is pleasing to him, through Jesus Christ, to whom be glory for ever and ever. Amen."
> Hebrews 13:20–21 (NIV)

Epistle 76

In our first Epistle we were given some exercises to develop a prayer life communicating with our Father in heaven. Various following epistles looked at different types of prayer—Charles Spurgeon's arrow prayers; Peter the Disciple's panic prayer; Hudson Taylor's purpose to rest in Christ alone; Eric Liddell's prayer life based on complete surrender; Lancelot Andrewes likening prayer to the burning of incense; John Calvin sprinkling his prayers with the perfume of Jesus' sacrifice; Spurgeon again, just sitting still and looking up!

Benignus O'Rourke, an Augustinian friar and member of the community at Clare Priory in Suffolk, once had an elderly lady talking to him about her problem with prayer. She was at a stage where she found it impossible to pray. She would come to church and, in the peace and silence of the sanctuary, she would valiantly try to pray but the words would not come. O'Rourke said: "What my parishioner was discovering, in fact, was one of God's loveliest gifts, the purest form of prayer. She rejected it because it was not what she had been taught."[1]

Silence is not merely an absence of noise; it actually has a substance. In the constant commotion of this modern world, we may attend church regularly, become involved in Bible Study groups, and partake in prayer meetings, yet sometimes we are so burdened with troubles in our personal life that, instead of feeling refreshed with these activities, our hearts feel constantly heavy. Thus, it is hard to find the words to express our pleas to our Father in heaven. Sit in the silence! At the heart of silence is the God of all stillness and peace. And God, in our silence, penetrates deeply into our hearts.

When God created the heavens and the earth; the light and the darkness; the waters and all the creatures that lived in the sea; the land and all that roamed on it; the wild animals and domestic livestock; he

---

1. O'Rourke, *Finding Your Hidden Treasure*, 15.

said it was good. But then, when he created male and female, he blessed them and charged them to be custodians of all he had created. The male and the female he created in his own image, in his own likeness. "In the Ancient Near East it was widely believed that a god's spirit lived in any statue or image of that god, with the result that the image could function as a kind of representative of, or substitute for the god, wherever it was placed."[2] Often a king was regarded as the representative/substitute. However, a Hebrew perspective is distinctly different. Here, in Genesis, it is implied that man is not a king like the kings of nations, but he is to look after creation as a king should—and be responsible to the ultimate King for its development and care. The word "image" signifies that man is not like any other creature; he alone is able to communicate with the divine personage. But the added phrase, "in his own likeness," stresses the fact that man is distinct from God. We are made in God's image, but we are only a likeness; in our likeness we talk to him. Christ is the only true image of God.

Augustine of Hippo was an advocate of prayer in secret. By this he did not necessarily mean being hidden away from others but rather, that we need to go to the secret places of our hearts. In this silent depth we will find God. When Jesus was with his disciples near the end of his earthly sojourn, he said:

> *I will ask the Father, and he will give you another advocate to help you and be with you forever—the Spirit of truth. The world cannot accept him, because it neither sees him nor knows him. But you know him, for he lives with you and will be in you. I will not leave you as orphans; I will come to you. Before long, the world will not see me anymore, but you will see me. Because I live, you also will live. On that day you will realize that I am in my Father, and you are in me, and I am in you.* John 14:16–20 (NIV)

And this is what Augustine believed. We do not need to go searching for God, reaching out as if to touch him. Wherever we are, whatever we pray, our God who hears us is hidden within, in our secret place. He longs for us to dwell there with him. We are in him and he is in us.

From the *Confessions of Augustine*, Benignus O'Rourke presents the Bishop of Hippo's words in a modern translation:

> *Late I have loved you, beauty ever old yet ever new! Late I have loved you! You were within me, but I was outside.*

---

2. Hart, *Genesis 1:1–2:3*, 318.

> *There I sought you, as I rushed among the beautiful things you had made.*
>> *You were with me, but I was not with you.*
> *The beautiful things of this world kept me far from you.*
>> *You called. You cried.*
> *You burst through my deafness. You scattered my blindness.*
>> *I breathed your fragrance, and now I pine for you.*
> *You touched me, and I burn with desire for your peace.*[3]

These were the words Augustine penned when he realized his search for God in the world around him was futile. It became a great adventure for him and resulted in a journey inside his very soul, into his waiting heart. Christ told his disciples—and us—that "you are in me, and I am in you." We are the Father's likeness made in his image so we will truly recognize him through our Savior.

---

3. O'Rourke, *Finding your Hidden Treasure*, 22.

Epistle 77

What do we mean by the term "Fear of God"? We hear it often but how is it understood in the Bible, for example? If we are afraid of God, how can he be our loving heavenly Father? How can we approach him with confidence? We understand the word in the secular sense—there are many things in this world that we find most fearful. There are daily events that fill us with dread and terror not only because of their power, but also because we can see no solution being possible. To face the fact that "Fear of God" is also present could leave us with nowhere to turn for courage and hope!

> *There should be a genuine fear of God, but this is instilled to alert people with dispositions that are cruel or malicious to the realization that there will be an accounting for violence, oppression, and every kind of premeditated malice. But once anyone has been converted to God and has begun the spiritual journey, fear is useless, while faith expanding into boundless confidence in God is life-giving.*[1]

We come across hundreds of mentions of fear in both the Old and New Testaments. The term often gives us a visual aspect of some catastrophic event or an emotional aspect of how people respond to a specific fear—by trembling, quaking, writhing, weeping! Men and women are struck with fear; seized with alarm; overcome with cowardice. In the Old Testament fear often brings a questioning of God and his purposes. Many of these are from a fear of an expectation of punishment for sin. Fear of death brings a plaintive cry:

> *We are consumed by your anger and terrified by your indignation. You have set our iniquities before you, our secret sins in the light of your presence. All our days pass away under your wrath; we finish*

---

1. Keating, *Intimacy With God*, 13.

> *our years with a moan. Our days may come to seventy years, or eighty, if our strength endures; yet the best of them are but trouble and sorrow, for they quickly pass, and we fly away. If only we knew the power of your anger! Your wrath is as great as the fear that is your due. Teach us to number our days, that we may gain a heart of wisdom.* Ps 90: 7–12 (NIV)

However, whilst many of the Psalms may begin with negativity, they have a clear perception of the glory of God and can bring a strong emotion of joy to us when we realize that, right throughout the Old Testament, no matter how sinful God's people were, his love and concern was intense and faithful. When David was fleeing from the jealous wrath of Saul, he spoke to the Lord in the words of Psalm 18. David felt he was entangled by the cords of death but he could sense that, out of the LORD's thunder and lightning: "He reached down from on high and took hold of me; he drew me out of deep waters." Psalm 18:16 (NIV) The biblical mode of thinking in the scriptures is difficult to be understood by secular men and women. "For the ancient Hebrew, a member of the holy people, covenanted with a holy God for a unique purpose in history, there is no paradox in the liturgical command, 'Serve Yahweh with fear, and rejoice with trembling.' Psalm 2:11"[2] Respectful fear can bring an experience of great joy!

In the New Testament the disciples constantly experience fear and danger. But, when Jesus calms the storm, heals the sick, casts out demons, and raises people from death, they are overcome with fear at the holiness of their Master. They are in deep awe of his majesty. They cry out: "God has come to help his people." Luke 7:16b (NIV) even though they were yet to understand the scope of the redemptive nature of their teacher. Fear is holy awe. When the expression "fear of the Lord" is used in the Bible it comes with a sure and certain hope and a dedication to God's law and God's way. With human frailty we can be delivered from our worldly fears, but, we must still fear evil in all its forms. We must constantly turn away from sin and come before a holy God in awe and trembling. We must understand that the fear of God means coming into a right relationship with God. That relationship is the abhorrence of sin and the growing of complete trust in a loving Father full of glory and holiness. We need to grow a maturity of faith so that we don't judge God by secular power or

---

2. Buttrick, *The Interpreter's Dictionary of the Bible. Volume 2. D–J*, 258.

by authoritarian earthly fathers. God is God and there is no person nor any worldly establishment that can be compared to him.

When we come to pray to this awesome God, we must prepare ourselves. Be silent and seek a holy word, a sacred word—or a sentence of scripture—to open ourselves to his presence. This will become a symbol for our communication with him. We begin with ourselves but the Spirit will take over and guide us on our journey. We will not lose our own personality for we are all unique, but the Spirit will be with us leading us up the steps of contemplative prayer to feel closer to our holy God in the heights. We will stand in awe in his fearful presence. Out of our prayers will come our actions:

> *Brothers and sisters, whatever is true, whatever is noble, whatever is right, whatever is pure, whatever is lovely, whatever is admirable—if anything is excellent or praiseworthy—think about such things. Whatever you have learned or received or heard from me, or seen in me—put it into practice. And the God of peace will be with you.* Phil 4:8–9 (NIV).

Think about such things; pray about such things.

Epistle 78

There is an old joke about the parable of the Prodigal Son. The question is: "Who was most upset at the welcome the prodigal son received?" The obvious answer is the wrong answer!! There is also an old perception that the main message of the parable is that the young son saw how wayward his life had become, and returned to the family fold to live a more worthy life—but had he really repented? Some cynical people might also say that he realized home was a better option than wallowing in pig swill!

The *Pesikta Rabbati* is a Hebrew document composed about 845 CE. A collection of homilies on the Pentateuchal and prophetic readings, it tells one story of a king whose son had gone away from his father on a journey of a hundred days. Feeling remorse, the boy's friends said to him to return to his father. However, he says that he cannot. Then word comes to him from the king to return as far as he can, and he will come the rest of the way to meet him. The homily is likened to God saying that a lost person only has to repent and turn back and *God will hasten to welcome him!*

Interesting that a ninth-century Jewish homily echoes a New Testament parable.

In our story of the Prodigal Son in Luke 15:11–31, there is an addendum. It concerns a churlish older brother. This son has kept the Law, worked energetically and dutifully, and always obeyed his father. He has never been given a reward—a great feast of celebration like his runaway brother. "'My son,' the father said, 'you are always with me, and everything I have is yours. But we had to celebrate and be glad, because this brother of yours was dead and is alive again; he was lost and is found.'" 31 (NIV) However, if we look closely at the attitude and words of the older brother, we could quite easily come to the conclusion that there may have always existed a problem. He does not call his father, "Father" and he refers to his brother as "this son of yours." It appears that all he has done for his father in the past may have been motivated solely by self-interest. Even the fact that his father, as host of the celebration, has left the feast to placate him with gracious love is disregarded. His final attitude is not revealed—his heart was not stirred by his father's plea.

In Christian families today we often find children who have wandered away from the faith in which they were reared. It appears to happen in young adulthood when they move to live in a secular world often with a far different mindset from that of Christianity. In the halls of learning, intellectualism and scholarship seem to be the ultimate; in the world of business, prestige and wealth appear to be the goal. Their faith fades to the distress of the parents. But the groundwork is not totally lost—take heart! If they return what a great celebration there will be—and a celebration in which siblings must partake. The one who had gone far away is restored!

Years ago, a young man was offered a business opportunity in Japan for two years. The night before he was due to depart, he celebrated his good fortune with friends. In the morning his parents were at the airport to farewell him—they had traveled down from Berkely Vale on the Central Coast of New South Wales. But he did not appear—his partying had been so great that he overslept. One of his friends went round to wake him and took him to meet his parents who had gone to a relative's abode. But they did not stay to meet him—they were so angry they traveled back to the Central Coast. All day whilst he waited for an evening flight, he tried to contact them to apologize. Finally, when just about to board, they took his call and grudgingly forgave him. This might be the action of an earthly father but not the response of our heavenly father. "I tell you that there is more rejoicing in heaven over one sinner who repents than over ninety-nine righteous persons who do not need to repent." Luke 15:7 (NIV) Like the father of the prodigal son and the king who awaited his son's return, God will come swiftly to the lost: "While he was still a long way off, his father saw him and was filled with compassion for him; he ran to his son, threw his arms around him and kissed him." Luke 15:20 (NIV) This, then, is the main message of the parable!

Proverbs 22:6 says: "Start children off on the way they should go, and even when they are old they will not turn from it." (NIV) Children can be prepared for life in the world but then when they voluntarily (and momentarily) stray, they have to take the total burden of their chosen path themselves. But remember, "In their hearts humans plan their course but the LORD establishes their steps." Proverbs 16:9 (NIV) Often we are left only with prayer to our loving Father. "We do not know what to do, but our eyes are upon you." 2 Chronicles 20:12b (NIV) We have to build our own strength purely in our Savior and, in doing so, find the tenacity to keep going. God is good and he is sovereign. He knows each one of us and keeps us in his heart, rejoicing when we turn to him. Pray for your loved one; find others to pray with you. We were never meant to struggle alone.

> *Be joyful in hope, patient in affliction, faithful in prayer.* Rom 12:12 (NIV)

Epistle 79

God showers many blessings on us throughout our lives and even when we only see trials and tribulations the blessings are still there; he surrounds us with his compassionate love—is that not a great blessing? And throughout all the years he extends to us the ability to pray—that wonderful opportunity to converse with him in friendship—to thank him for the blessings and seek him for the comfort. Is this not a great gift? Prayer is the path to experiencing the indwelling of God in our hearts and thus in our lives. We need to open up to our Father in a very deep way—to understand that he alone is the answer to all our prayers. We need to stand still awhile and breathe—to breathe in the Spirit in everything we see and do. "Be still, and know that I am God." Psalm 46:10 (NIV)

In this frantic world of today we seldom sit and rest from all our endeavors. We are always busy—even when we finish a project we immediately move on to another task. A family with all its demands leaves little time to reflect; to contemplate; to rest our souls. We need to let go and let be! We need to reflect on our daily life with deep and careful thought.

> *The contemplative person responds to the complexities of existence by simply awakening to God's ever-present life, as if rousing from a bad dream into the clear light of morning. Awakening in the ever-present life of God is the simplest thing you can do. Other actions generate complex strategies, convoluted machinations of effort. Awakening in God is simple.*[1]

Is praying to God a great effort we have to work hard at to achieve success? Ponder on Jesus talking about the Good Shepherd and his sheep: "My sheep listen to my voice; I know them, and they follow me. I give them eternal life, and they shall never perish; no-one can snatch them out of my hand." John 10:27–28 (NIV) What do you discover in the

---

1. Frenette, *The Path of Centering Prayer*, 143.

sequence? *My* sheep *hear* my voice; they *follow* me; I *give* them eternal life. Because we are chosen to be his sheep we will hear his voice—we belong to him right from the beginning. When we acknowledge that we are his, we will follow. Then the Shepherd does all the giving with the greatest gift of all, Eternal Life. Plus, no-one can snatch us away! We love God because he first loved us. We are his people—stop to hear his voice and to receive his promises.

This passage illustrates that we should not approach prayer with our heads—thinking, talking, discussing. Prayer is the province of the heart—of feeling, loving, sensing. Listen with your heart to the voice of God; to the words of Jesus; to the breath of the Spirit. When life seems to be mightily confusing, remember: "He makes me lie down in green pastures, he leads me beside quiet waters; he restores my soul. He guides me in paths of righteousness for his name's sake." Psalm 23:2–3 (NIV) In the stillness listen and heed.

It is difficult to hand over all to God and just sit in contemplative silence. The primary reason most people reject a prayer life is to do with control. Even though life is difficult and situations continually arise, which seem to be beyond our knowledge and our capabilities, nevertheless, we strive to keep everything under our control. We think that if we micro-manage every situation and diligently keep to set goals we will be successful in life. But when we stop to evaluate our efforts, we may often be left with only a desperate weariness instead of the rewards we strove for. Can prayer be the simple answer?

> *We do not step out of the world when we pray; we merely see the world in a different setting. Prayer is the way to master what is inferior in us, to discern between the signal and the trivial, between the vital and the futile, by taking counsel with what we know about the will of God, by seeing our fate in proportion to God. Prayer is no panacea, no substitute for action. It is, rather, like a beam thrown from a flashlight before us unto the darkness.*[2]

Look for God's blessings, God's love, and God's comfort in his Word. Find strength with the following verses from God's Word which reveal his compassion for us in our need.

> *Look to the LORD and his strength; seek his face always.* 1 Chr 16:11 (NIV)

---

2. Heschel, *Modern Spirituality*, 9.

> *The LORD is good to those whose hope is in him, to the one who seeks him; it is good to wait quietly for the salvation of the LORD.* Lam 3:25–26 (NIV)

> *Do not be anxious about anything, but in every situation, by prayer and petition, with thanksgiving, present your requests to God. And the peace of God, which transcends all understanding, will guard your hearts and your minds in Christ Jesus.* Phil 4:6–7 (NIV)

With these words in your heart, be confident in prayer.

Epistle 80

Are there some days when prayer seems remote? There are probably times when you struggle to find the right words to begin. But, take heart, there are many resources in God's Word to set your pattern for the day. In the Book of Acts, for example, we find the wonderful praying of the Fellowship of Believers in Jerusalem. Acts 4:24b–31. This follows the healing of the paralyzed man; the continued preaching of Peter and John; and their resultant imprisonment.

The apostles continued to boldly preach in the same place where they had healed the paralytic—in the Temple Courts. Many people were following their teaching and this, of course, greatly troubled the authorities. The Pharisees who had been the chief opponents of Jesus, had been somewhat tolerating Peter and John, perhaps hoping they would not have the same influence as Jesus. But Peter was emphatic that it was through Jesus himself that the man had been healed. They preached a Christ who had risen from the dead and this brought forth a greater enemy—the Sadducees. They were not a legal body but, being mostly from the aristocracy, they had a great deal of influence. Specifically, they did not believe in resurrection, so that Peter's preaching of a risen Jesus stirred them up into a strong and growing opposition. Thus, with the amount of people now beginning to follow the apostles, the Pharisees knew they needed to take some action. No doubt they probably began to realize that the people might start to rightly accuse them of being the executioners of Jesus! Therefore, Peter and John were arrested and imprisoned. The next day they appeared in court and were challenged to answer who gave them the power to preach and heal.

It is interesting here to note that the man who was healed was there—standing in court beside the apostles. He hadn't traveled far and wide to broadcast his healing like the man healed of a demon possession by Jesus. Nor had he gone home to rejoice with family and friends. "Heal" reflects the same Greek word as is used elsewhere in this passage with the wider meaning of "save." Also, in his defense, "We notice the ease with which Peter moves from healing to salvation."[1] Luke, the author of Acts, does not elaborate on why the healed man was there, standing beside Peter and John in the courtroom. It seems he is the proof to all the audience that Jesus was the Savior—the very Messiah the Jewish people had been waiting for. We can feel that presence of a Savior silently standing beside us, giving us the courage—the boldness—to proclaim him to all! For this is what the whole passage is about—the fearlessness to proclaim Jesus no matter whatever the consequences might be. "'What are we going to do with these men?' they asked." Acts 4:16a (NIV) So, in an attempt to prevent Peter and John from proselytizing, the rulers, the elders, and the teachers of the law commanded them to cease their teaching in the name of Jesus. So, the apostles were released—but with a stern warning.

They returned to their followers and everyone raised their voices in prayer. This was the immediate reaction to a time of turmoil and release. This too should be our response to the opposition and pitfalls that occur in our lives. Contemplate how the believers prayed and model our prayers on theirs.

Firstly, they fill their minds with thoughts of the King of kings, "a ruler of unchallengeable power."[2] They praise this mighty God who is the Creator of all:

> *"Sovereign Lord," they said, "you made the heavens and the earth and the sea, and everything in them. You spoke by the Holy Spirit through the mouth of your servant, our father David: Why do the nations rage and the peoples plot in vain? The kings of the earth rise up and the rulers band together against the Lord and against his Anointed One."* Acts 4:24b–26 (NIV)

Their words are confirming the coming of the Messiah throughout the Hebrew scriptures while nations raged against him. This very God who created all things, and revealed himself through David, is also the God of history:

> *Indeed Herod and Pontius Pilate met together with the Gentiles and the people of Israel in this city to conspire against your holy servant Jesus, whom you anointed. They did what your power and will had decided beforehand should happen.* 27–28 (NIV)

---

1. Stott, *The Message of Acts*, 97.
2. Stott, *The Message of Acts*, 99.

Only then do the believers bring their petitions before God—firstly, "Consider their threats" secondly, "Enable your servants to speak your word with great boldness" thirdly, "Stretch out your hand to heal and perform miraculous signs and wonders through the name of your holy servant Jesus." 29–30 (NIV) They approach a holy God in praise and humility; they plead for protection for the fledging church amongst great opposition; and, finally, ask for the strength and courage to carry out the work of the gospel including the ability to perform signs and wonders to confirm the message of Jesus and his divine mission.

In our prayers let us first praise our great and wondrous God and give him the royal homage that is due. This confirms our belief that he is able to answer all our needs. Then bring our requests to the throne and pray for fortitude and strength to rest in his peace and consolation. Pray with others; be united; be bold.

> *After they prayed, the place where they were meeting was shaken. And they were filled with the Holy Spirit and spoke the word of God boldly.* Acts 4:31 (NIV)

This earthly reaction illustrated God's response—they were renewed by the Holy Spirit to go out and preach the salvation of the Cross.

Epistle 81

In James 4:8 we read: "Come near to God and he will come near to you." (NIV). In John 15:4 (NIV) Jesus says: "Remain in me, as I also remain in you. No branch can bear fruit by itself; it must remain in the vine. Neither can you bear fruit unless you remain in me."

What more do we need? Jesus provides us with the blessings, the joys, the courage, and the faithful support, when we come to him and when we stay with him. Did we not find this when we first turned to him? Is it the case now that we still experience failed expectations, disappointment with others, turmoil, and sadness? Do you wonder why the brightness and safety is no longer there? Andrew Murray, a prolific Christian writer at the turn of the twentieth century, says: "The answer us very simple. You wandered from him. The blessings he bestows are all connected with his 'Come unto me,' and are only to be enjoyed in close fellowship with him. You either did not fully understand, or did not rightly remember, that the call meant, '*Come to me and stay with me.*'"[1]

When we come to God, we find rest. The rest of forgiveness and acceptance as his loved ones; and, the rest for our souls when we fully become his in our daily walk—staying with him; abiding in him. We can learn from him constantly in the reading of his Word "we should meditate on its meaning, until the understanding, that gate to the heart, opens to apprehend something of what it offers and expects."[2] We need to constantly renew our spirits by continually praying for this wonderful timeless rest. Close our ears to the distractions of the world and find that peace that passes all understanding. How we pray and what is in our hearts that leads us to prayer, must be the gentleness and humility of the precious Son who gives us our rest.

---

1. Murray, *Andrew Murray on Prayer*, 17.
2. Murray, *Andrew Murray on Prayer*, 19.

Vines and vineyards were common motifs in ancient religions. In the Old Testament the vine was a common symbol for Israel, the covenant people of God. In Isaiah 5:1–4 we have the beginning of the Song of the Vineyard which exposes the disobedience and unfaithfulness of the Israelites:

> *I will sing for the one I love a song about his vineyard:*
> *My loved one had a vineyard on a fertile hillside.*
> *He dug it up and cleared it of stones and planted it with the choicest vines.*
> *He built a watchtower in it and cut out a winepress as well.*
> *Then he looked for a crop of good grapes, but it yielded only bad fruit.*
> *Now you dwellers in Jerusalem and people of Judah, judge between me and my vineyard.*
> *What more could have been done for my vineyard than I have done for it?*
> *When I look for good grapes, why did it yield only bad?* (NIV)

Vineyards also feature in all synoptic gospels but none there concentrate on the vine itself. John's gospel presents the vine as the important motif. And this vine does not produce bad fruit because Jesus himself is the vine and God is the gardener who continually prunes the vine:

> *I am the true vine and my Father is the gardener. He cuts off every branch in me that bears no fruit, while every branch that does bear fruit he prunes so that it will be even more fruitful. You are already clean because of the word I have spoken to you.* John 15:1–3 (NIV)

The reading continues with the commandment
to remain in him!

When we think of the vineyard in the Old Testament as the people of Israel and see the vine in the New Testament as Jesus the Messiah, we can turn to a foreshadowing of this in Psalm 80. 7–8, 14–17:

> *Restore us, God Almighty; make your face shine on us,*
> *that we may be saved.*
> *You translated a vine from Egypt; you drove out the nations and planted it . . .*
> *Return to us, God Almighty! Look down from heaven and see!*
> *Watch over this vine, the root your right hand has planted,*
> *the son you have raised up for yourself.*
> *Your vine is cut down, it is burned with fire; at your rebuke your people perish.*

> *Let your hand rest on the man at your right hand,*
> *the son of man you have raised up for yourself.* (NIV)

Jesus, the son who is seated on the right hand of the Father, is the true vine; his followers are the branches and they derive their life from the vine and produce good fruit. The Gardener disciplines when he prunes and cuts off the dead wood. Pruning brings on stronger growth on the vine. We the followers must persevere in our belief. But we must be always aware that no branch has life in itself. We must remain in him if we are to bear fruit! Jesus is clear that no-one can bear fruit by itself—the branch *must* remain on the vine. Thus, we know that we cannot bring forth fruit unless we open our hearts to the Holy Spirit and faithfully pray—dependent on Christ alone. Ponder deeply that, because of Christ's momentous sacrifice, we have become part of the vine. "Believers, meditate on this, until your soul bows to worship in the presence of the mystery of the perfect union between Christ and the believer."[3]

"Do we not remember seasons of labour and trial in which we received such special strength that we wondered at ourselves? In the midst of danger we were calm, under bereavement we were resigned, in slander we were self-contained, and in sickness we were patient."[4] This was because we remained in him; remained in perfect union with him through the Holy Spirit.

---

3. Murray, *Andrew Murray on Prayer*, 30.
4. Spurgeon, *The Cheque Book of the Bank of Faith*, 5.

Epistle 82

We are now in the time of Advent—the season of expectant waiting and preparation for both the celebration of the birth of Christ at Christmas and the return of Christ at the Second Coming. All through the Old Testament, the people were yearning for the coming of a Messiah promised hundreds of years before—what ecstasy it would be when that promise was fulfilled! In the fourth and fifth century in Spain and Gaul, Advent was a period of preparation for the baptism of new Christians at the January feast of Epiphany—encompassing the celebration of the incarnation represented by the visit of the Magi to the baby Jesus; his baptism in the Jordan River; and, his first miracle at the wedding at Cana. In this season of preparation Christians would spend forty days in penance, prayer, and fasting. By the sixth century Roman Christians had tied Advent to the coming of Christ both at Bethlehem and in the Last Days.

How different Advent is today. Only some denominations recognize this celebration in their liturgy and practice! Sadly, the coming of Christmas occurs in the retail world long before Advent but we know that during this time much in this world does not even mention the birth of Jesus. There are very few nativity scenes these days and, when there are, would many children understand what they represented? Jolly songs about Father Christmas take precedence over carols. But when we anticipate the coming of Jesus at Advent and experience the joy of his birth at Christmas, we must also contemplate the glory of his Second Coming. Probably Dietrich Bonhoeffer was correct when he said: "There are only two places where the powerful and great in this world lose their courage, tremble in the depths of their souls, and become truly afraid. These are the manger and the cross of Christ."[1]

---

1. Bonhoeffer, *God Is in the Manger*, 26.

When David became King over Israel, the LORD God said: "You will shepherd my people Israel, and you will become their ruler." 2 Samuel 5:2b (NIV)

In Matthew 2:6 we read: "But you, Bethlehem, in the land of Judah, are by no means least amongst the rulers of Judah; for out of you will come a ruler who will shepherd my people Israel." (NIV) From the David, the shepherd of the Old Testament, will come Jesus, the Shepherd of the New Testament. Descended from the line of David comes the long-awaited Messiah, born in David's city, Bethlehem. David's vision of building a magnificent temple for the LORD God, will be fulfilled by a heavenly son. The central sanctuary will be Jesus himself.

For: "In those days and at that time I will make a righteous Branch sprout from David's line; he will do what is just and right in the land. In those days Judah will be saved and Jerusalem will live in safety. This is the name by which it will be called: The LORD Our Righteous Savior!" Jeremiah 33:14–16 (NIV)

An advent is a coming into place; into view; or, into being—an arrival. And what a wondrous arrival is the birth of Jesus, our Savior, in the nondescript village of Bethlehem. For thousands of years this Savior had been anticipated and now he arrives quite differently from that which was expected.

Each week of our Advent period should be a building of great anticipation for the fulfillment of God's loving plan for our redemption and restoration.

During the days we are observing Advent, Judaism is commemorating Hanukkah, which is an eight-day celebration also called the Festival of Lights. It is an acknowledgment of the victory of a small group of Jewish rebels, led by Judas Maccabee and his brothers, over the armies of Syria in 165 BC. As a result of this action the Temple in Jerusalem was liberated and rededicated. However, the Maccabees, having just returned from the battlefield, were deemed impure and therefore could not make the pure oil required to light the Menorah until they underwent seven days of ritual purification. One cruse of pure oil was found. There was only enough oil to light a lamp for one day but miraculously this amount lasted for eight days until the warriors were purified. In Leviticus 24:1–3 we read:

> The LORD said to Moses, "Command the Israelites to bring you clear oil of pressed olives for the light so that the lamps may be kept burning continually. Outside the curtain that shields the ark of the

> *covenant law in the tent of the meeting, Aaron is to tend the lamps before the LORD from evening till morning, continually. This is to be a lasting ordinance for the generations to come."* (NIV)

The candles of the Hanukkah today celebrate the miracle of the lasting pure oil. But the light dispensed by these candles cannot ever compete with the light of that glorious star in the sky at Bethlehem which we celebrate when Advent culminates in the birth of the Messiah.

Here is the Collect for the first Sunday in Advent found in one of the early editions of the Book of Common Prayer with the added note: This Collect is to be repeated every day until Christmas Eve. Will this not build your anticipation?

> Almighty God, give us grace that we may cast away the works of darkness, and put upon us the armour of light, now in the time of this mortal life, in which thy Son Jesus Christ came to visit us in great humility; that in the last day, when he shall come again in his glorious Majesty to judge both the quick and the dead, we may rise to the life immortal, through him who liveth and reigneth with thee and the Holy Ghost, now and ever. *Amen* [2]

---

2. Church of England. *The Book of Common Prayer*, ca1863.

Epistle 83

The conception of the baby Jesus came about by miraculous means. Consequently, it is a scenario that is often discarded by atheists and agnostics who are always ready to maintain the impossibility of a virgin birth and any other of the miracles of Jesus, the son of Mary and the Son of God. Even so-called Christians pick and choose what they are prepared to believe! Then there are the many traditions about Mary that abound in narratives from the second century onwards—stories that have no established proof.

The first two chapters of Luke give us the most detailed description of the conception and subsequent birth of Jesus. In the midst of this, we also have the story of Elizabeth and Zechariah who have been granted the gift of a child in their old age—this child is to be John the Baptist; the voice in the wilderness who announces the coming of the Messiah. Mary is yet to be married but is betrothed to Joseph who is descended from the line of David. The angel Gabriel announces to Mary that she is to be the mother of a son she is to call Jesus.

> "How will this be," Mary asked the angel, "since I am a virgin?" The angel answered, "The Holy Spirit will come on you, and the power of the Most High will overshadow you. So the holy one to be born will be called the Son of God." Luke 1:34–35 (NIV)

A miraculous event—yet that one word "overshadow" is wondrous! When Mary arrives to visit with the aged Elizabeth the child in Elizabeth's womb quickened. "Blessed is she who has believed that the Lord would fulfill his promises to her!" Luke 1:45 (NIV) For Mary, faced with the shame of what would be viewed in her society as the humiliation of an illegitimate birth, submits to God. A very young virgin finds protection and empowerment and, in her vulnerability, she finds the courage to joyously praise her God:

> *My soul glorifies the Lord and my spirit rejoices in God my Savior,*
> *for he has been mindful of the humble state of his servant.*
> *From now on all generations will call me blessed,*
> *for the Mighty One has done great things for me—holy is his name.*
> *His mercy extends to those who fear him, from generation to generation.*
> *He has performed mighty deeds with his arm;*
> *he has scattered those who are proud in their inmost thoughts.*
> *He has brought down rulers from their thrones but has lifted up the humble.*
> *He has filled the hungry with good things but has sent the rich away empty.*
> *He has helped his servant Israel, remembering to be merciful to Abraham*
> *and his descendants forever, just as he promised our ancestors. Luke 1:46-55*
> *(NIV)*

> The song is modelled, in structure and expression, upon the Song of Hannah in 1 Samuel 2:1–10 with numerous reminiscences of the Psalms and other OT poetry. The Magnificat is a beautiful summary of the OT hope of God's redemption of his people, as it is brought to concrete realization in the Incarnation, in the womb of God's handmaiden of "low estate." [1]

Despite having exultant moments, it is full of the piety of Mary and her gratitude for the coming fulfillment of God's promises to Israel.

When we are looking to our life of prayer, how great is the feeling and expression in this glorious song of praise. Coming before our God with thanks for our blessings and his faithful care, is the greatest way to begin prayer.

> I pray that prayer would follow praise, and praise grow into prayer. That there may be a movement to magnify and adore the riches of your grace. That the name of Jesus may be always in my mouth—from that one blessed source, that Jesus lives in my heart, and rules, and reigns, and is formed there in the hope of glory . . . I will praise you every day; morning by morning will I praise your name, and night by night testify to your faithfulness.[2]

It is difficult to imagine the thoughts of a virgin being chosen by God for this holy commission. But we can be assured that God does not give his people anything that they cannot do—today God our Father gives *us* the strength and courage for every task *we* face. When Moses

---

1. Buttrick, *The Interpreter's Dictionary of the Bible. Volume 3. K–Q*, 226.
2. Hawker, "Where Praise Grows to Prayer," and "Who Is Our Praise But Jesus" in Elmer. *Piercing Heaven*. 222, 231.

reached the edge of the Promised Land, he summoned Joshua to take the people over the Jordan and said to him—in the presence of all Israel:

> *Be strong and courageous, for you must go with this people into the land that the LORD swore to their ancestors to give them, and you must divide it among them as their inheritance. The LORD himself goes before you and will be with you; he will never leave you nor forsake you. Do not be afraid; do not be discouraged.* Deut 31:7–8 (NIV)

The LORD God was faithful to his chosen people Israel throughout the times of the Old Testament; he was there for his new Elect in the New Testament. He is here for us—now and always. Let us open our hearts to the Holy Spirit and be mightily strengthened, praising the Father in prayer for his love and protection, and pledging our gratitude for the gift of the baby Jesus coming as our Savior.

Epistle 84

Advent—the waiting—is moving onto the Incarnation, the great mystery of it all, and, the promise of redemption. Seven hundred years before the birth of the Christ Isaiah wrote:

> *For to us a child is born, to us a son is given,*
> *and the government will be on his shoulders.*
> *And he will be called Wonderful Counselor, Mighty God,*
> > *Everlasting Father, Prince of Peace.*
> *Of the greatness of his government and peace there will be no end.*
> *He will reign on David's throne and over his kingdom,*
> > *establishing and upholding it with justice and righteousness*
> > > *from that time on and forever.*
> *The zeal of the LORD Almighty will accomplish this.* Isa 9:6–7 (NIV)

On the shoulders of a baby will be the government of the earth. From this child comes the whole theology of the New Testament and the fulfillment of the whole theology of the Old Testament. And who was at the birth of Jesus; who came to see the holy miracle? The first were the poor and the lowly—the shepherds on the hills who, overcome with fear at the proclamation of the host of angels, hurried with amazement to the city to find the manger. There were no powerful, rich, or well-educated people there that night. Thus, we must reflect in humility and wonder at the coming of the Promised One in the most humbling of circumstances and we must keep that humility and wonder in the year ahead. How many of us are enchanted with the child in the manger but how many of us outgrow the Jesus story without really understanding the depth and the mystery of it all. Dietrich Bonhoeffer contended that: "If there was no mystery in his miracles and healing Jesus would not be God. We cannot understand fully but his coming in the flesh means he can be touched: he is real!"[1] We cannot solve the enigma of his Lordship

---

1. Bonhoeffer, *God Is in the Manger*, 64.

by human experience and wisdom. We can only touch the surface. Revisit the manger—this child has our eternal life in his hands and this is the real mystery.

> *The Word became flesh and made his dwelling among us. We have seen his glory, the glory of the one and only Son, who came from the Father, full of grace and truth.* John 1:14 (NIV)

> *God sent his Son, born of a woman, born under law, to redeem those under law, that we might receive adoption as children. And, because you are his children, God sent the Spirit of his Son into our hearts, the Spirit who calls out, "Abba, Father." So you are no longer a slave, but God's child; and since you are his child, God has made you also an heir.* Gal 4:4b–7 (NIV)

The Lord of the Ages is God
The turning point of the Ages is Christ
The right spirit of the Ages is the Holy Spirit

As we take the hope, the peace, and the joy of the coming of Jesus into the new year may we recognize the full worth of our undeserved gifts. The Sovereign LORD "wakens me morning by morning, wakens my ear to listen like one being instructed." Isaiah 50:4b (NIV) Let us pledge our first word in the morning to our Father. "God wants to open the heart before it opens itself to the world; before the ear hears the innumerable voices of the day, the early hours are the time to hear the voice of the Creator and Redeemer. God made the stillness of the early morning for himself. It ought to belong to God."[2] Honor and receive this silence; learn to have a listening silence. It will bring clarity—a bringing together with no sorrow or fear, just quietness and security. If prayer is the first priority of the day, our day ahead will be full of renewed hope and joy. It will give us a confident strength knowing that God is leading us in every step of the minutes and the hours. Even if we are faced with a day of trouble or stress and we are unable to change the circumstances in our own strength, we can dedicate the break of day to him: "In the morning, LORD, you hear my voice; in the morning I lay my requests before you and wait expectantly." Psalm 5:3 (NIV) We can do this because, "I, by your great love, can come into your house; in reverence I bow down

---

2. Bonhoeffer, *God Is in the Manger*, 88.

toward your holy temple. Lead me, LORD, in your righteousness because of my enemies—make your way straight before me". 7–8 (NIV)

Turning to slumber each night in his presence we can continue with assurance:

> *I will praise the LORD, who counsels me; even at night my heart*
>   *instructs me.*
> *I keep my eyes always on the LORD.*
> *With him at my right hand, I will not be shaken.*
> *Therefore my heart is glad and my tongue rejoices;*
> *my body also will rest secure*
> *because you will not abandon me to the realm of the dead,*
> *nor will you let your faithful one see decay.*
> *You make known to me the path of life;*
> *you will fill me with joy in your presence,*
> *with eternal pleasures at your right hand.* Ps 16:7–11 (NIV)

Pray morning and night with surety because of the coming
of a holy baby!

Epistle 85

Over the next three weeks, during which we are embracing a new year, the Epistles will be in recess, but Perpetua leaves you with a three-part Epistle this week to tide you over! The past year has been one full of unforeseen events. With the spread of COVID we have been experiencing loneliness and anxiety whilst still being surrounded by the ongoing conflicts and traumas of our present-day world. With prayer we have been able to take our fears to our wonderful Father in Heaven and find strength and courage to persevere. Our prayer life can enlighten our hearts, enrich our souls, and bring wisdom to our minds. With quiet study of the hearts, souls, and minds, of people in the Bible, we can find an immense depth of feeling and a vast well of encouragement.

Week 1 In the Old Testament, David was God's anointed King. But for much of his life he was a fugitive, firstly from the jealous King Saul and secondly, from his power-hungry son, Absalom. The great aspect of this is that David tells us about his experiences in his own words. We do not just have the engrossing narrative in 1 and 2 Samuel—we also know how the man himself felt when he lived in this narrative. The following is a list of readings from the Books Samuel enlightened by David's own words in the Psalms.

1 Samuel 19:11-17   *Psalm 59*
   When Saul sent men to watch David's house in order to kill him
1 Samuel 21:10-11   *Psalm 56*
   When the Philistines had seized David in Gath
1 Samuel 21:10-15   *Psalm 34*
   Feigning insanity before Achish who drove him away and he left
1 Samuel 22:6-23   *Psalm 52*
   When Doeg the Edomite told Saul "David has gone to Ahimelek"

1 Samuel 23:26-29   *Psalm 18*
    David sang to the LORD the words of this song when the LORD delivered him from the hand of his enemies and from the hand of Saul
1 Samuel 24:1-7   *Psalm 57* and *Psalm 142*
    When he had fled from Saul into the cave
1 Samuel 30:6
2 Samuel 15:30   *Psalm 69*
    A cry of distress when feeling overcome by his enemies
2 Samuel 8:13-14   *Psalm 60*
    When he fought Aram Naharaim and Aram Zobah and when Joab returned and struck down 12,000 Edomites in the Valley of Salt
    See also *1 Chronicles 18:12* where the account varies slightly.
2 Samuel 12:1-27   *Psalm 51*
    When the prophet Nathan came to him after David had committed adultery with Bathsheba
2 Samuel 16:5-12   *Psalm 7*
    Concerning Cush, a Benjamite—this is probably Shimei, a follower of Saul, who cursed David and pelted him with stones
2 Samuel 17:9a   *Psalm 3*
    When David was hiding in a cave when fleeing from Absalom
We also have three Psalms *concerning* David the Warrior
    Psalm 20   Praying for protection in the impending battle
    Psalm 21   Great rejoicing after the battle
    Psalm 144   Praise to the LORD who gives victory to the king
A more detailed Song of Praise from David is in *2 Samuel 22:1-51*

Week 2 If God came to you and said: "Ask for whatever you want me to give you," what do you think you would reply? We are not talking about the day-to-day worries we want solved, but specifically about what treasure in the world would we really love to have? This is the question the LORD God asked Solomon when he became King of Israel 1 Kings 3:5b Solomon replied: "give your servant a discerning heart to govern your people and to distinguish between right and wrong." 3:9 (NIV) Because Solomon asked for wisdom God was pleased—he not only granted him wisdom but also gave him gifts he did not ask for—great wealth, honor among kings, and a long life.

The Book of Proverbs, a guide for our God-fearing life, abounds with the wisdom of Solomon. Chapters 1-24 are listed under Solomon's authorship whilst Chapters 25-29 are more proverbs of Solomon, copied by the men of Hezekiah, the King of Judah. The remainder are termed *Sayings of the Wise* and *Further Sayings of the Wise*. Proverbs in modern conversations are a congenial way of getting a point across. Sometimes they can be contradictory, for example—"Look before you leap," which contrasts with "He who hesitates is lost"! A similar confusion can arise with Old Testament proverb—"Do not answer a fool according to his folly, or you will be like him yourself." Proverbs 26:4 (NIV) followed by "Answer a fool according to his folly, or he will be wise in his own eyes." 26:5 (NIV) These are not actually contradictory! We have to read and absorb proverbs of wisdom carefully and we also need to have the wisdom to know in which situations we apply each! They will always carry wisdom if used with the appropriate level of wisdom!

Of course, the Proverbs we read for instruction must be written by one who is already wise. We know that Solomon's wisdom was God-given, thus his proverbs are reliable for all generations. The words of Jesus are authoritative. Paul writes for the people of Laodecia:

> *My goal is that they may be encouraged in heart and united in love,*
> *so that they may have the full riches of complete understanding,*
> *in order that they may know the mystery of God, namely Christ,*
> *in whom are hidden all the treasures of wisdom and knowledge.*
> Col 2:2–3 (NIV)

Even with our limited gifts we can test proverbs to see if they appear false—if not by the author, then by the content. Is the content biblical for example; does it agree with similar passages? We often hear quoted— "spare the rod and spoil the child." Some people interpret this as we must be spared from using the rod and rather spoil the child with gifts and unquestioned freedom. In Psalm 23:4b the LORD's rod (of loving discipline) and his staff (of support and protection) comfort us. This proverb is not an excuse for child abuse but for the sensibility of setting boundaries for the young so that they will grow to adulthood in security.

Let us consider some biblical proverbs to guide us through the year ahead:

Chapters 2–3: Moral Benefits of Wisdom
Chapter 4: Wisdom is Supreme
Chapter 8: Wisdom's Appeal

There are some quirky proverbs—"He who winks with his eye is plotting perversity; he who purses his lips is bent on evil." 16:30 (NIV)

> *And some that, on the surface, beggar belief—"Gray hair is a crown of splendor; it is attained in the way of righteousness." 16:31 (NIV)*
>
> *And ones that are tantalizing to think about—"The words of the mouth are deep waters, but the fountain of wisdom is a rushing stream." 18:4 (NIV)*
>
> *Or distressing to think about—"The words of a gossip are like choice morsels; they go down to the inmost parts." 18:8 (NIV)*

Week 3 When we come to the New Testament, we find a writer who really opens up his deepest feelings when he speaks to the new followers of Christ. He also greets and prays for his fellow workers illustrating how well he knows each one of them. Paul concentrates on teaching a theology of Jesus and his work of redemption and, in so doing, can sometimes appear to be unconcerned with the stories of the life of Jesus. "Some people find Paul lacking in comparison with the Master; others simply find Paul distasteful, offensive, oppressive, exclusive, confusing, arrogant, or just plain wrong."[1] But a concentration on Paul's personal excerpts exposes a deeply loving man dedicated to guiding the new Christian (and us) on the right path to salvation.

In 2 Corinthians 11 Paul is warning the people of Corinth about false prophets who will lead them astray. By regaling his sufferings in v.23–33—imprisonment, shipwrecks, floggings, lashings, beatings, stoning, danger everywhere and from every race and creed, plus hunger and thirst, Paul is crying out in distress at the foolishness of the people in failing to keep the faith. They must be convinced about his authority to preach the gospel when they understand what cruel depths he has encountered to persevere with his ministry. He talks also about his "thorn in the flesh," which has been sent to torment him further. Yet he can say: ". . . for Christ's sake, I delight in weaknesses, in insults, in hardships, in persecutions, in difficulties. For when I am weak, then I am strong." 2 Corinthians 12:10 (NIV) When we read this section of Paul's letters we cannot ignore his selfless dedication to his Savior—a dedication he wants for all of us.

Not only do we have the details of his persecutions in the above verses but we also read how, at times, he feels deserted by fellow workers—specifically those he mentions by name and whom we have looked at in a previous epistle. 2 Timothy 4:9–18 Some had just left; some had

---

1. Kirk, *Jesus Have I Loved, but Paul?* 3.

failed to defend him; some had actually done him harm. Nevertheless, he is convinced, "The Lord will rescue me from every evil attack and will bring me safely to his heavenly kingdom. To him be the glory for ever and ever." 2 Timothy 4:18 (NIV) There are also those whom he sought but did not find, for example, when he went to preach in Troas and Titus was not there as he expected! 2 Corinthians 2:12; and, those who loved and followed him in the past but now seem to have turned away to some new cult, "My dear children, for whom I am again in the pains of childbirth until Christ is formed in you, how I wish I could be with you and change my tone, because I am perplexed about you." Galatians 4:19–20 (NIV) He discovers some who are arguing amongst themselves; who are his fellow workers and "whose names are in the book of life." Philippians 4:3b (NIV)

At the beginning or end of each of his letters Paul sends personal greetings and support for those who work with him in the Gospel. These greetings are full of love and concern. Romans 16 is the most extensive of these lists. Here Paul includes warnings about deceivers and finishes with the most wonderful benediction—the words of which we could joyfully embrace to finish our prayers to our heavenly Father at the close of each day!

> *Now to him who is able to establish you in accordance with my gospel, the message I proclaim about Jesus Christ, in keeping with the revelation of the mystery hidden for long ages past, but now revealed and made known through the prophetic writings by the command of the eternal God, so that all the Gentiles might come to the obedience that comes from faith—to the only wise God be glory forever through Jesus Christ! Amen. Rom 16:25–27 (NIV)*

Epistle 86

In Epistle 1 from Perpetua a suggested pattern for a Prayer Life was laid out. Hopefully some may have found this helpful and it has led to a model of daily prayer with our Father God. It did involve a set of physical and mental prerequisites. However, every individual needs to find the way that works most effectively. Here are the suggestions from Epistle 1.

- Set a time each day or on set days or nights that suits.
- Put a notice on your front door—"Please do not knock or ring at this time,"
- or something similar.
- If you are a business man or woman who is constantly engaged in meetings, inform your colleagues you are not available at this prescribed time. Make your prayer time as regular as your business meetings.
- Inform your family and friends you cannot be in touch at certain times.
- Turn your phone and computer onto silent.
- Turn off the radio and the television.
- Close off any other noise in your home or office.
- Set a timer (perhaps on the oven)—starting with 10 minutes.
- Choose the most comfortable chair you have.
- Spend the first five minutes thinking about the weekly happenings.
- Engage your heart and your mind.
- Spend the next five minutes talking to God.

Eventually you will find it easier to prepare yourself for prayer. With constant application you will want to spend more time thinking and praying. It will often progress into a real sense of anticipation of this closeted prayer time and your eyes and ears will be opened so that your heart will engage with the Spirit.

No doubt these procedures may not appeal or even work for you. With that in mind, in this Epistle, another attractive list of prayer practices appears for you to contemplate. These were devised by Peter and Judy Taylor for a Prayer Retreat entitled: *Praying With Paul*, which was held in October 2021, and the suggestions are printed here with their permission.

Ten Practical Ideas for Better Intercessory Prayer

Lessen interruptions by choosing a specific quiet time and place to pray.

1. Structure your prayer time. Keep lists or a prayer diary. Record God's answers if you sense them.
2. Set achievable goals: Instead of planning to pray for two hours, plan to pray five times today.
3. In addition, create triggers for prayer throughout the day, for example, whenever you start your car, put on your shoes, have a cup of coffee, clean your teeth, see a red light. Pray for someone in particular.
4. Create reminders that you cannot avoid, for example, put *Galatians 5:22–23* on the door of the refrigerator. Pray for one or more of the fruits of the Spirit for someone every time you open the refrigerator.
5. Pray sentence prayers for people as you meet them—for the sender of emails as you receive them, for Christians in each school or church you pass on the way to work, for the person who serves you at the supermarket, or makes the coffee you pick up on the way to work. Pray for your friends or family every time you check their text messages or Facebook or Instagram posts.
6. Pray for the work of the gospel in countries which are in the television news, for example, while you listen to the item about hurricane damage in Haiti, pray at the time for the people affected. If you put it off until later you may forget.

7. Build prayer into what is already in your schedule. Plan to pray in your car on the way to work. Pray as you walk, for example, from this corner to the next, or for the people at the dog park as you walk past. On the way home from dropping a child at school, pray for the families you met at the school gate. Pray for your minister and everyone involved in the Services as you drive to church.
8. Memorize prayers from the Bible and pray them. Psalms are especially good for this.
9. Try breathing prayers. Breathe in and out deeply and pray simple prayers as you inhale and exhale, for example, take the names of each of your family members and pray their name as you inhale and one phrase for them as you breathe out—I pray for Lucia. May she grow to love you!

> May your prayer life grow and deepen as you faithfully follow the Father, the Son, and the Holy Spirit. May you continually learn from the Word and daily experience true and enriching fellowship with other Christians on your earthly pilgrimage.

Epistle 87

Perhaps you feel overwhelmed with all the instructions for establishing and continuing a strong prayer life with God our Father. You may think that you have tried all the suggestions on many lists but still do not feel delivered from the frustration of prayerlessness! Is it a prize never to be attained? Is Paul's exhortation in 1 Thessalonians 5:17 "Pray continually" (NIV) impossible to follow? However—is there no strong desire; is there no real urgency?

In his sacrificial death Christ cleansed us from all sin. He delivered us from a life clinging to the Law of the Old Testament to a life living in the Spirit of the New Testament. Everything we have and everything we achieve is given to us by grace. We don't have to strive to gain all the blessings of life; they are given to us in love. We should step down from the world and hear Jesus say to us:

> *Just as I will cleanse you from all other sins, so also will I deliver you from the sin of prayerlessness—only do not seek the victory in your own strength. Bow before me as one who expects everything from his Savior. Let your soul keep silence before me, however sad you feel your state to be. Be assured of this—I will teach you how to pray.*[1]

Andrew Murray, who lived from 1828–1917, ministered as both a pastor and author in the towns and villages of South Africa. His faith was a testimony to his solid foundation in a living Savior amidst all the turmoil and tragedy of that country in those turbulent times. He commented on prayer: "What folly to think that all other blessings must come from Him, but that prayer, on which everything else depends, must be obtained by personal effort!"[2] To him Jesus was constantly at our side—responsible

---

1. Murray, *Andrew Murray on Prayer*, 165.
2. Murray, *Andrew Murray on Prayer*, 165.

for teaching us how to approach the Father. It is only through Jesus that we can do this. We know that he revealed this vital truth to his disciples: "I am the way and the truth and the life. No-one comes to the Father except through me. If you really know me, you would know my Father as well. From now on, you do know him and have seen him." John 14:6–7 (NIV)

> Wait upon him, glorify him, abide with him.
>
> We do not have to struggle—we just need to turn our emptiness over to our Savior. We rest in his strength; in his peace, and; in his grace. We open our whole beings to receive his Spirit to dwell in our hearts and our minds.

Our prayer life has to be an integral part of our whole Christian life. And, as Christians, we are different from the world around us. We live in the world but must not be of the world. We have to live differently, to live almost as a stranger to the world. That takes courage—the courage to see everything around us through eyes and hearts dedicated to God. We must turn away from the darkness of ignorance, of evil, and of sin, and live in the light that Jesus shines into each one of us. This light must become a continual distinguishing characteristic for all those who stumble in the darkness—for those who need and value encouragement and kindness. Let us always be alert to the world but leading our lives with souls filled with the Spirit no matter how mundane our surroundings may be or how worryingly our troubles may develop.

We look back at Paul's words telling us to pray continually. Nicky Gumbel expounds this section of 1 Thessalonians 5:17–28 in the following way: "You are a citizen of a different world. You have to learn a new language. What Paul describes here is effectively the grammar of a new language: 'Be joyful always; pray continually; give thanks in all circumstances.' Prayer should be like breathing—something we do continually, but often unconsciously. Instead of always complaining 'give thanks in all circumstances'—expressing your thanks to God and other people—in little things as well as big things. 'Do not put out the Spirit's fire; do not treat prophecies with contempt. Test everything. Hold on to the good. Avoid every kind of evil.' All this can seem a very daunting prospect. But you are not on your own. Paul prays, 'May God himself, the God of peace, sanctify you through and through' and he finishes on a resounding note of hope and help—'He who calls you is faithful, and he will do it.'"[3]

Remember, in your prayerlessness, bring God into your heart and bow down before the great Redeemer. Listen in silence. When you speak know that God always hears his people when they really mean what they are praying.

For those who had been cleansed from sin in the days of the prophet Zechariah God declared:

> *They will call on my name and I will answer them;*
> *I will say, "They are my people,"*
> *and they will say, "The LORD is our God." Zech 13:9b (NIV)*

However, in the times before-hand when the people were led to hear the words of the LORD through his prophet Zechariah:

> . . . *they refused to pay attention, stubbornly they turned their backs and covered their ears. They made their hearts as hard as flint and would not listen to the law or to the words that the LORD Almighty had sent by his Spirit through the earlier prophets. So the LORD Almighty was very angry.*
>
> *"When I called, they did not listen, so when they called, I would not listen," says the LORD Almighty. Zech 7:11–13 (NIV)*

Approach the LORD your God in the sanctity of the cross.

---

3. Gumbel, *The Bible in One Year*, 605.

Epistle 88

Sometimes, when we sing hymns, psalms, and other spiritual songs, we don't really register with the meaning of certain phrases. In the hymn "Take my life and let it be," the third verse is worded as follows:

> Take my motives and my will,
> all your purpose to fulfil;
> take my heart—it is your own,
> it shall be Your royal throne.[1]

As in readings of Scripture, hymns convey a great depth of meaning—an extent of intensity; an abundance; a completeness. God is in the soaring heights of the heavens; he is in the unfathomable depths of the earth. He is so great he can be a mystery to mere mortals. How can we comprehend the content here? How can our hearts be royal thrones for a God who is so seemingly unattainable?

The verse in this hymn is challenging us to search our hearts and examine who—or what—actually occupies it. Who sits on the central seat of our being?

Can we say with confidence?

> *I seek you with all my heart; do not let me stray from your commands. I have hidden your word in my heart that I might not sin against you.* Ps 119:10–11 (NIV)

Can we claim with authority that the Word is in our hearts?

> *As water reflects a face, so one's life reflects the heart.* Prov 27:19 (NIV)

Are we at the stage when we can re-iterate Paul's words?

---

1. P. C. A., *Rejoice!*, 477.

> *For it is with your heart that you believe and are justified, and it is with your mouth that you profess your faith and are saved.* Rom 10:10 (NIV)

Do we acknowledge that the Word is mighty in its strength?

> *For the word of God is living and active. Sharper than any double-edged sword, it penetrates even to dividing soul and spirit, joints and marrow; it judges the thoughts and attitudes of the heart. Nothing in all creation is hidden from God's sight. Everything is uncovered and laid bare before the eyes of him to whom we must give account.* Heb 4:12–13 (NIV)

Will our hearts suffer a reckoning?

Nothing must inhabit our souls—our hearts—except the Triune God. In this present world there are many other competing gods and beliefs. But our God has revealed himself as the only true God: Father, Son, and Holy Spirit. The word trinity in relation to the Godhead may not be implicitly stated in the Bible but it is quite obvious that it is the only truth—from the actions of God with his people Israel in the Old Testament; the messages of God's appointed prophets to a disobedient nation; the coming of the Messiah in fulfillment of all the former promises; the life, teaching, and sacrifice of Jesus; and, the sending of his Spirit to earth after he ascended into heaven to sit on the right side of God. Even in the creation Jesus and the Spirit are present—hovering over the waters in Genesis and in the active Word of John's Gospel—both with God in the beginning.

The Apostles' Creed and the Nicene Creed are strong in the foundational truths of the Bible. They clearly ascertain a belief in a Triune God. Their words are powerful and significant, yet fundamental. They speak of the intimate nature of our faith. Plus, they stand alone. At the same time, they are resolute—declaring that we will remain firm in the challenges of this earthly life. With our affirmation we must never desert its tenets. When we stand to recite these Creeds, we must savor every word; take every premise into our hearts; deepen our belief in the content; and seek to invigorate our earthly lives! The question of what we believe is daunting, but it is a question that we must answer. Nowhere is there a more important requirement for our souls.

In Isaiah, Ezekiel, and the *Revelation to John*, the throne of God is depicted as glorious and holy, with God in the midst of heavenly beings and accompanied in sound by great songs of praise. Isaiah relates that

God declares that Heaven is his throne and the earth is his footstool. But following this, God asks where will his resting place be? It will be in he or she who is humble and contrite in spirit; the one who trembles in awe and adoration at God's word—in the hearts of such earthly beings. In biblical terms the heart of each man or woman is representative of the soul and spirit of the body. The heart represents the center of life and rules over the whole person emanating to the world the fruits of the spirit. Thus, when we take God into our hearts we establish him on a throne of trust, love, and obedience.

In Westminster Abbey there is a memorial to the actor and playwright, David Garrick, who died in 1779. His memorial shows him standing on the throne of his profession—taking a final bow on the stage. It includes the following words: "Shakespeare and Garrick like twin stars shall shine, and earth radiate with a beam divine." We are yet to see a divine light from this source.

Truly our God is the only one who can radiate a beam divine!

> *LORD, my God, you are very great; you are clothed with splendor and majesty. The LORD wraps himself in light as with a garment; he stretches out the heavens like a tent and lays beams of his upper chambers on their waters. He makes the clouds his chariot and rides on the wings of the wind. He makes winds his messengers, flames of fire his servants.* Ps 104:1–4 (NIV)

Take his radiance into your heart; fill your soul with his promises; believe only in him and he will be your guide even unto death.

Epistle 89

The Reverend Samuel Choi was recently thinking of his Seminary training in Korea when he wrote the following:

> Whenever there would be lots of snow, it would be our job as students to clear the snow after morning prayer. This was part of our training in spirituality. We were reminded to clear our hearts as we cleared the snow away. On summer days, we would pick up sticks and sweep the campus . . . we read that John the Baptist came to prepare a way of the Lord. The call was certainly clear—to repent and turn away from the self-gratifying way of life for the pagans, turn from religiosity to a real relationship with Jesus. The call was to empty hearts in order to be ready for the Kingdom of God.[1]

In last week's Epistle we talked about emptying our hearts so God could be enthroned there. Today, with our hearts ready for the work of the Kingdom, we look at the mandate of Jesus when he said: "Then come, follow me." Luke 18:22 (NIV) But following Jesus does not only mean walking in his steps and enjoying the peace and security we attain when we do this. It involves much more! It involves taking the message of Jesus and his salvation to all the peoples in the world so they too can enjoy all the benefits of salvation.

> *All authority in heaven and on earth has been given to me. Therefore, go and make disciples of all nations, baptizing them in the name of the Father and of the Son and of the Holy Spirit, and teaching them to obey everything I have commanded you. And surely I will be with you always, to the very end of the age.* Matt 28:18–20 (NIV)

---

1. Choi, *Keeping in Touch*, v.3, 2022.

We can fill empty hearts with the words of Jesus and find the strength and purpose to carry out the Great Commission.

Like John the Baptist we must prepare the way. Yes, we can evangelize, but this does not mean we grab someone and force-feed them all the reasons why they should repent and come to Jesus. Sometimes we might only introduce Christ to someone; other times we might accompany them on part of the way; or, we might be there when they take the final step to commitment. It reminds one of the Dr Seuss story about the seven bears climbing out the window to investigate a noise—they go out, in, through, around, above, under—a journey of adventure in sections. But whichever part of the journey we are involved in, we need good preparation—repenting; reading the Word; praying; maturing in faith; and adapting our plan to attract all the many different people we encounter in life.

Throughout history we see the success for people who prepare well and failure for those who do not. When we look at the race for the South Pole between the Briton, Robert Falcon Scott, and the Norwegian, Roald Amundsen, we see completely different approaches to attaining the prize. Amundsen was a driven, meticulous explorer, reared in the snow and cold of his native land. He was an experienced sailor in icy conditions, even attaining a captain's certificate so that there would be no conflict with the captain and the expedition leader when crucial decisions had to be made. He was also an experienced cross-country skier and sledger. Amundsen researched the building of adequate shelters—even igloos—experimented with dog teams, and dressed in furs like the Inuit of the north. Scott, on the other hand, had only been in snow country once before, could not master skis, and dressed in navy-issue woolen clothing. He thought it was cruel to use dogs preferring to use the men to haul sledges irrespective of the fact that these men needed to conserve all their energy for the expedition itself. And those sledges were, in the end, somewhat bereft of vital supplies so that he could include rocks from the Pole area. Scott did take ponies, which struggled fruitlessly in the conditions plus the expedition had some motorized sledges but without a mechanic to maintain them! Nor did he seal his fuel efficiently leading to evaporation of a vital necessity. Amundsen set out for the Pole from a base camp set amidst some dangerous ice formations but as close as possible to the goal. Scott left from a base some ninety-three miles further from the Pole, a position that had been recommended by the librarian of the Royal Geographical Society! Scott was arrogantly confident: "I don't hold that anyone but an Englishman should get to the South Pole."[2]

A similar poor preparation involved the Australian, Douglas Mawson. On a three-man trek, only he survived. The first loss involved one of the trio falling into a crevasse with his sledge—a sledge loaded with the majority of the vital stores instead of the most needed provisions being divided amongst both the sledges—plus the fallen explorer was not wearing widened snow shoes or riding on the sledge, either of which may have successfully spread the weight in the treacherous conditions. The second loss involved the most experienced of the men because his best weather gear was on the lost sledge and Mawson would not allow this man, an expert skier, to immediately leave him to fetch help for them both from the base camp.

In life it is important that we prepare well—it involves our mortal lives. In the Christian life it is far more important that we prepare well—it involves our eternal lives.

We need to prepare our minds—praying that God may reveal a potential structure for studying the Word and the provision of mentors to guide us.
We need to prepare our hearts—praying to God to give us hearts of compassion for the lost and an earnest desire for their salvation
We need to prepare the way—praying to ask God to give us the boldness and wisdom to minster effectively, and for the strength to stay the course.

---

2. Langner, *Scott and Amundsen*, 1.

Epistle 90

This week we are going to have a look at words and their meanings. We find that the meanings of specific words have changed over the centuries sometimes to have quite different connotations. In the 1950s the word "nice" meant "precise." Also, in this present age of political correctness words and terms have been devised to the point of becoming ridiculous, for example, there is a present thought that the use of the term "body bags" should be changed to "transport tubes"? The mind boggles a little. Then there are words that have been adapted from a long-recognized use to mean something entirely different, for example, "marriage"—a biblical word now abused. Let us look at words that denote values and moral rules and see how they vary. Our values from the Old and New Testament have often gone on a wide and winding route throughout history—sometimes discarded; sometimes accepted in a wider meaning. In 1960 when C. S. Lewis wrote *The Four Loves*, he emphasized four different meanings of the word "Love." Lewis explored the nature of love from a Christian and philosophical perspective through thought experiments. The book was devised from a series of radio talks by Lewis and was criticized in some countries for its frankness about sex. But of course, sex does involve love—or—should involve love. How different is our lifestyle today where sex tries to bombard our senses constantly on media and even in conversation; and the sex usually purely involves lust rather than love. First Lewis looks at the situation of God as the source of all love in the aspects of our need-love and our Gift-love. Then, in detail, he looks at the Four Loves—Storge (empathy bond); Philia (friend bond); Eros (romantic love); and, Agape (unconditional sacrificial "God" love). Definitely a book worth reading and studying!

Consider the words used over time to donate virtues and values. The four virtues of the classic Greeks were temperance, prudence, courage (or fortitude), and justice. Roman virtues revolve around spiritual authority, i.e., the sense of one's social standing built up through experience and hard work. Highly regarded were an ease of manner, courtesy, openness, friendliness, mercy, gentleness, and dignity. But sadly, overall, there was a sense of self-worth and personal pride.

Throughout history societies of various nations have developed their own code of morality—or in some cases—immorality pretending to be morality: "a wolf in sheep's clothing"! We see this in Tudor times in the court of Henry VIII. Shrovetide was one of the Christian events that was celebrated with much that was bordering on the exact opposite of the coming of Lent. In 1522 these celebrations were held in Cardinal Wolsey's York Place. A large chamber was decorated as a castle with towers. In the towers were beautiful ladies, each representing a quality of chivalry: "beauty, honour, perseverance, kindness, constancy, bounty, mercy and pity."[1] Mary, the Dowager Queen of France, and the favorite sister of Henry, played beauty; Anne Boleyn was perseverance; and her sister Mary was kindness.

> Opposite these eight women were eight men representing the perfect male virtues: nobleness, amorousness, youth, attendance, loyalty, pleasure, gentleness, and liberty. The eight female virtues were protected from assault by eight members of the royal chapel representing danger, disdain, jealousy, unkindness, scorn, sharp tongue, and off-handedness.[2]

Eventually the male virtues had to attack the castle to rescue the virtuous women. Henry VIII himself led a successful onslaught to rescue his sister. Then they all sat down to feast! It is pertinent, like C. S. Lewis, to study each of these "virtues" to realise some of the implications that evolve.

During the twentieth century the reaction to a prudish Victorian society and the "War to End all Wars" was to indulge in a frenetic world of dancing, drinking, and sexual dissipation. Gradually, throughout this century a movement called the "me generation" grew until now some people have begun to realise the extent of the damage that we have inflicted on themselves and God's creation. But our values appear to continue on man-made solutions.

Where today can we find a list of virtues which are God given and not of human inventiveness? These virtues are the fruit of the Spirit of the triune God.

1. Bryson, *La Reine Blanche*, 205.
2. Bryson, *La Reine Blanche*, 205.

> ... the fruit of the Spirit is love, joy, peace, forbearance, kindness, goodness, faithfulness, gentleness, and self-control. Against such things there is no law. Those who belong to Christ Jesus have crucified the flesh with its passions and desires. Since we live by the Spirit, let us keep in step with the Spirit. Let us not become conceited, provoking and envying each other. Gal 5:22–26 (NIV)

Nicky Gumbel says:

> *Now that the Spirit lives in us, involve him in all your decisions and follow his prompting. If you are thinking, saying, or doing something that makes you feel uncomfortable inside, that may be the prompting of the Holy Spirit to stop. On the other hand, when you make a decision and feel a deep sense of peace, know that that comes from keeping in step with the Holy Spirit.*[3]

At the Harry Potter film studios there is a huge room with over three thousand wands used in the movies. J. K. Rowling wanted each wand to reflect the personality and characteristics of its owner. Our personality and characteristics should reflect the fruit of the Spirit so that our lives shine through to the world. Keep in step with the Holy Spirit when you go to God in prayer. Pause and prepare; listen and heed!

---

3. Gumbel, *The Bible in One Year*, 144.

Epistle 91

The Gloucester Candlestick, dating from 1104–1113, is a masterpiece of English metalwork; a gilt tangle of beasts clambering and clawing through fleshy foliage. These figures represent the struggle of vice and virtue, of sin and purity, as creatures strive to reach the light or sink into the darkness below. But we know that these figures cannot climb to the light with solely earthly attributes! In 600 AD a saintly monk, John Climacus, wrote an ascetical treatise for monasticism in Catholicism and Eastern Christianity entitled *The Ladder of Divine Ascent*. A glorious golden twelfth-century icon, showing the monks, led by Climacus, ascending the ladder to Jesus, is held in Saint Catherine's Monastery in Egypt. The rungs of the ladder are divided into thirty steps representing the thirty years of the life of Christ and illustrate virtues to be attained by the climber until, at last, he or she will attain the highest degree of religious perfection! Beginning with the renunciation of the world, the ascent moves through penitence and affliction, defeat of vices and acquisition of virtues, avoidance of traps of asceticism, and acquisition of the peace of the soul through *Prayer*.

During the Sermon on the Mount—concerning prayer—Jesus said: "And when you pray, do not keep on babbling like pagans, for they think they will be heard because of their many words." Matthew 6:7 (NIV)

Similarly, John Climacus instructed his followers to pray with pure simplicity, as when praying excessively the penitent's mind would be distracted by the search for words! During the fourth century, Saint Evagrios taught that the value of prayer lay not in its quantity but in its quality. In fact, he wrote much on the practice of prayer. The following are a few of his gems!

> *Pray with tears for the Lord rejoices greatly when you pray with tears!*
> *Try to make the intellect deaf and dumb, you will then be able to pray.*
> *Prayer is the flower of gentleness and of freedom from anger.*
> *Prayer is the remedy for gloom and despondency.*

If you have not received the gift of prayer, persevere patiently to receive it. If you long for prayer, renounce all to gain all.

One of the shortest and most wonderfully effective prayers of all time is the prayer of the criminal on the cross beside the dying Christ: "Jesus, remember me when you come into your kingdom." Jesus answered him, "Truly I tell you, today you will be with me in paradise." Luke 23:42–43 (NIV)

Neither the beasts of *The Gloucester Candlestick* nor the monks on *The Ladder of Divine Ascent* can achieve their goals of reaching the heavenly heights under their own strength. They all see it as a reward for attaining virtue over sin. We cannot achieve this; even attempting it demonstrates our pride and conceit. In our life of prayer, we need to acknowledge how we should approach our God. The great prayer of the Jewish people was the Shema, which begins: "Hear, O Israel, the LORD our God, the Lord is One. Love the LORD your God with all your heart and with all your soul and with all your strength." Deuteronomy 6:4–5 (NIV) This is the prayer that many faithful Jews recited as they entered the gas chambers of the concentration camps.

> The noble old Rabbi Akiba, one of those who stood against the Emperor Hadrian's anti-Jewish legislation and died horribly at the hands of his torturers, went on reciting the Shema quietly until he could do so no more. Like the angels ceaselessly chanting "Holy, holy, holy," the Shema had become, for Akiba, as habitual, and as vital, as breathing.[1]

A different prayer is that of the Eastern Orthodox Church:

> There the 'Jesus Prayer' has been rightly popular: 'Lord Jesus, Son of the living God, have mercy on me, a sinner'. . . . This, like the Jewish Shema, is designed to be said over and over again, until it becomes part of the act of breathing, embedding a sense of the love of Jesus deep within the personality. . . it focuses on the mercy which the living God extends through his Son to all who will seek it.[2]

Tom Wright, a modern-day theologian, acknowledges that the Jesus Prayer implicitly contains the doctrine of the Trinity, but he believes we need to pray explicitly to the Trinity—the Father, the Son, and the Holy

---

1. Wright, *Spiritual and Religious*, 165.
2. Wright, *Spiritual and Religious*, 166.

Spirit. We must acknowledge each: the great Creator God, whom Israel longed for to bring justice and peace to his chosen people; Jesus, who through his earthly work and sacrifice on the cross brought saving grace to the whole world; and the Holy Spirit, Comforter and Counselor, who was sent to be with us in our life today. Importantly Paul says: "You, however, are not in the realm of the flesh but are in the realm of the Spirit, if indeed the Spirit of God lives in you. And if anyone does not have the Spirit of Christ, they do not belong to Christ." Romans 8:9 (NIV)

Wright gives us the words to begin our prayers each day:

> Father almighty, maker of heaven and earth:
> set up your kingdom in our midst.
> Lord Jesus Christ, Son of the living God:
> have mercy on me, a sinner.
> Holy Spirit, breath of the living God:
> renew me and all the world.[3]

---

3. Wright, *Spiritual and Religious*, 166.

Epistle 92

When you come to read this Epistle, we will still be in the midst of a home-grown catastrophe on our eastern shores and an overseas tragedy in Ukraine. Some of us are experiencing leaking windows, swollen doors, and water running down our walls at home, plus scary driving situations and constant wet shoes when we venture outside. This is just a smudge on our personal landscape. We think of those further north who have lost all their earthly possessions—their homes, their furnishings and personal contents, their cars—even their clothes. Precious lives have been lost leaving grief and despair. A post on Instagram captioned a wet exterior as "how I love a good storm when inside my comfy home" illustrated the sadness of ignorance. Remember constantly all who are experiencing such losses. It will be many months before any kind of normality can be restored. Pray also for those who have dedicated themselves to rescue work and ask for on-going protection for them. We must thank them in our hearts for their selflessness. Some of these are mere boys going in school groups to help in the clean-up.

In view of the frightening situation in Ukraine, all at St Swithun's have been urgently invited to join in a week of prayer for peace. A silent Prayer Vigil will be held in the church at 12 noon on Saturday, March 12.

We must pray for Vladimir Zelensky, President of Ukraine, as he stands against the invasion of his country—for wisdom, strength and protection for him, his family, and his people.

We must pray against the will of the President Putin of Russia; that he might be stopped in his intentions by the wishes of his people, the resistance of the people of Ukraine, and the fervent desires of the rest of the world.

Even the Russian soldiers go into Ukraine in ignorance of their leaders' intentions—pray that they may come to realise the depth of their actions.

Pray for all civilians who seek shelter and escape from the weapons of war.

Pray particularly for children who are torn from all that is familiar and precious.

Pray for the elderly who, in their frailty, are so vulnerable to ongoing chaos.

If you read the epistle when this time is past, continue to pray for all countries that still exist in the midst of the fear and the danger of war.

In today's world we are exposed to the realities of these events seeing first hand the fighting and losses regularly on our media. We have no excuse, as Christians, to be guilty of not becoming involved in prayers for the suffering.

Unlike past generations nothing is concealed from our eyes and our beings. When the First World War began in 1914 the general cry was—"It will be over by Christmas"—how drastically wrong was this. Rupert Brooke, who penned that famous poem that begins with the words: "If I should die . . ." originally wrote to "his friend, John Drinkwater, 'Come and die. It'll be great fun'. . . Lord Northcliffe, proprietor of the *Daily Mail*, was put in charge of propaganda. In an essay called 'What to Send Your Soldier', full of helpful tips for those back home, he suggested sending peppermint bulls' eyes: the bulls' eyes ought to have plenty of peppermint in them, for it is the peppermint which keeps those who suck them warm on a cold night. It also has a digestive effect, though that is of small account at the front, where health is so good and indigestion hardly ever heard of. The open-air life, the regular and plenteous feeding, the exercise, and the freedom from care and responsibility, keep the soldiers extraordinarily fit and contented."[1]

In our present time, Ukraine is only the latest of wars! Columbia, Myanmar, and Syria are in the midst of civil wars, as well as Libya and Mali. South Sudan is at war due to ethnic violence. Russia's war with Ukraine is possibly only the beginning of Putin's desire to stretch his country's boundaries to those of the past—to regain territories lost when peoples strove for independence from a cruel taskmaster and developed

---

1. Lambert, *Unquiet Souls*, 171.

a freer lifestyle. There are so many wars that it is easy for some people to ignore the news so that they can live their lives unhindered by such unpleasantness. But we are in a constant war against the powers of darkness who rail against a loving Father. We need to put on the armour of God so that we can stand firm:

> *with the belt of truth buckled around your waist, with the breastplate of righteousness in place, and with your feet fitted with the readiness that comes from the gospel of peace. In addition to all this, take up the shield of faith, with which you can extinguish all the flaming arrows of the evil one. Take the helmet of salvation and the sword of the Spirit, which is the word of God. And pray* ... Eph 6:14–17 (NIV)

Scripture, both the Old and the New Testaments, overflows with an essential truth that we have a loving, patient, and compassionate God. This is a God who is righteous and faithful. He can foil the plans of any nation; he can thwart any purpose undertaken by humans.

> *No king is saved by the size of his army;*
> *no warrior escapes by his great strength.* Ps 33:16 (NIV)

At this time, and always, we must put our trust in his holy name for his love is unfailing. Only in him can we renew our hope.

Epistle 93

Once again Perpetua is blessed with an epistle from Ann Powell. She is looking at a section of Scripture we have often visited especially when we were younger. However, it is very appropriate at this time considering the constant storms, rains, and floods that we have been experiencing on the eastern coast of our country. We remember the people who are grieving such great losses.

About 20 years ago a remarkable young woman hit the headlines, first in France, although she's English—but then, as you can imagine, the British press rushed to jump on the bandwagon. As Jesus himself once said: "A prophet is not without honour except in his own country!"

She was, and still is, diminutive—the headline in the French newspaper, *Figaro*, called her "the little fairy of the oceans." Her name is Ellen Macarthur and, at the age of twenty-four, she sailed solo in her yacht *Kingfisher* 25,000 miles, non-stop around the world in the Vendee Globe race. She didn't win the race, but she broke so many records that her fame almost eclipsed the winner and for some days even pushed the national and international news off the front page of most of the papers.

A tiny boat in mighty seas!

You might say that there have been other stories of great daring since then and perhaps she didn't feature in the Australian Press in quite the same way, but her story comes into my mind as we look at a passage in Luke's gospel, about an even tinier boat in one stormy sea. We find only a few verses but the incident appears in some form in all four gospels. It's important!

We pick up the story in Chapter 8:22 in Luke's Gospel: "One day, Jesus said to his disciples, 'Let us go over to the other side of the lake' so they got into a boat and set out." (NIV) It has the deceptive simplicity of a children's story. It reminds me of one of my favourite children's books called *Little Pete Stories*. Each take begins: "One day" and Pete's exploits for that day follow!

This is Dr Luke in story mode. Listen, he says, and I'll tell you a story about Jesus. "One day"—not a specific day you notice, "Jesus went with his disciples" . . . How many disciples? Who were they? In a boat? What sort of boat?

Curiosity tempts us to look for answers in the other gospels—to identify the disciples as Peter, James, and John, and the boat as belonging to one of them—a small fishing boat like the one in the museum in Tiberias. But my guess is that this is not important. It is what *happened* and the disciples' reaction that is important!

It's like Ellen Macarthur saying: It's not about fame, it's about sharing what you've done, with people.

So, one day Jesus and an undefined number of disciples climbed into an unidentified boat to sail across the Sea of Galilee.

The water lapped gently.
There was just enough wind.
The boat rocked like a cradle and—Jesus fell asleep.
How tired he must have been.

At the beginning of the chapter, we are told that they have been traveling from one town to another—crowds everywhere—
> asking questions, arguing,
>> seeking answers to their problems,
>>> jostling, demanding—

In the midst of that,
> Jesus sought a quiet place on the either side of the Sea of Galilee
>> and he fell asleep in the boat.

So, let's think of another example. As you well know, the Great Ocean Road travels along the Shipwreck Coast. There are many tragic stories around Australia of people who never made their destination, but one from that coast is particularly moving. In 1874 the fifty-two passengers and crew on board the sailing ship *Loch Ard* were celebrating their safe arrival, when winds, waves, and concealed rocks wrecked the ship in a sudden storm. Of all the immigrants of family and friends only two were saved. Their memorial is on the cliff top.

But it has always puzzled me why experienced fishermen—as we believe many of the disciples were, should, in the first place, set sail if there was a storm brewing and then get in such a panic when the storm broke. But let me remember Ellen Macarthur again: Death is the last thing any sailor thinks about. No-one would ever get in a boat at all, if all they could think about was whether they were going to die. But, at the top of the ninety-foot mast when *Kingfisher* was hit by a squall—she was scared! She thought she would die!

With their tiny boat tossed up and down and water coming in faster than the disciples could bale it out, there could be no illusions. A storm like that could capsize the boat and suck them under without trace. They thought they would die. And Jesus slept!

Like the story of Jonah, where he lay down and fell into a deep sleep when a violent storm arose: "The Captain went to him and said: 'How can you sleep? Get up and call on your God! Maybe he will take notice of us and we will not perish.'" Jonah 1:6 (NIV) Was Jesus' sleep the sleep of exhaustion or the sleep of confidence? I wonder!

There is no specific mention of fear, but you can hear it in the disciples' voices as they wake Jesus, crying out—"Master! Master! We're going to drown!" Luke 8:24 (NIV) And Jesus got up.

He rebuked the wind and the raging waters—the storm subsided and all was calm. Whatever the disciples expected I guess it wasn't that!

I wonder what they did expect?

Perhaps they were giving Jesus a chance of survival.

Or was it a dim hope that he might be able to help?

The disciples' track record wasn't very good! If we look back at Luke's gospel, faith is specifically mentioned in relation to forgiveness and healing. The paralysed man walked because of his friends' faith. The centurion's servant was healed due to his master's faith. "Where is your faith?" said Jesus to his disciples. Where is our faith? In the tangible? In the comfort we surround ourselves with? *Earthquakes, floods, war, can destroy that in an instant!*

Is our faith in relationships, in our families, in our friends? Circumstances change and even in our mobile society their physical presence may not be just around the corner. The past two years of lockdowns and restrictions have made us aware of that. Is our faith in our resources? Rising costs, a fall in share prices, redundancy can change all that. Is our faith in our health/our physicality? Well, we know that can't be taken for granted. Young and old alike have lived with the fear of COVID for a long time.

The calm sea of security can quickly become a storm, and the fragile boat of our being can capsize and leave us with—what? We are all in the same boat!

In Hebrews 10:1 we read: "Faith is being certain of what we believe in and sure of what we hope for." (NIV) Where is our faith? Are we in the same boat as Jesus?

The disciples were filled with fear—and amazement. Isn't it strange that the word fear isn't mentioned until this point in the story. The word fear isn't mentioned in the storm; it was implied only by their cries for help.

But this is a different kind of fear. Perhaps better described as awe. The awe of the unknown, the incomprehensible, the presence of power, the authority—who is this Jesus?

I began with Ellen Macarthur's story. It is an inspiring one of courage and determination and humility. A French newspaper said that she commands the waves. But she knows that she does not. It is God who stills the roaring of the seas; the roaring of the waves! The Psalmist even says that when LORD stills the storm to a whisper even the waves of the sea are hushed! We don't have to sail our lives' fragile boats singlehanded, placing our faith in the tangible. Jesus will accompany us. He is no less than the Son of God who stills the roaring seas of disaster, the crashing waves of circumstance, and guides us into a safe harbor. He is worthy to receive glory and honour and praise!

Where is your faith? Is Jesus in your boat with you?

Let us pray this prayer:

> Heavenly Father,
> we often feel that our life is like a fragile boat on the stormy sea
> Forgive us and heal us.
> Lord Jesus,
> please be with us when the winds
> and waves of life threaten to drown us
> Calm us and strengthen us.
> Holy Spirit,
> Your presence is like the wind in our sails
> giving purpose to our lives.
> Breathe on us and restore us. A-men

Epistle 94

When we think about sheep, we tend to come to the conclusion that sheep are silly animals who will blindly follow a leader without individual thought of any kind. However, one of the many advantages of sheep as a successful domestic animal, is that they generally have a social structure. They can be controlled by a leader and that may be a shepherd, a sheepdog, or even by one of their own kind—known as a bellwether sheep. Plus, one of their traits in flocking closely together gives them a survival advantage from marauding wolves or large cats. Ancient peoples found that sheep, no matter what their failings, were worthy of care and respect.

In a fascinating book, *A Short History of the World According to Sheep*, Sally Coulthard states that "of any animal that has lived on this planet, sheep have shaped the course of human history."[1] Over centuries sheep have provided humans with wool, which is a brilliant robust and fire-resistant insulator; sheepskins; meat; milk high in fat and protein and with healthy levels of calcium and magnesium; butter, yogurt, and cheese; lactose; and lanoline, with uses ranging from waterproofing to cosmetics. Curiously the need for effective shearing of the fleece led to the invention of the scissors. The use of lanoline led to the development of the gabardine coat by Thomas Burberry. Who did not have a gabardine coat in the 1950s?

Ancient Mongolians used woolen felt to create their homes known as yurts; Romans used felt under their helmets and their armor. The Vikings, intrepid sailors and fighters, wove huge sails for their ships making it possible to travel incredible distances.

> Amy Lightfoot, textile researcher and head of the Tømmervik Textile Trust in Hitra, Norway, worked out that to make a sail big enough to power a 98-foot boat, which could carry 60 men, you'd need the fleeces of about 700 sheep. It would also take

---

1. Coulthard, *A Short History of the World According to Sheep*, 3.

longer, she calculated, to make a sail than to build the actual ship—by about a factor of twenty.[2]

Coulthard sourced this information from a journal article by Claire Eamer with the wonderful title: *"No Wool, No Vikings: The Fleece that Launched a Thousand Ships."*

Although some rams can occasionally become aggressive, sheep are gentle creatures—even affectionate. In the Old Testament, Nathan rebuked David with the story of "the poor man [who] had nothing except one little ewe lamb that he had bought. He raised it, and it grew up with him and his children. It shared his food, drank from his cup and even slept in his arms. It was like a daughter to him." 2 Samuel 12:3 (NIV) In addition to the list of attributes they possessed, sheep also served as a medium of exchange: "Now Mesha king of Moab raised sheep, and he had to pay the king of Israel a tribute of a hundred thousand lambs and the wool of a hundred thousand rams." 2 Kings 3:4 (NIV)

In Medieval times monasteries in Britain, which had increased their income by sheep farming, "became so adept at the 'business of wool' they started to sell futures in their own products,"[3] though some did get into debt. The Medici family in Italy were involved in lucrative wool-trading as well as money-lending—leading to the growth of their enormous wealth and power.

Though sheep might sometimes have had a bellwether sheep they were in constant need of care and protection: "So they were scattered because there was no shepherd, and when they were scattered they became food for all the wild animals." Ezekiel 34:5 (NIV) But, the Sovereign LORD says: "I will rescue them from all the places where they were scattered on a day of clouds and darkness." 34:12b (NIV)

What is the overall message of the Old Testament? Is it not the promise of the coming of the Savior? He is the Great Shepherd of Psalm 23, and . . .

> *He tends his flock like a shepherd:*
> *He gathers the lambs in his arms and carries them close to his heart;*
> *he gently leads those who have young.* Isa 40:11 (NIV)

In the Old Testament, unblemished lambs were essential for sin offerings, guilt offerings, and peace offerings. This was the precursor of

---

2. Coulthard, *A Short History of the World According to Sheep*, 144.
3. Coulthard, *A Short History of the World According to Sheep*, 181.

Jesus, the ultimate sin offering: "I am the good shepherd. The good shepherd lays down his life for the sheep." John 10:11 (NIV) The New Testament iterates and develops further the illustration of the Good Shepherd in Matthew 18:10–14, Luke 15:3–6 but predominately in John 10:1–18, *The Shepherd and His Flock*. Throughout this gospel chapter is revealed the shepherd who loves his sheep so dearly that he lays down his life for them. "No-one takes it from me, but I lay it down of my own accord. I have authority to lay it down and authority to take it up again. This command I received from my Father." John 10:18 (NIV)

In following the example of the Good Shepherd and his sheep do we provide warmth, food, loving care, and life-saving direction, to our fellow travelers in the world of today? Are we regularly praying for the lost—those who have been scattered in dark and shrouded lands?

> *May the God of peace, who through the blood of the eternal covenant brought back from the dead our Lord Jesus, that great Shepherd of the sheep, equip you with everything good for doing his will, and may he work in us what is pleasing to him, through Jesus Christ, to whom be glory for ever and ever. Amen.* Heb 13:20–21 (NIV)

Epistle 95

These days we all tend to check the daily weather report and gaze upwards to see if there are any rain clouds! Sometimes we dread the clouds which frequently darken the skies. But our God is a faithful God—our troubles have always brought us blessings even though we often need the gift of hindsight to recognize this. Charles Spurgeon says that the clouds "are the dark chariots of bright grace . . . Our God may drench us with grief, but he will not drown us with wrath; nay, he will refresh us with mercy."[1] In the first book of the Bible, God gave us a sign of the covenant he made with Noah after the Great Flood: "I have set my rainbow in the clouds, and it will be the sign of the covenant between me and the earth . . . Never again will the waters become a flood to destroy all life." Genesis 9:13,15b (NIV) When the Israelites were fleeing from their lives of slavery in Egypt:

> *By day the LORD went ahead of them in a pillar of cloud to guide them on their way and by night in a pillar of fire to give them light, so that they could travel by day or night. Neither the pillar of cloud by day nor the pillar of fire by night left its place in front of the people.* Exod 13:21–22 (NIV)

Even when suffering, Job recognized the glory and power of God:

> *He spreads out the northern skies over empty space; he suspends the earth over nothing. He wraps up the waters in his clouds, yet the clouds do not burst under their weight. He covers the face of the full moon, spreading his clouds over it.* Job 26:8–9 (NIV)

Yet his friend Elihu scorns the God of the clouds: "Look up at the heavens and see; gaze at the clouds so high above you. If you sin, how does that affect him?" Job 35:5–6 (NIV) But the Psalmist knows that God is not a remote God! Yes, he determines the number of the stars and calls them

---

1. Spurgeon, *The Cheque Book of the Bank of Faith*, 142.

each by name. He covers the sky with clouds." But this is the same God who "heals the broken-hearted and binds up their wounds." Psalm 147: 4, 8, 3 (NIV)

In 2004, Gavin Pretor-Pinney founded the Cloud Appreciation Society. By 2011 there were nearly 28,000 members and as of 2020 the Society had over 50,000 members. (If this had been around in an earlier century probably one of its most prominent members would have been the painter, John Constable!)

The Manifesto of the Society states: "We believe that clouds are unjustly maligned and that life would be immeasurably poorer without them."!! Many of its members link their appreciation of clouds with Christianity—its founder believed that clouds and Christianity were intrinsically connected. Yet sometimes hymnwriters have often portrayed clouds as a barrier or an impediment between God and man—writing of clouds of sorrow and clouds of doubt! Perhaps that is how Elihu saw the clouds of heaven?

But so many biblical references portray the glory of clouds being present at momentous events. After Jesus predicted his suffering and crucifixion to the disciples, he took Peter, James, and John up a high mountain. "There he was transfigured before them. His face shone like the sun, and his clothes became as white as the light." Matthew 17:2 (NIV) Moses and Elijah appeared, talking to Jesus. The disciples were overcome; Peter said to Jesus that they should build three shelters for this holy group. But while he was speaking, "a bright cloud enveloped them, and a voice from the cloud said, 'This is my Son, whom I love, with him I am well pleased. Listen to him!'" Matthew 17:5 (NIV) After the resurrected Jesus appeared to the disciples over a period of forty days, he spoke to them about the Kingdom of God. Then, before he ascended to heaven, he promised them he would send a Counsellor and Comforter, the Holy Spirit—who would give them the strength and the power to be his witnesses to the ends of the earth. "After he said this, he was taken up before their very eyes, and a cloud hid him from their sight." Acts 1:9 (NIV)

In his letter to the Thessalonians Paul tells his brothers and sisters in Christ that Jesus will come again:

> *For the Lord himself will come down from heaven, with a loud command, with the voice of the archangel and with the trumpet call of God, and the dead in Christ will rise first. After that, we who are still alive and are left will be caught up together with them in the clouds to meet the Lord in the air. And so we will be with the*

Lord for ever. Therefore encourage each other with these words.
1 Thess 4:16–18 (NIV)

>He is coming again—with the clouds!

Epistle 96

Do you believe that the devil is a real being or merely the personification of evil in the world today? Over the last century, with the enormous expansion of the Press and the vast development of automation in printing, and the rapid progression of modern information technology, we have innumerable theories and philosophies battling for supremacy in our brains. In times past there was right and there was wrong, which also led to belief and unbelief. Simplistic but straightforward! Now our thoughts are often "in a muddle" as Mr Emerson often said in the book *Room with a View*. This is a great advantage for the Evil One. It is also an advantage for him if we make caricatures of the devil with horrid grins, pitchforks, and red tights abounding. Then it can become hard to believe in a real devil. Perhaps the celebration, or even the mere recognition of Halloween, falls into this category. Plus, those of us who do believe the devil is real do not know how to handle him effectively.

The devil himself is an archfiend; the chief of devils (fallen angels); an instigator of all that is evil and a tempter. He is God's adversary—the Anti-Christ. Strangely, in the Old Testament, the devil does not appear as a distinctive demonic figure, but the word "satan" is used. This word does not appear as a proper noun but as a common noun—one who is an adversary; an obstructor of people's happiness; a seducer; an opponent; a cause of sickness; a wicked man. The angel of the LORD acted as Balaam's satan, his adversary in Numbers 22:22. And, of course, the most well-known depiction of a satan in the Old Testament is the serpent who tempts Eve. Although not named here, he is the devil in the Old Testament. "He originates in Heaven, standing outside earth's natural order. He is malevolent and wiser than humans, bringing them under his rule. He knows divine matters and uses speech to introduce confusion."[1] And, in his speech, he uses emotional words to deceive us. In the New

---

1. Waltke, *Genesis*, 90.

Testament the devil is mentioned thirty-three times by name—as the tempter of Jesus in Matthew 4:1; the prince of demons in Mark 3:22; the ruler of this world in John 12:31—to note just three. He enters into humans and influences them to have evil passions and commit evil deeds. He is sometimes called Beelzebub! Beelzebub is a name derived from a Philistine god and later adopted by some Abrahamic religions as a major demon. The name is also associated with the Canaanite god Baal.

The devil is so very clever in his activities: in regaling his influence on a Christian, the affectionate uncle Screwtape writes to his nephew: "He must not be allowed to suspect that he is now, however slowly, heading right away from the sun on a line which will carry him into the cold and dark of utmost space."[2]

When the Christian strays, ever so slightly, through carelessness or neglect, it is not always with a recognizable sin, but often with a "vague, though uneasy, feeling that he hasn't been doing very well lately . . . Indeed, the safest road to Hell is the gradual one—the gentle slope, soft underfoot, without sudden turnings, without milestones, without signposts."[3] We must keep renewing our faith through prayer and our prayers must be grounded in Christ and his sacrificial love for us. When we feel our prayers are not answered we cannot say they were in vain; nor when we feel they are answered we cannot say that the result would have happened anyway. We cannot manipulate the Father. His love is constant—he answers our prayers in his way and in his time for he is all-knowing and all-giving. We will always find strength for today and bright hope for tomorrow if we come to him in humility and faithfulness. When we connect consistently in prayer the devil cannot grasp us even in our lowest times. Christianity is not a temporary crutch—it must be living and communing through the Spirit—day by day, hour by hour. And our prayer must be that which Jesus prayed to his Father for those he left behind: "My prayer is not that you take them out of the world but that you protect them from the evil one." John 17:15 (NIV)

Luther believed that the most dangerous aspect of the devil was that he enticed Christians to deviate from sound doctrine. Our teaching of the Word must be accurate and forthright. It must not be adapted to make it more amenable to the those outside the family of the church. The devil runs amok in our world instilling doubt in the hearts of unbelievers—and

---

2. Lewis, *The Screwtape Letters*, 57.
3. Lewis, *The Screwtape Letters*, 58.

believers. Our foundation has to be able to resist all his wiles. We don't have to build churches or houses that are octagonal. In the nineteenth century five cottages in Cornwall were built this way, without any corners, so that there was nowhere for the devil to hide. God can always protect us from the evil one and, at the end times, he will destroy him! The devil is real but he will never fully succeed.

Epistle 97

We are now moving toward the great day of salvation!

*For Christ, our Passover lamb, has been sacrificed; therefore,
let us keep the festival.*
1 Cor 5:7 (NIV)

He is alive and reigns forever!

We have had five Sundays in Lent, then Palm Sunday, followed by Holy Week ending in Maundy Thursday and Good Friday then Easter Sunday. Tom Wright, New Testament scholar comments:

> But my biggest problem starts on Easter Monday. I regard it as absurd and unjustifiable that we should spend forty days keeping Lent, pondering on what it means, preaching about self-denial, being at least a little gloomy, and then bringing it all to a peak with Holy Week, which in turn climaxes in Maundy Thursday and Good Friday . . . and then, after a rather odd Saturday, we have a *single day* of celebration.

Wright continues:

> *But Easter week itself ought not to be the time when all the clergy sigh with relief and go on holiday. It ought to be an eight-day festival, with champagne served after morning prayer or even before, with lots of Alleluias and extra hymns and spectacular anthems. Is it any wonder people find it hard to believe in the resurrection of Jesus if we don't throw our hats in the air?*[1]

Sadly today, most people don't experience the depth of any of the Easter happenings. With Christmas Day, it is often the only time they attend

---

1. Wright, *Surprised by Hope*, 267–68.

church. Those that do might observe Lent, but do they accompany it with due repentance or just feel good about their self-denial? Of course, along with acknowledgment of Lent, much of our ancient liturgy has been cast aside—sometimes replaced with a relevant modern liturgy or, perhaps, with nothing of real impact. But if we do retain Lent; if we give things up in Lent—let us take things up with Easter. New life, new beginnings, new promises, new tasks, new wonder! Alleluias!

Interestingly if you take away the birth of Jesus in the gospels you lose four chapters. But if you take Easter away there is no New Testament at all! There would be no Christianity—we would all still be wandering in the desert and drowning in our sins.

Albeit, whether you agree with Tom Wright or not, let us take Easter Sunday deep into our hearts and keep it there forever! After the Crucifixion many were brave: Joseph of Arimathea, a kind and upright man, went to Pilate and asked for the body of Jesus. He took down the body from the cross, wrapped it reverently in a linen sheet, and took it to a tomb in the rock.

> *The women—those who had come with Jesus from Galilee—followed close behind, and saw the tomb and how His body was placed. Then they returned, and prepared spices and perfumes. On the Sabbath they rested in obedience to the Commandment. And, on the first day of the week, at early dawn, they came to the tomb bringing the spices they had prepared. But they found the stone rolled back from the tomb, and on entering they found that the body of the Lord Jesus was not there. At this they were in great perplexity, when suddenly there stood by them two men whose raiment flashed like lightning. The women were terrified; but, as they stood with their faces bowed to the ground, the men said to them, "Why do you search among the dead for Him who is living? He is not here. He has come back to life. Remember how he spoke to you while He was still in Galilee, when He told you that the Son of Man must be betrayed into the hands of sinful men, and be crucified, and on the third day rise again." Then they remembered his words."* Luke 23:55–24:8 (WNT)

When the women hurried to relate this great news to the disciples "the whole story seemed to them an idle tale; they could not believe the women." Luke 24:11 (WNT)

We must remember his words—all the prophecies of the Old
Testament were to be fulfilled according to God's eternal
purposes.

How brave and faithful were these women in such frightening times. We live in frightening times when the world seems to be in chaos for one reason or another. But Christ is risen! He was crucified for us! What a wondrous discovery so early in a morning when the many followers thought all was lost! During the First World War and in the Second World War, many soldiers found that with the coming of each new day there could be the hope of peace with a release from the brutal experiences amongst which they were existing—whether in bloodied trenches or in heinous Prisoner of War camps. After the wars ceased returned soldiers sought the comradeship they had felt in those brief quiet moments before the dawn. From 1919 onwards a dawn vigil became the basis for commemoration in the years that followed.

Each dawn that comes after Easter Sunday can be a quiet celebration in our hearts. What better time is there to praise our God for his redemptive love. "Because of the LORD's great love we are not consumed, for his compassions never fail. They are new every morning; great is your faithfulness." Lamentations 3:22–23 (NIV)

Epistle 98

There are many symbols that have been used in Christianity times over the ages. The "tetramorph," meaning four shapes, is the traditional name for the "four living creatures" who surround the throne of God. "The first living creature was like a lion, the second was like an ox, the third had a face like a man, the fourth was like a flying eagle." Revelation 4:7 (NIV) These shapes were also taken as the symbols of the four gospel writers. The winged lion holding a book was a traditional image of Mark. In the opening chapter of Mark, John the Baptist is described as one crying in the wilderness, like a lion roaring as king of the desert. Symbols of Luke usually showed a winged ox. The second chapter of this gospel speaks of two instances of Jesus being taken to the Temple in Jerusalem—in infancy and as a twelve-year-old. The ox, which was an animal sacrificed in the Temple, came to be associated with Christ's own sacrifice. The centered human face was understood to be an image of Matthew whose gospel opens with the human genealogy of Christ. The eagle in the tetramorph was interpreted as John, the gospel writer who wrote of the lofty heights of Jesus' divinity. Like eagles who soared toward the sun, John's commentary was seen as radiating the light of divine knowledge.

What symbol would you see as appropriate for the Books of Acts? Jesus, as he prepared to leave to ascend to Heaven commanded the disciples:

> On one occasion, while he was eating with them, he gave them this command: "Do not leave Jerusalem, but wait for the gift my Father promised, which you have heard me speak about. For John baptized with water, but in a few days you will be baptized with the Holy Spirit." Acts 1:4–5 (NIV)

When Jesus was baptized by John in the Jordan, as he came up out of the water: "he saw heaven being torn open and the Spirit descending on him like a dove." Mark 1:10 (NIV)

Most would see the dove as a fitting symbol for Acts—the Holy Spirit coming down on the disciples on the Day of Pentecost. But:

> *Suddenly a sound like the blowing of a violent wind came from heaven and filled the whole house where they were sitting. They saw what seemed to be tongues of fire that separated and came to rest on each of them. All of them were filled with the Holy Spirit and began to speak in other tongues as the Spirit enabled them.*
> Acts 2:2–4 (NIV)

Perhaps the wind—or the fire?

Sometimes there is an attempt to distinguish between baptism with water and baptism with the Holy Spirit. But there is none—there is not a second or higher blessing. Paul tells those in the Corinthian church that all are baptized by one Spirit into one body. Baptism with water expresses our repentance and our faith in a living Savior. It also acknowledges "the powerful and discernible presence of the gift of the Spirit."[1] Taking the Spirit into our hearts is a challenging but vital necessity. We must "pray that the Spirit of God will deeply and fully baptise the new believer in Christ . . . Baptism in water is the sign and seal of baptism in the Spirit, as much as it is of the forgiveness of sins."[2] In churches that practice infant baptism the later rite of confirmation is the strengthening of the promises made on the Christian's behalf at baptism.

Through prayer there is an *increased* gifting of the Holy Spirit.

The great message of the Book of Acts is the establishment and growth of the Christian Church. The Holy Spirit enabled the apostles to find the strength and commitment to carry out the Great Commission. Matthew 28:19–20

They needed to often refresh themselves in the Spirit. How did they do this? The priority of the apostles was prayer—they devoted themselves to prayer. There is a tremendous amount of prayer in Acts; it was the mainstay of the apostles. They prayed before the coming of the promised Spirt; they prayed about the choice of the apostle to replace Judas Iscariot; they prayed on the Day of Pentecost; they prayed constantly for the host of new believers. To the writer, Luke, prayer was the convincing sign of a spiritual life and it was the essential way of life. "When people pray, the Spirit comes, the place where they pray is shaken, prison doors break

---

1. Green, *Thirty Years that Changed the World*, 257.
2. Green, *Thirty Years that Changed the World*, 257.

open, and people dare to die with radiance."[3] Stephen died in radiance with the words of the crucified Jesus on his lips. The man guarding the coats that the Jews put aside when they stoned Stephen, was Saul of Tarsus. Here was a man who was a dedicated religious Jew; a Pharisee who prayed many times during the day in the midst of actively persecuting Christians. It was not until Saul encountered Jesus on the road to Damascus that the prayers of his mouth became the prayers of his heart. He was filled with the Holy Spirit and was baptized.

Paul developed a great passion for the lost. Do we have that same passion? We need to pray to God to open our hearts that we may be filled with his Spirit and may constantly pray for all who are seeking deliverance and protection from the Evil One. In these times when so many ways of the world can hold them in its thrall, we must continually ask for God's blessing on all those we love so that the wonder of Christ's sacrifice will be revealed to them.

---

3. Green, *Thirty Years that Changed the World*, 269.

Epistle 99

Is there a special book that you have always treasured—you might only read parts of it occasionally but its content stays with you and you bring it out every now and again to read it completely? *The Everlasting Mercy* is a long poem written John Masefield and published in 1911. It is styled as the confession of Saul Kane, a young country lad in the mid-nineteenth century, who is a rebel to his parents, a drunkard, a womaniser, and a poacher, who has been jailed nineteen times. He engages in boxing bouts with no consideration for the rules, fights over women, destroys public property, and decries God and prayer. His solution to every episode is to drink himself into oblivion. This was a work that first made Masefield famous although it shocked early twentieth-century sensibilities with its direct, honest, and therefore harsh language and its cursing of God himself.

Saul looks at his lonely, destructive life . . . *until* . . .

> *Out into darkness, out to night,*
> *My flaring heart gave plenty light,*
> *So wild it was there was no knowing*
> *Whether the clouds or stars were blowing;*
> *Blown chimney pots and folk blown blind*
> *And puddles glimmering like my mind,*
> *And chinking glass from windows banging,*
> *And inn signs swung like people hanging,*
> *And in my heart the drink unpriced,*
> *The burning cataracts of Christ.*
> *I did not think, I did not strive,*
> *The deep peace burnt my me alive;*
> *The bolted door had broken in,*
> *I knew that I had done with sin.*
> *I knew that Christ had given me birth*
> *To brother all the souls on earth,*

And every bird and every beast
Should share the crumbs broke at the feast.
O glory of the lighted mind.
How dead I'd been, how dumb, how blind.
The station brook, to my new eyes,
Was babbling out of Paradise;
The waters rushing from the rain
Were singing Christ has risen again.
I thought all earthly creatures knelt
From rapture of the joy I felt.
The narrow station-wall's brick ledge,
The wild hop withering in the hedge,
The lights in huntsman's upper storey
Were parts of an eternal glory,
Were God's eternal garden flowers.
I stood in bliss at this for hours.[1]

Jesus talks, in a parable, about one who has lost a lamb:

> "Rejoice with me; I have found my lost sheep." I tell you in the same way there will be more rejoicing in heaven over one sinner who repents than over ninety-nine righteous persons who do not need to repent. Luke 15:6b–7 (NIV)

> *I have no greater joy than to hear that my children are walking in the truth.* 3 John 1:4 (NIV)

Conversion is a deep experience so when you experience this through God's grace, your senses are aroused and move to contemplation. The birth of the religious transgresses to studying the message and the message is about a loving, faithful, and compassionate Father. How do you react when you meet someone you feel could become a perfect friend? You develop that friendship by talking and sharing with each other. So, when you wish to know God your Father, you talk deeply to him—you pray! Conversion crosses the bridge to prayer. But sometimes new believers begin to flounder—they need to be supported and encouraged:

> *Trust in the LORD with all your heart and lean not on your own understanding; in all your ways submit to him, and he will make your paths straight.* Prov 3:5–6 (NIV)

> *Therefore, my dear brothers and sisters, stand firm. Let nothing move you.* 1 Cor 15:58a (NIV)

---

1. Masefield, *The Everlasting Mercy*, 67–68.

We must pray earnestly for new believers. Paul wrote:

For this reason, since the day we heard about you, we have not stopped praying for you. We continually ask God to fill you with the knowledge of his will through all the wisdom and understanding that the Spirit gives, so that you may live a life worthy of the Lord and please him in every way, bearing fruit in every good work, growing in the knowledge of God, being strengthened with all power according to his glorious might so that you may have great endurance and patience, and giving joyful thanks to the Father, who has qualified you to share in the inheritance of his holy people in the kingdom of light. For he has rescued us from the dominion of darkness and brought us into the kingdom of the Son he loves, in whom we have redemption, the forgiveness of sins. Col 1:9–14 (NIV)

All will come together in Christ—the believer and the newly converted: "Therefore encourage one another with these words." 1 Thessalonians 5:11 (NIV)

Epistle 100

Every now and again we may have a flat period in our prayer lives. Usually, we can open our hearts to the Spirit and renew our communion. There is always a sure and certain way to embrace our prayer life again . . .

The following is the testimony of a young woman who grew up in an atheist family under a Communist state system in Latvia:

> *At funerals we were allowed to recite the Lord's Prayer. As a young child I heard these strange words and had no idea who we were talking to, what the words meant, where they came from or why we were reciting them. When freedom came at last, I had the opportunity to search for their meaning. When you are in total darkness, the tiniest point of light is very bright. For me the Lord's Prayer was that point of light. By the time I found its meaning I was a Christian.*[2]

In Matthew 6 Jesus tells us how we should pray—not like the Jews who pray like hypocrites praying in public places so that people will be impressed. We must pray to our Father away from all this and should not babble with excessive words. Our God knows our needs even before we voice them.

Jesus gives us the words to pray by encompassing the gospel message.

Our Father in heaven

"Abba" is the defining term for father in the Aramaic language, spoken by Jesus as an informal term to describe his personal relationship with God. We are now privileged to call our Father God, Abba; it is now a personal relationship to us with a Father who is both near and in the heavens.

---

2. Bailey, *Jesus Through Middle Eastern Eyes*, 91.

Hallowed be your name

God's name is holy—it has been defiled in the past Ezekiel 16:16–23 but we know Isaiah was overcome with God's holiness. Isaiah 6:1–5 He is holy; he expects us to live holy lives because: "For you are a people holy to the LORD your God. The LORD your God has chosen you out of all the peoples on the face of the earth to be his people, his treasured possession." Deuteronomy 7:6 (NIV)

Thus, we must treasure his holiness!

Your kingdom come, your will be done on earth as it is in heaven

Jesus preached continually on the Kingdom of God and declared that he was instigating the Kingdom on earth. Luke 11:20 Yet we seem to be looking to the future believing it has yet to take place—it is both "now" and "not yet." It is a preliminary blessing of the things to come in the last days. Men and women can be delivered from evil in the present and brought under the blessings of God's reign. The church is not the kingdom; the kingdom creates the church; it is the church's mission to witness to the kingdom; the church is also the custodian of the kingdom—an awesome responsibility for the people of God.

Give us today our daily bread

We are to ask for the basic food for our needs for today. God told Moses that each morning bread would rain down from heaven for the Israelites in the desert. The people were only to collect as much bread as they needed for that day and to keep none of it for the next day. Exodus 16:4 The *Old Syriac* version translates to: Deliver us, O Lord, from the fear of not having enough to eat. Give us bread for today and with it give us confidence that tomorrow we will have enough.

Forgive us our debts, as we also have forgiven our debtors

Jesus reaffirms this relationship between forgiving and being forgiven. Matthew 6:14–15 If we do not reach out to our neighbor who has wronged us, our love for God is incomplete. When we look at the world today there are heinous crimes being committed each day that are hard to forgive. Do we say with Jesus and Stephen—forgive them for they know not what they do? The world hates this theology because it feels that anger is necessary to fight for justice.

We must pray for ourselves and for those whom we find so hard to forgive.

And lead us not into temptation, but deliver us from the evil one

This petition in the Lord's Prayer "expresses the confidence of an earthly pilgrim traveling with a divine guide."[3] We need the strength to keep to the path—we need to vigilant; to watch and pray. Mark 14:38 The devil lurks everywhere. We are weak thus we constantly need God's protection. How many times did Peter weaken? "Simon, Simon, Satan has asked to sift all of you as wheat. But I have prayed for you, Simon, that your faith may not fail. And when you have turned back, strengthen your brothers." Luke 22:31–32 (NIV) Jesus prays for us to keep the faith; pray always that we will thwart Satan—in our lives and in the world around us.

For thine is the kingdom and the power and the glory forever, Amen.

This is an affirmation of praise to God; an abridgement of 1 Chronicles 29:11–13 where David said:

> *Praise be to you, LORD, the God of our father Israel, from everlasting to everlasting. Yours, LORD, is the greatness and the power and the glory and the majesty and the splendor, for everything in heaven and earth is yours. Yours, LORD, is the kingdom; you are exalted as head over all. Wealth and honor come from you; you are the ruler of all things. In your hands are strength and power to exalt and give strength to all. Now, our God, we give you thanks, and praise your glorious name.* (NIV)

As we dwell on this—receive the greatest prayer of all:

> *May "The LORD bless thee and keep thee; the LORD make his face shine upon thee and be gracious unto thee; the LORD lift up his countenance upon thee and give thee peace."*
> Num 6:24–26 (KJV)

Threefold; in three persons; God will bless you!

---

3. Bailey, *Jesus Through Middle Eastern Eyes*, 128.

Epistle 101

When we approach a complex task, especially in a professional situation, we spend time analyzing, critiquing, studying, and outlining our approach, before beginning to put any theories into practice. Being well prepared is more likely to attain a successful result. But if we don't prepare well, we could flounder around retrying old methods and not thinking through a more enterprising and enlightening program. Our personal "modus operandi" has generally worked well in the past and doesn't involve any challenging of our confidence or lack of expertise! When we don't achieve the results we hoped for we are almost bewildered—and certainly frustrated.

Is this sometimes how our prayer life appears? We pray faithfully for the same things each day—our family, our security, our personal professional life, even for the happiness that sometimes appears to evade us. We may even become bored with the same old prayers which don't seem to bring results.

We must pray effectively by knowing what the Bible says—we must know God's nature; we must know his promises; we must be aware of what pleases and what displeases him, and; we must know how he handles those who fall away. We need to be learning all the time; we need to remain in the faith; we need to prepare ourselves. Jesus said:

> *I tell you, then, whatever you ask for in prayer, believe that you have received it and it will be yours. And when you stand praying, if you have a grievance against anyone, forgive them, so that your Father in heaven may forgive you the wrongs you have done.*
> Mark 11:24–25 (NEB)

Here is an additional aspect to prayer we may not have accounted for: effective prayer requires faith, faith requires love, love requires forgiveness.

> *Every inspired scripture has its use for teaching the truth and refuting error, or for reformation of manners and discipline in right living, so that the person who belongs to God may be efficient and equipped for good work of every kind.* 2 Tim 3:16–17 (NEB)

Thus all scripture is inspired by God and is useful for teaching us how to pray, for reproof on how we behave, for correction when we stray, and for training in the holy life that God has prepared for us. We do not become bored with praying—we become bored with the same old words we use. Our methods are at fault. Pray about these same things that are close to your hearts but use the words of the Bible! Pray your needs through the Book of the Psalms, for example. We can take a specific psalm or specific parts of a number of psalms and make them the words of our petitions. Or we can take a section of one of the epistles of the New Testament into our hearts and express those words from our mouths.

The Lord is my shepherd—pray that God will shepherd your family with his love and that they may know that the Shepherd is always there for them in all the troubles of this world. Remember also that we, as followers of Christ, are instructed to protect the sheep of his flock:

> *Tend that flock of God whose shepherds you are, and do it, not under compulsion, but of your own free will, as God would have it; not for gain but out of sheer devotion; not tyrannizing over those who are allotted to your care, but setting an example to the flock. And then, when the Head Shepherd appears, you will receive for your own the unfading garland of glory.* 1 Pet 5:2–3 (NEB)

Pray that we may truly and deeply believe what the disciples witnessed so that we will always have the trust and fellowship to come close to our Father in prayer with the right words and living the decreed lives. When we come to the light of Christ and immerse ourselves in the words of the Bible we truly commune with the Father.

Older people remember the days in Sunday School when we learned our memory verses and even received prizes for remembering them well and faithfully. Those memory verses are rarely forgotten. Take a moment to recall those precious words! Words of old hymns sing in our hearts— "I've a Father in heaven whom my eyes have not seen, and whose voice never falls on my ear—but I know He is there and is listening to me when I whisper my prayer in the night." Doxologies and benedictions comfort our souls! Sometimes affirmations of our faith, Creeds, are so well taught in Confirmation classes, that we never forget these words—what better way to approach our God than to profess what we believe! In the words of the wise we read:

> *My child, do not forget my teaching,*
>   *but guard my commands in your heart;*
>   *for long life and years in plenty*
>   *will they bring you, and prosperity as well.*
> *Let your good faith and loyalty never fail*
>   *but bind them around your neck.*
> *Thus will you win favour and success*
>   *in the sight of God and man.*
> *Put all your trust in the LORD*
>   *and do not rely on your own understanding.*
> *Think of him in all your ways,*
>   *and he will smooth your path.*
> *Do not think how wise you are,*
>   *but fear the LORD and turn from evil.*
> *Let that be the medicine to keep you in health,*
>   *the liniment for your limbs.*
>
> Prov 3:1–8 (NEB)

Let us trust always in the words of the LORD—take hold of his words with all your strength. The Father will lead us in wisdom and insight so that our prayers will be refreshed and our way will be in the light of his love and not in the darkness of fear. God will protect us in days of panic; he will lift us up when we stumble and fall; he will hear our pleas; he will answer us with compassion.

Epistle 102

Terry Waite, a committed Christian from his youth, originally contemplated a monastic life but instead joined the Church Army, a social organization of the Anglican Church in the United Kingdom. He worked in Christian education in the UK; then in development issues connected with education and health in Africa, Asia, the Americas, and Europe. In 1980 he returned home where he was appointed as a special envoy to the Archbishop of Canterbury with responsibility for diplomatic and ecclesiastical exchanges. In this capacity he successfully negotiated for the release of several hostages in Iran and later, in 1984, he further negotiated for the release of four British hostages held by Libya. However, during negotiations in Lebanon the following year, 1985, his efforts were compromised and he himself was taken hostage.

Terry Waite remained in captivity for 1,763 days; the first four years in solitary confinement. Chained to a wall for twenty-three hours and fifty minutes each day he suffered physically from lack of sunlight and exercise. Mentally he lived in a silent world with no inter-personal communication and had no books or writing materials. Many Church Army officers back home wore a badge with the letter H on their uniforms, to encourage people to pray with them for Terry Waite's release. His release came about in November 1991—amazingly, in December 2012, he returned to Beirut to reconcile with his former captors!

Only complete ongoing trust in a Savior God could carry one through such a horrendous ordeal . . . trust in the Father and confidence in his care.

> *For in him our hearts are glad, because we have trusted in his holy name.* Ps 33:21 (NEB)

> *We can take courage and say, "The Lord is my helper, I will not fear; what can man do to me?"* Heb 13:6 (NEB)

We should constantly keep these words in our hearts—the more we repeat them; the deeper our prayers will become. We should daily meditate on the Lord's holy name so that we can understand the breadth of his character.

We can pray in confidence; we can overcome our fear.

Jehovah-Jireh will provide. When Abraham reached out his hand with the knife to sacrifice Isaac, the LORD called out and, because of Abraham's faith, told him to desist: "Abraham looked up, and there he saw a ram caught by its horns in a thicket. So he went and took the ram and offered it as a sacrifice instead of his son. Abraham named that place Jehovah-jireh." Genesis 22:13b–14 (NEB)

Jehovah-Shalom will send peace. Shalom is more than just simply peace; it is complete peace; often after turmoil and hostilities. It is a feeling of blessed contentment, completeness, wholeness, well-being, and harmony—perfect God-given peace. Jesus promised: "Peace is my parting gift to you, my own peace, such as the world cannot give. Set your hearts at rest and banish your fears." John 14:27 (NEB)

Jehovah-Tsidkenu will justify. God is a God of righteousness: "In his days Judah will be kept safe, and Israel shall live undisturbed. This is the name to be given him: the LORD is our Righteousness." Jeremiah 23:6 (NEB) Our Righteous Savior!

Jehovah-Shammah will be forever near. When Ezekiel received his vision from God, the Jews had been in captivity in Babylon for twenty-five years. God had promised that the people would be restored and that the city and the temple would be rebuilt. This is the vision of Ezekiel—the restoration of the land, the city, the temple. And in the midst would be the LORD: "and the city's name for ever after shall be, Jehovah-shammah." Ezekiel 48:35b (NEB) These are the closing words of the Book of Ezekiel—That is, the LORD is there!

Jehovah-Nissi will conquer every foe. This is the name given by Moses to the altar which he built to celebrate the defeat of the Amalekites:

> *Then Joshua defeated Amalek and put its people to the sword. The LORD said to Moses, "Record this in writing, and tell it to Joshua in these words: I am resolved to blot out all memory of Amalek from under heaven." Moses built an altar and named it Jehovah-nissi and said, "My oath upon it: the LORD is at war with Amalek generation after generation."* Exod 17:13–15 (NEB)

We can shelter under the refuge of the banner of the LORD and exult him for his deliverance from all that is evil from generation to generation.

We talked about using "God language" in our prayers in the last epistle. During his imprisonment Terry Waite never used his own words in prayer, realizing quite early that he would just be constantly pleading for God to get him out of his dungeon of fear and deprivation. Instead, he became incredibly grateful for the years he had learning by the old-fashioned method of rote. He failed to remember one sermon but could easily use the words of The Psalms and other books from his vast store of memory. The words of the *Prayer Book* became a precious lifeline. Most mornings he was able to save a little bread and water and repeat the communion service to himself. Look ever to the Word; trust in our God and our Savior, and we will grow in assurance and maturity.

Epistle 103

James Montgomery (1771–1854) was the son of Moravian parents who both died on a West Indian mission field during the time he was at boarding school in the UK. Throughout his life Montgomery was a great supporter of Christian missions abroad and of the dispossessed and suffering at home. His greatest legacy perhaps was the wonderful hymn he wrote about prayer.

> Prayer is the soul's sincere desire,
> Uttered or unexpressed—
> The motion of a hidden fire
> That trembles in the breast
> *Do not stifle the Spirit's fire or despise prophetic utterances . . . but*
> *bring all to the test; keep what is good in them.* 1 Thess 5:19, 21
> (NEB)
>
> Prayer is the burden of a sigh,
> The falling of a tear—
> The upward glancing of an eye,
> When none but God is near.
> *Listen to my words, O LORD, consider my inmost thoughts;*
> *heed my cry for help, my king and my God.* Ps 5:1–2 (NEB)
>
> Prayer is the simplest form of speech
> That infant lips can try—
> Prayer the sublimest strains that reach
> The majesty on high.
> *Thou art my hope, O LORD, my trust, O LORD, since childhood.*
> *From birth I have leaned upon thee; my protector since I left my*
> *mother's womb.* Ps 71:5–6 (NEB)
>
> Prayer is the contrite sinner's voice
> Returning from his ways,
> While angels in their songs rejoice,

And cry, "Behold he prays!"
Therefore confess your sins to one another, and pray for one another, and then you will be healed. A good person's prayer is powerful and effective. Jas 5:16 (NEB)

Prayer is the Christian's vital breath—
The Christian's native air—
His watchword at the gates of death—
He enters heaven with prayer.
And the Lamb went up and took the scroll from the right hand of the One who sat on the throne. When he took it, the four living creatures and the twenty-four elders fell down before the Lamb. Each of the elders had a harp, and they held golden bowls full of incense, the prayers of God's people. Rev 5:7–8 (NEB)

The saints in prayer appear as one
In word, and deed, and mind,
While with the Father and the Son
Sweet fellowship they find.
Greet one another with the kiss of peace. All God's people send you greetings. The grace of the Lord Jesus Christ, and the love of God, and the fellowship of the Holy Spirit, be with you all. 2 Cor 13:12–14 (NEB)

Nor prayer is made by man alone—
The Holy Spirit pleads—
And Jesus, on the eternal throne,
For sinners intercedes.
In the same way the Spirit comes to the aid of our weakness. We do not even know how we ought to pray, but through our inarticulate groans the Spirit himself is pleading for us, and God who searches our inmost being knows what the Spirit means, because he pleads for God's people in God's own way; and in everything, as we know, he co-operates for good with those who love God and are called according to his purpose. Rom 8:26–28 (NEB)

O Thou by whom we come to God—
The life, the truth, the way!
The path of prayer Thyself has trod;
Lord, teach us how to pray![1]
Very early next morning he got up and went out. He went away to a lonely spot and remained there in prayer. Mark 1:35 (NEB)

---

1. Montgomery, "What Is Prayer?" in P. C. C. *The Book of Praise*. 432.

Epistle 104

When we pray, we enhance our words with hope. This is not the hope of the world when we use the word almost as a wistful wish. That is when we would like something to happen; we really want a certain thing to happen; we may even put our personal strength to try and bring such a thing to fruition. But personal hope is often frustratingly rarely rewarded. We, as Christians, need to put our hope in our God—he is the God of all hope: "May the God of hope fill you with all joy and peace by your faith in him, until, by the power of the Holy Spirit, you overflow with hope." Romans 15:13 (NEB)

Real hope is often a neglected part of the Christian life. But we can always determine from God's Word the reality of hope. Here, although we constantly learn about faith, we so often fail to realise the great treasure of hope in our faith: "And what is faith? Faith gives substance to our hopes, and makes us certain of realities we do not see." Hebrews 11:1 (NEB)

Faith and hope are intrinsically linked—faith is grounded in the reality of the past where hope is looking to the reality of the future. The wisdom of the Old Testament testifies to the anchor of the past: "Put all your trust in the LORD and do not rely on your own understanding. Think of him in all your ways, and he will smooth your path". Prov 3:5–6 (NEB) In the New Testament Peter directs us: "You must therefore be mentally stripped for action, perfectly self-controlled. Fix your hopes on the gift of grace which is to be yours when Jesus Christ is revealed." 1 Peter 1:13 (NEB)

We must acknowledge that the future is assured in the sacrifice of Christ. In fact, if we lose our understanding of the resurrection, we lose the central conviction that gives shape to the hope we proclaim—plus we lose sight of the God in whom we put our trust. Remember Jesus was the first-fruits of those who had fallen asleep and we who believe are now the redeemed people of God in his wonderful creation. Our hope is forged by his sacrifice.

John Piper says hope is faith in the future tense!

If our prayers are versed in hope—a hope that is structured around the depth of our faith—how much closer will we come to the loving and compassionate Father. It expresses a maturity of our faith in that we truly believe that our God is trustworthy and will grant what we need rather than what we want. "We have waited eagerly for the LORD; he is our help and our shield. For in him our hearts are glad, because we have trusted in his holy name. Let thy unfailing love, O LORD, rest upon us, as we have put our hope in thee." Psalm 33:20–22 (NEB)

When William of Orange decided to embark on the invasion of Britain, the kingdom of his father-in-law, James II, he did so after many months of deliberation. He refused to go unless he had a formal invitation from the English. This he received from a number of lords, bishops, politicians, plus an Admiral of the Fleet! These conspirators were attempting to prevent the country descending into a Commonwealth as the monarch strove to forcibly press the people into accepting and practicing the Roman Catholic faith. William, conscious of the need for home support considering the territorial ambitions of the French King, also sought the support of the States of Holland, which he eventually gained. With the hope of a successful endeavor, he nevertheless put his affairs in order and made his will. This hope he entrusted to his Lord and Savior, being prepared to accept whatever befell. Lastly, he summoned Mary to his study:

> *He said to me that in case it pleased God, that I should never see him again (words that pierced my heart and caused me such a pang, that at the hour I write it has scarcely worn off) if that happened, he said it will be necessary to marry again . . . He himself could not utter these words without shedding tears, and throughout the conversation he showed me all the tenderness I could wish.*[1]

William's perilous venture succeeded and at his arrival at Brixham, "the Prince and his men sang the 118th Psalm in the half-dozen languages of the multi-national army."[2]

---

1. Van der Zee, *1688: Revolution in the Family*, 118–19.
2. Van der Zee, *1688: Revolution in the Family*, 143.

Sadly, it was fourteen long years of resentment and sorrow before William felt national feeling was completely united behind him. Hope was eventually fulfilled but not in the ways he had anticipated:

> *The memory of my distress and my wanderings is wormwood and gall. Remember, O remember, and stoop down to me. All this I take to heart and therefore I will wait patiently: the LORD's true love is surely not spent, nor has his compassion failed; they are new every morning, so great is his constancy. The LORD, I say, is all that I have; therefore I will wait for him patiently. The LORD is good to those who look for him, to all who seek him; it is good to wait in patience and sigh for deliverance by the LORD.* Lam 3:19–26 (NEB)

Yet this I call to mind and therefore I have hope!

Epistle 105

Have you often pondered on the number of domestic pets in your locality? Actually, there are approximately 29 million pets in Australia making our country home to one of the highest number of pet owners in the world! Obviously the most popular animals are dogs and cats, but in the United Kingdom, for example, donkeys are often kept as special pets on farms.

Do donkeys have the attributes to make good pets, though? In literature they have not always rated well. In Homer, Aesop, and Apuleius they are portrayed as stupid, stubborn, and servile; Eeyore in *Winnie the Pooh* is a melancholy fellow; Benjamin in *Animal Farm* is resilient and loyal but stoically accepting of whatever fate will bring; nevertheless, William Wordsworth, in his poem *Peter Bell*, writes of a loyal and patient donkey. In politics we have the term a "donkey vote," which occurs when the voter simply writes down preferences in order of the candidates. Plus, the bray of a donkey is used as a simile for loud and foolish speech in political mockery.

All this is probably how we generally react to donkeys!

Have you ever re-evaluated common opinion when you find donkeys mentioned in Scripture? Donkeys in the Bible are found to be symbols of service, suffering, peace, humility, hard work, willpower, and good manners.

For some 5,000 years before Christ, the donkey supplanted the ox as a working animal becoming a "beast of burden," a pack animal, because of its attributes. "They loaded the corn on to their donkeys, and went away." Genesis 42:26 (NEB)

They were also royal animals used by kings in preference to the majestic horse!

In Deuteronomy 17:16 the LORD promised to set a king over Israel but warned that kings "shall not acquire many horses" (NEB) and David, when King of Israel, appears to have kept this commandment—even riding a donkey himself. His son, Absalom, was caught in the thick branches of a great oak when riding his donkey; his son Solomon was instructed to ride his father's donkey. On his deathbed David said to Zadok the priest and Nathan the prophet and Benaiah son of Jehoiada:

> *Take the officers of the household with you; mount my son Solomon on the King's mule and escort him down to Gihon. There Zadok the priest and Nathan the prophet shall anoint him king over Israel. Sound the trumpet and shout, "Long live King Solomon!"* 1 Kgs 1:33–34 (NEB)

Later, in the Old Testament, we read that another King is to be proclaimed, coming on a donkey:

> *Rejoice, rejoice, daughter of Zion, shout aloud, daughter of Jerusalem; for see, your king is coming to you, his cause won, his victory gained, humble and mounted on an ass, on a foal, the young of a she-ass.* Zech 9:9 (NEB)

When approaching Jerusalem, Jesus instructed his disciples: "Go to the village opposite, where you will at once find a donkey tethered with her foal beside her; untie them and bring them to me." Then Jesus sat on them and entered Jerusalem to the cries of the crowd: "Hosanna to the Son of David! Blessings on him who comes in the name of the Lord! Hosanna in the heavens." Matt 21:2, 9 (NEB)

Our King proclaimed: coming on a humble donkey!

However, the most fascinating biblical episode of a donkey is the story of Balaam and his donkey! This donkey was the only animal (besides the serpent in the Garden of Eden) who speaks in the Bible. After the Israelites had defeated the Amorites and the people of Bashan, Balak, the King of the Moabites, feared greatly that the Israelites would wage war against his people. So, he sent for Balaam, a spiritual diviner who blessed and cursed people for a fee. Though not an Israelite, Balaam knew God but did not have a genuine heart for the LORD. After God rejected the proposed mission Balaam again pleaded to be allowed to be the bearer of curses. He thinks God can be persuaded! God then permits him to go and bear the consequences! Then follows Balaam's journey on his faithful donkey. Three times the donkey saw the angel of the LORD standing in their way with a drawn sword in his hand—twice the donkey turned aside and the third time she lay down under Balaam. Three times Balaam beat her mercilessly.

> *The LORD then made the donkey speak, and she said to Balaam, "What have I done? This is the third time you have beaten me." Balaam answered the donkey, "You have been making a fool of me. If I had had a sword here, I should have killed you on the spot." But the donkey answered, "Am I not still the donkey which you have ridden all your life? Have I ever taken such a liberty with you before?" He said, "No." Then the LORD opened Balaam's eyes: he saw the angel of the LORD standing in the road with his sword drawn, and he bowed down and fell flat on his face before him.* Num 22:28–31 (NEB)

We can evaluate Balaam and his donkey in the words of Peter when he talks about false prophets:

> *They have abandoned the straight road and lost their way. They have followed in the steps of Balaam son of Beor, who consented to take pay for doing wrong, but had his offence brought home to him when the dumb beast spoke with a human voice and put a stop to the prophet's madness.* 2 Pet 2:15–16 (NEB)

In our prayer life do we genuinely seek the Lord's will?
Do we heed the angel of the LORD standing before us—
with his sword drawn?

Epistle 106

In the wilderness God punished the Israelites for casting the Golden Calf and worshipping it. Moses interceded for the Israelites, seeking God's favor:

> *And Moses prayed, "Show me your glory." The LORD answered, "I will make all my goodness pass before you, and I will pronounce in your hearing the Name JEHOVAH. I will be gracious to whom I will be gracious, and I will have compassion on whom I will have compassion." But he added, "My face you cannot see, for no mortal man may see me and live." The LORD said, "Here is a place beside me. Take your stand on the rock and when my glory passes by, I will put you in a crevice of the rock and cover you with my hand until I have passed by. Then I will take away my hand, and you shall see my back, but my face shall not be seen."* Exod 33:18–23 (NEB)

The Book of Exodus appears to be telling the reader that to see the LORD's face is too dangerous:

> *As looking at the sun destroys a person's sight, so looking at God in full divine splendor would destroy the person . . . It is entirely intelligible that Yhwh's face should be the focus of Yhwh's splendor. The splendor of the sun shines out from the sun's face. The face reveals the majesty of the person. Therefore, it is too dangerous to see the face.*[1]

Nevertheless, Yhwh provides protection for those he loves—there is a place by him—a place of perfect security and complete safety!

Moses is told to stand on the rock; in the New Testament Jesus is the rock—the living stone. He is the foundation, the cornerstone of the spiritual church—that which God promises in Isaiah 28—a *precious* cornerstone; a *sure* foundation. Remember also, when the Israelites had no

1. Goldingay, *Old Testament Theology. Volume 1. Israel's Gospel*, 405.

water in the desert, Moses was instructed to strike a rock and the water gushed out to quench their raging thirst. The water that comes from Jesus is the living water for our spiritual lives.

In the Psalms, David says: "What god is there but the LORD? What rock but our God?" This rock is David's salvation: "The LORD is my stronghold, my fortress and my champion, my God, my rock where I find safety, my shield, my mountain refuge, my strong tower." Psalm 18: 31, 2 (NEB) Not only is the rock the strong fortress—it is also the place of refuge; the crevice; the cleft in the rock.

How many times have we sung that old favorite hymn by Augustus Toplady, written in 1776, and which he entitled *A Living and Dying Prayer for the Holiest Believer in the World*. It contains a complete and perfect message for us as a testament of refuge in Jesus, our Savior. We must hide ourselves in the cleft of his blood, shed for us. We labor in vain to fulfill the Law but only in faith in Christ's sacrifice can we be restored to life with the Father. Toplady says of the third verse:

> *We do not think it strange or preposterous to wear clothes, the materials of which we borrow from other creatures; and why should it be deemed absurd, that we should hide our spiritual shame, by appearing before God in the garment of another—even the righteousness of Christ.*[2]

Unless we look to Jesus for the defeat of our sin, we die. There is no better refuge and no possible escape from our sins than Christ himself.

He alone clothes us in righteousness.

Rock of Ages, cleft for me,
Let me hide myself in Thee;
Let the water and the blood,
From Thy riven side which flowed,
Be of sin the double cure,
Cleanse me from its guilt and power.

Not the labours of my hands
Can fulfill Thy law's demands;
Could my zeal no respite know,
Could my tears forever flow,
All for sin could not atone;
Thou must save, and Thou alone.

---

2. Terry, *Stories Behind 50 Southern Gospel Favourites. Volume 2*, 192.

Nothing in my hand I bring,
Simply to Thy cross I cling;
Naked, come to Thee for dress;
Helpless, look to Thee for grace;
Foul, I to the mountain fly;
Wash me, Saviour, or I die.

While I draw this fleeting breath,
When my eyes shall close in death,
When I soar through tracks unknown,
See Thee on Thy judgment throne,
Rock of Ages, cleft for me,
Let me hide myself in Thee.[3]

>Let this be our prayer for the days and years ahead—
>until the end!

---

3. Church of Scotland, *The Church Hymnary*, 413.

Epistle 107

When we pray, what is it that we are expecting? Actually, when we pray, the "first implication is that God is *really there,* personal and addressable in worship. Prayer is communication with God in worship according to his revealed will."[1] To pray according to God's will is to seek him through his Word. We know that prayer in the Old Testament is an integral part of the lives of God's people, the Israelites. In the New Testament it is an integral part of the life of Jesus. He taught his disciples to pray; he teaches us to pray. Paul prays himself and instructs converts to Christianity how to pray. "And the persecuted and martyred church in Revelation continually prays."[2]

We are, as humans without God, poor in spirit.

> *There can be no question where the blame must be placed for our spiritual poverty. Every sin problem reveals a prayer problem. There is no sin that the Christians will ever commit that could not have been avoided by prayer. Jesus instructed his disciples: "Pray that you enter not into temptation." Mark 14:38* [3]

Therefore, we must be prepared to examine ourselves as we come with prayer to the Father. Another problem that we have in regard to prayer is that we sometimes think that—if God is sovereign and ordains the means and results of all on earth, what is the point of praying? Charles Hodge, a Reformed theologian who was Principal of Princeton Theological Seminary between 1851 and 1878, analyses this premise as follows:

> God has not determined to accomplish his purposes without the use of means; and among these means, the prayers of his people have their appropriate place. If the objection to prayer, founded

---

1. Reymond, *A New Systematic Theology of the Christian Faith*, 969.
2. Reymond, *A New Systematic Theology of the Christian Faith*, 971.
3. Reymond, *A New Systematic Theology of the Christian Faith*, 973.

on the foreordination of events be valid, it is valid against the use of means in any case. If it be unreasonable to say, "If it be foreordained that I should live, it is not necessary for me to eat," it is no less unreasonable to say, "If it be foreordained that I should receive any good, it is not necessary for me to ask for it." If God has foreordained to bless us, he has foreordained that we should seek his blessing. Prayer has the same causal relation to the good bestowed, as any other means has to the end with which it is connected. [4]

Patrick, born in Scotland in 385 as a Roman citizen, became known as the patron saint of Ireland. At age sixteen he was captured by pirates and taken to Ireland where he was sold into slavery as a shepherd. Living in isolation with little human contact, Patrick began to turn to the God of his parents. A love and fear of God inflamed his heart, and his faith grew through continuous prayer amidst his loneliness. Even in snow, frost, and rain he claimed to have the spirit of God to warm him. He fought to attain his freedom and amidst journeys back to Scotland, and then to Gaul, he eventually returned to Ireland as a missionary. There are many myths and legends about the life of Patrick and historians, scholars, and theologians, debate whether many of them actually occurred. However, in his life, his strong faith in Christ could not be denied.

In an early confession he acknowledged he carried a sin in his conscience from youth, and this acknowledgment enabled him to turn to God in prayer.

Some of the words he wrote illustrate the depth of his belief.

> I arise today
> Through God's strength to pilot me;
> God's might to uphold me,
> God's wisdom to guide me,
> God's eye to look before me,
> God's ear to hear me,
> God's word to speak for me,
> God's hand to guard me,
> God's way to lie before me,
> God's shield to protect me,
> God's hosts to save me
> Afar and anear,
> Alone or in a multitude.

---

4. Hodge, *Systematic Theology. Volume 3*, 169.

> Christ shield me today against wounding
> Christ with me, Christ before me, Christ behind me,
> Christ in me, Christ beneath me, Christ above me,
> Christ on my right, Christ on my left,
> Christ when I lie down, Christ when I sit down.
> I arise today through the mighty strength of the Lord of creation.[5]

When we ponder on the providence of God and how it often includes human actions, may we realise that God is always at work accomplishing his plans. Sometimes we are conscious of this; other times we unwittingly co-operate!

> Little did Caesar Augustus know when he made his decree (Luke 2:1) that the census he was ordering would make possible the fulfilment of the prophecy that the Messiah would be born in Bethlehem, but he helped fulfil it nonetheless.[6]

---

5. lords-prayer-words.com, 2021.
6. Erickson, *Introducing Christian Doctrine*, 143.

Epistle 108

Scarlett is a little girl who loves running. She runs all day when outside. If there is a race with other children she keeps running after the race is over. And she laughs as she runs—her delight is in being "fleet of foot"!

In Greek mythology, Homer introduces us to Polites, the legitimate son of King Priam and Queen Hecuba of Troy, who was known for his swiftness. So, Polites, being "fleet of foot," was stationed as a watchman for the Trojans to look for the approach of the Achaeans, one of the major tribes of Greece.

The Roman god of commerce, Mercury (Mercurius), often served as a mediator between the gods and mortals, his winged feet giving him the advantage of speed. Eventually he become the symbol of message-bearing of all types even to the point of today being the logo for British Post. However, Mercury was also known for being cunning and shrewd—a deceiver of many. This is ironic considering we are faced today with scamming messages on our electronic devices. His Greek counterpart was the swift Hermes and both supposedly escorted the dead to the underworld.

Feet, whether swift or not, are mentioned often in the Bible. We find security in where our feet are placed!

> *The LORD God is my strength, who makes my feet nimble as a hind's and sets me to range the heights.* Hab 3:19 (NEB)

> *I have not strayed from the course of duty; I have followed thy path and never stumbled.* Ps 17:5 (NEB)

We are given vital guidance:

> The LORD *will guard the footsteps of his saints, while the wicked sink into silence and gloom; not by mere strength shall a person prevail.* 1 Sam 2:9

> *Look out for the path that your feet must take, and your ways will be secure. Swerve neither to right nor left, and keep clear of every evil thing.* Prov 4:26–27 (NEB)

We also attain deliverance:

> *He brought me up out of the muddy pit, out of the mire and clay; he set my feet on a rock and gave me a firm footing.* Ps 40:2 (NEB)

> *For you have delivered my soul from death, and my feet from falling, so that I may walk before God in the light of life.* Ps 56:13 (NEB)

We can rejoice that the messenger who foretells our Savior is "fleet of foot":

> *How lovely on the mountains are the feet of the herald who come to proclaim prosperity and bring good news, the news of deliverance, calling to Zion, "Your Lord is king."* Isa 52:7 (NEB)

Our feet are the instrument of our direction—join with the herald:

> *let the shoes on your feet be the gospel of peace, to give you firm footing.* Eph 6:15 (NEB)

> *Your word is a lamp to guide my feet and a light on my path.* Ps 119:105 (NEB)

Never fear if your enemies persecute and harass you; if they dog your footsteps continually—walk always in the presence of God and fear them not.

We know that feet in the days that Jesus walked on this earth, were filthy—open sandals treading dusty and muddy thoroughfares. Yet the Son of God knelt before his disciples at the Last Supper and washed their feet. In humility he washed them all—even those of the betrayer. He loved his disciples, weak and questioning as they were. He loves us in our sins. He purchased us with blood and we became his treasure. By laying down his life he could not have loved us more.

Using our feet these days is a popular past-time! The fitness craze abounds—running, jogging, or just walking—to keep our physical bodies healthy. In many countries of the world people embark on pilgrimages as an additional way of pursuing fitness; but some of the walkers perhaps are attempting to find spiritual answers for their minds. These pilgrimages follow the paths of pilgrims of ancient times. The most well-known is probably the Camino de Santiago, known also as the Way of St. James as it leads to the Cathedral of Santiago where tradition holds that the remains of the apostle James are interred. It is actually a network of pilgrim's ways encompassing several routes in France, Spain, and Portugal. Since 2013 the Camino de Santiago has attracted more than 200,000 pilgrims each year. The French Way gathers two-thirds of the walkers and is probably the most arduous. We may enjoy the challenge of some of these pilgrimages in the beautiful surroundings of God's creation, when we traverse more than one country, but, as Christians, our real delight is in the messenger who, "fleet of foot," brings us the great news of salvation and shows us the eternal path to tread.

Always remember the words of Augustine of Hippo when he warns that to turn away from the Lord is to fall!

Pray today that our feet stay on the path of righteousness in Christ, walking in his ways and laying ourselves in humility at his feet. And when we think of our loved ones who have strayed from the good news ask that he will call their wandering hearts home. He alone is able to fulfill all our spiritual yearnings and bring completeness. He alone is able to keep us all from falling.

Epistle 109

When we face great difficulties in life how do we overcome them? Is our first instinct to look to the practice of the modern world—by immediately developing a positive mental attitude? Do we turn to our loved ones or to professionals to give us the best advice? Importantly, do we ever consider that the first step is to turn to our faithful and compassionate Father in Heaven?

We read in God's Word of people who, in arrogance and pomposity, made their own decisions in contrast to the plan God had for them. Saul, for example, sometimes followed the instructions of God but too often became impatient and tried to direct his own path. A great contrast was the action of his son Jonathan when the Israelites were surrounded by thousands of Philistines preparing for battle. Now the Israelites and the Philistines lived side by side for many years but even in times of peace the Philistines were careful to maintain control. They made sure that there were never any Israelites who were capable of being blacksmiths. This way the Israelites had to come to them to sharpen their plowshares, mattocks, axes, and sickles, and were always without the skills to make weapons of war. Philistines also controlled commodities for which the Israelites had to pay highly in their times of need. Consequently, Saul's army was ill-prepared to say the least. In 1 Samuel 13 Saul counted the people who were with him to face the enemy—there were only about six hundred! What is more is that "So when war broke out none of the followers of Saul and Jonathan had either sword of spear; only Saul and Jonathan carried arms." 1 Samuel 13:22 (NEB) So, Saul sat under a tree with his men!

Meanwhile, Jonathan, with his sword and his armor bearer, left the camp and went toward the Philistine garrison. Jonathan went in complete faith that the LORD would act for him saying, "He can bring us safe through, whether we are few or many." His armor bearer pledged himself to his master:

> *"Do what you will, go forward; I am with you whatever you do."*
> *"Good!" said Jonathan, "we will cross over and let them see us. If they say, 'Stay where you are till we come to you,' then we will stay where we are and not go up to them. But if they say, 'Come up to us'; we will go up; this will be the sign that the LORD has put them in our power."* 1 Sam 14:7–10 (NEB)

With complete humility, faithfulness, and obedience to the LORD, the two young men climbed the rocky crag to confront the Philistines holding the garrison. With one sword between them they killed about twenty well-armed men. The remaining Philistines panicked—they trembled; the earth quaked; they fled!

Our Savior Jesus, without any great army and in complete humility, faithfulness, and obedience, faced the fallen world with only a wooden cross and destroyed death. God saves through a humble king—a king like Jonathan but not like Saul—a glorious King called Jesus. It is in God that we must put our complete trust when we face the world and its painful challenges. When we do this, we will have the strength to persevere and will find the peace of God.

> *The Lord is near; have no anxiety, but in everything make your requests known to God in prayer and petition with thanksgiving. Then the peace of God, which is beyond our utmost understanding, will keep guard over your hearts and your thoughts, in Christ Jesus.* Phil 4:6–7 (NEB)

Charles Spurgeon says:

> Run not to man. Go only to your God, the Father of Jesus, who loves you in him. You shall not be able to understand the peace which you shall enjoy. It will enfold you in its infinite embrace. Heart and mind through Christ Jesus shall be steeped in a sea of rest. Come life or death, poverty, pain, slander, you shall dwell in Jesus above every ruffling wind or darkening cloud. Will you not obey this dear command?[1]

This great peace is a presence. It is a sense of being protected. It guards us like a great fortified wall or an army that will never flee. It doesn't remove that which is greatly troubling us, but calms and strengthens us when we

---

1. Spurgeon, *The Cheque Book of the Bank of Faith*, 90.

pass our distress over to our heavenly Father. It is a peace and protection that the world cannot give us. Initially, we may find that this peace alludes us, but it is a peace to be learned. We must hand ourselves over wholly to God in prayer.

Anne, a Christian lady had spent time with her very ill sister, enticing her to eat and persevere. On her way home she went into her church, sat in the silence, and prayed a simple prayer to God to put his arms around her loved one. She experienced a great comfort of peace in her being. The next day God, the loving Father, wrapped her sister in his arms and took her home.

Epistle 110

For those of us who are growing old, our perspective on life is changing. We no longer seem to be making grandiose plans for our future but are perhaps spending more time looking inward and reminiscing about the past. How often do we remember older people telling us stories of their younger life; how often did we switch off, to our detriment, when this happened? We have often closed our minds to the wisdom they may have imparted—perhaps not obviously; but through the muddle of experiences. Sometimes, of course, this retelling was an older person trying to establish some relevance in the midst of the busy world of the young. But was this not a call for compassion? Aloneness is the bane of the elderly and always has been.

Augustine of Hippo in Chapter 8 of his *Confessions* talks "of images, knowledge and experiences accumulated over a lifetime being like a great field or a spacious palace . . . a storehouse for countless images, a cloister, a vast sanctuary, an inner place."[1] When we ponder on these memories, we find a deeper self in our own story. But, in today's society, when we are so often experiencing, either directly or indirectly, the onset of dementia issues such as Alzheimer's, we frighteningly face a prospect of being unable to dwell in our memories or to connect with the memories of our loved ones.

In the Bible we discover—time and time again—that *God always remembers.*

This is crucial for our existence both physically and spiritually. Psalm 88 is entitled: *Prayer for Help in Despondency.* Here the suppliant feels deserted by God with the result that there is wretchedness and desperation:

---

1. Lysaught, "Memory, Funerals, and the Communion of Saints," 275.

> *Thy burning fury has swept over me, thy onslaughts have put me to silence; all the day long they surge round me like a flood, they engulf me in a moment. Thou hast taken lover and friend far from me, and parted me from all my companions.* Ps 88:16–18 (NEB)

But God does not abandon his loved ones; he remembers all his people—he remembered Sarah, Hannah, Rahab; he remembered Abraham, Samuel, David. And—God remembered his people Israel, even though for centuries they oscillated between worshipping him and turning away from him. Reading the Old Testament in its completeness brings home to us how compassionate and forgiving is our LORD. Throughout, God remembered the covenant with his nation and expected Israel to faithfully remember also. He constantly sent prophets to speak his words—but the people did not heed them. "Hark you heavens, and earth give ear, for the LORD has spoken: I have sons whom I reared and brought up, but they have rebelled against me." Isaiah 1:2 (NEB)

> *I brought you into a fruitful land to enjoy its fruits and the goodness of it; but when you entered upon it you defiled it and made the home I gave you loathsome. The priests no longer asked, "Where is the LORD?" Those who handled the law had no thought of me, the shepherds of the people rebelled against me; the prophets prophesied in the name of Baal and followed gods powerless to help.* Jer 2:7–8 (NEB)

We notice also, amidst the Old Testament, that there is often constant repetition. Sometimes it is the same request—as in the criticism of Adonijah, firstly by Bathsheba as a mother of Solomon, and then by Nathan as a prophet; or, it may be similar words adapted to be spoken to a family member and then to a servant. Overall, however, "it is the inescapable tension between human freedom and divine historical plan that is brought forth so luminously through the pervasive repetitions."[2]

> God remained faithful, even though Israel did not. Today, as in all times, God continues to remember even when he is forgotten.

> *Remember the word spoken to me, thy servant, on which thou hast taught me to fix my hope. In time of trouble my consolation is this, that thy promise has given me life.* Ps 119:49–50 (NEB)

---

2. Alter, *The Art of Biblical Narrative*, 113.

We must always remember the ultimate reconciliation between God and us:

> ... *the Lord Jesus, on the night of his arrest, took bread and, after giving thanks to God, broke it and said: "This is my body, which is for you; do this as a memorial of me." In the same way, he took the cup after supper, and said: "This cup is the new covenant sealed by my blood. Whenever you drink it, do this as a memorial of me." For every time you eat this bread and drink this cup, you proclaim the death of the Lord, until he comes.* 1 Cor 11:23–26 (NEB)

We must daily remember each other in prayer. Paul remembered Timothy constantly in his prayers, day and night; he thanked the churches for the prayers they voiced for him; in particular he remembered Philemon in his prayers: "I thank my God always when I mention you in my prayers, for I hear of your love and faith towards the Lord Jesus and towards all God's people." Philemon 4 (NEB)

Remember all those in physical need; remember those who are suffering from spiritual need; and always, in prayer, remember those who do not have the joy of remembering. God will remember them and take them in his loving arms.

> The angel of the Lord said to Cornelius: "Your prayers and acts of charity have gone up to heaven to speak for you before God."
> Acts 10:4 (NEB)

Epistle 111

On July 6, 1919 the British Airship R-34 arrived at Long Island, USA, after leaving the United Kingdom some 108 hours before. When the Airship reached its destination, it had virtually no fuel left. However, the American ground crew had no experience in landing such a large Airship! Consequently, British Major John Pritchard jumped by parachute from R-34 to instruct the ground crew on how to guide it to its mooring.

After sixteen members of the Old Christian's Club Rugby Team (Old Boys of the Stella Maris College in Uruguay) survived the crash of their chartered plane in the Andes, they struggled to survive in the snow with only the battered fuselage as shelter for almost ten weeks. Finally realizing that help was not coming, two of the team—Nando Parrado and Roberto Canessa—taking readings on the plane's spherical compass, scaled a mountain of 13,500 feet then turned west and trekked downhill for days until they reached a valley where they were sighted by some Chilean cowherds. After contact was made with the authorities, helicopters were able to airlift the rest of the survivors. Parrado, now terrified of any type of flying, bravely went with the rescuers to guide them in under the horrendous conditions of weather and altitude.

Do we fear to take risks? We do have to be prudent and take precautions. But we are called to take certain risks.

Abraham agreed to take risks for God by giving up his comfortable life and venturing into the unknown.

Esther risked her life by coming before King Ahauerus and exposing her origins in order to plead for her people.

When Isaiah saw the vision of God in the Temple he cried:

> Woe is me! I am lost, for I am a man of unclean lips and I dwell among a people of unclean lips; yet with these eyes I have seen the King, the LORD of Hosts. Then one of the seraphim flew to me carrying in his hand a glowing coal which he had taken from the altar

> *with a pair of tongs. He touched my mouth with it and said, "See, this has touched your lips; your iniquity is removed, and your sin is wiped away." Then I heard the LORD saying, "Whom shall I send? Who will go for me?" And I answered, "Here I am; send me."* Isa 6:5–8 (NEB)

We read in the last epistle how God's people had constantly turned away from him and practiced evil. Yet, all through these times, when the LORD God called faithful followers to be prophets—they took up the mantle and went forth!

The disciples took risks daily when they followed the words of the Great Commission.

> *Jesus then came up and spoke to them. He said: "Full authority in heaven and on earth has been committed to me. Go forth therefore and make all nations my disciples; baptize people everywhere in the name of the Father and the Son and the Holy Spirit, and teach them to observe all that I have commanded you. And be assured, I am with you always, to the end of time."* Matt 28:18–20 (NEB)

These disciples, who terrified, had once hidden behind locked doors when they lost their leader in death, took risks under the power of the Holy Spirit.

When we read the *Letters of Paul*, we discover that the Church at Philippi was not only being persecuted by the Romans, but was also under doctrinal attack by the legalists, causing much division in the church family. Paul charges the congregation to be worthy of the gospel. He tells the people that God is always at work in them enabling their will to work continuously for his good pleasure. He is sending to them Epaphroditus, his spiritual brother, his faithful co-worker, and, his fellow soldier in fighting the wiles of the devil. Epaphroditus was a man of courage who traveled to Rome at great risk to himself to support Paul when he was in prison.

> *Welcome him then in the fellowship of the Lord with whole-hearted delight. You should honour men like him; in Christ's cause he came near to death, risking his life to render me the service you could not give. And now, friends, farewell; I wish you joy in the Lord.* Phil 2:29–3:1 (NEB)

We are blessed in that we live without the persecution suffered by many in the world today. We might often think we don't need to take risks for the gospel. But we must be faithful and vigilant. We must take the opportunity to be disciples of Jesus in personal evangelism and support to those in the church and those outside. Nor do we have to do this alone. We are a family of believers held together in true fellowship. Even coming to church is vital. Yet in this constantly changing world there is often a different way to think about going to church . . . we come to church if we are able, for the sake of other people. We are a needed part of a whole. If attendance is impossible, then we must make use of every other means to connect, speak, pray, and encourage. We are each different but deliberately placed by God, essential and valuable. We need each other!

> In all things connect, speak, and encourage—but most of all,
> Pray for each other constantly!

Epistle 112

There was a tourist on her first visit to Europe who, like many people, took numerous photographs. However, the majority of her photographs were of doors! These were primarily historical doors—wooden doors, iron doors, even stone doors. Supposedly wooden doors were used in Europe from 3000 BC and stone doors throughout Asia from 2000 BC. The first doors in history were made from fabrics or animal hides—when Cain was contemplating murdering his brother Abel, God warned him that: "sin is a demon crouching at the door. It shall be eager for you, and you will be mastered by it." Genesis 4:7 (NEB) In these early days of creation this would have been an animal hide door. We read further on that Abraham sat at the entrance to his tent; he ran from the tent door to greet the three strangers. Genesis 18:1–2 Soon we progress to wooden doors. Noah had numerous intricate details to carry out when building the ark—one of them involved the entrance door: "You shall make a roof for the ark, giving it a fall of one cubit when complete; and put a door in the side of the ark, and build three decks, upper, middle, and lower". Genesis 6:16 (NEB) In St. Mary's Church, Long Crichel in Dorset, there is a charmingly carved Noah's Ark set into a niche. There are number of animals peering out the windows and the door looks very much like a church door. The bow of the ark is decorated with a large camel's head—the ship of the desert!

When the Israelites were living in Egypt and later in the Promised Land, their homes became more permanent dwellings. In fact, the earliest depictions of doors appear in the paintings in Egyptian tombs. In Ancient Greek and Roman times, doors became more involved—single, double, triple doors, and sliding or folding doors on hinges. Folding doors were found in the ruins of Pompeii. Variety of doors in bronze, wood, marble, and glass were developed, some with extensive carving, decoration, and etching. As instructed by God, Solomon:

> *At the entrance to the inner shrine he made a double door of wild olive; the pilasters and the door-posts were pentagonal . . . he carved cherubim, palms, and open flowers on them, overlaying them with gold and hammering the gold upon the cherubim and the palms.* 1 Kgs 6:32 (NEB)

Doors can sometimes cause conflict! The Royal Crescent in Bath, built some 240 years ago, is a semi-circular row of terraced houses. Often housing Royal personages in the beginning, the row today is still remarkable for its symmetrical architecture and its uniformity in color, as well as its notable residents. One of the owners in recent years painted her door a fairly bright yellow. The Bath City Council issued a notice insisting it should be repainted. A court case ensued, which resulted in the Secretary of State for the Environment declaring that the door could remain yellow! We can be different but we must stay in the unity.

In modern times receiving the "key to the door" generally signifies a change in status from outsider to insider; definitely from teenager to adult! Often in literature opening and closing of doors indicate a portent of change. Importantly, doors very often have aesthetic, symbolic, or ritualistic purposes and this is no more evident than in the Bible. Jesus tells us that *he is the door* and anyone who enters by him will be saved! Furthermore, not only saved by him, but dwelling with him in eternal life:

> *Here I stand knocking at the door; if anyone hears my voice and opens the door, I will come in and sit down to supper with him and he with me.* Rev 3:20 (NEB)

> *After this I looked, and there before my eyes was a door opened in heaven.* Rev 4:1 (NEB)

The sacrifice of Jesus is the door that leads to our salvation. The gift of the Holy Spirit becomes, through prayer, the door to living in certain faith on earth today. When the Spirit calls us, we must step through the doorway.

> *When they arrived and had called the congregation together, they reported all that God had done through them, and how he had thrown open the doors of faith to the Gentiles.* Acts 14:27 (NEB)

In today's world the *Open Doors Ministry for Persecuted Christians* asks for our prayers more than anything else. Prayer is the most powerful force with the irrefutable hope of a Heavenly Father who can accomplish all things.

Recall that, when Paul and Silas were imprisoned, they were praying and singing hymns to God, and the other prisoners were listening to them:

> *Suddenly there was such a violent earthquake that the foundations of the jail were shaken; all the doors burst open and all the prisoners found their fetters unfastened.* Acts 16:26 (NEB)

Not only are the doors opened for us but we can free ourselves from all that the world holds dear and walk into the true life.

Let us open the doors of our hearts—listen, heed, pray, and act.

When Paul was in Philippi, he went outside the city gate to the riverside, to talk to a group of women gathered there.

> *One of them named Lydia, a dealer in purple fabric from the city of Thyatira, who was a worshipper of God, was listening, and the Lord opened her heart to respond to what Paul said.* Acts 16:14 (NEB)

The earth, and everything in it, belongs to God; the devil shall not prevail against him. *Let us begin our prayers boldly* that due praise will be lifted up to our Redeemer King...

> *Lift up your heads, you gates,*
> *lift them up, you everlasting doors!*
> > *that the King of Glory may come in.*
> *Who then is the King of Glory?*
> *The King of Glory is the LORD of Hosts.* Ps 24:9–10 (NEB)

Epistle 113

> Human societies are based on the human tendency to want things, and are geared to satisfying those wants: possessions or facilities to bring ease and personal satisfaction. The results are frequently disappointing, and always terminate in the embarrassing non sequitur of death.[1]

In the early days of Christianity many sought a different life to this "seeking after earthly fulfillment." But it was an extremely radical option and gave birth to a movement known as monasticism. Communal monasticism was begun about 320 AD by a converted soldier. This man, Pachomius, had originally spent some time as a hermit before he set up his community in Egypt. He had strict rules and insisted his followers had to hand over their personal wealth and then undertake assigned work to support the community. Initially to join the monastery, it was necessary to stand outside the door for several days to establish commitment before entry was granted. Then the novice had to work as a servant for three years before he would be accepted. Pachomius determined that members each day prayed twelve times, at evening twelve times, at night twelve times—on each occasion confessing their uncleanness and reciting a psalm.

Other Christians followed the example of Pachomius by setting up houses of pure devotion to God. However, many people chose to remain as hermits, living alone in deserts or caves, away from the world and its temptations. One of these gained much fame for his endurance in such a life. Simon Stylites spent his last years existing on the top of a pillar. Obviously, admirers of his lifestyle supplied him with sustenance of some kind. The remains of this pillar can be found in the ruins of a church in Syria.

---

1. MacCulloch, *A History of Christianity*, 200.

As Christianity spread so too did the establishment of monasteries for men and convents for women with the main priority for both being prayer. But some of these institutions brought forth wonderful sources of spiritual encouragement with the writings of monks and prioresses. During the High Middle Ages Hildegard of Bingen, a Benedictine Abbess, was active as a writer, composer, philosopher, mystic, visionary, and medical practitioner. She also studied cosmology and is considered to be the founder of scientific natural history in Germany.

> *Hildegard was speaking and writing at the end of the age when women in monasteries were likely to have as good an access to scholarship as men. In her lifetime, the first universities were taking shape, all-male institutions which were to gather them most of the intellectual activity of Western Latin culture.*[2]

As a result, women of these times were greatly attracted to the unconstrained study of spirituality and many became influential mystics. Hildegard's prayer for the comforting fire of the Spirit still resonates for us today.

> *Holy Spirit, Comforting fire, Life of all creation.*
> *Anointing the sick, cleansing body and soul,*
> *Fill this body!*
> *Holy Spirit, Sacred breath, Fire of love,*
> *Sweetest taste, Beautiful aroma,*
> *Fill this heart!*
> *Holy Spirit, Filling the world, from the heights to the deep,*
> *Raining from clouds, filling rivers and sea.*
> *Fill this mind!*[3]

By the time we come to the twentieth century we find there are fewer such institutions and, in those that remain, there is an impetus to go out into the world to teach and pastor in addition to a continuing prayer life. Change in modern times is inevitable. Churches are changing also. In Devon in the UK there is a new rural church plant on a farm: the vision is to become a center for spiritual renewal and innovative creativity—a new creation in the midst of God's creation. This plant has been inspired by an early Christian, St. Basil, who was known to have a real reliance on the power of prayer and the Holy Spirit. His farm outside a city was a haven for the hungry, the sick, and the unloved. Our churches today, whether

---

2. MacCulloch, *A History of Christianity*, 420–21.
3. Thiele, *Justprayer.org*

they change in format or not, must always be true centers of loving prayer and worship.

St. Hilda's at Whitby in Yorkshire is home to a family of Anglican nuns. Their original historical home has been sold to a wedding reception group. With the money from the sale, they have built a beautiful center behind with accommodation for travelers. There are numerous services of prayer and worship each day and opportunities to partake in meals. All meals, except for those on Tuesdays, are eaten in silence. This gives a wonderful sense of contemplation on the grace before the repast. The sisters are so welcoming and loving that comfort, peace, and renewal flow through, and prayer becomes a daily companion.

Many churches today hold regular Prayer Retreats—these have become wonderful opportunities for all Christians to renew their strength and come closer to their Savior in today's frenetic world. You will find in your own part of the world there are many centers devoted solely to the holding of Prayer Retreats, which you can attend for weekends or for longer periods, There you can share with others prayer and spiritual experiences, or; you can choose a more solitary path where deep personal reflection and prayer can help you grow in the Holy Spirit. Various groups organise annual conferences at such centers encouraging members of their congregation to participate. Even just attending a Quiet Day can refresh and strengthen your faith.

Epistle 114

When John Wesley was at Oxford University in the early 1730s, he became involved in many Christian works of charity. He had with him a small band of university friends. Wesley visited and preached at a nearby prison: "Wesley and the laymen took turns to visit the prisons daily: twice a week they read prayers."[1] Wesley also started a small school for poor children and visited poor families in the locality. "The friends took turns to hear the children read, or say their prayers."[2] He established a small fund for providing prisoners, the poor, and the children with any material items they might need. John Wesley was a very methodical person with his followers and in every task he undertook. To aid his friends he wrote a handbook entitled *A Collection of Forms of Prayer*, which they were pressed to study in their spare moments. Wesley himself was a man of prayer who liked to "shoot up a prayer, an 'ejaculation,' on the first second of every hour."[3] This band of committed Christians became known as the *Holiness Club* or the *Godly Club*.

In 1736 John and his brother Charles, on behalf of SPCK (Society for Promoting Christian Knowledge), embarked on a journey to Georgia, a newly founded English colony in America. There was a fearful storm during the voyage. Wesley, fearing death, became greatly influenced by the piety and courage of a group of Moravians who calmy sang hymns throughout. On reaching the colony he became engaged in conversation with one of the Moravian leaders who asked Wesley if he knew Christ. "Wesley paused in some confusion, then replied lamely: 'I know he is the Saviour of the world. . . But do you know he has saved *you*?' Wesley replied uncomfortably, 'I hope he has died to save me.'"[4]

1. Pollock, *John Wesley*, 48.
2. Pollock, *John Wesley*, 48.
3. Pollock, *John Wesley*, 49.
4. Pollock, *John Wesley*, 68.

This man, who had devoted his life to good works in the name of Christ, only came to know Jesus fully when he attended a Moravian prayer meeting back home in London. He claimed his heart was lit by God. He then began to earnestly pray for those who persecuted him and were trying to prevent him from preaching and evangelizing.

Who were the Moravians? They were Protestants who traced their origins to ancient Bohemia, the present-day Czech Republic. Theologically they were followers of Jan Hus who preached Reformation principles opposing many of the church's practices a century before Luther posted his ninety-five theses on the church doors in Wittenberg. Hus was burned at the stake in 1415 for his preaching and his ashes thrown in the Rhine—however his church, with its pulpit and original furnishings, still remains in Prague. The Moravians did have an early period of dissent and unhappiness and faced many struggles. By the 1720s many had become refugees in other countries. In Germany some settled in land owned by Nicolaus Zinzendorf in Herrnhut. Zinzendorf, an eventual bishop of the Moravian church, was responsible for a great revival amongst the people, developing their love for prayer and their commitment to evangelism. Their resultant missionary zeal sent many to the Americas. In respect of prayer, on August 27, 1727, twenty-four men and twenty-four women of the Herrnhut Brethren pledged themselves to observe one hour each day to prayer.

> *The thought struck some brethren and sisters that it might be well to set apart certain hours for the purpose of prayer, at which seasons all might be reminded of its excellency and be induced by the promises annexed to fervent persevering prayer to pour out their hearts before the Lord.*[5]

The Brethren based its premise, which it called the *Warrant for Prayer Watch*, on Leviticus 6:12–13:

> *The fire shall be kept burning on the altar; it shall never go out. Every morning the priest shall have fresh wood burning thereon, arrange the whole-offering on it, and on top burn the fat from the shared-offerings. Fire shall always be kept burning on the altar; it shall not go out.* (NEB)

A perpetual prayer shall be raised to the Lord, it shall not cease!

---

5. Church of the Brethren, *The Memorial Days of the Renewed Church of the Brethren*, 1822.

This faithful community commenced a prayer watch which lasted for over one hundred years. Only sixty-five years after it began this same community had sent 300 missionaries to the far reaches of the world.

Could our present-day Christian community maintain a prayer vigil for one hundred years? Surely there is a plethora of reasons why it should be done.

> Do we have the belief in the vital importance of prayer?
> > Do we have the courage and commitment?
> > > Do we have the love in our hearts to attempt it?

John Wesley translated these words from a German hymn by Paul Gerhhardt.

> Jesus, thy boundless love to me
> No thought can reach, no tongue declare;
> O knit my thankful heart to Thee,
> And reign without a rival there:
> Thine wholly, Thine alone, I am:
> Lord with Thy love my heart inflame.[6]

---

6. Church of Scotland, *The Church Hymnary*, 432.

Epistle 115

We Christians are not the only people who pray. But, unlike the majority of religions in the world today, our praying is a vital communion with a living, loving God. Greek and Roman religions, Nordic religions, and ancient and modern Eastern religions all invoke prayers to imaginary and mythical gods. Even a religion that uses Christian in its title does not believe prayer is a supplication between humans and the Creator God. Christian Science teaches that prayer is a spiritualization of thought or an understanding of God from a human perspective. Prayer just gives man a clearer view of life!

Different religions use a variety of body postures to pray as do different denominations of Christianity. Early Christians knelt or even spread themselves prostrate on the floor to pray. Hands were clasped or arms raised. Interestingly when Paul advised women on their demeanour in worship, he said: "It is my desire, therefore, that everywhere prayers be said by the men of the congregation, who shall lift up their hands with pure intention, excluding angry or quarrelsome thoughts." 1 Timothy 2:8 (NEB) Generally we sit with heads bowed and possibly with hands folded or clasped to pray in Church Services, though there are still many who kneel. A few in closed communities still prostrate themselves when praying. For many generations Presbyterian congregations in Scotland would stand to pray. There were biblical reasons for this, one being in 2 Chronicles 20:5–9:

> *Jehoshaphat stood in the assembly of Judah and Jerusalem, in the house of the LORD, in front of the New Court, and said, "O LORD God of our fathers, art thou not God in heaven? Thou rulest over all the kingdoms of the nations; in thy hand are strength and power, and there is none who can withstand thee. Didst not thou, O God our God, dispossess the inhabitants of this land in favour of thy people Israel, and give it for ever to the descendants*

> *of Abraham thy friend?" So they lived in it and have built a sanctuary in it in honour of thy Name and said, "Should evil come upon us, war or flood, pestilence or famine, we will stand before this house and before thee, for in this house is thy Name, and we will cry to thee in our distress and thou wilt hear and save."* (NEB)

In Mark 11:25, Jesus says: "And when you stand praying, if you have a grievance against anyone, forgive him, so that your Father in heaven may forgive you the wrongs you have done." (NEB)

But there are also biblical reasons to follow the practice of kneeling—Ezra and Solomon in the Old Testament; Stephen, Peter, and Paul in the New Testament, all knelt in prayer. In Philippians 2:10 we read ". . . that at the name of Jesus every knee should bow—in heaven, on earth, and in the depths." (NEB)

The following verse gives us a solid reason for kneeling in humility:

> *—and every tongue confess, "Jesus Christ is Lord" to the glory of God the Father.* 2:11 (NEB)

Early Church Fathers contributed their beliefs—Justin Martyr preached: "They all rose together and prayed." Augustine of Hippo wrote: "We pray standing, which is a sign of the resurrection." The Free Church of Scotland continues the practice of standing and often encourages other denominations to follow what they term is the Apostolic pattern!

Is the manner in which we pray the essential part of prayer?
It is not the mode of our physical body but the condition of our spiritual body.

There are only two vital requirements we need to come before God in prayer:

True humility and complete surrender

Surrender in the war was devastating. Soldiers felt ashamed that they were now under the power of an enemy. Japanese soldiers committed suicide rather than surrender because of family honor. Russian soldiers knew that it was better to be dead as their own country would completely abandon them in this plight. Russian prisoners-of-war who were sent back to their country at the cessations of hostilities were either executed or sent to the Gulags. Surrendering was the acceptance that the fight had been lost by the combatant and all hope of life appeared to be gone: "To suffer under restraint is deadly. It is like chaining a man to the scaffold on which he is to be hanged."[1]

During the Second World War, civilians too lost their freedom. Hans and Sophie Scholl were a brother and sister who went to the Ludwig Maximilian University to leave flyers that called for the overthrow of National Socialism in Germany. Both were arrested but Sophie was initially considered innocent of the charge. However, she surrendered her freedom to protect others who were involved. She was executed by guillotine immediately after her trial. Sophie messaged a friend that God was her refuge into eternity. As she walked to her death, she was heard to remark that it was a splendid sunny day!

What does surrendering to God really mean?

It means that we accept that the battle we have been fighting in the world is now over—we have lost the struggle. By embracing a spiritual surrender, we let go of our lives and give control to a God who is trustworthy in all he says and does.

> *For through the law I died to the law—to live for God. I have been crucified with Christ: the life I now live is not my life, but the life which Christ lives in me; and my present bodily life is lived by faith in the Son of God, who loved me and gave himself up for me.* Gal 2:19–20 (NEB)

Surrendering to God involves no distress, no persecution, no shame.
Surrendering to God means a certain hope, comfort, and peace.
In humility let us pray that the Holy Spirit will guide us to
complete surrender.

---

[1]. Purdom, *On the Front Line*, 430.

Epistle 116

"A cup of tea, a Bex, and a good lie down." This was once a well-known quip to anyone in Australia who was having a bad day full of worry and stress! In years gone by a cup of tea was an accompaniment to practically every pause in the day. On the cross-channel ferry from France, a passenger was overheard telephoning her daughter to ask her to purchase some milk and leave it by the back door—a cup of tea would be desperately needed on the traveler's return! In 1913 the suffragette, Emmeline Pankhurst, traveled to America to publicise her cause. In one of her speeches, she said: "When you have warfare things happen; people suffer; the non-combatants suffer as well as the combatants. And so it happens in civil war. When your forefathers threw the tea into Boston Harbour, a good many women had to go without their tea . . ."[1]

How do you deal with family or friends who are suffering with problems in their daily lives? Do you advise them to be strong and cope with the setbacks; or, do you tell them how you or someone you know has a similar problem so you know how they feel? No two problems are the same and no two people react to problems in the same way—you cannot fully understand!

Listen and berate; listen and sympathize; or, *heed and encourage*?

Is a cup of tea, a Bex, and a good lie down going to solve our problems?

Barnabus, a companion and co-worker with Paul, was known as "the son of encouragement" by the Apostles. He was a Levite who hailed from Cyprus and was a person of means—he sold his land and placed the proceeds at the feet of the apostles for the use of the church. Barnabus appears to be part of a Hellenist movement back to Jerusalem from Gentile lands. When Paul was converted on the road to Damascus he was not well received when he began to preach about the risen Christ

---

1. Addis, *I Have a Dream*, 61.

in Jerusalem; but Barnabus spoke in support for him and his evangelism. It was Barnabus, being an upright man, who was commissioned by the church in Antioch to undertake a missionary journey with Paul and John Mark to the island of Cyprus and the cities of the north mainland. During this journey Mark left and returned to Jerusalem much to Paul's displeasure. In later times when Paul was in Antioch preparing to leave on another missionary journey to see how his former converts were managing, Barnabus wanted to take Mark with them:

> but Paul judged that the man who had deserted them in Pamphylia and had not gone on to share in their work was not the man to take with them now. The dispute was so sharp that they parted company. Barnabas took Mark with him and sailed for Cyprus, while Paul chose Silas. He started on his journey, commended by the brothers to the grace of the Lord. Acts 15:38–40 (NEB)

We are not told why Mark deserted Paul but we know that Barnabus was devoted to him, not only because he was his cousin, but possibly to encourage him to once again take up the work of the Church of Christ. In fact, in spite of disruptions in the church the friendship between Paul and Barnabus did not fail. When we read of Mark being with Paul in Rome in later years (Col 4:10) we see the encouraging work of Barnabus in such a reconciliation.

Throughout the Old Testament the Israelites found strength and encouragement from a faithful God: David said to his son Solomon:

> Be steadfast and resolute and do it; be neither faint-hearted nor dismayed, for the LORD God, my God, will be with you; he will neither fail you nor forsake you, until you have finished all the work needed for the service of the house of the LORD. 1 Chr 28:20 (NEB)

Isaiah is told by God: "fear nothing, for I am with you; be not afraid, for I am your God. I strengthen you, I help you, I support you with my victorious right hand." Isaiah 41:10 (NEB)

Micah, the prophet, wrote: "O my enemies, do not exult over me; I have fallen, but shall rise again; though I dwell in darkness, the LORD is my light." Micah 7:8 (NEB)

Barnabus found his courage and hope in a risen Christ as we can. But we, as members of the body of Christ in our renewed strength, must also encourage each other constantly:

> *For God has not destined us to the terrors of judgement, but to the full attainment of salvation through our Lord Jesus Christ. He died for us so that we, awake or asleep, might live in company with him. Therefore hearten one another, fortify one another—as indeed you do.* 1 Thess 5:9–11 (NEB)

> *We ought to see how each of us may best arouse others to love and active goodness, not staying away from our meetings, as some do, but rather encouraging one another, all the more because you see the Day drawing near.* Heb 10:24–25 (NEB)

Let us be vigilant in our prayers for each other. May we ever reach out in love through Christ our Savior to endue others with hope, courage, and strength. Be joyful always; pray continually; give thanks in all circumstances.

Do this for ourselves and for all God's people.

Epistle 117

Howard Somervell and George Mallory were close climbing friends who both made incredible attempts to conquer Mt. Everest in the 1920s. Somervell was born into a devout Presbyterian family in the Lake District. Nevertheless, whilst studying science at Cambridge, he:

> *... flirted with atheism, joining the Heretics, a society in which, as he recalled, "all my cherished religious beliefs were dashed to the ground. For two years I strenuously refused to believe in God." But then, toward the end of his second year, he slipped by chance into a prayer meeting at a local church. There he experienced a revelation and emerged to become an ardent and passionate evangelical. "It was not long," he noted, "before I was preaching, with shaking knees and beating heart, at open air meetings in the Cambridge market place."*[1]

Over the years, probably because of Somervell's horrific experiences treating the wounded and the dying in the First World War, his evangelical practice of preaching somewhat faded, "he remained nevertheless a man of intense religious faith, convinced of the power of prayer, which he took as a visceral reality."[2]

The power of prayer is the power of God who hears and answers prayer:

> *Again I tell you this: if two of you agree on earth about any request you have to make, that request will be granted by my heavenly Father. For where two or three have met together in my name, I am there among them.* Matt 18:19–20 (NEB)

It isn't simply in the words! Prayer is an act of worship. We glorify our God and humbly accept that we have need of him. He is our Creator;

---

1. Davis, *Into the Silence*, 19–20.
2. Davis, *Into the Silence*, 20.

he is the reason we exist and, by communicating with him, we find the reason and purpose of our existence. By consistently being faithful in prayer it becomes our prescription for the way we live. We have a powerful God thus there is none better with whom to entrust our precious life: "for God's promises never fail." Luke 1:37 (NEB)

James commends to us how to pray:

> *If any of you falls short in wisdom, you should ask God for it and it will be given you, for God is a generous giver who neither refuses nor reproaches any-one. But you must ask in faith, without a doubt in your mind; for the doubter is like a heaving sea ruffled by the wind. A person of that kind must not expect the Lord to give him anything; he is double-minded, and never can keep a steady course.* Jas 1:5–8 (NEB)

We must never give way to temptation and troubles.

> *Since therefore we have a great high priest who has passed through the heavens, Jesus the Son of God, let us hold fast to the religion we profess. For ours is not a high priest unable to sympathize with our weaknesses but one who, because of his likeness to us, has been tested every way, only without sin. Let us therefore boldly approach the throne of our gracious God, where we may receive mercy and in his grace find timely help.* Heb 4:14–15 (NEB)

Fear makes us weak and confused—prayer gives us strength and wisdom: Jesus said, "I am the vine, and you the branches. Those who dwell in me, as I dwell in them, bear much fruit, for apart from me you can do nothing." John 15:5 (NEB)

We do not always see the answers to our prayers perhaps because we already have set answers in our minds. But God answers our prayer in his way not ours. Incredibly God's way can be the way we hoped for! When the barren Hannah prayed: "O LORD of Hosts, if thou wilt deign to take notice of my trouble and remember me, if thou wilt not forget me but grant me offspring, then I will give the child to the LORD for his whole life, and no razor shall ever touch his head." 1 Samuel 1:11 (NEB) God granted her wish. When she had weaned her son, she took him to the temple and said, "What I asked for I have received; and now I lend him to the LORD; for his whole life he is lent to the LORD." 1 Samuel 1:28a (NEB) God answered her prayer exactly as she requested and later blessed her greatly: "The LORD showed care for Hannah, and she conceived and gave birth to three sons and two daughters." 1 Samuel 2:21a (NEB)

Paul's prayer was also answered—but for God's purposes:

> *If I should choose to boast, it would be the boast of a fool, for I should be speaking the truth. But I refrain, because I should not like anyone to form an estimate of me which goes beyond the evidence of his own eyes and ears. And so, to keep me from being unduly elated by the magnificence of such revelations, I was given a sharp physical pain which came as Satan's messenger to bruise me; this was to save me from being unduly elated. Three times I begged the Lord to rid me of it, but his answer was: "My grace is all you need; power comes to its full strength in weakness." I shall therefore prefer to find my joy and pride in the very things that are my weakness; and then the power of Christ will come and rest upon me. Hence I am well content, for Christ's sake, with weakness, contempt, persecution, hardship, and frustration; for when I am weak, then I am strong.* 2 Cor 12:6–10 (NEB)

Both these prayers were answered. Hannah rejoiced in the gift of a son; Paul became content in his weakness for in this weakness he found strength.

We may not even glimpse the answer to our prayer but we can still hold in our hearts the power of prayer as did Howard Somervell. From an evangelical awakening; to a doctor in the War to end all wars; in the dangers of mountaineering leading to the loss of his companion climber Mallery on Everest; during the long years of working as a medical missionary in India, and; in the midst of his compulsive work as an artist—he placed his strength in his belief in the power of prayer.

Epistle 118

For seventy years and 214 days Queen Elizabeth II has reigned; the longest reign of any British monarch and the second-longest recorded of any monarch. Her constant presence is now an almost unfathomable absence. To most people they have known her as Queen for the entirety of their lives. To the much older—her father the King, can be remembered. The day of his death had an unexpected effect for some Australian children. Practicing the Maypole Dance would come to an end because the Princess was no longer coming to watch such a performance on a huge cricket ground in Melbourne! Amazingly, the father of one of these children, having been born in 1896, was now entering the reign of a sixth monarch!

When we face the death of a loved one the grief brings an immense sadness; sometimes a strange anger; often many plaintive questions. Most of all, as time stretches on, the longest emotion is probably a yearning—a yearning for a life as it was; "saudade" being a deep emotional state of melancholic longing for a person who is now absent. Sometimes another person fulfills the duties and the care but can never fill the deep void. In the case of the Queen, there is now a King to carry on the monarch's role. We have seen how involved the transfer of power has been and will continue to be in the months ahead. Even the smallest detail is not to be overlooked! The day after Elizabeth's death the royal beekeeper had to tell the bees that the Queen was gone. Following an ancient tradition, John Chappelle informed the hives at Buckingham Palace that their mistress had left this world. All of the five hives were tied with a black ribbon and, knocking on each one, he charged the bees to be good to the new master.

> Joy and woe are woven fine,
> a clothing for the soul divine.
> Under every grief and pine,
> runs a joy with silken twine.[1]

Similarly, it is often said that to truly love means to experience deep grief —joy and woe are intrinsically linked—by nature they are inseparable qualities. Jesus told his disciples that their sorrow will turn to joy. Predicting his coming death on the cross he said:

> *In very truth I tell you, you will weep and mourn, but the world will be glad. But though you will be plunged in grief, your grief will be turned to joy. A woman in labour is in pain because her time has come; but when the child is born she forgets her anguish in her joy that a child has been born into the world.* John 16:19b–21 (NEB)

This is not the grief the disciples will experience contrasted with the rejoicing the Jewish leaders will have when they come to dispose of Jesus so decisively. No—this is the joy that will come to the disciples themselves after the anguish of their loss, "for the moment you are sad at heart; but I shall see you again, and then you will be joyful, and no one shall rob you of your joy." 16:22 (NEB) Furthermore, Jesus promises his disciples—and he promises us—that: "In very truth I tell you, if you ask the Father for anything in my name, he will give it to you. So far you have asked nothing in my name. Ask and you will receive, that your joy may be complete." 16:23–24 (NEB)

Joy beyond the troubles that daily assail us in this present world!

If we turn our eyes on Jesus, if we ask of God in his name, the things of the earth will go strangely dim in the light of his glory and his grace.

This is the only way we will be able to journey through our grief; through our losses in life. Often, we just have to hand everything over to Jesus when the pain is so great and there seem no words to express how we feel. Sometimes our theology of life seems only as sturdy as a house of cards but, even in the overwhelming emptiness, we must put our trust in our loving, faithful, compassionate Father. If prayer seems to evade us, dwell well in the silence.

> *The LORD is my strength, my shield, in him my heart trusts.* Ps 28:7 (NEB)

---

1. Blake, *The Complete Poems*, 172–173.

God is always there even when we do not hear an answer to our prayers of distress.

Hannah found a wonderful answer; Paul found an answer of refusal.

> Our answer surrounds our very being:
> "Peace, child! I am here!"

Epistle 119

On television; on YouTube; on Instagram; we watch all the ceremonies pertaining to the death and funeral of a Queen. Much of it is overwhelming and yet those who partake express a stoicism and perseverance in their duties of reverence and love. As we see the vigils around the catafalque do we wonder what is going through the minds of those standing in vigil? We could say we see profound and loving sorrow. What are we thinking when we witness these scenes? Oswald Chambers uses a word that could relay to us the breadth of these thoughts—*brood*! To brood is to grieve deeply; but also, to meditate with morbid persistence; to carry a heavy load; even to torment oneself! Prayer to uphold and carry one through the darkest hours that lie ahead would provide the strength and perseverance to endure. "We are able to persevere only because God works within us, within our free wills. And because God is at work in us, we are certain to persevere."[1]

Paul urges the Corinthians to persevere in their faith . . .

> *Be alert, stand firm in the faith, be valiant and strong.* 1 Cor 16:13 (NEB)

> . . . *stand firm and immovable, and work for the Lord always, work without limit, since you know that in the Lord your labour cannot be lost.* 15:58 (NEB)

How does our faith come to us? Chambers sees it materialise when we *brood* on another death—*when we brood on the cross.* The cross is the center where the power lies. He points out that Charismatic and Pentecostal Movements place the emphasis on the effects of the cross. We must brood on the cross itself for we have not brooded enough on its tragedy and its meaning of redemption.

---

1. Sproul, *The R. C. Sproul Collection. Volume 1*, 364.

> *So now my friends, the blood of Jesus makes us free to enter boldly into the sanctuary by the new, living way which he has opened for us through the curtain, the way of his flesh. We have, moreover, a great priest set over the household of God; so let us make our approach in sincerity of heart and full assurance of faith, our guilty hearts sprinkled clean, our bodies washed with pure water. Let us be firm and unswerving in the confession of our hope, for the Giver of the promise may be trusted.* Heb 10:19–23 (NEB)

Plus—we strengthen our faith by meeting together in fellowship and prayer. Through both of these we learn to persevere no matter what trials we face.

Let us consider two large animals who exist together. The elephant has only one pace—a walk—although sometimes he can speed up for a short burst; to a hurried shuffle of about twenty miles an hour. His normal pace is three or four miles an hour. In comparison a rhinoceros can trot, gallop, and jump, and often seems to run as fast as a horse. A rhinoceros is not necessarily prone to attacking an elephant but it may decide to drive in front of him:

> . . . some nervous elephant who has turned tail at his approach. The elephant bolts at her best pace, followed by the rhino, whose speed of course allows him to overtake her whenever he wishes. Apparently, however, he feels like the dog who gives chase to a motor-car without considering what he is going to do with it if he catches it. As each rush brings his snout close to the elephant's rump he checks and stands listening to her retreat through the swishing grass before again pounding on in pursuit . . . In this fashion the pair of them may cover a quarter of a mile before the rhino's curiosity is satisfied and he swings off into a course of his own.[2]

Do we feel that we are often pursued by endless problems which seem impossible to overcome?

Can we persevere in the strength of our faith knowing we can take our troubles to our God in prayer?

We can persevere when we know the power of the cross.

Similarly, when an elephant has lost his tusks (most likely in a fight) another elephant will generally walk behind him looking out for him! Elephants develop strong, intimate bonds with other elephants in their family!

---

2. Shebbeare, *Soondar Mooni*, 51.

> We must care for each other constantly in fellowship
> and prayer.

The biography of the Indian elephant *Soondar Mooni* (Beautiful Disposition) from which the above extract is taken, is entrancing; illustrating the fascinating complexity of one of God's creatures—yet uncovering characteristics that we believe only belong to human beings! It was written by a very individual personality; a forester and Game Warden in India, Malaya, and Bengal.

We must always go back to the cross! "The centre of salvation is the Cross of Jesus, and the reason it is so easy to obtain salvation is because it cost God so much. The Cross is the point where God and sinful man merge with a crash and the way to life is opened—but the crash is on the heart of God."[3]

> Brood on this in prayer!

---

3. Chambers, *My Utmost for His Highest*, 4/6.

Epistle 120

The LORD's true love is surely not spent,
 nor has his compassion failed;
 they are new every morning,
 so great is his constancy.
The LORD, I say, is all that I have;
 therefore I will wait for him patiently.
The LORD is good to those who look for him,
 to all who seek him;
it is good to wait in patience and sigh
 for deliverance by the LORD. Lam 3:22–26 (NEB)

No wonder we do not lose heart! Though our outward humanity is in decay, yet day by day we are inwardly renewed. Our troubles are slight and short-lived; and their outcome an eternal glory which outweighs them far. Meanwhile our eyes are fixed, not on things that are seen, but on the things that are unseen; for what is seen passes away; what is unseen is eternal. 2 Cor 4:16–18 (NEB)

Both these readings, one from the Old Testament and the other from the New, convey the assurance that the love of God never ceases—no matter what the circumstances of our life we must not lose heart. Often, we feel that even in our quiet times of prayer, there appears to be a worrying silence. Should we be questioning this silence or might it be God's deliberate silence. Does he want us to pause from life and dwell in his encompassing silence? Could this be God trusting us to understand that his desires for us are always tightly bound by his steadfast love. "If God has given you a silence, praise Him, He is bringing you into the great run of His purposes."[1] Our prayers may not be answered the way we anticipate but they are always answered in God's way. This stillness that comes from

---

1. Chambers, *My Utmost for His Highest*, 10/11.

the Father gives us the confidence to say: "I know that God has heard me." Silence leads us to a deep intimacy. The silence we experience when we are alone with a loved one in their dying moments is enriched when we know that there are three there together—one leaving the care of the earthly to rise to the arms of the heavenly.

> *. . . a deep reverence is in this silence.*

We come to this place of a welcome silence through the growth of our relationship with God—learning about God with all his attributes and actions in the Bible; seeking our God through gratitude and obedience; and coming to know God fully in our heart and souls. We can go away to a place where the noise of the world does not intrude but we can also find silence in our daily busy life. We can look for him in our joys, in our tribulations, and in our loneliness. God is wherever we seek him!

In Revelation 8:1, we read: "Now when the Lamb broke the seventh seal, there was silence in heaven for what seemed half an hour." (NEB) This is an event that seems incomprehensible. Most commentators write that this is to prepare us for the terrible judgments that are about to be related. "So fearful and awful is even this initial retribution that the inhabitants of heaven stand spell-bound, lost for a long time—half an hour—in breathless, in silent amazement."[2]

We remember from the affirmation of our faith in the Creed of the Apostles that, in regard to the judgments, Jesus is sitting on the right hand of the throne of God, ordained to judge the "quick and the dead." In the following verses William Hendricksen notes that the seven angels standing before God were given seven trumpets, and:

> *Then another angel came and stood at the altar, holding a golden censor; and he was given a great quantity of incense to offer with the prayers of all God's people upon the golden altar in front of the throne. And from the angel's hand the smoke of the incense went up before God with the prayers of his people.* Rev 8:3–4 (NEB)

Hendricksen understands this to mean: "These saints in persecution and tribulation are praying. But their prayer-life is imperfect. It needs to be incensed with the intercession of Christ, the one now enthroned in heaven. Once these prayers have been incensed, the seer notices that the

---

2. Hendricksen, *More Than Conquerors*, 141.

smoke ascends to the very presence of God; that is, the prayers of the saints, which accompany the smoke of the incense, are heard in heaven."[3]

Could we therefore infer that a time of silence as we begin to prayer—pondering deeply on the crucifixion of Christ for our salvation—would provide a true intercessory for our prayers; sanctifying and purifying our very words?

> Therefore, may our hearts always be directed to the steadfast love of God through the intercession of Jesus.

> *The LORD is in his holy temple; let all the earth be hushed in his presence! Hab 2:20 (NEB)*

---

3. Hendricksen, *More Than Conquerors*, 142.

Epistle 121

In Durham Cathedral there is an exquisite modern stained-glass window depicting the Last Supper. Called the Daily Bread window, it is an abstract representation looking down from above at Jesus and the twelve disciples seated at a long table. This perspective draws on our imagination as well as our sight. Vibrant colors all play a significant part—the purple border, a regal color, symbolizes the majesty of Christ; the deep blue, the sky; the fresh green, the earth. Christ is seated at the head with disciples down each side. The figure seated second on the left is slightly back from the table—this represents the traitor, Judas Iscariot. Although the actual betrayal and arrest is yet to take place, it illustrates that he has already made his decision and is moving out in spirit from the rest of the disciples. The objects of bright yellow on the table are the representatives of the broken bread and the table itself, deeply red, represents the shedding of Christ's blood. Over the head of Jesus is a cross and on each corner of the table are the nails that were driven into his hands and feet. We cannot immediately travel to Durham to witness this but with the marvel of modern technology we can find this window and dwell in its beauty and its symbolism.

Jesus went to the cross to die for each one of us—to atone for our sins. It is only because of his sacrifice that we can have a sure and certain hope.

We have: "That hope we hold. It is like an anchor for our lives, an anchor safe and sure. It enters through the veil, where Jesus has entered on our behalf as forerunner, having become a high priest for ever in the succession of Melchizedek." Hebrews 6:19–20 (NEB) We need a high priest to enter the holy of the holies to plead for us: "Now this is my main point: just such a high priest we have, and he has taken his seat at the right hand of the throne of Majesty in the heavens, a ministrant in the real sanctuary, the tent pitched by the Lord and not by man." Hebrews 8:1–2 (NEB) In joy we celebrate that our high priest defeated death and rose to life eternal. In gratitude we celebrate that the writer of the *Letter to the Hebrews*, besides the picture of Jesus as Messiah and High Priest, also gives us such wonderful glimpses of the character of Jesus—his compassion, his gentleness, and his understanding of human weakness.

> ... and a compassion *for* Jesus, our Savior.

Dietrich Bonhoeffer, who actively spoke and worked against the Nazi regime in Germany, was arrested by the Gestapo in April 1943. This began an incarceration in prisons and concentration camps until his execution in April 1945. "... less than twenty-four hours before he left this world, Bonhoeffer performed the offices of a pastor. In the bright Schönberg schoolroom that was their cell, he held a small service. He prayed and read verses for that day Isaiah 53:5 'With his stripes we are healed' and 1 Peter 1:3 'Blessed be the God and Father of our Lord Jesus Christ!' By his great mercy we have been born anew to a living hope through the resurrection of Jesus Christ from the dead." (RSV) He then explained these verses to everyone. Best recalled that Bonhoeffer "spoke to us in a manner which reached the hearts of all, finding just the right words to express the spirit of our imprisonment and the thoughts and resolutions which it had brought."[1] Payne Best, one of his fellow prisoners "described Bonhoeffer as 'all humility and sweetness, he always seemed to me to diffuse an atmosphere of happiness, of joy in every smallest event in life, and of deep gratitude for the mere fact that he was alive ... He was one of the very few men that I have ever met to whom his God was real and ever close to him.'"[2]

This hope upon which Bonhoeffer preached—where else can we find such a secure and certain hope? No earthly person or undertaking can provide such a surety. On December 17, 1927, the United States Submarine S-4 was accidentally rammed by the US Coast Guard destroyer, Paulding. There were only six known survivors out of the forty submariners on board. These men were trapped in the forward torpedo room and they desperately relayed a series of morse code signals by tapping on the hull of the vessel. "Is there any hope?" The carefully worded response was: "There is hope. Everything possible is being done." This was a hope founded on an empty promise—although there have been instances of men being rescued from such an underground tomb in modern times,

---

1. Metaxas, *Bonhoeffer*, 528.
2. Metaxas, *Bonhoeffer*, 514.

in those early days there was no possible means of saving these men. The living hope that Christ gives us is not an empty promise!

Today, when we pray, may we speak the following words:

> Father God I will not be afraid to follow you;
> For only in living in you Lord, can I have true life;
> In your precious son, Jesus, I have a hope that never dies;
> With you Spirit I have a sure and faithful counsellor.

May the hope which comes through Christ ever burn in our hearts.

Epistle 122

During his incarceration Dietrich Bonhoeffer wrote the following poem.

WHO AM I?
Who am I? They often tell me
I stepped from my cell's confinement
Calmly, cheerfully, firmly.
Like a squire from his country-house.
Who am I? They often tell me
I used to speak to my warders
Freely and friendly and clearly,
As though it were mine to command.
Who am I? They also tell me
I bore the days of misfortune
Equally, smilingly, proudly,
Like one accustomed to win.
Am I then really all that which other men tell of?
Or am I only what I myself know of myself?
Restless and longing and sick, like a bird in a cage,
Struggling for breath, as though hands were
compressing my throat,
Yearning for colours, for flowers, for the voices of birds,
Thirsting for words of kindness, for neighbourliness,
Tossing in expectation of great events,
Powerlessly trembling for friends at an infinite distance,
Weary and empty at praying, at thinking, at making,
Faint, and ready to say farewell to it all?
Who am I? This or the other?
Am I one person today and tomorrow another?
Am I both at once? A hypocrite before others,
And before myself a contemptibly woebegone weakling?
Or is something within me still like a beaten army,
Fleeing in disorder from victory already achieved?
Who am I? They mock me these lonely questions of mine.
Whoever I am, Thou knowest, O God, I am Thine

Epistle 123

Every day we read about the disastrous war in Ukraine—since the Russian invasion began in February 2022 nearly 14,500 people have been killed; just over 6,000 of these are civilians. Devastation of homes and whole cities has become the norm and those who have not fled are living in badly damaged basements with no water or electricity. Many families have made their way to neighboring countries. In fact, Poland has recorded seventeen million crossing the border into their territory. The most poignant suffering is that of the children. They are always the most vulnerable in any war.

But turn from these incredible figures and focus on the intense fear of one Ukrainian Christian aboard a ship trying to navigate treacherous waters. This seafarer sent a desperate message to the Reverend Tay, Principal of the Missions to Seafarers at Millers Point in Sydney:

> *Father we r here now in Ukraine Odessa*
> *We see a lot of seamines also the oilrig is burning and aboundon*
> *also the building is burning hit by missiles*
> *Include us too in yur prayers.*

The reply went back to our Christian brother:

> I know how difficult it is at such time like this to be at sea.
> Your safety is paramount and is our concern.
> I'm praying for you below and please take time to share with me any prayer requests or testimonies. Thank you.
> Dear Lord Jesus, we pray for protection for all seafarers at sea especially those at Odessa and at war zone areas. Help the navigation crew to be vigilant in their navigating to avoid hitting any sea-mines.
> Grant safe passage in and out of the war zones.
> Protect their vessel from being hit by any missiles or drones.

The *Mission to Seafarers* describes seafarers as an "unreached people group" because of their isolation during their time at sea, separated from their loved ones for months; sometimes even years. In today's world with the high efficiency of loading and unloading of freight plus the often-tight security of countries in regard to refugees seeking asylum, seafarers often are unable to disembark at a port when their ship docks. Those that are able to do so here in Sydney, go to the Mission where they know their needs—both practical and spiritual—will be catered for by a blessing of chaplains. They will find a place to relax and will have the ability to communicate with people at home either free of charge or at a very low rate. It would seem that this Ukrainian sailor has been to Sydney in the past, to know to reach out for prayer from "Father Tay," who can guide him to his heavenly Father.

> *Others there are who go to sea in ships and make their living on the wide waters. These men have seen the acts of the LORD and his marvellous doings in the deep. At his command the storm-wind rose and lifted the waves high. Carried up to heaven, plunged down to the depths, tossed to and fro in peril, they reeled and staggered like drunken men, and their seamanship was all in vain. So they cried to the LORD in their trouble, and he brought them out of their distress. The storm sank to a murmur and the waves of the sea were stilled. They were glad then that all was calm, as he guided them to the harbour they desired. Let them thank the LORD for his enduring love and for the marvellous things he has done for men.* Ps 107:23–31 (NEB)

In Ramsgate, where in the beginning months of the Second World War, the "little ships" departed to sail to Dunkirk to bring back the defeated British army, there is a Harbour Mission and Sailors Home. Founded in 1878 it was originally for the boys, some as young as 10, who were apprenticed to smack fishermen. They lived above the Sailors' Church when ashore. Many people who were rescued from shipwrecks also found safety and solace there and in the adjacent building, where they were clothed, sheltered, and medically treated. The lovely little church is open for prayer for seamen every day.

In the New Testament Luke tells a story in meticulous detail of his and Paul's shipwreck off the coast of Malta in Acts 27. All on board were saved through God's providence. When Paul himself tells his readers of the hardships he has endured in 2 Corinthians 11 he points out he was shipwrecked three times! All through the ages, ships ply the oceans in war not just to fight the enemy but to take food and other vital supplies to countries in need. When Paul was with Luke, he was being taken to Rome for trial, but the ship was also carrying a cargo of wheat. Sometimes the voyage of a ship is undertaken just to keep trade ongoing to maintain necessities for the beleaguered country.

Our frightened Ukrainian sailor is possibly on such an essential voyage—he calls out over the vast oceans to ask for our ongoing prayers. Take time to think on him in his danger and pray that he can find the courage and strength in God, through our Savior Jesus, to face his uncertain future. Please pray continuously for all those in peril on sea and, also on land—far away from our blessed and secure country. Thanks be to God for our safety in our homeland.

Epistle 124

The Book of Habakkuk begins with a lament from Habakkuk to God. God responds to his prophet. Again, Habakkuk regales God with further laments and again God responds. The first lament consists of the record of oppression of the people Israel—specifically the severity and the extreme length of this oppression. The second lament calls on the holiness and justice of God and the question of God's mode of punishment in the light of his character. When God responds to the laments, the first response is in the form of an oracle; the second response in the telling of a vision. The faithfulness of God is compared with the arrogance of the people. The righteousness of God is a gift; the people must respond in gratitude with their hearts and not by carrying out pious acts. In the final chapter of the book, we are led into Habakkuk's proclamation to God—it is in the form of a prayer. David Baker, an Old Testament commentator, says: "He glorifies God for his person and his actions in creation. In response to his experience of the presence of Yahweh, Habakkuk provides one of the most moving statements of faith and trust found in scripture"[1]:

> *When thou dost tread the sea with thy horses the mighty waters boil.*
> *I hear, and my belly quakes; my lips quiver at the sound;*
> *trembling comes over my bones, and my feet totter in their tracks;*
> *I sigh for the day of distress to dawn over my assailants.*
> *Although the fig-tree does not burgeon, the vines bear no fruit,*
> *the olive-crop fails, the orchards yield no food,*
> *the fold is bereft of its flock and there are no cattle in the stalls,*
> *yet I will exalt in the LORD and rejoice in the God of my deliverance.*
> *The LORD God is my strength, who makes my feet nimble as a hind's*
> *and sets me to range the heights.* Hab 3:15–19 (NEB)

Habakkuk acknowledged his low estate and weakness.
He remembered the Babylonians were coming.

---

1. Baker, *Nahum, Habakkuk and Zephaniah*, 68.

He saw the loss and desolation which would result.
But GOD—the Lord—was his strength.

In the midst of all these calamities he will not only be safe but he will be *joyously* safe—like a deer frolicking and gambolling over rocks and crevices.

When we look at Habakkuk's prayer in detail, we see that he begins by glorifying God—he is in complete awe of his holiness and in the wonder of his creation. He prays for God's mercy; he prays for God's revival in him. In the midst of his wrath, he pleads with God to be merciful and send revival amongst all his people. But the people must revive their reverence for the Lord GOD!

Habakkuk records how God has gone into battle for a chosen race even though it had been unfaithful.

> *With threats thou dost bestride the earth and trample down the nations in anger. Thou goest forth to save thy people, thou comest to save thy anointed; thou dost shatter the wicked man's house from the roof down, uncovering the foundations to bare rock.* Hab 3:12–13 (NEB)

The race which was to bring forth God's anointed was to be protected.

But all must glorify their God and confess their waywardness.

In a past epistle, we learnt about the beginning of prayer—how, like Habakkuk, we must acclaim praise to a wondrous Creator God who is all powerful and ever faithful. But we understand that confession is also an integral part of prayer. This does not involve a listing of our sins to God, ticking them off as we go. Rather it is the acknowledgment that we have fallen short in our walk with him and we need to come back with our hearts, our minds, and with resolute fortitude. It is the opening up to him in humility—accepting his mercy and grace through forgiveness. When we have laid open our souls; we have re-established our relationship—then we can approach his throne with boldness and reveal our petitions. Still, as we do this, we are aware how well the Father knows his children: "Even before a word is on my tongue, O LORD, you know it completely." Psalm 139:4 (NEB) There is a warmth and closeness in this verse. God is always attuned to all our needs yet he waits for us to bring them to him. Thus this is the joy of reassurance in our prayer lives.

Blessed be the LORD, for he has heard my cry for mercy.
The LORD is my strength, my shield, in him my heart trusts;
so I am sustained, and my heart leaps for joy,
and I praise him with my whole body.
The LORD is strength to his people,
a safe refuge for his anointed king. Ps 28:6–7 (NEB)

Epistle 125

We come to the time of the year when we observe Remembrance Day. Originally named Armistice Day to commemorate all those who died in the First World War, it has now become a Day of Remembrance for all wars. The Great War, as it was known originally, was thought to be the war to end all wars! It is desperately sad to realise that this was not the outcome and our world is constantly at war in many countries. The results of these on-going battles and revolutions—death, disfigurement, mental stress, grief, relocation, separation, torture, imprisonment, starvation of people, and devastation of the earth—are always present somewhere in this wonderful creation of our God.

Many people in recent times have criticized Remembrance Day and the establishment of memorials. They see these as a glorification of war. In 2014, the Governor of Tasmania, Peter Underwood, used the Dawn Service of Anzac Day to express his disgust in the so-called celebration of the day. To men, women, and children who had come together to mourn their loved ones, he told them that their tears were for murderers—for the men and women who had suffered the ultimate fate when their country had directed them to fight and kill. But such days come with an unspoken prayer that all leaders will take every step to avoid such destruction and sorrow in the future. Significantly, it helps those who have participated in the unimaginable horror of war to have the strength to find the purpose of it all—even where that seems impossible.

When nations fail to honor this remembrance, such as in the war in Vietnam, those who return can never come to terms with their part in the unspeakable carnage that is war. In the United States, for nearly twenty years, the government refused to publicly recognize those who had returned from Vietnam. There had been no monuments erected and no memorial marches held. People wanted to forget. Therefore, there was nothing tangible to prompt their memory. In gripping prose, Philip

Caputo maintains a fellow warrior's sacrifice was more than worthy and validated that those who choose to turn their backs should be filled with shame:

> *You were part of us, and a part of us died with you, the small part that was still young . . . whatever the rights or wrongs of the war, nothing can diminish the rightness of what you tried to do. Yours was the greater love. You died for the man you tried to save, and you died pro patria . . . You were faithful. Your country is not . . . it wishes to forget and it has forgotten. But there are a few of us who do remember because of the small things that made us love you—your gestures, the words you spoke, and the way you looked. We loved you for what you were and what you stood for.*[1]

Remembrance is a gift to the dead. The sacrifice needs to be recognized as worthwhile. Those who return alive must honor those who are brought home in body bags, or, as in former wars, those left behind in some foreign grave. There must be a sense of propitiation otherwise the deaths are in vain. Those who fell kept the faith; those who live must keep the faith with them by commemorating the fallen in their hearts.

When we pray for the families who are always grieving their lost ones, we must also pray for those who returned broken in body and anguished in spirit—struggling to restore some semblance of their former selves.

A Russian soldier wrote:

> *No one returns from the war. Ever. Mothers get back a sad semblance of their sons—embittered, aggressive beasts, hardened against the whole world and believing in nothing except death. Yesterday's soldiers no longer belong to their parents. They belong to war, and only their body returns from the war. Their soul stays there.*[2]

We must pray for those who have no answers to how or why—families of the *Missing in Action* where no body has ever been found, or if found, it is not possible to be identified. We must pray for the countless innocent victims of sexual violence—not only women, but children also—by the aggressors.

But the most important component of our prayer must be the continual prayer for peace in the world. As we do, we must always remember

---

1. Caputo, *A Rumor of War*, 223–24.
2. Babchenko, *One Soldier's War*, 388.

the following words: "fear nothing, for I am with you; be not afraid, for I am your God. I strengthen you, I help you, I support you with my victorious right hand." Isaiah 41: 10 (NEB)

Pray that all those in peril know these words from one of the thousands of gravestones in France—they will not be forgotten.

> We would give the world, and more . . .
> to see his smiling face come through the door.

Epistle 126

We can see from our reading on prayer that, often we are so overwhelmed by the busyness of life or the loneliness of our circumstances, that we cannot find the words we need to speak to God. When we sometimes lose our pattern of regular prayer, we can still keep our hearts and souls alive.

David Adam suggests that we treat the beginning of each day like the incoming tide of the sea—just a short prayer to acknowledge the beginning of each morning that God has given us and—to rejoice in it:

> *Awaken me, Lord*
> *To your light,*
> *Open my eyes*
> *To your presence.*
> *Awaken me, Lord*
> *To your love,*
> *Open my heart*
> *To your indwelling.*
> *Awaken me, Lord*
> *To your life,*
> *Open my mind*
> *To your abiding.*
> *Awaken me, Lord*
> *To your purpose,*
> *Open my will*
> *To your guiding.*[1]

Then rest a moment knowing that nothing that happens during the day can separate you from the love of God. Even in the worst hours our God is there.

---

1. Adam, *Tides and Seasons*, 7.

God is my fortress
God is my might
God is my Saviour
God is my right
God is my helper
All the day long
God is the power
Making me strong [2]

Joseph Freeman's earliest years were the worst hours and days. Joseph was born in 1826 in New Orleans; the son of a slave, he was born into slavery. At age thirty-four he managed to escape and stowed away on a tobacco ship, which was sailing to Tobacco Dock in London. He eventually settled in Chemsford, Essex, where he found work in an iron foundry. As a slave Joseph carried the name of his American owner so he took the name of "Free man" to celebrate his freedom. When attending the local Meeting House he met his future wife, Sarah. They had a short and happy marriage but Joseph died in 1875 of consumption. The funeral was paid for by his employer and workmates. His friends from the Non-Conformist Church erected the following gravestone:

TO THE MEMORY OF
J O S E P H
ONCE A SLAVE IN NEW ORLEANS
WHO ESCAPED TO ENGLAND AND
BECAME ALSO A
FREE MAN
IN CHRIST
READER! HAVE YOU BEEN MADE FREE
FROM THE SLAVERY OF SIN?
The Lord God
Forgives our sins.
Frees us from evil.
Delivers us from bondage.
Releases us from captivity.
Protects us throughout each day
Is with us as the night approaches
Shelters and comforts us in the fading light
Gives us the strength and joy for the morrow.

---

2. Adam, *Tides and Seasons*, 59.

At the end of the day direct your heart rightly:

Then you could hold up your head without fault, a man of iron, knowing no fear. Then you shall forget your trouble; you will remember it only as flood-waters that have passed; life will be lasting, bright as noonday, and darkness will be turned to morning. You will be confident, because there is hope; sure of protection, you will lie down in confidence; great men will seek your favour. Job 11:15–19 (NEB)

Epistle 127

We often hear people say "I have seen the light!" This term, dating from the late 1600s, originally referred to religious conversion, the light referring to the appearance of light before a sinner in the Bible. However, by the 1800s it was used more broadly for any kind of understanding (a sudden insight) or the finality of a difficult journey (the light at the end of the tunnel)!

The coming of the dawn each day confirmed to the Hebrews that darkness will never last forever. God was the creator: "I am the LORD, there is no other; I make the light, I create darkness, author alike of prosperity and trouble. I, the LORD, do all these things." Isa 45:7 (NEB)

The light shining each morning at sunrise was for the benefit of man and woman. It brought surety and promise.

> *Come, let us return to the LORD; for he has torn us and will heal us, he has struck us and he will bind up our wounds; after two days he will revive us, on the third day he will restore us, that in his presence we may live. Let us humble ourselves, let us strive to know the LORD, whose justice dawns like morning light, and its dawning is as sure as the sunrise. It will come to us like a shower, like spring rains that water the earth.* Hos 6:1–3 (NEB)

Throughout the Bible, light symbolises faith, holiness, knowledge, wisdom, grace, hope—in God's revelation. Darkness symbolises evil, sin, despair.

> Light and darkness co-exist in the world, but light restrains the darkness;
> the darkness cannot overcome the light.

In the New Testament we see the original meaning of "seeing the light." In Acts, Luke relates the religious conversion of Saul, the Christian persecutor, to Paul, an apostle of the risen Christ.

> *Meanwhile Saul was still breathing murderous threats against the disciples of the Lord. He went to the High Priest and applied for letters to the synagogues at Damascus authorizing him to arrest anyone he found, men or women, who followed the new way, and bring them to Jerusalem. While he was still on the road and nearing Damascus, suddenly a light flashed from the sky all around him. He fell to the ground and heard a voice saying, "Saul, Saul, why do you persecute me?" "Tell me, Lord," he said "who you are." The voice answered, "I am Jesus, whom you are persecuting. But get up and go into the city, and you will be told what you have to do." Meanwhile the men who were travelling with him stood speechless; they heard the voice but could see no one. Saul got up from the ground, but when he opened his eyes he could not see; so they led him by the hand and brought him into Damascus.* Acts 9:1–8 (NEB)

In John's gospel we understand a different aspect of "seeing the light." John sees it as being alive in Christ. "All that came to be was alive with his life, and that life was the light of men." John 1:4 (NEB)

Further along, John records the words of Jesus: "Jesus addressed the people: 'I am the light of the world. No follower of mine shall wander in the dark; he shall have the light of life.'" John 8:12 (NEB)

Further, John warns us that walking in darkness means rejecting God's message of eternal life through Jesus. When we walk in the light, we also learn to manifest God's love to others.

In history we see people who claim to have seen the light and become true followers of Jesus. Constantine was one of these. If you are studying Church History you will invariably find a question on the examination paper which says: "Do you believe Constantine was a Christian?" or words to that effect. "The Emperor Constantine associated the Christian God with the military successes which had destroyed all his rivals, from Maxentius to Licinius."[1] Constantine saw God as the God of Battles; he really didn't seem to understand Christianity at all. He "told Eusebius of Caesarea that one of the crucial experiences in his Milvian Bridge victory had been a vision of 'a cross of light in the heavens, above the sun, and an inscription, *Conquer by this* . . .' Constantine was probably

---

1. MacCulloch, *A History of Christianity: The First Three Thousand Years*, 191.

not very clear about the difference between a universal sun cult and the Christian God."[2]

During his reign he gave the church equal recognition with the traditional official cults of the day. He favored Christian leaders, even though they belonged to a battered and minority church; he preached sermons, and; was even baptized before his death. Constantine renamed the city of Byzantion, Constantinople, which he then quadrupled its size, and sponsored the building of magnificent Christian churches, which nevertheless were set up as temples more in keeping with traditional cults. His great plan was to gather the bodies of the twelve Apostles to accompany his own corpse in one of these "temples," which seems to be a strange way to interpret the Christian story!

Thus, we must always be wary of interpreting visions of conversion without comparison with the teachings of scripture. In the non-canonical Gospel of Thomas, we read: "There is light within a man of light, and he lights up the whole world. If he does not shine, he is darkness." There are deceivers, like Constantine, with their own agenda: "Everyone who does not abide in the teaching of Christ, but goes beyond it, does not have God; whoever abides in the teaching has both the Father and the Son." 2 John 9 (NEB)

> Pray that we may never fall under the influence
> of the deceivers!

---

2. MacCulloch, *A History of Christianity: The First Three Thousand Years*, 191.

Epistle 128

Sergei Kourdakov grew up as a dedicated Communist in his homeland of Russia. He idolized Lenin, visiting his remains in Moscow:

> *As I entered the quiet sanctuary and approached the mortal remains of Father Lenin, I was overcome with a sense of awe and reverence. I stood close, quietly looking at the body of the man about whom I had studied so much and who was a god to me. He was the founder of my "religion" which had given me something to believe in for the first time in my life. He taught me equality, brotherhood and the strong helping the weak. I bowed my head and prayed to him.*[1]

Because of his commitment and leadership skills at the Naval Academy, Kourdakov was selected by the KGB to form a special police squad to seek out law-breakers; beat them up; and take them to the prisons. Selecting strong brutish fellows—cadets who relished fighting—he had much success in carrying out such operations. Constantly coming in contact with the worst kind of people, all of his men soon developed a complete disregard for them as human beings.

Kourdakov and his men were so successful that they were now directed to carry out what was termed as far more important work—attacks on a different problem group: ". . . there are criminals who are a far greater threat to our country's security and our way of life. They are more dangerous because they work quietly in our midst, undermining the foundations of our system and threatening the existence of our country."[2] These people were the "religiozniki," the religious believers. Christians were meeting secretly in their homes thus they were considered devious. The authorities really did not know what to do about the numbers who were regularly joining such believers. Their answer was the obviously that

---

1. Kourdakov, *Forgive me, Natasha*, 71.
2. Kourdakov, *Forgive me, Natasha*, 101.

which they used for every situation—direct action of beating, bashing, and imprisoning but—this time—all done in secret so the public would not feel they were punishing innocent men, women, and children.

Gradually Kourdakov came to believe that this brutality was unjust. And as he was promoted in the Soviet chain of command, he came to see many leaders in private situations—drinking themselves to oblivion and appearing no better than the drunkards and louts he and his men had originally persecuted. He began to become more and more distressed about beating the believers—people who did not fight back in any way. One particular young girl, Natasha, appeared at three successive meetings and he himself took part in stripping and viciously lashing her. When instructed to destroy boxes of confiscated literature he began to read some handwritten notes in an attempt to understand the faith of the believers. He had discovered some scripture on prayer from the Gospel of Luke, chapter 11. It was not like anything he had read before. He became engrossed in the words of Jesus: ". . . the words bit deeply into my being. It was as though somebody was in the room with me, teaching me these words and what they said."[3] He read them again and again and realized what the girl Natasha believed in her heart—believed enough to suffer such torments that he and his men had inflicted upon her. He discovered that he still had some humanity in his heart.

From that time onwards, Sergei Kourdakov planned his escape from his homeland. Through service in the Navy, he was able to flee his ship when it was anchored off the coast of Canada during extreme weather, swimming through treacherous seas. He was permitted by the Canadian authorities to stay there and then proceeded to spend the rest of his short life telling Christians all over North America—in churches, on television, in newspaper interviews, and in talks with government officials—about the plight of Russian Christians. He raised money to send Bibles back to his homeland. During this period, he wrote a testimony of his life entitled, *Forgive me, Natasha*. He had found forgiveness from a living God and wanted her to forgive him also. Whether she ever survived her persecution he never knew. It was a short life and a brief time of witnessing. At the age of twenty-two he died instantly from a gunshot.

Softly and tenderly Jesus calls – sinner come home.

---

3. Kourdakov, *Forgive me, Natasha*, 172.

In our life today where we are able to worship freely with no threat of persecution, we may find it hard to understand such hatred of Christians. But just as it is based on fear in all these "closed" countries, we do experience an inkling of the fear that secular Australians have of Christianity. This fear is often motivated by the threat of having to change their lifestyle and their love of earthly wealth and possessions. It also creates the possibility that they may have to walk away from their indulgence in questionable life patterns.

> God of everlasting love, who provides all things, we pray for all people:
> make your way known to them, your saving power among all the nations.
> We pray for the welfare of your church here on earth:
> guide and govern it by your Spirit, so that all who call themselves Christians
> may be led in the way of truth and hold the faith
> in unity of spirit,
> in the bond of peace,
> and in righteousness of life.[4]

---

4. Anglican Church of Australia. Archbishop of Sydney's Liturgical Panel, *Sunday Services*, 29.

Epistle 129

We are coming to the end of the year: the approach of a celebration of the culmination of the promises that God made to his people Israel. God the Creator sends his Son the Redeemer. From re-creation to salvation through the birth of the baby Jesus—fully man and fully God.

The traditional events we know, but they are clouded with traditions of misinterpretation and misunderstanding—not always dramatically but subtly. This does not mean that the words of the narrative of the birth of Jesus in the gospels are incorrect but rather that we see them through modern eyes rather than Middle Eastern eyes. Much of early Christian tradition is based almost solely on Greek and Latin culture and expression:

> *This assumption distorts historical reality and weakens greatly our understanding of the roots of Christian theology and spirituality. In the third and fourth centuries Syriac was the third international language of the church. It served as the major means of communication in the Roman diocese of the "East," which included Syria, Palestine, and Mesopotamia.*[1]

> *Syriac is a sister language to the Aramaic of Jesus . . . [plus] Arabic-speaking Christianity began on the day of Pentecost . . . it gradually became the major theological language for all Eastern Christians.*[2]

Kenneth Bailey, who wrote these words, has lived in the Middle East all his life. He has studied the language and literature of Arabic Christians to learn their culture and their traditional ways, which come from the days of Jesus and the apostles, and has lectured extensively.

---

1. Meyendorff, *Ephrem the Syrian: Hymns*, 1.
2. Bailey, *Jesus Through Middle Eastern Eyes*, 12.

In Luke 2 we find Joseph returning to his town of origin. Because of his genealogical background Joseph would have been welcome in most of the houses of Bethlehem. He was also "royal" from the family of King David. Like Jerusalem, Bethlehem was regarded as a "city of David" so this would be another reason that Joseph would have no trouble finding accommodation. We know that, in every culture today—primitive and modern—a woman about to give birth is greatly valued and protected. Therefore, Bailey reasons that the pregnant Mary, with a descendent of David at her side, would be very much respected. No-one in Bethlehem would be aware that they were yet to be married. We must also remember that Mary had close relatives with accommodation not far from Bethlehem—Elizabeth and Zechariah lived in the hill country of Judaea. This is an area which surrounds Bethlehem.

Joseph "went up to Judaea from the town of Nazareth in Galilee, to register at the city of David, called Bethlehem, because he was of the house of David by descent; and with him went Mary who was betrothed to him. She was expecting a child, and while they were there the time came for her baby to be born, and she gave birth to a son, her first-born." Luke 2:5-6 (NEB) While they were there does not suggest a dramatic search because the birth was imminent. Because of the abruptness of the text, we tend to think there was no accommodation when they arrived and the poorest shelter had to suffice because there was no time. It does make for a more exciting pageant! It is thought that these misinterpretations have come from an anonymous account of the birth of Jesus: *The Protevangelium of James*, written two hundred years after the event. This work is filled with some very hard-to-believe events with Joseph running around trying to find a midwife and arriving back after the birth. In addition, a witness scores a leprous hand because of unbelief in the virgin birth!

Bailey also discusses the picture of Jesus being born in a stable because Joseph could not find any other accommodation. But traditional Middle Eastern houses were generally composed of two rooms—one a room where the family cooked, ate, lived, and slept; the second a room slightly lower than the first where the animals would be brought into for shelter and warmth at night and taken out each morning. This room was daily cleaned and used for guests when needed. Yes, there would have been a manger but laid with fresh straw when needed. Into such a room were invited the shepherds—members of the lower scale of society. For this reason, they were mightily afraid but the angels of the Lord reassured them, and so they came to a home such as they themselves might have had—"The outcasts became honored guests."[3]

Proceeding with Bailey's study we delve into the visit of the Wise Men from the East. "Any Christian living in Rome in the early centuries of the church would naturally think of the East as Persia, and indeed the word Magi in Greek literature does refer to people from Babylonia or Parthia." But for Jewish Christians in the first century; the East would refer to the Jordanian deserts and the deserts of Arabia. The Wise Men were wealthy; they brought gifts of gold, frankincense, and myrrh. ". . . gold was mined in Arabia. But more specifically, frankincense and myrrh are harvested from trees that only grow in southern Arabia."[4] Today there are millions of Arabic Christians.

Poor Jewish shepherds and rich Gentile Arabs came together in adoration.

> *Arise, Jerusalem, rise clothed in light; your light has come*
> *and the glory of the LORD shines over you.*
> *For, though darkness covers the earth and dark night the nations,*
> *the LORD shall shine upon you and over you shall his glory appear;*
> *and the nations shall march towards the light*
> *and their kings to your sunrise.* Isa 60:1–3 (NEB)

When we read the gospel narrative with modern eyes our hearts are excited with the words, but when we read it with Middle Eastern eyes the text is enriched—we live in the ancient world and rejoice in God's gift of salvation.

---

3. Bailey, *Jesus Through Middle Eastern Eyes*, 37.
4. Bailey, *Jesus Through Middle Eastern Eyes*, 52.

A Final Epistle from Perpetua

Joel calls on the Israelites to come to prayer:

> *Blow the trumpet in Zion,*
> *Proclaim a solemn fast, appoint a day of abstinence;*
> *gather the people together, proclaim a solemn assembly;*
> *summon the elders,*
> *gather the children, yes, babes at the breast;*
> *bid the bridegroom leave his chamber*
> *and the bride her bower.*
> *Let the priests, the ministers of the LORD,*
> *stand weeping between the porch and the altar*
> *and say, "Spare thy people, O LORD, thy own people,*
> *expose them not to reproach,*
> *lest other nations make them a byword*
> *and everywhere men ask*
> *'Where is their God?'"* Joel 2:15–17 (NEB)

David calls the people to worship and obedience:

> *The LORD is king, let the earth be glad,*
> *let coasts and islands all rejoice.*
> *Cloud and mist enfold him,*
> *righteousness and justice are the foundation of his throne.*
> *Fire goes before him and burns up his enemies all around.*
> *The world is lit up beneath his lightning-flash;*
> *and earth sees it and writhes in pain.*
> *The mountains melt like wax as the LORD approaches,*
> *the LORD of all the earth.*
> *The heavens proclaim his righteousness,*
> *and all the peoples see his glory.*
> *Let all who worship images, who vaunt their idols,*
> *be put to shame; bow down, all gods, before him.*
> *Zion heard and rejoiced, the cities of Judah were glad*

at thy judgements, O LORD.
For thou, LORD, art most high over all the earth,
far exalted above all gods. Ps 97: 1–9 (NEB)

Bibliography

Adam, David. *Tides and Seasons*. London: SPCK, 1989.
Addis, Ferdie. *I Have a Dream: The Speeches That Changed History*. London: Michael O'Mara, 2011.
Alter, Robert. *The Art of Biblical Narrative*. New York: Basic, 1981.
Anglican Church of Australia. Archbishop of Sydney's Liturgical Panel. *Sunday Services: a Contemporary Liturgical Resource*. Sydney South, NSW: Anglican Press Australia, 2001.
Austen, Jane. *Persuasion*. London: Collins, 1913.
Babchenko, Arkady. *One Soldier's War*. Translated by Nick Allen. New York: Grove, 2007.
Bailey, Kenneth E. *Jesus Through Middle Eastern Eyes: Cultural Studies in the Gospels*. London: SPCK, 2008.
———. *Paul Through Mediterranean Eyes: Cultural Studies in 1 Corinthians*. Downers Grove, IL: IVP Academic, 2011.
Baker, David W. *Nahum, Habakkuk and Zephaniah; An Introduction and Commentary*. Leicester, UK: Inter-Varsity Press, 1988. Tyndale Old Testament Commentaries.
Benedict, Saint, Abbot of Monte Cassino. *The Rule of Saint Benedict*. Translated into English. London: SPCK, 1931.
Blake, William. *The Complete Poems*. Editor, Alicia Suskin Ostriker. London: Penguin, rev. repr. 2004.
Bonhoeffer, Dietrich. *God Is in the Manger: Reflections on Advent and Christmas*. Translated by O. C. Dean, Jr. Compiled and edited by Jana Reiss. Louisville, KY: Westminster John Knox, 2010.
———. *My Soul Finds Rest: Reflections on the Psalms*. Editor and translator, Edwin Robertson. Grand Rapids, MI: Zondervan, 2002.
Bonhoeffer, Dietrich and Maria von Wedemeyer. *Love Letters from Cell 92*. Edited by Ruth-Alice von Bismarck and Ulrich Kabitz. Translated by John Brownjohn. London: HarperCollins, 1994.
Brontë, Anne. *Agnes Grey*. Edited with an introduction by Angeline Goreau. London: Penguin, 1988.
Brooke, Rupert. *The Poetical Works of Rupert Brooke*. Edited by Geoffrey Keynes. London: Faber and Faber, 1946.
Broomhall, Marshall ed. *Martyred Missionaries of the China Inland Mission: With a Record of the Perils and Sufferings of Some Who Escaped*. London: Morgan & Scott, 1901.

Bryson, Sarah. *La Reine Blanche: Mary Tudor: A Life in Letters.* Stroud, Gloucestershire: Amberley, 2018.
Buchan, Ursula. *Beyond the Thirty-Nine Steps: A Life of John Buchan.* London: Bloomsbury, 2019.
Bunyan, John. *The Pilgrim's Progress: An Illustrated Christian Classic.* Nashville, TN: Thomas Nelson, 2019.
Buttrick, George Arthur [et al.] eds. *The Interpreter's Dictionary of the Bible. Volumes 1–4.* Nashville, TN: Abingdon, 1962.
Byron, George Gordon Byron, Baron. *Selections from Byron: Poetry and Prose.* Edited by D. M. Walmsley. London: Methuen, 1931.
Calvin, John. *Prayer.* Kingsford, NSW: Matthias Media, 1996.
Caputo, Philip. *A Rumor of War.* London: Arrow, 1978.
Carman, Bliss [et al.] eds. *The World's Best Poetry. Volume 4. The Higher Life.* Philadelphia, PA: John D. Morris, 1904.
Carson, D. A. *The Gospel According to John.* Leicester: Apollos, 1991. Pillar New Testament Commentary.
———. *Praying with Paul: A Call to Spiritual Reformation.* Grand Rapids, MI: Baker Academic, 2nd ed. 2014.
Chambers, Oswald. *My Utmost for His Highest.* Uhrichsville, OH: Barbour, 1963.
Choi, Samuel. *Keeping in Touch, v. 3, no .3.* St Ives, NSW: St Ives-Pymble Presbyterian Church, 2022.
Church of England. *The Book of Common Prayer: and administration of the sacraments, and other rites and ceremonies of the church according to the use of the Church of England.* London: Society for Promoting Christian Knowledge, ca 1863.
Church of the Brethren. *The Memorial Days of the Renewed Church of the Brethren.* London: Forgotten Books, 2017 (1822). Classic Reprints.
Church of Scotland. *The Church Hymnary.* London: Oxford University Press, rev. ed. 1927.
Cornwell, Bernard. *Waterloo: The History of Four Days, Three Armies and Three Battles.* London: William Collins, 2014.
Coulthard, Sally. *A Short History of the World According to Sheep.* London: Head of Zeus, 2020.
Dahl, Roald. *Going Solo.* Camberwell, VIC: Penguin Australia, 2008.
Davis, Wade. *Into the Silence: The Great War, Mallory and the Conquest of Everest.* New York: Vintage, 2012.
Dawn, Marva J. *A Royal Waste of Time: The Splendor of Worshipping God and Being Church for the World.* Grand Rapids, MI: Eerdmans, 1999.
———. *In the beginning, God: Creation, Culture, and the Spiritual Life.* Downers Grove, IL: IVP, 2009.
Deal, Tim. *Livingstone.* New Haven, CT: Yale Nota Bene, 2001.
Demarest, Bruce. *Satisfy Your Soul: Restoring the Heart of Christian Spirituality.* Colorado Springs, CO: NavPress, 1999.
De Vinck, Christopher. *The Power of the Powerless: A Brother's Legacy of Love.* New York: Crossroad, 2002.
Dickens, Charles. *A Tale of Two Cities.* Edited by Richard Maxwell. London: Penguin, 2000.
Dickinson, Emily. *[Poems]* selected by Geoffrey Moore. Oxford: Oxford University Press, 1986. The Illustrated Poets.

Dorman, Marianne. "Lancelot Andrewes and Prayer, 1998." *Project Canterbury: Bringing Anglican History Online.* http.//www.anglicanhistory.org/essays/dorman.1.html
Elmer Robert ed. *Piercing Heaven: Prayers of the Puritans.* Bellingham, WA: Lexham, 2019.
Erickson, Carolly. *Great Harry: [The Extravagant Life of Henry VIII].* London: Robson, 1998.
Erickson, Millard J. *Introducing Christian Doctrine.* Edited by L. Arnold Hustad. Grand Rapids, MI: Baker Academic, 2nd ed. 2001.
Fee, Gordon D. and Douglas Stuart. *How to Read the Bible Book by Book: A Guided Tour.* Grand Rapids, MI: Zondervan, 2002.
Fraser, Antonia. *Cromwell: Our Chief of Men.* London: Phoenix, 2002.
Frenette, David. *The Path of Centering Prayer: Deepening Your Experience of God.* Boulder, CO: Sounds True, 2012.
Friends of Friendless Churches. *Introduction to New Members.* London: F.F.C., 2021.
Garvey, John. ed. *Modern Spirituality: An Anthology.* London: Darton, Longman and Todd, 1985.
Goldingay, John. *Old Testament Theology. Volume 1. Israel's Gospel.* Downers Grove, IL: InterVarsity, 2003.
Green, Michael. *Thirty Years that Changed the World: A Fresh Look at the Book of Acts.* Leicester, UK: Inter-Varsity Press, 2002.
Gumbel, Nicky. *The Bible in One Year: A Commentary.* London: Hodder & Stoughton, 2019.
Hamilton, Duncan. *For the Glory: The Life of Eric Liddell.* London: Doubleday, 2016.
Hanes, David ed. *My Path of Prayer.* Worthing, West Sussex: HE Walter, 1981.
Hart, I. "Genesis 1:1–2:3 As a Prologue to the Book of Genesis." *Tyndale Bulletin.* 46 (1995), 318.
Hauerwas, Stanley [et al.] eds. *Growing Old in Christ.* Grand Rapids, MI: William B. Eerdmans, 2003.
Hendricksen, William. *More Than Conquerors: An Interpretation of the Book of Revelation.* Grand Rapids, MI: Baker Book House, 1939.
Heschel, Abraham. "On Prayer." In *Modern Spirituality: An Anthology.* Edited by John Garvey. Viii–13. London: Darton, Longman and Todd, 1985.
Hodge, Charles. *Systematic Theology. Volume 3.* Peabody, MA: Hendricksen, 2003.
Jacobs, Alan. *The Narnian: The Life and Imagination of C. S. Lewis.* San Francisco, CA: HarperSanFrancisco, 2005.
Keating, Thomas. *Intimacy With God: An Introduction to Centering Prayer.* New York: Crossroad, 2009.
Keller, Timothy. *Walking with God through Pain and Suffering.* London: Hodder & Stoughton, 2015.
Kirk, J. R. Daniel. *Jesus Have I Loved, but Paul?: A Narrative Approach to the Problem of Pauline Christianity.* Grand Rapids, MI: Baker Academic, 2011.
Kourdakov, Sergei. *Forgive me, Natasha.* Basingstoke, Hants: Marshall Pickering, 1975.
Kozlowski, Bryan. *What the Dickens?!: Distinctively Dickensian Words and How to Use Them.* Philadelphia, PA: Running Press, 2016.
Ladd, George Eldon. *A Theology of the New Testament.* Grand Rapids, MI: Eerdmans, 1974.
Lambert, Angela. *Unquiet Souls: A Social History of the Illustrious, Irreverent, Intimate Group of British Aristocrats known as "The Souls."* New York: Harper & Row, 1984.

Langner, Rainer K. *Scott and Amundsen: Duel in the Ice*. Translated by Timothy Beech. London: Haus, 2007.

Lee, Harper. *To Kill a Mockingbird*. London: Arrow, 2006.

Levering, Matthew. *The Theology of Augustine: An Introductory Guide to His Most Important Works*. Grand Rapids, MI: Baker Academic, 2013.

Lewis, C. S. *How to Pray: Reflections and Essays*. London: William Collins, 2018.

———. *Mere Christianity*. London: Geoffrey Bles, 1952.

———. *The Problem of Pain*. London: Centenary, 1940.

———. *The Screwtape Letters*. London: HarperCollins, 2002.

Lewis-Stempel, John. *Six Weeks: The Short and Gallant Life of the British Officer in the First World War*. London: Weidenfeld & Nicolson, 2010.

Lloyd-Jones, Martyn. *Living Water: Studies in John 4*. Wheaton, IL: Crossway, 2009.

lords-prayer-words.com. *St Patrick's Breastplate*, viewed 2/6/21

Lysaught, M. Therese. "Memory, Funerals, and the Communion of Saints: Growing Old and Practices of Remembering." In *Growing Old in Christ*. Edited by Stanley Hauerwas [et al] Grand Rapids, MI: William B. Eerdmans, 2003.

MacCulloch, Diarmaid. *A History of Christianity: The First Three Thousand Years*. London: Penguin, 2010.

Marshall, I. Howard. *The Acts of the Apostles: An Introduction and Commentary*. Leicester: Inter-Varsity Press, 1980.

Masefield, John. *The Everlasting Mercy*. London: Sidgwick & Jackson, 1911.

McKernan, Michael. *Padre: Australian Chaplains in Gallipoli and France*. Sydney: Allen & Unwin, 1986.

Merton, Thomas. "The Inner Experience: Christian Contemplation." *Cistercian Studies* 18.3 (1983), 210.

Metaxas, Eric. *Bonhoeffer: Pastor, Martyr, Prophet, Spy: A Righteous Gentile vs. The Third Reich*. Nashville, TN: Thomas Nelson, 2010.

Meyendorff, John. *Ephrem the Syrian, Hymns*. Translated by Kathleen McVey. New York: Paulist, 1989.

Morden, Peter. *C. H. Spurgeon: The People's Preacher*. Farnham, Surrey: CWR, 2009.

Murray, Andrew. *Andrew Murray on Prayer*. New Kensington, PA: Whitaker House, 1998.

Musurillo, Herbert ed. *The Acts of the Christian Martyrs*. Introduction, texts and translation by Herbert Musurillo. Oxford: Clarendon, 1972. Oxford Early Christian Texts.

Nelson, Sara. *So Many Books, So Little Time: A Year of Passionate Reading*. Sydney, NSW: Hodder, 2004.

Newton, Gary. *Heart-Deep Teaching: Engaging Students for Transformed Lives*. Nashville, TN: B & H Academic, 2012.

Nouwen, Henri J. M. *Reaching Out*. Garden City, NY: Doubleday, 1975.

O'Rourke, *Finding Your Hidden Treasure: The Way of Silent Prayer*. London: Darton Longman and Todd, 2010.

Paton, John G. *John G. Paton: The Autobiography of the Pioneer Missionary to the New Hebrides (Vanuatu)*. Edinburgh: Banner of Truth, 2013.

Peterson, Eugene H. *Eat This Book: A Conversation in the Art of Spiritual Reading*. Grand Rapids, MI: Eerdmans, 2006.

Piper, John. *God Is the Gospel: Meditations on God's Love as the Gift of Himself*. Wheaton, IL: Crossway, 2008.

Pollock, John. *Hudson Taylor and Maria: A Match Made in Heaven*. Fearn, Ross-shire: Christian Focus, 1996.
———. *John Wesley*. London: Hodder & Stoughton, 1989.
Pratt, Richard L. Jr. *Pray with Your Eyes Open: Looking at God, Ourselves and Our Prayers*. Phillipsburg, NJ: Presbyterian and Reformed, 1987.
Presbyterian Church in Canada. *The Book of Praise*. Toronto, ON: the Author, 1972.
Presbyterian Church of Australia. *Rejoice! A Collection of Psalms, Hymns and Spiritual Songs*. Sydney, NSW: the Author, 1987.
Purdom, C. B. Ed. *On the Front Line: True World War I Stories*. London: Constable, rev. ed. 2009.
Raiter, Michael. *Stirring of the Soul: Evangelicals and the New Spirituality*. Kingsford, NSW: Matthias Media, 2003.
Rappaport, Helen. *Ekaterinburg: The Last Days of the Romanovs*. London: Hutchinson, 2008.
Reis, Pamela Tamarkin. *Reading the Lines: A Fresh Look at the Hebrew Bible*. Peabody, MA: Hendrickson, 2002.
Religious Tract Society. *Writings of Edward the Sixth, William Hugh, Queen Catherine Parr, Anne Askew, Lady Jane Grey, Hamilton and Balnaves*. London: The Society, 1836.
Reymond, Robert L. *A New Systematic Theology of the Christian Faith*. Nashville, TN: Thomas Nelson, 1998.
Ricoeur, Paul. *The Symbolism of Evil*. Boston, MA: Beacon, 1967.
Ronald, Susan. *Heretic Queen: Queen Elizabeth I and The Wars of Religion*. New York: St Martin's, 2012.
Sadler, Glenn Edward. "Defining Death as 'More Life'": Unpublished Letters by George MacDonald. *North Wind* 3 (1984) 4–18.
Sankey, Ira D. *Gospel Hymns and Sacred Songs*. New York: Biglow & Main, 1875.
The Scottish Psalter, 1929: Metrical Version and Scripture Paraphrases with Tunes. London: Oxford University Press, 1929.
Shebbeare, E. O. *Soondar Mooni*. London: Victor Gollancz, 1958.
Shelley, Percy Bysshe. *Selected Poems of Percy Bysshe Shelley*. London: Oxford University Press, 1919.
Simpson, Joe. *Touching the Void*. London: Vintage, 1997.
Small, James G. *I've Found a Friend, Oh, Such a Friend,1863*. Timeless Truths Free Online Library: Hymns, 3/3/21.
Sproul, R. C. *The R. C. Sproul Collection. Volume 1. The Holiness of God/Chosen by God*. Carol Stream, IL: Tyndale House, 2017.
Spurgeon, C. H. *The Cheque Book of the Bank of Faith: Precious Promises for Daily Readings*. Tan, Ross-shire: Christian Focus Publications, 1996.
Stott, John R. W. *Men Made New: An Exposition of Romans 5–8*. London: Inter-Varsity Fellowship, 1966.
———. *The Message of Acts: To the Ends of the Earth*. Nottingham: Inter-Varsity Press, 2nd ed. 1991.
Tennyson, Alfred, Baron. *The Works of Alfred Tennyson*. London: Kegan Paul, 1879.
Terry, Lindsay. *Stories Behind 50 Southern Gospel Favorites. Volume 2*. Grand Rapids, MI: Kregel, 2005.
Tersteegen, Gerhard. *Thou Hidden Love of God, 1729*. Timeless Truths Free Online Library: Hymns 24/5/2021.

Thomas À Kempis. *The Imitation of Christ*. Translated with an introduction by Leo Sherley-Price. Harmondsworth, Middlesex: Penguin, 1952.

Tozer, A. W. *The Pursuit of God*. Harrisburg, PA: Christian Publications, 1982.

Van der Zee, Henri and Barbara. *1688: Revolution in the Family*. London: Viking, 1988.

Wallace, Ronald S. *Calvin, Geneva and the Reformation: A Study of Calvin as Social Reformer, Churchman, Pastor and Theologian*. Grand Rapids, MI: Baker Book House, 1988.

Waltke, Bruce K. *Finding the Will of God: A Pagan Notion?* Grand Rapids, MI: Eerdmans, 2002.

Waltke, Bruce K. with Cathi J. Fredricks. *Genesis: A Commentary*. Grand Rapids, MI: Zondervan, 2001.

Weymouth, Richard Francis. *The New Testament in Modern Speech: An Idiomatic Translation into Every-day English from the Text of the Resultant Greek Testament*. London: James Clarke, 3rd ed. 1914.

Williams, Peter J. *Can We Trust the Gospels?* Wheaton, IL: Crossway, 2018.

Witherington, Ben III. *Paul's Letter to the Romans: A Socio-Rhetorical Commentary*. Grand Rapids, MI: Eerdmans, 2004.

Witkop, Philipp ed. *German Students' War Letters*. Translated and arranged from the original edition by A. F. Wedd. London: Methuen, 1929.

Wordsworth, William. *The Works of William Wordsworth*. Ware, Hertfordshire: Wordsworth Poetry Library, 1994.

Wright, N. T. *Spiritual and Religious: The Gospel in an Age of Paganism*. London: SPCK, 2017.

———. *Surprised by Hope*. London: SPCK, 2007.

www.ingramcontent.com/pod-product-compliance
Lightning Source LLC
Chambersburg PA
CBHW071436300426
44114CB00013B/1464